signed by author

Max Putzel

St Louis

Oct . 1963

THE MAN IN THE MIRROR

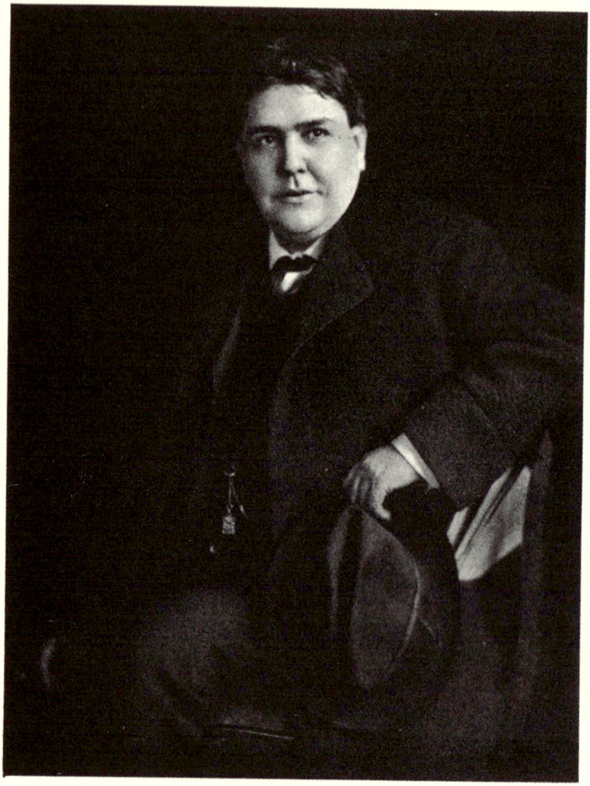

THE MAN IN THE MIRROR

William Marion Reedy
AND HIS MAGAZINE

BY MAX PUTZEL

HARVARD UNIVERSITY PRESS
Cambridge, Massachusetts · 1963

© Copyright 1963 by the President and Fellows of Harvard College
All rights reserved

Distributed in Great Britain by Oxford University Press, London
Library of Congress Catalog Card Number 63-17208
Printed in the United States of America

Publication of this book has been aided by a grant
from the Ford Foundation

TO MY PARENTS
AND MY TEACHERS

ESPECIALLY

Viola Davies Graves
Herschel Baker
Richard Sewall

PREFACE

For almost thirty years William Marion Reedy edited the *Mirror*, a St. Louis weekly magazine which came to exert a subtle, provocative influence in America and abroad. One is constantly running across allusions showing how closely certain leaders attended to his exuberant irony during the fateful years between the start of our war with Spain and the end of our first war with the Central Powers. "Not to know Reedy argues yourselves unknown," said a fellow editor, unwittingly posing Reedy's notoriety beside the devil's. But if he *was* sometimes devilish as a political satirist, the editor of *Reedy's Mirror* was better known as a humorist, a critic, and a discoverer. Pater, Yeats, and Emily Dickinson were among his early literary finds. Theodore Dreiser and Edgar Lee Masters were proud to count themselves among his later ones.

"Where can I find Reedy?" is said to have been Frank Harris's first question on stepping off the gangplank in New York, in 1916. Some say the British editor was only momentarily nonplused to learn that he still had nearly a thousand miles to go, and set off at once.

How then explain the obscurity that has settled like dust on Reedy's name? In St. Louis, where he spent his life, he is still fairly well known. Elsewhere he is familiar only to a handful of specialists in literary or political history. Perhaps the reason is that he was a seeker of values in poetry and public life which his contemporaries considered unimportant—and his successors took for granted. In any event the fame he attracted in the last five or six years of his life flickered

PREFACE

like heat lightning on a droughty night, and passed beyond the horizon. Since no one had thought to keep a complete file of the *Mirror* and the only two passable ones remained in St. Louis, where his standing was controversial, he had to await a biographer who would be his fellow townsman—someone involved in the life he knew—yet no zealous apologist.

Even in that city the scarcity of source material for such a study is almost unbelievable. Reedy wrote little about himself and never wrote a book or consented to have his best essays collected. Copies of his nickel pamphlets are offered by booksellers at five dollars, and no library has an entire set. James T. Babb spent fifteen years vainly trying to acquire a fair file of the *Mirror* for Yale Library. Other periodicals Reedy edited have disappeared without a trace. Of a literary monthly he published for several years after 1900 I could find only one volume of six issues in a library, and a single stray copy in a bookstore. Yet the twenty-seven volumes of the *Mirror* at the St. Louis Public Library comprise a sufficient record and monument.

For what Reedy wrote is more important than anything that happened to him. Indeed, perhaps the best service his biographer could perform would be to bring firsthand evidence of the boldness and wit of his fighting style. Hence I have been profuse in quoting from the *Mirror*.

In fact I have made the magazine and its contributors rather than just the life of its editor the focus of my study. Assuming that little is known of the cultural life of St. Louis, I have included the magazine's journalistic and intellectual environs in my opening chapters. Decadence in literature and politics colored that environment. I have given roughly a third of my pages to it. Reform in politics and naturalism in literature around the turn of the century take up somewhat less than a third. The revival of poetry in the years 1905 through 1920

PREFACE

takes up somewhat more than a third, Reedy's part in forwarding that trend being his most memorable contribution to American life. While this three-part pattern of simplification has entailed sweeping omissions and arbitrary inclusions, a single theme has evolved as I pursued my inquiry.

Even before he shook off the limitations of the *fin de siècle* Reedy was unhappily aware of the gulf that separated prevailing literary attitudes from the practical concerns of life in America. Philosophers, critics, writers of verse and fiction, all prided themselves on their genteel aloofness from the economic and political realities of provincial life. Reedy did not. His function as critic and editor was to bring life and letters into phase with one another, and he never lost the local, the common, touch. This trait won him the admiration of a generation of writers through whom he became internationally influential.

His function as an emulsifying agent bringing literature and the common life into suspension has not been apparent to my predecessors in the examination of Reedy and his magazine. Some of them have done his reputation the disservice of overstating his admirable traits or admiring him for unadmirable ones. Charles J. Finger in the *Dictionary of American Biography* went much too far, for example, when he claimed that Reedy "combined the genial improvidence of a Richard Steele with the polish of an Addison and the humor of a Charles Lamb." John T. Flanagan, in a valuable article for the *Missouri Historical Review* (1949), gave a more sensible estimate, appreciative of Reedy's wit yet rather too grudging in its appraisal of the editor's literary acuity and the wide sway he exercised. Fred Wilhelm Wolf's doctoral dissertation (Vanderbilt University, 1951) deserves our gratitude for attempting to preserve even the most trivial details of Reedy's memory, but its evaluation of Reedy's critical achievement leaves much to be desired. Frank Luther Mott, who picks the *Mirror* as

PREFACE

one of thirty-four "important magazines" of its period to discuss in his standard *History of American Magazines,* corrects a number of exaggerated claims. He considers Reedy to rank somewhere between his friend W. C. Brann and his rival H. L. Mencken. (Elbert Hubbard is thrown in for good measure.) Indispensable as Dean Mott's great work has been to me, I cannot find that grouping serviceable. The four editors shared a certain stylistic intemperance which invites comparison. But when one compares them one finds that Reedy's critical judgment was backed by a humanistic sensibility and by intellectual substance and learning the others lacked.

This conclusion is supported by documentary sources which, meager as they are, were available to me and not to my forerunners. Apart from having at hand my own microfilm notes on the *Mirror* I have had access to several collections of correspondence. Since all are listed in my footnotes and bibliographic notes I shall mention here only the most considerable: the Albert Bloch, Thekla Bernays, Byars, and Bynner papers at the Missouri Historical Society; the Mosher and Amy Lowell papers at Harvard; the Ficke, Lindsay, and Sara Teasdale papers at Yale; the Dreiser papers at the University of Pennsylvania; and collections of varied content in Chicago and New York.

Those interested in further investigation of Reedy and his associations will be more concerned to know what important sources I have not examined; for some of these are sure to become available. The most informative sealed collections will doubtless prove to be the Masters papers on deposit at the University of Pennsylvania and the Zoë Akins papers at the Huntington Library. The literary executors in charge of these tell me that the former contains 188 sheets of Reedy's letters to Masters plus carbon copies of Masters' letters to Reedy and others; the latter about 100 letters from Reedy to Miss Akins.

PREFACE

Reedy's letters to Ezra Pound, Theodore Roosevelt, and Vachel Lindsay have not turned up, though there is a good possibility that they will. His extensive correspondence with Mitchell Kennerley has been lost, probably irretrievably, with the exception of a handful of letters in the possession of Dr. Wolf and the New York Public Library. His letters to Carl Sandburg will doubtless be deposited at the University of Illinois but were not available to me. There is still the faint hope that Reedy's incoming correspondence will be found, though I have been unable to lay hands on any scrap of it.

My interest in Reedy began when I was a contributor to a little review and a graduate student at Washington University, in 1933. The *St. Louis Review* printed two piquant essays on Reedy by Jean Winkler. When I returned to that university as an instructor, many years later, John Francis McDermott guided my earliest fumbling effort at a literary appraisal of the *Mirror*, and Ralph Bieber supervised a historical study of its comments on the Spanish-American war. Thomas T. Hoopes, curator of the City Art Museum in St. Louis, taught me camera techniques to use in my research. Later Richard Sewall gave invaluable supervision to my Yale doctoral thesis on Reedy and the poets. He has continued to gird me with his wisdom, good taste, and good sense. My good friends Norman Holmes Pearson, Herman Wardwell Liebert of the Yale Library, and Thomas B. Sherman of the *St. Louis Post-Dispatch* have also been tactful counselors to one "long choosing and beginning late."

Librarians have been extraordinarily indulgent. Among them I want to express particular gratitude to Lawrence Miller, librarian emeritus and friend to Reedy, who made helpful suggestions while I was working at the Mercantile Library of St. Louis, where Miss Elizabeth Tindall pointed out many unexpected morsels of information. My obligations to Mrs. G. G. Drury, when she was director of reference services at the St.

PREFACE

Louis Public Library, and to her successor and many colleagues, can never be listed, much less repaid. Charles Van Ravenswaay and other friends at the Missouri Historical Society have gone out of their way to find me material I could not have done without. Donald Gallup at Yale, Stanley Pargellis at the Newberry Library in Chicago, Mrs. Neda Westlake at the University of Pennsylvania, and several members of the Houghton Library staff have not only attended to proper requests but often had to put up with visits that were more like invasions than orderly research. The portrait of William Marion Reedy (c. 1901), shown in the frontispiece is from a print in the Mitchell Kennerley Collection in the New York Public Library.

Miss Babette Deutsch was generous to let me have copies of the many letters she received from Reedy. Mrs. Richard Ederheimer not only permitted me to reproduce her late husband's portrait of Reedy but, at my suggestion, presented it to the new American room at Yale. Francis A. Dunnagan and dozens of other friends have sent me information, references, and documents for which I am deeply grateful. The help I received from editors at the Harvard University Press has been invaluable. Finally I must express appreciation for the admirably detached going-over that was given this manuscript by one of my students, Margaret Manfred.

M. P.

University of Connecticut
Storrs
January 1963

CONTENTS

	1. Persona non grata	3
PART ONE	2. A Boy in Kerry Patch	11
The Shaping	3. Literati in the City Room	23
Years	4. The Decadence—From Oscar Wilde to an "American Baudelaire"	35
	5. The Founding of the *Mirror*	47
	6. Toward Naturalism	62
	7. The *Mirror's* "War Boom"	77
PART TWO	8. Streetcars and Corruption	92
Turning	9. At the Fair	104
Points	10. Roosevelt and the Free Press	114
	11. Theodore Dreiser	120
	12. Real Women and Love Lyrics	135
PART THREE	13. Three Critics in Search of an Art	150
The Mirror	14. Ezra Pound, Poet in Exile	162
and the Poets	15. Poets in the Market	168
	16. Vachel Lindsay, Poet on Native Ground	177
	17. Crossing Spoon River	193
	18. The War of the Imagists and Their Antagonists	217
	19. Attack from the Rear	226

CONTENTS

	20. War and Reaction	245
PART FOUR	21. Dreiser and Harris Merton Lyon	255
The After-Image	22. Poets and Politics: *da capo al fine*	265
	23. Last Reflections	279
	Abbreviations Used in Bibliography and Notes	296
	Selected Bibliography	297
	Notes	311
	Index	343

PART ONE

THE SHAPING YEARS

CHAPTER 1

PERSONA NON GRATA

A STUDENT of Renaissance literature who ran across the office files of *Reedy's Mirror* at the Mercantile Library in St. Louis, some ten years ago, confided his excitement to an older friend he met going out the door. The friend was president of the trustees of that venerable sanctuary, where Emerson, Arnold, Thackeray, and Mark Twain had lectured and where William Marion Reedy (like Joseph Pulitzer and Carl Schurz) had got some of his postgraduate education.

"I had no use for Reedy," said the president of trustees. "I don't want to know about him. He was a whoremonger and a bum. Anyway, Reedy was only a critic. He couldn't create."

It is hardly surprising that St. Louis opinion has always been sharply divided on the topic of Reedy. The student had been impressed by the extraordinary literary sophistication of his magazine. The trustee had grown up in Kerry Patch, the drab Irish faubourg where Reedy, too, was born and got his political seasoning. Anyone overhearing their exchange might have supposed they were talking about two men called Reedy. Yet it is the thesis of this book that there was only one. Mingling some traits of a well-fed Villon with those of a Falstaff in modern dress, he wrote of gibbets and babbled of green fields.

Born in 1862, the son of a policeman, William Marion Reedy attended public and parochial schools, graduated at eighteen from St. Louis University, a venerable Jesuit establishment, and immediately went to work as a reporter. A brilliant though erratic newspaperman, he became within ten years the editor of a weekly newspaper later known as the *St. Louis Star.* Soon afterward, while still engaged in newspaper work, he was one of the founders of a disreputable gossip sheet, the *Sunday Mirror,* founded in February 1891.

About three years later Reedy became its sole editor and began turning the *Mirror* into a lively journal of opinion. But despite the sprightliness of his style and the increasing vigor of the magazine's political and literary content, Reedy had fallen victim to debts and alcoholism, which led him to the verge of catastrophe. He awoke from one protracted spree to find himself married to the keeper of a brothel. The magazine went into bankruptcy. Fortunately he had friends who believed in his talent and character; one of them bought in the magazine at auction and three months later presented it to Reedy as a gift. Less than a year after these unsavory episodes Reedy was divorced, soon afterward marrying a young lady of good family. Almost at once the magazine began to be successful. By the start of the Spanish-American War it had achieved national circulation, attaining a peak of 32,250 copies at a time when the *Dial's* circulation was five thousand, the *Atlantic's* seven, the *Nation's* twelve.[1]

Clearly, the magazine was less important for its modest success in gaining a public than for the writers it attracted and the influence Reedy exerted on them. As critic and editor Reedy had a measurable effect on those he published, encouraged, or took down. Writers were drawn to the *Mirror* less by its circulation or by the small sums Reedy eventually got around to paying them, than by the editor's talent for stimulation and friendship, his wit, his liberality of outlook, and—above all—his zest. However ordinary his magazine may have seemed in its early years, his style relieved the drabness of its format; it kept drawing attention to the man himself and

PERSONA NON GRATA

his prodigious sympathies. He was always earthy and plainspoken. But he felt for great literature the same reverence he had for the common clay of suffering humanity out of which such literature is fashioned.

In the last years of the nineteenth century literature and practical life had become sundered by traditions of mutual contempt. Even after Reedy's influence had been felt by a generation of vigorous writers it was possible for politicians and businessmen to remain illiterate and for writers to exile themselves from the rough-and-tumble. But to assume either pose was increasingly regarded as escapism and a confession of weakness. Reedy's part in bringing about the change becomes more evident as one examines his career. His effect remains, though the magazine he created no longer exists. So closely were the two identified that within five weeks of his death, in 1920, *Reedy's Mirror* followed its editor to the grave.

But what was he truly like? Last impressions are less reliable than first, and Reedy is remembered as the fat, half-blind old man of fifty-eight, who laughed too much and walked with a rolling limp. He had long foregone the gourmandizing dinners and nights of garrulous drinking when he would enchant some visiting poet—Richard Le Gallienne or Bliss Carman—with his talk. Only a few old friends even then could recall the dashing stripling with those delicate features—the dark shock of tumbling hair always parted in the middle, the sensuous mouth, the hands small as a girl's. What all who knew him remembered and mentioned were the eyes—intense and probing, now laughing, now smoldering, searching and never still. They regarded the world with skepticism, as if no man's fraud and no trick of fate could ever take him by surprise. "He is all eyes," said his friend Edgar Lee Masters. An early portrait by James Montgomery Flagg has him resemble young Oscar Wilde in a brooding humor. But he laughed in the eyes of many cameras. Always there was in his face another quality that skepticism and mockery could not veil: a naked look, as if ardent flesh and spirit had stripped to wrestle there.

He was a *big man* as well as portly, and was so recognized. He would go to Washington and dine at the White House or to New York and be elected "mayor" of Greenwich Village. He would go to a Democratic national convention and write in his breezy, caustic way of all the posturing and the hugger-mugger. Political friends once retaliated for what he wrote by proposing him as a favorite-son candidate for President of the United States, and he was often seriously mentioned as a possible senator. He would be received in Chicago or New York as a kind of minor prophet, a humorous sage and arbiter of literary elegance, always good for a column—or even a full-page interview in the *New York Times*. He would serve on a prize jury with university scholars and be deferred to as a scholar in his own right, though he made a habit of deflating academic self-importance. For a time he was the nation's most respected authority on modern poets, and he was popular even with the warring poets themselves. At a meeting of the Poetry Society of America he called himself a lion—in a den of Daniels.

Until he was forty Reedy was an avowed conservative in politics and in literary taste. From that time on events forced him into an ever more radical position. He became a supporter of Theodore Roosevelt, an advocate of the economic views of Henry George, and a partisan of Masters, Theodore Dreiser, and other spokesmen of literary dissent. Yet in essential ways he remained a conservative all his life, even though it was the rebels who always claimed him for their own. Carl Sandburg said he never missed an issue of the *Mirror*, because he *had* to know what Reedy was thinking. Dreiser called him a "Balzac *manqué*," read his magazine for twenty-five years, and begged to be allowed to write a regular New York column for him—even gratis, though Reedy refused both the offer and the novelist's gratitude for his early support. Reedy seems to have felt that the debt was all on *his* side. Ezra Pound would retort angrily when Reedy ridiculed his novel poetic theories and the obscurity of his poems, yet Pound praised him for having the courage to print *Spoon River Anthology*. Masters, who could not have written that pivotal work without Reedy's early tart rejections and subsequent applause, boasted of Reedy as both his best friend and the "Literary Boss of the Middle West."

Spoon River altered the course of American verse much as Dreiser's *Sister Carrie* had begun to alter the course of our prose fiction some ten years earlier, and in the same direction. Each touched off a lively debate, much of it conducted in the *Mirror*. Each represented a new departure, raising moral and aesthetic, sexual, psychological, and stylistic problems. The broadening and liberalizing effect of the resulting naturalistic trend redirected American letters, and in so doing changed American lives. The trend is now well known. Reedy's part in it is not. In the standard reference works, where his name is mentioned at all, the account of him is invariably inadequate and ill-informed.

Historians are unaware, and will doubtless deny, that before his moment of fame as a critic and the obscurity that closed in so soon thereafter, William Marion Reedy had also helped establish Hawthorne and Emily Dickinson as classic American writers. He had helped bring to America the knowledge of Pater, Hardy, Yeats, Shaw, and the French symbolists. Together with only two other publishers, his close friends Thomas Bird Mosher of Portland, Maine, and Mitchell Kennerley of New York, he had paved the way for a revolution in book publishing. The sentimentality of *Trilby* and *Quo Vadis* had given way to cynicism and that in turn to a refreshing acceptance of realities. Meanwhile Reedy had helped form and introduce some fifty poets, among them Vachel Lindsay, Sara Teasdale, Witter Bynner; he had influenced Conrad Aiken and Amy Lowell. This he accomplished by a process of slow, grudging acknowledgment, a gradually expressed sympathy, then enthusiastic interpretation.

Since he was always more important for the independence and perceptiveness of his judgments than for the way he expressed them, there has been all too little interest in his critical essays. His style had a gusty warmth that was irresistible, but he marred his finest prose by verbal excesses he could not learn to overcome. He told his friends he never really cared for his own writing, but what he wrote showed a keen sensitivity to the inner meanings of what he read, an impish irony, and a shrewd ability to classify a new work and measure it by reference to an undimmed recollection of vast reading. Like his friends Percival Pollard and James Gibbons Huneker, he never seemed to forget a book. A young writer who came to collect a few novels for review said he appeared to read a book without ever having opened it, so swift were his intuitions. He was seldom caught off guard by the unexpectedness or mere daring of an unfamiliar writer off on a new tack. He was not disconcerted by the strident modernism others found baffling or beguiling. It amused him to find antique parallels in Greek or Japanese, that seemed to anticipate the New Poetry and make it look traditional in spite of itself. "All good poetry is essentially imagism," he said in 1917 in defense of Miss Lowell, who doubtless denied the allegation. "This 'new force in letters' is, like all such things, very old," he had written of Yeats in 1898.

He was mistaken in denying Yeats's greatness a few years later. He was often mistaken when he doubted the correctness of his first judgments. Humility in the presence of excellence made him disarmingly quick to admit his mistakes. In politics his shifts were sometimes bewildering, and he had a genius for showing up on the wrong side after deserting the winner. But his laughter was directed more often against himself than against the loser.

The *Mirror,* he said, is the organ of nobody but its editor, "who is himself a 'nobody.'" So he often deprecated fads he himself had started, but in the end he invariably judged each book against a scale of classic excellence. Thus, at a time when Thomas Hardy was driven to abandon fiction by the vilification of most critics, Reedy compared Hardy's supposed impiety with Sophocles' faith and had no hesitation in declaring the tragic vision of *Tess* and *Jude* to be prophetic and religious.

It is his critical sensibility rather than his private or his political life that justifies our reappraising Reedy as a man of intrinsic refinement. "He married a whore," answers respectable St. Louis, and thinks that puts an end to the matter. Yet it was precisely the imprudence of his dealings with women and with money that accounts for Reedy's gradual accretion of tolerance and wisdom. He was tempered by the anxiety of living always on the brink of a disaster—either a romantic scandal or a bankruptcy. Having lived down both, Reedy discovered a passion for defending men he himself had sometimes cruelly attacked. He ridiculed Henry George even as the old campaigner lay on his deathbed, then turned suddenly into an eloquent advocate of George's single tax. Poets like Francis Thompson and Paul Verlaine seemed to demand his special protection because he had passed through ordeals so like their own. He once warned Mosher not to expect to hear anything good about Reedy from St. Louis, where he was considered "hopelessly depraved."

It may be said to the credit of Reedy's home town, however, that it contained gentlemen of the highest professional rank, of nationwide reputation and integrity, who never wavered

THE MAN IN THE MIRROR

in their public loyalty to Reedy. Jurists, financiers, and professors took pride in his friendship at times when his actions were bound to scandalize the bourgeois. So it was with pure glee that he quoted in a letter the waspish comment about himself that he had overheard after introducing Emma Goldman, the anarchist advocate of free love, at the St. Louis Artists' Guild. Emma, said a wag, was probably the only woman in the world whom Billy Reedy could render respectable by his patronage. "Pinked me there, eh?" Reedy chortled.

But if he had his defenders at home, his relations with the community over the years were like a lifelong marriage marked by lovers' quarrels of Celtic ferocity. He was hated by men whose weakness he exposed, and their sons find it necessary to hate him still. He told the city that it had no soul—"or if it has, that soul sings small." He declared its leading citizens devoid of all "affectionate desire to make the city great and beautiful," and accused them of "dismal respectability." His nettle jeremiads were heeded, reread, and reprinted, but their barbs rankle still.

It would be absurd to suggest that Reedy was a great man misunderstood. He was by no means a small man, but in some ways he was all too well understood. His faults were as obvious as his talents. If they sometimes seemed to cancel one another out, still they did not rob him of one quality that is even more rare than greatness. He had the gift of true magnanimity.

CHAPTER 2

A BOY IN KERRY PATCH

BORN in December 1862 in the north-side Irish quarter known as Kerry Patch, William Marion Reedy was a child of Reconstruction, living in the shadow of the Civil War. One of its momentous, if inglorious passages at arms occurred the year before he was born and only a mile or two from his birthplace. That was the fall of Camp Jackson.

As the strategic gateway between East and West, North and South, Missouri had been for a generation the battleground where the slavery issue was fought out in court and Congress. A secessionist governor, Claiborne Jackson, took office during the ominous months between Lincoln's election and his inauguration, in the spring of 1861. He had set up and given his name to an encampment along Grand Avenue commanding both the western approach and the downtown center of St. Louis. Francis Preston Blair, Jr., the free-soil leader, had put an abolitionist war veteran in command of the town's arsenal, near the river which is the eastern city limit. The St. Louis arsenal probably contained munitions enough to control the upper Mississippi and Missouri valleys. When Fort Sumter fell, Frank Blair asked the help of his brother Montgomery, a member of Lincoln's Cabinet, and succeeded in raising a force of five thousand men, who promptly marched on Fort Jackson and demanded and got its surrender. Missouri stayed in the Union.

This action, which both Grant and Sherman watched from

THE MAN IN THE MIRROR

the sidelines along with thousands of other civilians, including Reedy's mother, was followed by an explosion of pent-up feelings. Hooted and stoned by Southern sympathizers as they marched their prisoners off, the raw German farm recruits under Franz Sigel lost their heads and fired into the mob, killing twenty-eight. But the ensuing consternation had ended before Reedy's birth, and the war itself had run its dreadful course before he reached years of awareness. The bitterness left in its train was part of his store of childhood memories, vaguely echoed in a chapter he wrote for a regional history.

St. Louis was, for the most part, intensely Southern; but the revolution of 1848 had brought . . . a great many Germans, who were against slavery and secession. The storm broke, and the breaking was a severe setback to St. Louis, whose prosperity was founded chiefly on that of the South. Its sympathies, through social, political, and business ties, were mainly with the South. The war destroyed business. St. Louis, if not the enemy's country, was strongly suspected of disloyalty, and for a time it seemed as if the war would smite the city itself, while there hung in the balance . . . the alternative of Governor Claiborne Jackson . . . that he would "take Missouri out of the Union or into hell." [1]

Here Reedy wrote with feigned nostalgia of the gaiety and brightness of ante-bellum days in his native city; of bejeweled ladies who "wore a nigger on every finger," of steamboatmen and cotton planters, merchants and slave traders, who spent money like water in the city's pleasure houses. But his own people—refugees from the Irish potato famine—had nothing to do with the splendor he pretended to mourn.

His father Patrick, a man of formidable whiskers and chilling austerity, was an Irish policeman who patrolled a beat in the notorious Third District where Kerry Patch was located. He had left the ancient beauty of Clonmel, county Tipperary, in the hard times, toiled on Arkansas levees beside slaves, and gone as a laborer, first to Michigan, where he married Anne Marion of Dublin, then to St. Louis, where he joined the

A BOY IN KERRY PATCH

force. He was a strong man "whose affections were treasured almost as secrets," his son recalled; "a sad man and quiet."

"Walking a beat in the old 'Bloody Third District' was no pink tea affair," writes a departmental historian, pointing out that while the Irish inhabitants would not permit foreigners (German or Negro) in Kerry Patch after dark, they were even harder on fellow countrymen in uniform. A policeman was expected to lay aside coat and weapons on occasion and fight the Irish with his bare knuckles. The blood-soaked chronicle containing this detail is headed by the portraits of thirty-eight members of the force slain in action. Each page is emblazoned with the motto "Honor the Fallen Policemen: Right and Justice Will Prevail." Patrick Reedy was twenty-seven when his first son was born. He rose in time to the rank of sergeant and became clerk or "night chief" in the headquarters of the Bloody Third. William was to be the eldest of three sons, the darling of his mother's wistful aspirations and the victim (as he came to believe) of his father's rigid devotion to law and property.[2]

The society of postwar St. Louis was dominated by four cultural groups, with none of which the Reedy family had any affiliation. There were the French, a dwindling caste still preserving its language, its real estate, and its habit of Creole urbanity. Pierre LaClède, a New Orleans merchant, had brought his young partner Pierre Chouteau to the site ninety-nine years before and showed him which trees he wanted cleared for his trading post. There were the New Englanders, founders of vigorous Protestant churches, solid business houses, and a private nonsectarian university and school system. T. S. Eliot's grandfather was one of their leaders and spokesmen. There were the Southerners, more single-mindedly devoted to politics than the others, yet by no means unanimous in their loyalties. While most of them were conservative Democrats seeking to recover ground lost in the war, the Blairs, like

THE MAN IN THE MIRROR

Thomas Hart Benton before them, belonged in the yeoman tradition and had come west to extend free soil and fight for emancipation. Finally, there were the Germans, still cherishing the theater of Schiller and Lessing and nourishing themselves on the music of Wagner and Brahms. Carl Schurz was their foremost political leader, but though they still sent their most promising sons abroad to be educated, they also dominated the educational system of the city. Their Philosophical Society controlled the city schools; its head, Governor Henry C. Brokmeyer, left his mark on William Torrey Harris, who became United States Commissioner of Education and in turn gave John Dewey his first encouragement.

With the exception of a few eighteenth-century pioneers like the Mullanphy family, the Irish were slow to rival such leadership. Through preferment in the Roman Catholic Church and ward politics they had just begun to emerge as a recognizable fifth cultural entity. Unobtrusively, a man like James Campbell, the utilities and traction financier, became a power to reckon with in Wall Street, without leaving St. Louis. Such homespun, canny men would inevitably take over Catholic leadership from the French, who enjoyed few accessions of new blood and had less incentive to compete for wealth and prestige. Irish intellectual life centered around the Jesuit mission's long-established St. Louis University, founded to enlighten the Indians. Reedy's mother was determined to send her sons there. She took particular pains with the eldest, who bore her maiden name.

It took all her determination to see that Billy got an education at all, amid the distractions of Kerry Patch. He grew up almost like a country boy on the sprawling Irish common, where it was still permissible to keep goats and raise cabbage. He was baptized in the Church of St. Lawrence O'Toole, peddled newspapers, served as altar boy or sang in the St. Bridget's choir, attended public and then parochial schools, and read whatever came to hand. He was an omnivorous reader who never had any system in his explorations. Rummaging in the attic one day he found in an old trunk a copy of the *Atlantic Monthly* containing Whittier's "Barbara Frietchie." He was enchanted by George Eliot's novels. He was addicted to a magazine called *Chatterbox* and to *Oliver Optic's Magazine: Our Girls and Boys*. But the supply of books at home was sparse, and the beginnings of his vast acquaintance with literature remain something of a mystery. He probably did not start to read with any discrimination until he was eighteen. At school, though, he was given his initial introduction to the classics. He learned Latin under the surveillance of his mother, who knew none, but considered it a key to holiness and a better life. Mrs. Reedy would clench her clay pipe in her teeth and memorize the inflections as the boy recited them, sure to catch him out if he later made a slip.[3]

His best friend was Johnnie Cunningham, who once fancied he saw an angel hovering over the altar while the two boys were serving Mass. His sweetheart was Johnnie's sister. Johnnie was a pirate who would lie in wait for farmers coming in to the old Round Top Market from Florissant, and board their wagons to steal melons. In time there were rumors that he held up men in the streets at night, but William knew him as a boy touched with fantasy, who virtuously delivered milk for his mother.

Often I went with him on his rounds. He would lift and tilt the milk can while I held the pint measure and poured its contents into the housewife's measure and took the tin ticket . . . I have played truant with him, and in winter, when we tired of skating, we would go to a blacksmith shop to be near the fire, and the smith would make us help. Or we would burgle into stable lofts and nestle in the hay so the cops would not see us. He was a boy with a sweet smile, and he could cut up old bootlegs into long strips which he would plait beautifully into five-strand whips, with handles fairly carved out of pieces of broomsticks. He was, as I have intimated, a pious boy. I remember he believed a story about a man who was struck dead for swearing at his cattle. And he used to lend me Frank Leslie's *Boys' and Girls' Weekly,* which contained the interminable and never-to-be-forgotten Jack Harkness stories. Moreover he could invent stories of adventure with Indians and pirates and tell them effectively to me and his sister. He wore a shirt with a low roll collar, with fire engines in full career stamped on the cloth, a square coat with a broad collar, tight jeans trousers with bell bottoms . . . Many's the licking I got for going with Johnnie Cunningham and his pals. For my parents knew of his reputation, and they couldn't see him as a sort of hero-adventurer, as I did.[4]

In spite of the nostalgia that clings to that reminiscence, written many years later, Reedy's childhood was a troubled one. Doubtless this was due in part to the very different expectations his parents had of him. His mother seems to have recognized the quickness of his mind and done all in her power to force its growth. After attending three primary schools, he was sent to Christian Brothers College, the leading Catholic preparatory school. His father remained aloof and sardonic, in a world known to the boys through rumor—a world that was inimical and alien. Many of William's friends besides young Cunningham soon found themselves at odds with the law. Many, like Cunningham, took the consequences.

Meanwhile, childhood was cut short for Reedy. Though he seemed reluctant to grow up, he was precocious. He entered St. Louis University as a classical day scholar at fourteen. This in itself might have been no great hardship, but belonging as he did to a group not yet assimilated by the community at large, he was further isolated by being younger than his classmates. Hence he did not perform as brilliantly in his studies as he had been expected to do. He was elected to the Philalethic Society, a literary club, but won few other honors.[5] Presumably it was his mediocre grades that led his hardhanded father to intervene. After two years in the humanities course, William was ordered to change to the commercial. When he graduated in 1880 it was with a business certificate. This fact always struck Reedy and his friends as exquisitely ironic, for his life thereafter was one long financial emergency, and he never gave up reading Greek and Latin poetry.

While his father's lack of understanding may have caused some of the emotional disturbance Reedy suffered later, it was the conflict between his feelings toward both parents that must have marked him so indelibly. His father wanted him to go into business—doubtless his own frustrated ambition. His mother he regarded as a saint, yet he could never satisfy her exacting standards of achievement and conduct. Her favoritism, too, certainly had its effect in his subsequent attitude toward women. It imposed special responsibilities on him and inspired confused feelings of guilt toward his brothers. Such blurred and unhappy emotions drove him to seek escape in romantic make-believe or conceal his boyish misery behind a jovial mask. His reading carried him into a more manageable world.

He was drawn to Tom Sawyer rather than to Huck Finn: Tom the bookish one, the overimaginative, romantic boy who stayed home, rather than Huck the child of nature, of impulse and direct action, the boy who escaped. Reedy's sympathy went out even more strongly to Tom Tulliver in "that piteous story *The Mill on the Floss*." A sense of pathos and alienation clouded all that Reedy remembered of his own home life, yet he insisted on valuing boyhood as a treasure, even its punishments as blessings. Soon after he was graduated and became a reporter, his friend Cunningham was arrested and broke out of jail in company with a friend of theirs named Jack Shea, who ran straight into the arms of a patrolman Reedy knew, and shot him dead. Reedy saw Shea brought in captive a few minutes later. Cunningham seems to have eluded arrest, only to die in squalid circumstances, in a train

THE MAN IN THE MIRROR

accident. Shea spent years in the penitentiary, and when he was pardoned at last Reedy ruminated on the injustice of their respective fates.

> Shea was very much like me, and had a natural right to as much as I have had of the world. There was nothing in me entitling me to the good time I have had, while he was a pariah and a convict. In the matter of reckless adventure as a boy, I wasn't very much different from him. I know that I and Cunningham were much of a piece mentally . . . The only thing I can see in which I had the best of [them] was in parents that kept track of me and paddled me when I went off upon adventure.[6]

An irrational sense of guilt infects all he tells of his childhood. Yet in discussing the literature of childhood he remained the vehement partisan of the boy, denying the honesty and validity of adult apprehensions. "The child is poet and philosopher at once. He interprets the world by his own unprejudiced experience, and for him there is no distinction or difference between ideal and real . . . He sees the world with fresh eyes, and his faith is mighty in all the beautiful things that ought to be true . . . He is unsullied by knowledge, and the witchery of the charm of him, the touch of pity in the perfection of his enjoyment, is his ignorance of the fact that every new joy marks a step in his eventual exile."[7]

It was probably most unfortunate for Reedy that he lived at home while he was at college and for ten years or so thereafter. The fact that he did is itself evidence of some inner bondage to his parents. He wrote little about his two brothers. Daniel followed him to the university and later into newspaper work. Frank became a fireman, married, and had an only son.

Though he continued to live at home, William's life gravitated downtown. He became increasingly a stranger to the life of Kerry Patch, just to the north. He did not aspire to invade the polite world of the west end or scale the intellectual Himalayas of the German south side. He preferred the great hotels, the bars, and the expectant air of the press room at the Four Courts. His life was governed by cycles of depression, illness, tension, and wild carousing, but there must have been long intervals when he spent all his spare time in the libraries. For it was after he left the university that his reading began to attract the amazed interest of librarians. At the Public Library one of them remarked that only the man who had built up the collection knew more of what it contained.

It was not until he had violently broken his home ties that Reedy began to find himself in his profession. After his mother's death, which occurred in 1897 when he was in his thirties, Reedy grew even more remote from family and neighborhood life. To make up for this feeling of alienation he became intensely gregarious. He would tell his downtown friends of his mother's countless acts of neighborly charity and refer humorously to her fond efforts to paddle him into a life of rectitude. Sergeant Reedy had retired in bad health at the age of fifty-five, and now became obsessed with the accumulation of property and a craving for security. It must have been partly resentment of his father's parsimonious ways that led the son to abandon the conservative views of his youth. He could assert his innermost feelings by becoming increasingly imprudent in business, lavish in his generosity, and radical in his economic theories.

At the time of the old sergeant's death in 1909, Reedy wrote a conventional obituary notice for publication. In it he praised Patrick Reedy's inflexible conduct as an officer of the law and told of the hardships he had endured as an immigrant. Privately he laughed at the wealth the old man had accumulated and invested in slum houses that rented for some $2,000 a year. That income seemed a puny achievement, "a small thing to look at as the result of a life of seventy-four years." Writing to a friend Reedy told how exacerbated their relations had grown.

He positively feared me—from my utterances as to land and wealth in the *Mirror*. He thought I'd delight in taking his property and scattering it to the birds. He wouldn't make a will till he felt the icy hand reaching for him. He summoned a lawyer, made the will, ordered a carriage for the hospital, got to the hospital and collapsed—never regained consciousness. Relinquishing his grasp was the last straw. Then burst that mighty heart. *Isn't* it frightful, the property obsession.

But poor old Dad, it was his loneliness drove him to it, I fear. I often tried to make friends with him. He couldn't be made friends with. He was distant, dark, cold, and he must have felt for many years about me as a hen feels when her hatch of ducks takes to water—only mine wasn't water. I hope he forgives me all my mockery of his idols.[8]

Despite the poor health that dogged him as a youth, Reedy himself survived both his brothers. Frank died young, a few years before their father; Daniel a few years later. The fireman's little boy became Sergeant Reedy's principal heir. At Frank Reedy's funeral William was astonished to find many of his own friends, some now wealthy and distinguished, come to show sympathy for him in his bereavement. Other mourners were old friends of the family, and he felt a stab of remorse that he had grown so much away from them. He could not remember their names, and the dead brother they praised seemed a stranger, someone he had not known at all. Writing about the wake he opened a window into his most private feelings.

Some buxom matron speaks to you by your boyish nickname and begs to introduce two stylish young ladies, her daughters. You show you don't know to whom you are speaking. Then she mentions her maiden name, and your youth comes back in a flash with the memories of a sweetheart long forgotten. An old, old lady speaks to you as if you were a baby. You scan her closely. Why, it is the

A BOY IN KERRY PATCH

old granny who helped nurse you. She must be nearly a hundred years old, but she's not much changed. Substantial citizens recall themselves to your recollection by giving their names. They are the boys with whom you played hooky, stole apples, fought rough-and-tumble or over-the-belt, spelled down or was spelled down by in the match at school. A very aged man in thin, high voice greets you sympathetically and tells you his name, which is that of the once fierce policeman who chased you for swimming in the quarry pond, as you ran, hat in hand, pants and jacket under arm along the deep dust roads, a flying cupid shocking the little girls into flight more precipitate than your own. They come and come, and tell you their sympathy, and the memories they evoke only make you feel the meaner that you had forgotten them all . . .[9]

Throughout the tale Reedy wavers between nostalgia verging on bathos and an irony at his own expense expressing a kind of shame that he has become even modestly successful. The qualities that make his old neighbors look up to him now seem somehow disgraceful. He is oblivious of their pride in his learning, his wit, and his power as a journalist. To have forgotten their names is like a betrayal. Busy friends from downtown have come, one of them a man he was sure had never liked him. Reedy writes: "You despise yourself in a disguised anger that *he* should have deceived you thus." Going from his father's house to the church, hearing the Latin chant again, he regrets that he ever left the parish for the wider world of affairs.

The odor of incense recalls your own acolyte days! Why, you were once just such a wide-eyed, self-conscious, black-handed, close-cropped arab temporarily turned angel! Those were the days when the priest and the altar boys went to the cemetery [to] a rich bug's funeral and on the way back the priest bought you soda water and sugar crackers and a funeral was a picnic indeed . . . Those light effects through stained glass and incense are as magically bright as of old—brighter indeed for remembrance, for regrets, for self-pity and self-knowledge, rudely stirred by this return to an elder day, and expressed in tears that burn but do not come.[10]

THE MAN IN THE MIRROR

One fears that the self-pity is greater than the self-knowledge. The writer seems filled with an urgent need to confess, but the sins he accuses himself of would shrink away to nothing in a clearer light. The brother whose funeral is their occasion is never alluded to or identified. And what Reedy omits saying about the Church tells more than what he says. He is revisiting it for the first time since his excommunication.

CHAPTER 3

LITERATI IN THE CITY ROOM

THE boy had a nose for trouble, if not a hankering after it. He was tall, slender, olive-skinned. Men jollied him, and women were prompted to protect him. Sergeant Reedy lost no time in finding him a job when he graduated from the university. In the summer of 1880, some five months before his eighteenth birthday, William went to work as the *Missouri Republican's* reporter for the sleepy French suburb of Carondolet—the youngest member of the staff of the oldest newspaper west of the Mississippi. One of his first news stories, of a fist fight between a priest and a schoolmaster, caught the eye of William Hyde his editor-in-chief and won him a berth in the city room.[1]

The *Republican* claimed descent from the *Missouri Gazette*, founded in 1808, some forty years before the first telegraph line was strung over the prairie to St. Louis. The paper called itself "a reliable, painstaking Family Journal," but for Reedy joining its staff had the glamor of initiation into some ancient, knightly order. Its downtown offices were encrusted with tradition, though a more prosaic observer might not have seen that patina for the soot. Theodore Dreiser, who was employed there a dozen years later, after a few months' work on the rival morning paper, the *St. Louis Globe-Democrat* (in Reedy's day a thriving newcomer), found the *Republican's* building "so old and rattletrap that it was discouraging." Its city room was lofty, more spacious than the *Globe's*, but beyond that Dreiser could find no advantages.

THE MAN IN THE MIRROR

The windows were tall but cracked and patched with faded yellow copy paper; the desks, some fifteen or twenty all told, were old, dusty, knife-marked, smeared with endless ages of paste and ink. There was waste paper and rubbish on the floor. There was no sign of paint or wallpaper. The windows facing east looked out upon a business court or alley where trucks and vans creaked by day but which at night was silent as the grave, as was the entire wholesale neighborhood . . .* [2]

The *Republican's* prospectus for 1880 declares that its objectives were to unify the people of the West and South and to "allay sectional bitterness." Actually, the paper was sympathetic to the lost cause of the Confederacy. While the *Globe-Democrat* was conservative and Republican, the *Republican* was conservative and Democratic. Editor William Hyde was nevertheless an upstate New Yorker. He was a steady, reliable worker who had come up from the ranks and been in charge for fourteen years, but although he had once flown a balloon home to New York, he was almost wholly lacking in imagination. More attracted to politics than to journalism, Hyde was credited with formulating the strategy that broke the Republican hold on Missouri after the war. This achievement was presently recognized when President Cleveland made him postmaster of St. Louis. Meanwhile, however, the paper was losing ground.

Consisting of ten seven-column pages of the usual size, the *Republican* had a front page fairly divided between advertising matter and national politics. Its second and third pages gave the business news and other items telegraphed from distant places. Its fourth-page editorials were devoted to violent debates with its chief rivals, the *Globe-Democrat* and the *Post-Dispatch*, a peppery evening paper founded the year before. Since the back of the paper was given over to literary

* Reprinted by permission of The World Publishing Company from *A Book about Myself* by Theodore Dreiser. Copyright 1922 by Boni & Liveright. Copyright 1949 by Helen Dreiser.

CITY ROOM LITERATI

essays, society news, and reports of the bustling river traffic, there were only two pages containing local news to which a reporter like Reedy could contribute. All articles were anonymous, however, and only rarely can one be safely attributed to Reedy.

As a cub reporter Reedy can have had few opportunities to distinguish himself, though his city editor, W. A. Kelsoe, said that his brilliance was early apparent. "A big book could be filled with interesting reading matter about Mr. Reedy's reportorial days," Kelsoe later wrote. Unlike the usual city editor, Kelsoe was a man of almost saintly gentleness; Reedy came to call him his "real father." Long after the great scoops with which Kelsoe credits him had become tawdry and the pages had turned yellow and brittle, Reedy continued to regard his cub days as romantic. His fellow reporters were "a band of brothers." They were in fact a whimsical lot living in a buffer state between bourgeois respectability and bohemian license where Samuel Clemens and Eugene Field had passed before them. They dreamed of fame, and two of them did achieve it in a degree. Augustus Thomas became a successful playwright, and William Cowper Brann became editor and publisher of a prosperous monthly magazine. While Reedy may have aspired to follow in their footsteps, he was content for the time being with the adventurous world around him. Occasionally there would be feasts in the city room; Kelsoe would bring the silver-mounted drinking horn he had acquired at Heidelberg, and they would broach a keg of beer and drink to the confusion of their enemies at the *Globe-Democrat*. What Reedy remembered was all golden. "We had youth— and the world was ours."[3]

But it was already apparent that the days of casual good fellowship were numbered. During the seventies, while Reedy was growing up, the town had been intoxicated by the prophecies of L. U. Reavis and other enthusiasts who were convinced that St. Louis was destined to be the metropolis of the hemisphere and the "Future Great City of the World." The year Reedy went to work for the *Republican*, that dream came to an end. The Census, which had showed the population of St. Louis to have quadrupled in 1840 and to have doubled each succeeding decade, now in 1880 reported an increase of only eleven per cent. There was general dismay, even outrage. The newspapers charged carelessness or falsification, and the Post Office was asked to review the count. But while St. Louis would remain for some years the fourth city in the nation, its hope of becoming an inter-American railhead and a rival of Paris was permanently shattered.

Trade and the railroads were passing St. Louis by. That the newspapers of the city were doing their best to keep it in the forefront of national life was not the accomplishment of the *Republican*. The daily press was dominated by two giants among editors, Joseph B. McCullagh and Joseph Pulitzer. Their rivalry posed a threat to the very existence of Reedy's paper. It also prepared Reedy himself to become a shrewd observer not only of the press but of the events it chronicled.

It would be hard to conceive of two successful men more unlike than McCullagh and Pulitzer. Though both were hard-driving, thorough, and fired with intense curiosity about men and their motives, they were opposite in temper, in appearance, and in their personal tastes. McCullagh, the editor of the *Globe*, was a stubby man, withdrawn, intensely conservative, and quietly humorous. His own writing was mordant, but he kept the rest of the paper dry and conscientiously dull. Dreiser, who had begun his reporting on Chicago dailies, was appalled by the repressive schoolroom atmosphere he encountered when he came to St. Louis to complete his apprenticeship on the *Globe*. Reedy said McCullagh was the best newspaperman in St. Louis—not to work for. Dreiser and

CITY ROOM LITERATI

Reedy pitied the editor's terrible loneliness as they walked past the shivering carriage horses awaiting him outside the *Globe* building in the small hours of the morning, and both men regretted his inhuman aloofness. Yet even if he lived in icy privacy, McCullagh's reputation was based in part on the local tradition that it was he who had invented those prying personal interviews so shattering to the privacy of American life in general.

Forbidding as he may have been, Pulitzer was a gregarious soul beside McCullagh. Gawky, with a long neck and hooked nose, he was a caricature of the nervous perfectionist gnawed by dissatisfaction. After his early training under Carl Schurz, he had sold his interest in Schurz's *Westliche Post* for a substantial sum. While still in his twenties he then sold the *Globe* a defunct German daily it had to buy in order to acquire its Associated Press franchise; Pulitzer made good his speculation after publishing the little paper for only one day. A few months before Reedy went to work for the *Republican* Pulitzer had managed to buy two more bankrupt dailies and had merged them into the *Post-Dispatch*. Though he had realized vast profits on his previous transactions and paid down only $2,500 for his new paper, Pulitzer, recently married to a beautiful Southern lady and always extravagant in his habits, had little cash to meet his operating expenses. So it was necessary for him to devise a radically new editorial policy that would win subscribers and advertisers away from the two solid morning papers and several less stable evening ones, including the *Chronicle,* which W. E. Scripps was publishing as part of the world's first newspaper chain. Pulitzer's program —daring exposés of civic corruption coupled with high-minded crusades for civic betterment—served the purpose.

He was a gadfly. Where ordinary prudence would have led him to restrain his fire until he could build up a friendly following, Pulitzer instantly undertook to expose all the depravity overtaking a border town in the wake of war. He would spend long hours in the curtained office where he kept up his tortured rewriting. Then he would burst forth upon his staff with complaints, orders, and aspersions. In time he drove Scripps out of St. Louis and challenged the supremacy of the *Globe*.

His immediate success in building circulation was due, however, to a brisk and vivid style rather than to blatant subject matter. The *Post-Dispatch* had a tone of self-assurance. Its articles were terse, precise, and lively. More than that, they gave information that other papers missed and, going beyond this, sought to examine the causes of an event. While contrasting sharply with the drabness of the morning papers, its format and neat sans serif headlines were by no means gaudy or overemphatic. The editorials were crisper than McCullagh's and a third the length of Hyde's.

As an alert cub reporter Reedy learned a good deal by following Pulitzer's development of his paper. At a time when the growth of public utilities went hand in hand with the spread of political venality, the *Post-Dispatch* was relentlessly specific. It denounced those who gave bribes as well as those who took them; it castigated wealthy tax evaders as well as bawds and faro operators. Admirable as these methods might seem, they made Pulitzer even more unpopular than he had always been with rival journalists. As an apprentice he had engaged in bitter personal feuds, and once he had deliberately shot a lobbyist in the vestibule of a hotel. Now, as editor, he intensified his personal attacks. Twice he was assaulted in the street—on one occasion by a professional gambler; on the other by Reedy's employer, William Hyde.

One personal vendetta undertaken by Pulitzer's managing editor, John A. Cockerill, in 1882, shocked the community and won Reedy's lasting contempt. While Pulitzer was out of town the *Post-Dispatch* printed a libel against Colonel Alonzo

Slayback in the heat of a political campaign. The Colonel, a former Confederate officer and a lawyer popular in St. Louis society, was the originator of the Veiled Prophet's parade and ball, which opened the autumn fairs and the city's social season. The charge the *Post-Dispatch* reiterated was one a gentleman of his mettle could hardly ignore. "Far from being a brave man, the Colonel, notwithstanding his military title, is a coward." When Slayback walked into the *Post-Dispatch* office to demand a retraction, Cockerill shot him dead.

Every segment of the public took sides in the debate as to whether the killing was murder or self-defense. Hotheads, led on by editorials in the *Republican*, wanted to burn down the new *Post-Dispatch* building. While a grand jury failed to hand down an indictment, opponents of the Pulitzer paper insisted its editor had "planted" a pistol on the Colonel's body after shooting him merely to escape a well-deserved thrashing. Editors throughout the West attacked Pulitzer for his "personal journalism." Soon afterwards he was impelled to leave the town for good, harboring (as his official biographer says) a feeling he never lost: that he was "unwelcome" there.[4]

While Reedy had not yet come of age and had no direct connection with this war among Olympians, the partisan excitement it stirred in him had a lasting effect. He considered Pulitzer inhuman and ruthless. He lost no opportunity to attack Pulitzer's journalistic methods and to bring up the Slayback case against him. In the course of years two of the editors Pulitzer sent out to manage the *Post-Dispatch* became close friends of Reedy. Each of them had cause to detest the publisher; yet it was clear that all those who came in contact with Pulitzer's genius learned something from the experience, and Reedy was no exception. His first taste of success would come when he challenged Pulitzer's position in a national debate.

Meanwhile, he had more elementary lessons to learn. His or-

THE MAN IN THE MIRROR

dinary duties involved regular visits to the board of education, attendance at meetings of the municipal council, and coverage of lectures, sermons, funerals, and weddings. With his penchant for trouble, he also haunted the Four Courts and the jails. He would sit up all night with the warden as he watched beside a man condemned to be hanged in the morning. They would chat interminably about immortality and the atheism of Robert Ingersoll. In the morning reporters and jailers would march their victim out to face the crowd and the gallows, and Reedy would note how he glanced up at the sky or at a bird perched on a tower, then look straight ahead "with fluttering swallowings in his throat." Later he would write of witnessing twenty hangings. "The sun came over the jail roof with a sudden glory, and made the crowd look inexpressibly mean as it poured out of the gate to meet the newsboys, crying 'Extry: all about the execution!' "[5]

The closest Reedy came to a momentous news story was an incident in the city room the month Colonel Slayback was killed. While temporarily on duty at the city desk he reached into a drawer to find copy for a waiting foreman from the composing room. With copy short that night, Reedy was tempted to hand over the thick manuscript he found there, without reading it. Fortunately he changed his mind. What he had found was his editor's account of a secret interview with Frank James, during which the train robber had promised to give himself up.[6]

"I have come back to Missouri to try to regain a home and standing among her people," the bandit had told Reedy's editor. "I have been outside her laws for twenty-one years; I am tired . . . of seeing Judas on the face of every friend." Jesse James had recently been killed by a member of his band trying to collect the heavy price that had been placed on both brothers' heads. A premature announcement that Frank meant to give himself up might have had bloody consequences, besides costing the paper a notable scoop. Having glimpsed the statement soon to be telegraphed to the ends of the earth, Reedy became too frightened to confide his discovery to anyone. And presently, knowing nothing of the narrow margin by which he had escaped disaster, the editor accompanied Frank James to the state capital and saw him received as a hero.[7]

While such moments of excitement are what a reporter likes to recall, there were long gaps between them. These Reedy filled with much reading and literary talk. He was fortunate in finding a few friends able to guide him in his search for learning. Miss Alice Kroeger at the Public Library would set aside books she knew he would want to read. Mrs. Ellen Bernoudy, permanent secretary of the school board, in the same building, also took a hand in his education. Besides giving him helpful explanations of the inner workings of local politics, she recommended books and gave him some inkling of the areas of polite letters to which he had not yet been introduced. Her grace and "flawless tact" were another revelation. Unfortunately tact was not one of the accomplishments he acquired from their acquaintance. Years later his criticism of her chief, Superintendent of Schools Louis Soldan, cost Mrs. Bernoudy her post.[8]

An even more important friend was William Vincent Byars, an older reporter whom Reedy's city editor, W. A. Kelsoe, had hired away from McCullagh—a considerable feat, since Pulitzer, too, had his eye on Byars and later did employ him. Reedy recalled a night in the city room when Byars chanted the *Younger Edda* in his own translation from the Old Norse, and another night when his friend read him Herodotus in the Greek, in a police station. Byars encouraged Reedy's long visits to the libraries. He himself was an ascetic who preferred country walks and nature study to the saloons and fancy houses Reedy frequented. Reedy had such reverence for his tutor's erudition that he overlooked the difference in their tastes, and in forty years he never presumed to address Byars by his first name. Even when they found themselves in opposite political camps, after Byars had drafted the platform on which William Jennings Bryan first ran for president, Reedy felt he must qualify his opposition, saying that his admiration for Byars made him doubt his own stand. He said he considered Byars a poet and "the best classicist in the United States." Above all he was so "unaffectedly Christian" that Reedy said Byars was like those members of the early Church to whom Paul had addressed his epistles.

Byars' research had begun with linguistics and led him into a study of prosody, after he had mastered Sanskrit, Hebrew, Gothic, Old Norse—and had read the major poetry of Latin, Greek, and the modern European languages. Gradually he developed an obsessive conviction. There seemed to him a causal relation between the Indo-European languages and the poetic forms they developed. In 1895, while working as assistant to the managing editor of Pultizer's *New York World* Byars experienced a sense of revelation. He published his vision under big headlines:

A *WORLD* DISCOVERY
The Iliad and the Odyssey of Homer Rhymed Poetry

Byars said he had hit on a fact destined to "alter the intellectual life of civilization." Generations of schoolboys had been misled into regarding classical poetry as unrhymed, but Homer's hexameters were made up of short, rhyming ballad lines. Their rhyme scheme turned on inflectional vowels. Their melody must be chanted to be heard. Anyone could learn to hear it, though he feared it would be forever lost on the deaf ears of classical scholars.

While this discovery may have seemed to most readers of the *World* somewhat less enthralling than Peary's expedition to the North Pole, which was treated on the following page, Reedy congratulated Byars fervently. What he had done, Reedy told him, was what must awaken "the solid boneheads out here to your merits and achievements." He wrote to offer his help in overcoming the prejudices of St. Louis academicians who contended, Reedy said, that "if the facts are as you say, they would have been discovered in Europe and not out in Missouri."

Years later, when a new generation of poets began seeking freedom from rhyme-bound forms, Byars' influence on Reedy indirectly affected several of them. Meanwhile Byars encouraged Reedy to listen for the melodic values *he* heard in classic verse, and confirmed him in the belief that Greek standards of poetic expression set a scale by which to measure all later writing. Byers taught him to hope a time would come when modern poets would emulate Homer and Horace in "subjecting rhythm to the laws of melody."[9]

Reedy worked for the *Republican* for only four years, leaving there soon after he came of age. Often ill, perhaps suffering from tuberculosis, he was so weak on one occasion that his fellow reporter, Michael Fanning, had to carry him on board a river steamer bound for Minnesota, where Reedy hoped he might recover. Fanning did not expect to see him alive again, but on board ship Reedy fell in love with a pretty passenger, and this seems to have effected a speedy cure. Whatever the cause of his recovery, when his former city editor and Mrs. Kelsoe visited him later that summer, they found him in robust health.

Reedy's career during the late eighties is altogether obscure. For a time he gave up journalism and tried ward politics, hoping for an appointment as commissioner of parks. Then he returned to reporting, joined McCullagh's *Globe* in 1886, moved to a tawdry little Sunday paper, the *Star-Sayings* (later the *St. Louis Star*), and became its editor in 1892. Soon afterwards he must have returned to the *Globe,* where he is said to have been a successful feature writer during the rare intervals when he was sober. McCullagh discharged and rehired him again and again. By the time he was thirty Reedy had become the hero of a cycle of alcoholic myths, and it seemed most improbable that his early promise as a writer or an editor would ever be realized. The great quantity of reading he was doing was not likely to help his advancement, either.[10]

"There is a general law that dissociates successful newspaper life from bookishness," William Hyde once told a lecture audience. Most of the young men on his staff at the *Republican* would have disagreed. "Literature," as Reedy said, was their "common dream"; but their literary aspirations were pathetic and foredoomed, though traces were sometimes discernible in their accounts of street brawls and trials at the Four Courts. Feature writers would become lyrical in describing the autumn fair or the Veiled Prophet's ball at the Merchants Exchange, where a debutante would be chosen to rule the town's social life for a year as Queen of Love and Beauty. Most of them also wrote verse, as Reedy did—facetious parodies of Swinburne and Rossetti for the most part, but serious bad poetry as well. Most of them doubtless believed, as he did, that the prose quality of journalistic writing in the eighties was higher than it ever was before or later, an opinion not borne out by a reading of the papers.

Reedy was not the only newspaperman whose behavior grew wildly erratic as a result of frustrations inherent in the craft. Pulitzer became an irascible old man firing scorching cables at his editors from a yacht in the Mediterranean. Even McCullagh, by 1896, found the life too much for him and ended by throwing himself from a window. The surprising fact is that Reedy survived to be one of the great editor's pallbearers.

CHAPTER 4

THE DECADENCE—
FROM OSCAR WILDE TO
AN "AMERICAN BAUDELAIRE"

THE year 1882, when Reedy was twenty, saw one other event quite as startling and more illuminating than the end of the James gang or of Colonel Slayback. This was the St. Louis visit of Oscar Wilde, whose well-publicized tour of America made an indelible impression on Reedy. It was his first encounter with a literary movement from which—although Poe was its acknowledged precursor—America had until then been happily immune.

Décadence is a term more familiar to America than to France. *C'est dit des écrivains de l'école symboliste,"* says *Petit Larousse,* defining *décadent.* But it is better understood in France than it ever has been in America. Reedy's prolonged fascination with it may explain a few idiosyncracies he shared with some of his contemporaries. It is of more than biographical interest, for the impact of the decadence on every literature had pervasive consequences.[1]

This predominantly French phenomenon had begun as an outgrowth of Charles Baudelaire's admiration for Edgar Allan Poe, almost half a century earlier. It evolved out of earlier romanticism and its myth of the noble savage. But the hero of decadent fiction and poetry was neither noble nor savage. He was a Man of Feeling tainted by progress and materialism —jaded, disillusioned, and content to be corrupt because helpless to stem the spread of corruption around him. His cynical dandyism was a pose, a pretense of indifference. This thinly disguised protest shared the anti-sentimental (hence counter-romantic) bias of the naturalists. Naturalism grew up side by side with the decadence—so much so that a typical decadent writer like Joris Karl Huysmans might even call himself a naturalist, until Émile Zola, the lawgiver of that sect, read Huysmans out of his camp.

What naturalism and the decadence shared as they spread through England, Central Europe, and Russia, was a somewhat ambiguous repugnance for the vast forces of science and industry, which presumed to assert man's control over his environment and his destiny, while threatening to destroy it. Their repugnance was ambiguous because naturalism (much influenced by Comte and Darwin) was an outgrowth of science, while both it and the decadence were products of industrial civilization.

What they shared as heirs of romanticism was confidence in the ultimate validity of emotional data as opposed to the rational data of science. This item of faith had been the most nearly definitive trait of romanticism. For the parent movement as for its two offshoots the feelings had been final arbiters of conduct as well as the source of all true knowledge. Hence the poet must cultivate sensitiveness to feelings and must despise the conventions of society, which mask and annihilate emotion, killing the spirit. The decadent is a "sensitive." As Reedy puts it in one of his early essays on Pater: "The spirituality of the sensuous is the saner part of that movement in letters which has been called the Decadence." Decrying the "vicious asceticism" he attributes to Anglo-Saxon as opposed to Latin cultures, he goes on to say: "We [Anglo-Saxons] do not cultivate the senses to that acuteness and sensitiveness which, so to speak, enables the eye to apprehend the invisible, the ear to encompass the inaudible, and all the sensory organs to contribute pleasure through emotions that are almost as vague as premonitions. Our souls can be found only with a club, when our hearts should be reached with a stab of a shaft of perfume . . ."[2]

It is in their attitudes toward nature that the three movements part company. The romantic had been seeking to attune himself to its mysteries and find truth in the apprehension of its beauty. The naturalist was more impressed with nature's cruelty and indifference to man. The decadent was ambivalent. As a dandy he felt himself to be above and outside nature, while as the heir of romanticism he also despised the ugliness and mediocrity of urban-industrial life. In the most searching examination of French decadence made by an American, A. E. Carter says the decadent fuses "a hatred of modern civilization and a love of the refinements modern civilization made possible. He is a noble savage—*à rebours*."[3]

In his efforts to assert his superiority over both nature and bourgeois conventionality the decadent carries sensitivity to the limit of neurasthenia. Love being natural, he must rise above it. He explores every subtlety of experience, deals clinically with every aspect of love, tries to surmount every natural feeling. Clara, in Octave Mirbeau's *Jardin des supplices,* makes passionate love before a cage where men are enduring the most fiendish torments the imagination can devise. Des Esseintes, in Huysmans' novel *À rebours,* prefers orchids to native wild flowers, leaves a jewel-encrusted tortoise to die and stink in his study, and is enchanted when his physician orders that he be fed by enemas—a final repudiation of natural functions. The decadent hero is self-centered, introspective, unwilling to make any concession to the ethical demands or the etiquette of society, indifferent to his friends and alienated from humanity. At last, driven by terror, he flees hysterically to religion.[4]

Reedy recognized the rationale, if such it can be called,

in an appreciative essay on Paul Verlaine some years later. The sympathy with which he discussed the poet implied a measure of self-identification.

> [Verlaine] was a mighty poor specimen of a man, take him for all in all, but for that reason he was interesting. He was not practical. He had no common sense. He had no self-control. To-day he groveled before the altar of the Virgin. To-morrow he worshipped Priapus in mad orgies. He was a pendulum that swung between St. Anthony—Origen even—on the one hand, and de Sade on the other. There was no peace for him either on the heights or in the depths. He was a flesh-prisoned Hell.

Reedy went on to praise Verlaine's diction, and in so doing betrayed the intensity of scrutiny he had for years devoted to the decadent effort to merge and intensify all sensation through refinement of artistic intuition. He taught his readers that to know such a poet must be a creative exercise of their own sensibilities. But it was Verlaine's character that fixed his attention. "The light shone clear through him. He was a man without a mask, the only one since—not Rousseau, but Villon and Rabelais. He was a moral swamp that grew beautiful flowers. And the world wondered, not knowing that he was only a man a little less disguised than the others." [5]

Reedy himself came to deplore the bizarre attitudes struck by the decadents, so it is hardly surprising that other American critics who never came under their spell failed to see the connection between the decadent movement and the great achievements in the twentieth century to which it was an indispensable preliminary. The interest in neurosis and perversity to which Poe gave almost unprecedented belletristic expression resulted in a great deal of tedious minor writing. It is much simpler to lump all such *fin de siècle* vagaries under the innocuous name of "Bohemia," as Harry T. Levin has done, than to relate them to a basic trend. In the *Literary History of the United States* Professor Levin discusses them almost

THE DECADENCE

facetiously as fads lacking any "clear-cut direction." His term "Bohemia" has connotations of quaintness, amiable impracticality, and sentimental escapism.[6]

Yet as one examines a life like Reedy's that bridges the years of minor decadent writing and those of major accomplishment, so facile a terminology becomes untenable. The faint odor of decomposition that overhung the eighties presaged a prolific literature thriving on disease and neurosis. What Reedy called a moral swamp became the essential source to writers as powerful as Marcel Proust and Thomas Mann, Franz Kafka and Henry Miller, the Albert Camus of *La Peste* and the William Faulkner of "A Rose for Emily."

Reedy's first direct contact with the decadence probably came in the form of an assignment from Kelsoe [7] to get over to the Southern Hotel and interview Oscar Wilde, who arrived in St. Louis in February 1882. By wearing velvet knee breeches and drawling of blue china the young poet had capitalized shamelessly on the notoriety he had won as Bunthorne, the butt of Gilbert and Sullivan's satire in *Patience*. Americans had reacted with vehement disgust. The authors of a detailed study of Wilde's reception and the prevalent attitudes it revealed note that in St. Louis the *Republican* was more "genteel to Oscar" than were the McCullagh and Pulitzer papers.[8]

The *Post-Dispatch* cartoonist drew Wilde as an ape, remarking that if a man makes a monkey of himself he becomes living proof of Darwin's theory. The *Globe* described Wilde as a dandy in a fur overcoat, his light-brown locks falling to his shoulder, and declared that by such exhibitionism the poet had "counted himself out of the company of self-respecting men of letters." Its tone of heavy sarcasm implied that Wilde's effete dress and mannerisms were beneath the contempt of hearty, down-to-earth St. Louis.[9]

Yet the *Globe* could not wholly conceal the visitor's respectful familiarity with American customs and writers. Wilde's lecture at the Mercantile Library that night showed both courage and good sense. Indeed his patience and lack of pretentiousness were an unspoken rebuke to the hecklers noisily repeating the jibes of the press. He undertook to speak only as a modest disciple of John Ruskin, urging Americans to revive the handicrafts of the past and build beautiful cities for the future. Yet he took a bold, original line in telling America to stop imitating European models and to seek architectural and artistic forms of its own.[10]

In its editorial next day the *Republican* took the *Globe* to task for belittling not Wilde but the people of St. Louis and their institutions. Its own interviewer gave a more favorable demonstration of the city's manners. He said he had found Wilde totally unlike the " 'greenery yallery Grosvenor Gallery' young man" he had been painted. "There was never a better-natured, better-mannered collegian came out of Oxford." [11]

There was a meeting of minds between Wilde and his obviously very young caller from the *Republican*. Many characteristics of syntax, vocabulary, and thought make it almost certain that the caller was Reedy, though the interview was unsigned and one cannot be sure. Wilde said he disliked Eastern cities that looked like imitations of European ones. It was like Reedy to emphasize, as the interviewer did, Wilde's preference for the West, and to follow that by asking whether the accounts of Wilde's meeting with Joaquin Miller were accurate. Wilde answered that they were "one of the few true things" that had been written about his travels; the Oregon poet who had taken London by storm a dozen years before was "a very fine fellow" and admirably American. Wilde asked in turn what the reporter thought of Whitman. The reporter answered that though his own opinion was valueless, there were lines in Whitman's *Leaves of Grass* which, "insane as he is counted, remind one of Homer."

THE DECADENCE

This answer, so characteristic of Reedy, evidently delighted Wilde, who lit a cigarette and, puffing thoughtfully, agreed that Whitman was a great poet. "There is more of the Greek feeling in him than in any modern poet," Wilde said. "His poetry is Homeric in its large, pure delight in men and women, and in the joy the writer feels and shows through it all in the sunshine and breeze of outdoor life." Asked about Reedy's favorite poet, Swinburne, Wilde did not attempt to deny that he had learned from him. He said that Swinburne was, after all, the third great libertarian after Milton and Shelley. Imitation of such a master was a necessary stage in learning an art.

Wilde, as usual, inveighed against the press. American newspapers "would employ people to write about the arts whom in England we would not consider qualified to report on a case of larceny above the value of five shillings." He wondered why most interviewers troubled to talk to him at all, since they insisted on fabricating his side of every conversation. Asked whether he disliked having the public let in on every detail of his private life, Wilde repeated what he had told a Washington reporter: he only wished he had one.

The writer of the interview departed with the feeling that Wilde's much abused aesthetic theories were "strangely akin to that practical system of metaphysics so unaesthetically styled 'horse sense.'" [12]

This interview must have influenced Reedy profoundly. Here was a poet exposing himself to mockery and misunderstanding in order to get attention for a doctrine that was wholesome and genuine in itself. What Wilde did to get attention for his message seemed unimportant. Behind the poseur, the wit, the parodist of his own parody, who out-Bunthorned Bunthorne, was a man of character—a devastating critic of the cant and complacency of the times. Afterwards Wilde went to France and came directly under the influence of Huysmans, whose *À rebours* gave him the model for his *Picture of Dorian Gray.*

It was not long after encountering Wilde that Reedy gave up journalism and tried to get an appointment as city park commissioner. The move may have been partly the result of what Wilde had said in contempt of American newspapers and in favor of beautifying American cities. It may also have been suggested by Reedy's young friend, M. A. Fanning, a protégé of Kelsoe who gave up his job as city hall reporter for the *Republican* to become Mayor David R. Francis's secretary. A wealthy grain broker with political ambitions he could afford to indulge, Francis had bought an interest in the *Republican.* When he became governor Fanning would accompany him to Jefferson City.

Meanwhile, during their apprentice years, the two young men were on close terms. Reedy led Fanning to read the moderns just as Byars had led Reedy to read the classics. "He gave me my first copy of Swinburne and of Omar," Fanning says of Reedy. "He gave me a paper copy of *Progress and Poverty* while [Henry George] the author was still an unknown man. He gave me *Isis Unveiled* and [A. P.] Sinnett's book on *Esoteric Buddhism* before Mme. Blavatsky had dawned on America." [13] But that potpourri—Swinburne, FitzGerald, the single tax and theosophy—held less enchantment for Reedy and Fanning than the decadence. Their next contact with that movement seems to have been through a frivolous society magazine, *Town Topics,* founded in 1885 in New York.

It was here that they would encounter Francis Saltus Saltus, who wrote fashionable society verse under the pseudonym Cupid Jones. It is hard to see what either Reedy or Fanning found to admire in this young poet, the spoiled son of a wealthy arms manufacturer. He had lived in Paris and was

THE DECADENCE

well informed about its most esoteric literary cults; that was apparently enough. A modern commentator says that American decadence reached its lowest level in Francis Saltus, who "held the lightest pen of the century"—perhaps an exaggeration.[14]

Francis was the half-brother of Edgar Saltus the novelist; Edgar translated one of Barbey d'Aurevilly's classics of the decadence into English and was a friend of Wilde, who translated another. But Edgar was capable of more serious work. His *Philosophy of Disenchantment,* though light in tone, is a competent study of Schopenhauer. He wrote some thirty novels. Edgar envied his half-brother's talent but said that his facility was both "frightful" and fatal, since Francis would never revise. Francis would scribble an ode to the coloratura Adelina Patti in four languages within an hour. He would write an opera with one hand while composing sonnets with the other. James Huneker tells of his selling epigrams to *Town Topics* for fifty cents apiece, when he could have been making a fortune writing critical essays—or so Huneker believed.[15]

In a number of magazine articles, which appear not to have survived, Reedy hailed Francis Saltus as an "American Baudelaire." It was true that Saltus admired Baudelaire, whom he celebrated as "king of voyellous sounds." He was partial to Gerard de Nerval ("Serene beneath the splendor of sad stars"), and revered the Marquis de Sade, whom he invoked in French as "Sublime libertin!" But Saltus was the victim of his own *sprezzatura* and dissipated his talent in rich living, drink, and drugs. At sixteen he had produced a ghoulish romance, an imitation of Poe (though even Poe provides no precedent for a hero who ravishes his lady and sleeps with her unaware that she has been dead for two days). In his thirties, bored and melancholy, Saltus wrote thirty sonnets celebrating his thirty favorite drinks. He expired before reaching forty, leaving five thousand lyrics for posthumous publication. "They have the perfume of exquisite sadness," Reedy declared.[16]

In 1890, the year after Francis Saltus died, Reedy and Fanning made a holiday visit to New York. The father of the Saltus brothers was grateful for the generous things Reedy had written about his late son's verse and invited the two young men to dine with him at the Park Avenue Hotel. Saltus *père* was a cosmopolitan gentleman who had been knighted by Queen Victoria for inventing the rifled steel cannon, a boon to mankind. He had been created marquis by the King of Portugal for a grandiose philanthropic gesture. He began the dinner conversation in French and was startled to learn that Reedy did not speak French. As Fanning recalled the incident, "Mr. Saltus was astounded. Then he asked Reedy as to his experience in Paris and was told: 'I've never been to Paris; I've never crossed the Atlantic; this is my first visit to New York.' Mr. Saltus leaned back, stared and muttered, 'My God, what a genius.' He added that no one had ever interpreted his son as this young man had; that he had even revealed the son to himself."[17] Totally oblivious of the comic ramifications of the scene he has drawn, Fanning is gravely impressed when Mr. Saltus offers to entrust Reedy with the task of editing three volumes of his late son's poetry. "It was at that time I realized his greatness," Fanning says of Reedy. "He was twenty-seven years of age."

Reedy was evidently not inclined to take on that editorial responsibility, though Saltus was ready to make it worth his while and the fee might have enabled him to live in New York. He and Fanning doubtless considered remaining there and may even have thought of pushing on to Paris to sample the genuine decadence at its source. But they returned to St. Louis, where there was a rich compost of decaying French culture, and together started a magazine similar in many ways to the one to which young Saltus had been a contributor. One

THE DECADENCE

of its features was a running commentary on decadent literature—always allusive, facetiously disrespectful, and full of double meanings. Its method was what some wit has called "praising with faint damns."

Wilde was now lampooned for his determined cleverness. "To be an epigrammatist," Reedy mimicked, "is to excel in saying things worse than anybody else. To say them better is to be a prig." [18] But though Wilde was in disgrace following the disclosure of his homosexuality, and the degradation into which it had led him, Reedy was indignant at a suggestion that Wilde's plays should henceforth be shown anonymously. They were the brightest comedies of the century, he insisted, "constructed with a skill beyond the attainment of any contemporary." [19] About a year later a Chicago friend sent Reedy an unsigned copy of the *Ballad of Reading Gaol*, soon after its anonymous appearance in London. In an essay studded with long quotations Reedy announced that this agonized statement must be considered a literary event of the first importance—far more significant than the fate of its author, whose name he withheld up to the final sentence.

"I don't know how to class the poem," Reedy said; but it reminded him of "The Ancient Mariner," and he heard in it elements reminiscent of Villon and Hood. "It is something of all three," he continued. "It has some of Coleridge's mysticism and romanticism. It is as brutal as Villon and as harshly gay." What he found most impressive, though, was Wilde's new simplicity, reminiscent of Hood, which laid the basis for brilliant contrasts of tone and color. Even in its occasional banality the *Ballad* seemed to re-create intentionally the barren monotony of prison. Most appalling was the poem's "truly awful despair and emptiness of heart . . . The writer is a 'lost soul' if ever there was one," Reedy concluded, "but damned or trebly damned he is an artist, and he projects his mood, his atmosphere, into his work with a force that tells

45

you, in every line, the hanged murderer was, and is happier than he." [20]

Oscar Wilde had ushered Reedy into the anteroom of the decadence, and his tragic end helped show the way out. While Reedy from then on faced resolutely in another direction, the lessons he had learned from the strange, neurasthenic outpourings of the eighties and nineties were of lasting value. They broadened his ethical horizons. They enabled him to comprehend Yeats, who, like him, had studied Sinnett and Mme. Blavatsky. They enabled him (with the aid of his friends Mosher and Pollard) to establish the reputation of Pater in America. They deepened his appreciation of a quality in Villon, a sardonic essence, that was alien to the romantics. From the time of the Wilde trials in 1895 Reedy was careful not to identify himself with the decadence. Henceforth he would warn young writers against giving in to those exotic tastes which had first drawn him to Wilde and Saltus. At the same time he had grown immeasurably in tolerance and understanding because of his early contact with the movement.

When Vance Thompson made the first serious study of the French symbolists to appear in America, Reedy greeted it with reserve. He twitted the editor of *Mlle. New York* for trying to explain these obscure poets to themselves. "One can't blame Mr. Thompson," he concluded. "One suspects that the writers he is interpreting didn't know what they meant." [21]

What beguiled, diverted, and charmed him was Thompson's belief that these new French poets were "literary children of Poe and Whitman." It was fascinating to consider that in like fashion an American mode of writing might some day grow out of the "Frenchy decadence" of Paul Verlaine.

CHAPTER 5

THE FOUNDING OF THE *MIRROR*

THE magazine Reedy and Fanning started was one of several in various cities that called themselves journals of society. The oldest and most enduring of these was *Town Topics*. Founded in 1885, the New York weekly bore a prospectus under its original masthead: "The change in the methods of journalism during the past few years has been a marked one. The long editorial has given place to the short, pithy comment; the descriptive article or thoughtful essay to the pungent paragraph . . ."[1] The editor proposed to present news of high society to its members in the "slightly altered form" of paragraphs. Apart from its novelty and possible appropriateness to a time of hurry and bustle, the casual paragraph had a timely function. In an age when leaders of society felt bound to observe a strict code of decorum in public, it capitalized on the gossip that circulated all the more busily in private.

About half the content of *Town Topics* consisted of such gaily malicious or salacious anecdotes, under the title of "Saunterings." For the rest, the magazine contained poems and tales, news of clubs, resorts, entertainment, sport, and the stock market ("Other People's Money")—all calculated to appeal to an emerging leisure class, the wealthy merchant and his wife. While *Town Topics* soon earned a reputation as dubious as the gossip it disseminated (it skirted the libel laws and was said to derive part of its income from outright blackmail), it also gained some degree of genuine literary distinction. Among its anonymous or pseudonymous contributors, besides the Saltus brothers, were two of the most knowledgeable critics of their time, Percival Pollard and James Gibbons Huneker. Some of the fiction published in the magazine reflected their taste.

As a leader of its genre *Town Topics* took its distinctive coloring less from its lurid content than from the eccentricities of its founder's brother, who presently became its publisher. Colonel William D'Alton Mann said he had held a war-time commission in the Union Army. After the Civil War he must have gone south as a carpetbagger, for he took over three Alabama daily papers, turned them into the *Mobile Register,* and claimed to have been elected to Congress though never seated. He boasted of having been a pioneer in cottonseed oil production and railroading. He published in *Town Topics* his design for a luxurious railway sleeping car, which he had patented and afterwards sold or lost to the Pullman Company. He also claimed to be a founder of the Compagnie Internaltional des Wagons-Lits.

The editors of *Collier's Magazine* once challenged his veracity, saying that the publisher of that "sewer-like sheet," *Town Topics,* was no better than a horse thief or common burglar.[2] Yet so reliable a commentator as Ludwig Lewisohn has said that the future of American letters was rather to be discerned in the red-carpeted office where Colonel Mann sat—"a bulky old man with magnificent white hair and patriarchal beard, a pasha of the Gilded Age"—than in the polite literary salon of a Columbia University professor like Brander Matthews.[3] Reedy, too, admired *Town Topics.* He called it "that exceedingly well-written and sprightly journal,"[4] regularly borrowed at least a page of copy from it, and founded his own reputation on pseudonymous paragraphs like the "Saunterer's." Both "Saunterings" and Reedy's "Reflections" maintained a tone of bland indifference to consequences. But whatever Reedy's paragraphs may have been like initially, he soon broadened their scope and raised their level of discourse to a plane to which the "Saunterer" did not aspire.

Reedy and Fanning may have founded their first magazine under the title of "St. Louis Sunday Tidings," by 1890 or earlier. No copy of that or of the first three annual volumes of their *Sunday Mirror*, which began publication in February 1891, has come to light. In the absence of such evidence it is impossible to say how closely their efforts may have resembled those of Colonel Mann. But the *Mirror's* beginnings are clouded by the presence on its original staff of a third partner, James M. Galvin.

Theodore Dreiser, the most vivid and detailed historian of St. Louis journalism, came to town the year after the *Mirror* was started. His recollections of Galvin, given at great length, throw the whole venture into a murky light. Dreiser was shocked by the easy opportunities for blackmail that lay open even to so callow a novice at reporting as himself. He implies that Galvin would not have been shocked. Galvin was knowing, slick, and gross—as Dreiser says, "a sort of racetrack tout, gambler, amateur detective and political and police hanger-on." Dreiser had reasons for dealing harshly with this red-headed tipster, whose main function was to gather information not accessible to other reporters. Red Galvin scooped him with distressing regularity and seemed unimpressed with his literary genius. But it is questionable whether he was also, as Dreiser insinuates, a Jew posing as an Irishman, an illiterate boor, a stockholder in a chain of brothels, and a commercial dealer in slander. Galvin's family thought of suing for libel when Dreiser's highly colored account of his early rivalry with Galvin appeared in a magazine. Later, when the same chapters appeared in Dreiser's autobiography, the book publishers had deleted Galvin's name.[5]

To Fanning Galvin was a "groundling." There is little indication what the relations among the three men were, and no certainty about Galvin's editorial functions. But in one account of the *Mirror's* early days Reedy seems to admit that part of the magazine's revenue derived from blackmail. This "peculiar commercialism," as he calls it, was not what the editors had in mind during their high-minded first year. It would appear, however, that the venture was insufficiently capitalized, ran into financial difficulties, and was taken over by unscrupulous backers who put temptation in the editors' way. Reedy goes on to say that after three years "the idea of 'grafting' the public gave way"—in other words, that reform set in. But neither the crime nor its repudiation is entirely believable. Reedy was prone to admit to unfounded slanders; and even after his confession he wrote some paragraphs about local profligates with implications as salacious as any to be found in *Town Topics*.[6]

While its quality is below the usual level of Reedy's prose, the following sample illustrates the closeness of the parallel between the two journals. It purports to have been written for the *Mirror* by the St. Louis correspondent of *Town Topics*.

To the Northwest of the city there is a pretty suburb known as Normandy, a settlement made up of the homes of the old French families and their branches, and here it is that the scandal had its origin and has its continuance. Among the most exclusive families in this settlement is that of a wealthy gentleman sybaritic in his tastes. The gentleman is the father of a large family, but his children as well as his wife have not lived with him for a long time. The most conspicuous personage about his household is a woman of handsome presence, whose ostensible connection with the establishment is that of governess . . . She now has the house to herself and carries herself as its mistress. She drives along the pretty country roads in a splendid trap, and takes the keenest delight in making the women turn their backs from and the men turn theirs after her . . .[7]

It is said to have been the custom of *Town Topics* to present such an item to the victim, in proof or manuscript form, ask

FOUNDING OF THE *MIRROR*

whether he cared to make any corrections, and accept a consideration for altering or suppressing it. This may have been the *Mirror's* practice, too.

There is no need to minimize the odium which attaches to such enterprises, but the evidence against the *Mirror* is inconclusive. The possible complicity of the individuals who edited it must be weighed against their known good characters and subsequent careers. Fanning was an idealist, a man with an acute social conscience who later devoted himself to the cause of municipal reform. J. J. Sullivan, who rose from copy boy to business manager, may have been less naive than Fanning seems to have been, but he was a devoted and honest associate of Reedy's for almost thirty years. Frances Porcher, who worked with Reedy on the *Mirror* after serving as his assistant on the *Star*, was a respectable woman of a good Virginia family. Of R. A. Dyer, another early staff member, Kelsoe says he was one of the "most reliable reporters" in St. Louis, "accurate in his statements and a man of his word." [8] Other early participants in the Mirror Company are mere names. Nothing whatsoever has been learned of A. B. Cardoner and A. LeBerton or LeBerthon, who with James Foy and William Thomas (brother of playwright Augustus Thomas) may have been part owners of the publishing company. Of Galvin himself it should be added that he later played a crucial role in initiating the muckraking campaign that won Lincoln Steffens his fame, and that several writers besides Steffens praised his courage in doing so.

The *Mirror* seems to have been started as one of a group of casual publishing ventures in which Reedy had a hand. Of the *Tidings* and *As You Like It*, which he helped edit for some five years, nothing is known. The one certain fact is that the *Mirror* was a vigorous, often cogent, organ of protest against the genteel tradition in Midwestern journalism. During its first precarious years Reedy used it boldly to shatter the complacency of church-going bribe dispensers and to celebrate the "wistful, tristful spirit" of Walter Pater.

In St. Louis, as in other Western cities, new periodicals started off blithely every year. If they succeeded they moved east. If they failed they were soon forgotten. Surveying the scene as the century was drawing to a close, the dean of St. Louis magazine editors, Alexander Nicolas De Menil, saw no prospect that the "dreams and hopes of the pioneers" of his guild would be realized for at least another quarter-century. De Menil, editor of the *Hesperian,* had taken part in every likely periodical venture for twenty years. He was a great grandson of the city's founder and had been an attorney before becoming a man of letters. With gentlemanly forbearance he blamed the many failures not on inept writing but on public apathy or the "absence of local literary pride." It nettled him to recall that Mark Twain had won a public he himself scorned to woo. Twain, he said, was "absolutely unconscious of almost all canons of literary art"; else how explain "such coarse characters as Huckleberry Finn?" [9]

Any suggestion that a magazine like the *Mirror* might one day justify his pioneer hopes and dreams Dr. De Menil would have rejected out of hand. Discussing magazine literature in one of those civic biographical encyclopedias (opulently bound in leather, tooled and edged with gold, rich in steel engravings of founding fathers and newly self-made men), De Menil left out the *Mirror* entirely. In a separate article he lumped it condescendingly with the *Western Commercial Traveler,* the *Mississippi Valley Butcher,* and other "miscellaneous journals." Reedy he patronized as a "bright and aggressive young journalist, whose command of language and faculty of discrimination" had given the weekly "a name and a local habitation." Though Reedy might have cringed at the solecism, he would not have denied what De Menil went on to add:

FOUNDING OF THE *MIRROR*

that for all its literary flavor, the *Mirror* was occupied chiefly with "local and social interests."[10]

Of his own literary quarterly De Menil wrote that it was more serious than any periodical in the West. "The *Hesperian* does not publish stories," he said; "it is devoted entirely to the higher literature."[11] He had to confess, though, that before William Torrey Harris moved east with his *Journal of Speculative Philosophy,* that scholarly publication had distinguished itself for even higher seriousness. Published in St. Louis for a dozen years, it had included among its contributors Bronson Alcott, William Ellery Channing, William James, Charles S. Peirce, and John Dewey. Henry James, Sr., Ralph Waldo Emerson, and Charles Darwin had been among Harris's earliest readers and correspondents. For a number of years the *Journal* had been a philosophical organ in a class by itself. Though of far less literary merit, it antedated even the *Academy* of London and Oxford as a medium of neo-Hegelian criticism. Its philosophical and literary core was the old St. Louis Philosophical Society.

If one can detect a single impulse that gave direction to the editorial policy of the *Mirror* in the nineties it was its antagonism toward both the genteel tradition represented by De Menil and the pretentious intellectuality of the St. Louis philosophers. The two shared a determination to preserve the distance between literature and the common life of America. Just as De Menil despised "the uncritical masses" so Harris addressed himself to "the few who study works of literature for spiritual insight." While Reedy could be polite to De Menil, his delight as a satirist was to contrast the rarified idealism of the philosophers with their human failings as politicians, lawyers, and autocrats of the St. Louis school system, which Harris had superintended. It was to be Reedy's function as a critic to close the gap that separated the daily life around him from its reflection in contemporary letters.

THE MAN IN THE MIRROR

The nineties were a troubled decade, dominated by more than five years of economic depression. The strikes and bitter reprisals of the eighties continued. There were riots and political trials, unemployment in the towns and foreclosures in the country. Intellectually it was a time of profound insecurity, which could take even the agnosticism of an Ingersoll seriously. The columns of the *Mirror* touched on such disquieting themes as social Darwinism, anarchism, the confused murmurings of Populism, the novel sexual theories of Havelock Ellis and Cesare Lombroso, the radicalism of Edward Bellamy and Henry George, the dreams of manifest destiny fomented by Josiah Strong and Alfred Thayer Mahan, attacks against the trusts, Governor John Peter Altgeld's clemency to the Haymarket "bombers," in Illinois; and Altgeld's battle with President Cleveland over the Pullman strike. Faith and morality were vexing puzzles to readers of the *Mirror*, and their letters showed that political scandals and mounting evidence of corruption were shaking public confidence in the American dream. Elsewhere, the intoxicating rhetoric of a young professor of history, Frederick Jackson Turner, who proclaimed that the closing of our frontier had stopped a "gate of escape from the bondage of the past," enchanted all who longed to believe America enjoyed some peculiar immunity from problems that bedeviled the rest of the world. The newspapers carried sensational evidence to the contrary, featuring hunger and repression on the one hand, vainglorious and conspicuous consumption of riches on the other. The general unease was aggravated by another topic that bulked large in the *Mirror:* the rapidly shifting status of women—in education, in business, and at home.

That a time like this, when inarticulate masses clashed with self-taught masters, was also one when the insights of literature were not available to interpret disconcerting realities,

FOUNDING OF THE *MIRROR*

seemed ominous to Reedy. But he dealt with most problems in a light and provocative vein.

In St. Louis it was the weighty thinkers of the Philosophical Society who drew his sharpest barbs. They spoke of their doings rather fulsomely as The St. Louis Movement in Philosophy, Literature, and Education, and traced their origins to the fifties. Most of the members belonged to an older generation, predominantly German. All were close students of Hegel's *Wissenschaft der Logik*. This was their "Bible," which their founder and prophet, Henry C. Brokmeyer, had translated from the German. He spent years revising his translation but never published it. His bride, to whom he had given a copy for her wedding present, said she couldn't imagine what language he had translated it *into*.[12]

In literature the philosophers thought only Homer, Dante, Shakespeare, and Goethe were worth their serious critical discussion. In education they followed Froebel and Montessori, founded the first American kindergarten, and anticipated many of the ideas which their protégé Dewey later forged into the progressive school movement. In political philosophy they believed that institutions continually tend to approach a divine ideal, attaining conformity to it by a process of conflict and resolution—Hegel's *thesis, antithesis,* and *synthesis*. Their sententious utterance of these views, their implacable optimism in the face of all that went wrong in frontier political evolution, their love of generalization and preference for an abstruse jargon (partly Hegel's, partly their own) gave the philosophers an affinity with the transcendentalists. Harris brought Emerson and Alcott to St. Louis and eventually followed them to Concord. Brokmeyer, on the other hand, was scathingly contemptuous of the grade of logic the New Englanders found acceptable. By 1890, however the St. Louis Movement was as dated as St. Louis's pretentions to future greatness, and the philosophers retained only a unique ability to annoy the young.[13]

In his highly entertaining account of the relations between the St. Louis and Concord groups, Henry A. Pochmann praises Brokmeyer and his followers because they lived "strictly according to the vision" which Emerson and his theorists "contented themselves with advising others to follow." Brokmeyer had migrated from Germany alone and penniless, knowing no English. He had progressed from New York bootblack to Louisiana shoe manufacturer, only to give up industry and fortune and resume his studies. From Georgetown University in Kentucky he had gone to Brown, where in the course of disputations with the University president, Francis Wayland, he heard of transcendentalism. Then, contemptuous of the dilletantes of Brook Farm, though admiring Thoreau, he had moved to Warren County, Missouri, where Daniel Boone had ended his days. There Brokmeyer had lived by trapping and hunting, studied Hegel, and undertaken his painfully literal translation of the *Logik*. After the Civil War, in which he played a major role as leader of the German liberals, he studied law, rewrote Missouri's constitution, and ran successfully for lieutenant governor, serving for a year or so as acting governor of Missouri.

With his erudition, his keen intellect, his wide experience and aptitude for command, Brokmeyer could have matched the career of Carl Schurz. But, as his disciple Denton Jacques Snider says, he preferred to transcend the transcendentalists. Unlike Pochmann, Snider felt that politics proved Brokmeyer's undoing. Reedy, who knew Governor Brokmeyer, bore out Snider's view. He recalled the philosopher as "a big, rough, Indian-faced and Indian-speaking Rabelaisian," and in a portrait more alive and breathing than any other that has sur-

FOUNDING OF THE *MIRROR*

vived, he noted the wedge that parted Brokmeyer's beliefs from his performance.

The intellectual force in the red-granitic frame, the Gargantuan nose, the beady eyes, the sarcastic smile come up before you. And such talk! It was a cyclone of words—ordered words, in a dialect, every one counting . . .

Here was a German who couldn't speak English who could speak Choctaw, fresh from the backwoods, who had translated the greater part of Hegel's *Logic*—and understood it. Here was a great burgomeister sort of man, full of round oaths and strange obscenities, who soared into the spaces of cold thought and then cut loose with the boys at night and carried, after fixing, the primaries.

The nights at Baldy Holly's in Jefferson City or at Pat Carmody's Pontiac Club here, and "Old Brock" talking to one or two of us, when we could get him away from the political gang! I heard him even as Lamb must have heard Coleridge; the likeness was strong when Hegel gripped him hard and bore him away into things he could only speak of in Hegelian jargon.

And this man, who formed the gentle Snider, who influenced William Torrey Harris, who broke an intellectual spear with [Thomas Davidson] "the greatest scholar in the world," who could talk Hegel in Choctaw and spoke of translating him into the language of the Sequoyah—what think you he was doing? He was the head of the railroad lobby at the Missouri capital, passing out passes by the handful, running the legislature single-handed and alone. Yet he could soar with Plato! He was the friend of liberty. It was he, largely, and Frank P. Blair, who saved Missouri to the Union. He helped enfranchise the Confederates proscribed by Drake's Constitution. He was a leader. He was in line for a senatorship. But—all the idealism vanished. The railroads got him —he was gone . . .[14]

The only one of the St. Louis Movement for whom Reedy entertained any admiration was Snider, the most prolific author of them all. Reedy regarded him with a kind of wonder mixed with pity. The man pursued his Baconian aspirations toward mastery of all knowledge with such single-minded indifference to worldly regard or reward, yet fell so far short of his goals. Snider had already published some twenty books —commentaries on Shakespeare, Homer, Goethe, Dante; volumes of poems, a novel, pedagogical studies. He was about to start writing a sixteen-volume analysis of the psychological basis of all knowledge. "A most gentle, simple man," Reedy called him: "He lives in St. Louis, but he walks in Hellas in the morning of the world and thinks thoughts that ecstacized the first thinkers who attacked the mysteries of whence and whither." [15] Toward the others Reedy was less sympathetic. Thomas Davidson, a Scottish high school teacher and a charter member of the Fabian Society of London, had been Joseph Pulitzer's intellectual mentor. Reedy, like Snider, found him inhuman and cold, and referred to him sarcastically as "the greatest scholar in the world." He charged Davidson with advocating the abolition of love in marriage; said the Honorable Charles Nagel was not above making mercenary political deals in the corridors at City Hall; and insinuated that Louis Soldan, Harris's successor as superintendent of schools, might want watching in his dealings with the "text book trust."

By 1894 Harris had left St. Louis, served as president of the National Education Association, and become Bronson Alcott's collaborator in guiding the famous Concord summer school of philosophy. He was also United States Commissioner of Education and represented America at international gatherings. When this "truistic transcendentalist" (as Reedy called him) came home to lecture on Goethe, Reedy mocked the psychological terminology he had now superimposed on Hegel's.

Professor Harris is famous as an educator but more famous as one of the most voluble and learnedly unintelligible of the later members of the Concord school of philosophy. He is "away up in G," on the differentiation of the ego, qualitative subjectiveness, and the distinctiveness of the apprehension of the reason and the

FOUNDING OF THE *MIRROR*

perception of phantasmagoriae . . . He is the man who made the *Journal of Speculative Philosophy* a source of unfailing pleasure to a class of cryptogrammatists who delight in the location of the needle of thought in a haystack of sesquipedalian verbiage, and the explorers of mind who love to thread their way to the open air of common sense through a labyrinth of sentences.

Reedy compared Harris's St. Louis audience to that of the pedant in Goldsmith's "Deserted Village," whose "words of learned length and thund'ring sound, / Amazed the gazing rustics ranged around."

Being an eastern man now, all Westerners are "rustics." The veneration he evoked here was due largely to the wonder that a man who had once consented to live in St. Louis should have achieved the distinction of being so unintelligible as to impress Emerson with his philosophical profundity.[16]

The *Journal of Speculative Philosophy* suspended publication about the time Fanning left the *Mirror* and Reedy took over as its sole editor. The humorous German periodical *Puck* had gone through struggles like the *Mirror's* but was now reported to be thriving in New York, proving (said Reedy) that a magazine could achieve greatness "by leaving St. Louis in time." But Reedy was dismayed when his leading rival, the *Criterion,* followed the general drift eastward, leaving him in sole possession of the field. He felt the "unfortunate dwellers in Manhattan" would not know what to do with such talent.

Actually, the transplanted *Criterion* did well in New York. "How, as a youngster, I used to lie in wait for the *Criterion* every week, and devour Pollard, Huneker, Meltzer and Vance Thompson!" H. L. Mencken later recalled. "Scarcely a month failed to bring forth its new genius. Pollard was up to his hips in the movement . . . He had a hand for every débutante. He knew everything that was going on. Polyglot, catholic, generous, alert, persuasive, forever oscillating between New York and Paris, London and Berlin, he probably covered a greater territory in the one art of letters than Huneker covered in all seven." [17] But the *Criterion's* witty French editor, Henri Dumay, fell out with his prudish employer (a retired St. Louis school teacher) and the magazine went under. After that Pollard and Huneker sent Reedy the kind of contribution they had formerly sent Dumay. The peripatetic Pollard signified his devotion by listing "The *Mirror,* St. Louis," as his address in *Who's Who* for as long as he lived.

Reedy himself had no inclination to move east, with or without his magazine. His style and character as a writer depended on his vast acquaintance, and his intimate knowledge of the places and institutions among which he had grown up. The vagaries of a bartender or an elegant hostess, the mannerisms of a debutante, the appearance of a pompous mayor, the eccentricities of street characters he knew by name, the oratory of a reforming clergyman—such minutiae gave piquancy or tumultuous life to his "Reflections," which generally took up three or four pages at the front of the magazine and were signed familiarly "Uncle Fuller," whimsically, "Marion Reed" or satirically, "Pasquin." Yet if humorous or knowing accounts of law suits and club gossip, press comments, personal feuds and political contests were his staples, his paragraphs, each impaling some indignity or foible, were ballasted with more substantial topics gleaned from leading journals sent him in exchange for the *Mirror* from London, New York, Chicago, or San Francisco. These items from abroad he discussed with fantasy, mischief, and zest. It was Reedy's relish for human diversity—his quick scorn or tenderness or delight in the incongruous—that gave broad appeal even to his comments on local trivia. This "local" point of view, much like the perspective Steele gave the *Spectator* and Harold Ross insisted on maintaining in his *New Yorker,* was the intrinsic virtue rather than a limitation of his magazine.

By "the glorious middle nineties," as Mencken called them,

FOUNDING OF THE *MIRROR*

the *Mirror* had sloughed off all resemblance to *Town Topics* and was discovering writers others overlooked or underestimated. Reedy printed Emily Dickinson long before she was widely recognized; Kate Chopin, who now lived in St. Louis; and Alice French, who signed herself Octave Thanet. He printed Ambrose Bierce in 1894, and later was delighted to discover his *Tales of Soldiers and Civilians* in a paper-backed edition sold by a news butcher on a train. And he acquired translators who could acquaint his readers with the exotic literary wares of France, Russia, and Germany. Already he was promoting the exquisite books published by Thomas Bird Mosher in Portland, Maine, and exchanging suggestions with that ardent literary pirate. Mosher was advancing the American reputations of John Donne, William Blake, and Robert Browning, as well as such contemporaries as William Morris, Walter Pater, Rudyard Kipling, and Robert Louis Stevenson, British writers unprotected by American copyright.

Unlike Colonel Mann, Reedy kept reducing the amount of space assigned to gossip of "society" and altering the format, the content, and the subtitle of his magazine each year. What had been "A Journal Devoted to Literature, Art, Society, the Drama," became "A Journal of Comment on Anything of Human Interest," and by the turn of the century "A Weekly Journal Reflecting the Interests of Thinking People." Later the subtitle became "Reedy's Paper," and finally it was absorbed like the polliwog's tail, and the title became simply *Reedy's Mirror*.

CHAPTER 6

TOWARD NATURALISM

A YOUNG woman some five years his elder put the finishing touches to Reedy's education. In her middle thirties Miss Thekla Bernays was a plain but frank-featured lady, vivacious in manner and vivid of speech. The age difference between them was no barrier to a friendship that grew in candor and intellectual excitement with the years.

Born in an obscure Illinois village and educated abroad, Miss Bernays had turned out the English libretto of an oratorio on the rape of the Sabines, which was sung at the Mercantile Library the year Reedy joined the *Republican.* Subsequently she had lectured widely, contributed to the *Journal of Speculative Philosophy* and the *Criterion,* and written of her travels for the dailies, both English and German. A student of literature brought up in the tradition of her renowned kinsmen, the professors Jakob and Michael Bernays, Thekla Bernays chose many of the foreign language books given the Mercantile Library by its president, Robert Brookings, better known as benefactor of Brookings Institution. She also kept house for her brother, a brilliant though controversial surgeon, who was one of Reedy's close friends. Dr. A. C. Bernays had been the first American to earn a doctorate of medicine *summa cum laude* at Heidelberg. He was also a passionate racehorse owner, who on occasion performed surgical operations on thoroughbreds. Reedy once told Miss Bernays he enjoyed pulling the good doctor's leg as much as Dr. Bernays liked amputating other people's. While she could seldom brook such flippancy at the expense of a brother she idolized, Thekla Bernays had a lively sense of humor. She also shared Reedy's literary tastes, notably his enthusiasm for Pater.

Writing in the *Globe-Democrat* in 1894, Miss Bernays attempted to define the two governing tendencies among the "jumble of ideas" that made up the "Currents of Modern Literature," as she entitled her essay. The predominant influence for thirty years, she said, had been the Darwinian. In France this had routed romanticism soon after that movement won out over neoclassicism. "The analytical and comparative methods taken over from the exact sciences were at once adapted to poetry and fiction." Darwinism was the basis of the naturalist school, which, however, was inextricably interfused with others calling themselves "Impressionists, Decadents, Symbolists, Sensitivists." She quoted George Eliot's remark that speech is "but broken light upon the depths of the unspoken," and said that all these groups were engrossed in efforts to transcend speech, and voice the unspoken.

The decadent cults were less interesting as literature, however, than as a symptom of "the malady of our day—shattered nerves, neurasthenia." And she cited Huysmans, the Dutch novelist Louis Couperus, the Belgian Maurice Maeterlinck, and the Frenchman Paul Bourget (who had dedicated a book to Henry James) as typical of the subjective, impressionist tendency. She distinguished between these decadent writers and the primarily naturalist Darwinians, whom she found less "tainted" by the modern malady. Among the naturalists she placed Henrik Ibsen, Leo Tolstoy, Fyodor Dostoevski, Hermann Sudermann, and Gerhart Hauptmann.[1]

Three years later, in 1897, complimenting her on an appreciative essay about Pater's *Gaston de Latour*, Reedy confessed that he himself had grown weary of Pater's "maddening mistiness." He called Thekla Bernays a "most splendid critic,"

THE MAN IN THE MIRROR

but added, "Doesn't one tire of cream puffs? I like a good, rough, blurting style now and then. I like a fellow to forget . . . the way of saying a thing in the urgency to say it."[2] This in effect was his first plea for naturalism.

Reedy's reputation as a critic must rest partly on his success in evaluating the earliest primitive stirrings of naturalism in American fiction. Yet an examination of his essays and "Reflections" on what has come to seem a clear-cut tendency toward naturalism is bound to turn up some baffling contradictions and surprises. If he often expresses violent antipathy for what one might expect him to admire, it may reflect less on his judgment than on literary historians who have taught us to expect responses that are sometimes the product of theory rather than observation.

The line between decadent and naturalist writing was blurred in the nineties. At times Reedy was as unsympathetic toward Ibsen, Tolstoy, James, and Émile Zola (the accepted spokesman for naturalism) as he was in his taunting references to the decadents. His attacks on Hamlin Garland, an American follower of the naturalist trend, were intemperate and sarcastic. This want of sympathy is all the harder to understand when one finds Reedy writing an experimental story about Kerry Patch in a naturalist vein, in 1894; printing Ambrose Bierce and a story by Israel Zangwill from *Town Topics,* the same year; and acclaiming Stephen Crane's *Red Badge of Courage* as a work of genius. And, as we have seen, Reedy also defended Thomas Hardy at a time when adverse criticism had driven him to give up fiction. Similarly, Reedy's recognition of Dreiser's purpose and method five years later was as instantaneous as a conditioned reflex. And when he hailed James Joyce soon thereafter it was with the same spontaneous gesture of welcome, like a greeting waved to a friend met by appointment on a crowded street corner.

TOWARD NATURALISM

Despite his ten-year exposure to the decadence Reedy still had the romantic impulses of the idealistic boy who had defended Johnnie Cunningham of Kerry Patch as a hero adventurer. Such instincts, one would suppose, were sadly out of date at a time when romanticism was smothered in sentimentality and belittled by all the newer schools. But Reedy's idealism was philosophically based, a part of his Jesuit conditioning, and he never abandoned it. His sentimental bias, though a weakness he did not entirely overcome, was always counteracted by a saving love of irony. Thus he admired extravagantly Henry B. Fuller's *Chevalier of Pensieri-Vani*. Its exotic Italian setting was romantic but what appealed to him more was its ironic tone. Fuller's *Cliff-Dwellers* and other proto-naturalist Chicago novels had not the same charm for him. Later in the decade a similar combination of irony and romance in revolutionary Italy was what drew him to Ethel Lilian Voynich's *The Gadfly*, a work bought by two and a half million revolutionary romantics in Soviet Russia, long after it had been forgotten in naturalist America.[3]

Reedy's critical approach was not that of journalistic reviewers who base arbitrary judgments largely on personal taste. From the first he seems always to have begun his critical appraisal of a work or an author with a generic analysis. Each had to be "classed" before it could be interpreted, and interpreted before it could be judged. Reedy's prodigious memory made classification a fairly automatic process. He would have agreed with Virginia Woolf that "even the latest and least of novels" has the *right* to be judged with the best of its kind.[4]

"I wonder if anyone ever reads *The Scarlet Letter*," he remarked in 1896. "I judge not, for if it were read we should not hear queries as to when the great American novel will be written." Hawthorne's psychology, he wrote, was more acute than that of the modern French and Norwegians. "Balzac's creatures are manikins compared to the vital humanity of Hester and Rev. Mr. Dimmesdale, and nothing in literature since Ariel and Puck is quite so eerie as Hester's child. The spiritual tragedy in the book is more tense than anything since the Greek drama died." Its poetry, like the Greek "enshrines the poetry of life," he added, "its bravery in suffering and its weakness in everything." [5]

Similarly, in disagreeing with William Dean Howells on the merits of Mark Twain's *Recollections of Joan of Arc*, Reedy could admit that Twain had brought interesting insights to his reading of history, but, he added, "he has nothing of that faith in unfaith that is the peculiar savor of Montaigne and that one should expect in a story dealing with such a subject." These reactions to Hawthorne and Twain are typical. Reedy continually maintained that Hawthorne was still being underestimated, while Twain could not be considered a great humorist. Measured against Rabelais, Reedy found Twain parochial. Materialism, he contended, had blunted his wit.

Toward Twain's friend Howells Reedy maintained an attitude of deference, though they disagreed on almost every question. The old gentleman was a pioneer of realism, but it was not for this that Reedy venerated him. He respected the craftsmanship of Howells' novels. He accepted the fact of Howells' critical prestige and nicknamed him not altogether facetiously "the Dean" of American critics, often commending his kindliness. He reprinted approvingly an item from the *Mirror's* Chicago contemporary, the *Chap-Book,* written by its editor, Bliss Carman, which held that while Howells might be mediocre, dogmatic, and narrow, he nevertheless exercised a sway comparable to Dr. Johnson's, because of his deeply rooted charity. But Carman added, "He is rather the friend of youth than of literature." When Gertrude Atherton, in San Francisco, began the general attack on Howells as a repressive influence on American letters, Reedy came to his defense.

TOWARD NATURALISM

But by the middle nineties Howells' influence was chiefly discernible in the younger writers he had sponsored, and these Reedy did not concede the same immunity he accorded the Dean. He deplored their way of returning Howells' compliments in print, and reprimanded Stephen Crane, Harold Frederic, and Hamlin Garland for a kind of literary logrolling he took to be the mark of a coterie.

He first knew Crane as a *Chap-Book* poet, and praised *Black Riders* in 1895, though he made fun of the lines.

> Two or three angels
> Came near to the earth
> They saw a fat church . . .

"When so specific as to the church, why such incertitude as to the exact number of puzzled angels?" Reedy asked. "The poet's eye in a fine frenzy rolling, should be able to count straight." And he asked whether the popular song of the day would have been popular had it celebrated "two or three little girls in blue." [6]

The Red Badge of Courage, coming out the following year, won Crane Reedy's unqualified praise. The novel was "a production of genius, not the result of mere talent." Its freshness was like "newly greening woods in spring." Its directness, its appeal to every sense, its "analogical flashes," were all but Homeric. He did not choose to identify it with any contemporary trend. Passing over minor crudities and "infantile" blemishes, he praised Crane's honesty in rendering "the overpowering irony of things." But once *Red Badge* had become a critical storm center and Crane's early novel *Maggie: A Girl of the Streets* was brought out for the first time under Crane's signature, Reedy began to have misgivings. He considered *Maggie* not naturalism but a "kind of illegitimate symbolism." [7]

Reedy was prejudiced against the *Chap-Book,* the leading outlet for American naturalism, because it had become the medium of a literary cult. This little magazine, a thing of typographic delicacy and beauty, had been started in 1895, after Reedy became sole editor of the *Mirror* upon Fanning's departure. Its publisher was Herbert S. Stone of Chicago, son of the general manager of the Associated Press and at the time still an undergraduate at Harvard. Reedy called the *Chap-Book* excellent in its way, though "too everlastingly devoted to Mr. Hamlin Garland to be a continual delight to sane people." [8]

Garland's first collection of short stories, *Main-Travelled Roads*, had appeared in 1891 under copyright of that powerful New York organ of social protest, the *Arena*, but Stone presently announced a new edition with a preface by Howells. Garland's *Land of the Straddle-Bug* was serialized in the *Chap-Book* soon afterwards—a distinction accorded few writers besides Garland and Henry James. By the mid-nineties Garland was turning out two or three books a year—novels, stories, criticism, verse—and Howells predicted that he would end by creating a distinct new school of American literature. If there was one thing Reedy mistrusted more than a cult it was a school of literature.

What brought down Reedy's thunderbolts on Garland, however, was not so much his *Chap-Book* associations as certain condescending remarks he had made about Hawthorne in an interview. Stumbling on *Mosses from an Old Manse* had first given Garland the idea of becoming a writer, he had told a reporter from *Illustrated American*. "I had no idea that I should like him so much," Garland confessed; "for, as he was a classic, I supposed I should find him dry. I doubt if I should like him so much now; but at the . . . time, I found him inspiring." When the interviewer wondered how a realist like Garland could have been inspired by such a "pronounced romanticist" as Hawthorne, the young man burst out laughing and admitted he had once been very "conventional" himself. It was only when he had read Howells that he decided to become a realist or—as he preferred to say—a "veritist." Rudyard Kipling and Sarah Orne Jewett belonged in the same school, he said, and Henrik Ibsen had been "one of the first of the veritists," though Garland could not approve his "probing of social ulcers." [9]

"The way to make literature true is to give it verity," Garland had said, and Reedy called this definition "epigrammatic." Garland did well to admire Howells' English, he said in one of his "Reflections," for it was certainly at least as fine as Victor Hugo's, which the young man also praised. But as he read of Garland wondering if he would still like Hawthorne, Reedy lost his temper. "'I doubt if I should like him so much now,'" Reedy quoted. "Certainly not. Now, Mr. H. G. could give Nathaniel Hawthorne cards, spades, little casino, big casino, and three aces, and beat him." Garland had told the interviewer that his learning to become a writer had been a long story, "a process of years." "Rome was not built in a day." Reedy concluded.[10]

Critics had credited Garland with bringing to American literature an invigorating dash of youthful independence but it seemed to Reedy that he had no more than the brashness of adolescence coupled with a profound ignorance of America's genuine achievements in letters. Reedy looked with jaundiced eye on a collection of Garland's essays which Herbert Stone had brought out two years earlier under the title *Crumbling Idols*. These have since been called a bold manifesto giving a metaphysical basis for the new naturalism. Garland had declared the new West to be culturally self-sufficing. He had said that for most Americans Wordsworth, Dante, and Milton had become "mere names."

"Rise, O young man and woman of America!" Garland had declaimed. "Stand erect! All that Shakespeare knew of human life, you may know, but not at second hand, not through Shakespeare, not through the eyes of the dead. . . ."[11] To which Reedy replied, a month after commenting on the *Illustrated America* interview, that Garland was "prophesying through his hat."

Garland had appealed to the regionalism Frederick Jackson Turner looked to as the source of a new, pure American culture now that the frontier was closed. But the cry of the West for a new literature was not, Reedy said, the "wild yawp . . . Mr. Ham Garland hears in his secondary consciousness superinduced by contemplation of himself." What the people wanted was trash. Garland's own publishers, the firm of Stone & Kimball, had just dissolved. While Herbert Stone proved able to carry on his publishing business alone, Reedy listed firm after firm that had been forced to the wall by the public's indifference to the literature of the West. "It must not be understood that there is no culture in the West," Reedy concluded. But the thousands of discriminating readers there read what was best, regardless of its origin. They did not "debauch their minds with the febrile fiction, the undigested essays, the charlatan science, the exaggerated art," which, he implied, Garland was so boisterous in promoting.[12]

Reedy's own attitude toward regionalism comes out when he praises a Missouri novel he calls "weakest where it is most Missourian" for depicting "a world that will be recognized as real anywhere." When a reviewer in the *Mirror* praises a *Little Book of Missouri Verse* that includes three of his own poems, Reedy says the collection is "calculated to make the state ridiculous."

While Garland's critical essays provoked Reedy by their optimism, his fiction aroused general opposition by its pessimism. Where Howells had established himself as a realist by delineating an American scene whose conflicts were usually happily resolved in the end, Garland drew on rural life as he had known it in the Dakotas. There the unequal struggle generally ended with mortgage foreclosure, crop failure, drabness and disease. For Garland was following in the footsteps of Émile Zola.

Here again Reedy dissented, for in his eyes Zola depicted a "sordid, mephitic world" and had an unhealthy passion for ugliness and filth. He maintained toward Zola much the same scorn and revulsion he had now come to show the decadents. Where Reedy called himself the apostle of a cheerful philosophy, Zola "deliberately chose to depict the coarser aspects of life. He was infatuated with the unclean . . . He had no vision." This was Reedy's final judgment when Zola died in 1902; but earlier he had qualified his views because of his admiration for the stand Zola took in the Dreyfus case. When Zola published *J'accuse,* espousing the cause of Captain Alfred Dreyfus and becoming himself a victim of the anti-Semitic hysteria generated by the Jewish captain's trumped-up trial for treason, Reedy wrote a series of articles praising Zola's courage. This admiration led him to reread an essay on Zola's realism which Havelock Ellis had written for a London magazine, the *Savoy.*

Reedy interpreted Ellis as discarding the prevalent dichotomy between realism and idealism. For Reedy, as for Ellis, there could be no absolute realism, for the selection of significant detail constitutes art, and art is necessarily idealistic: it selects that which suggests the essence or idea and eliminates what is philosophically nonessential. Whether Zola used proper philosophical or artistic criteria in making his selection was another question. But fearing this qualification might be taken for prudery, Reedy hastened to add that Zola's decision to include the sexual and biological human functions in his writing was not inartistic: "To refine away those aspects in social intercourse is beneficial," Reedy said. "In literature it is disastrous." [13]

THE MAN IN THE MIRROR

Given these unfavorable and one-sided judgments of Zola and Garland, it is surprising to find Reedy unequivocally sympathetic toward the novels of Thomas Hardy. In 1896, the year Hardy gave up writing novels because of the hostile reception of *Jude the Obscure,* Reedy declared that book a tragic masterpiece. *Harper's Magazine* had bowdlerized it for American readers, but Reedy knew the unexpurgated text. He knew all Hardy's prose works, and for him they were "bound together by a strain of spiritual growth."

Spirit was what distinguished Hardy from the others—"the spirit that animates his mind and runs like a religion . . . through all the figures and scenery and changes of his world." As Reedy interprets it, the Fate which is the theme of all Hardy's novels is "neither a Moloch of blind tyranny nor the sublime avenger of Mosaic law." On the contrary, it is "eternal harmony, the eternal righteousness with which poor human nature comes in accord, not half so often through its volition as through the invitation and persuasion of circumstance." Hardy's characters encounter catastrophe not by accident but because they have violated "the serene ideal." Despite its apparent violence and disorder, Hardy's universe is as harmonious as Shakespeare's; its nature is the expression of a sublime intelligence. Thus Reedy makes Hardy out to be a deist, indifferent to an indifferent God, yet devoted to the impassive justice of His creation.

"Hardy is emphatically a teacher," he says, "and this not in any formal didactic sense, but as Thackeray and Balzac and Shakespeare are teachers, holding the mirror up to nature and clarifying the reflection through poetic imagination until the universal lesson emerges in majestic power. The author of *Tess* has often been compared to the Greek dramatists . . . Once the mere background [the English environment of the Wessex Tales] is put in its proper place, the virtue of the seemingly hyberbolical judgment is discerned . . . Hardy really has the impersonal and impartial grip of the classic dramatists." What Hardy had for Reedy that his contemporaries lacked was "the repose of wisdom." Zola and the others seemed to Reedy cynical in their emphasis on the predominance of evil, whereas Hardy wrote with "pity for the degradations and misfortunes of mankind, not in cynical dissection of them." Thus the beauty of the world and the dignity and high potentiality of human life were what Hardy emphasized. That such potential as pure love and cheerful renunciation were seldom realized was a fact Hardy could not ignore. Tolstoy, too, had dwelt on the power of love and the beauty of renunciation, but Reedy insisted that in Tolstoy's novels love always degenerated into self-contemplation, while renunciation was only a mask for sexual fear. Hardy, on the other hand, deflected his readers from thoughts of self and led them to consider mankind in the light of universals—pity and terror and grace. "He teaches the beauty of renunciation, the dignity of pain, and the transfiguring power of unblemished love." [14]

Such insights may have been fleeting, and Reedy in his thirties was frequently inconsistent, as his friend Thekla Bernays felt free to point out. He was going through a profound transition, and Hardy satisfied deep emotional, as well as philosophical, needs. But just as he found spiritual repletion in Hardy, so Reedy transferred to others (notably Zola) feelings of revulsion and disgust with himself. Once when Miss Bernays passed along to him someone's compliment on his learning, he said it made him hate himself. Had he encountered Dreiser and Joyce at this stage in his development Reedy might have been repelled by what later transported him.

It was necessary for him to go through a series of chastening experiences before he would be ready to accept and advocate the naturalist vision.

PART TWO
TURNING POINTS

CHAPTER 7

THE *MIRROR'S* "WAR BOOM"

BILLY Reedy, the easy-going newspaper humorist and barroom wit, turned quite suddenly into William Marion Reedy, the editor of a journal "for thinking people."

In 1892, when he left the *Star* and was about to become sole editor of the *Mirror*, he was living at his father's house in Cass Avenue, at the edge of Kerry Patch.[1] At thirty he was still the stately, plump Buck Mulligan, his black hair parted in the middle and nervously pushed back from his forehead, his huge dark eyes twinkling with cynical laughter. He was an impressive young man, tall and well built, but his face was already marked by dissipation—the skin too sallow, the eyes bloodshot and rimmed with shadow. When he wrote, his small hand gripped the pen shakily and his tiny script sloped fanwise down the copy page. He cursed his printer, saying "Distortion is his joy."

By the turn of the century Reedy had become the portly, settled proprietor, the editor of acknowledged local reputation whose views were starting to be heeded in New York and London. This metamorphosis took place late in the period between 1892, when Fanning gave up the co-editorship, and the spring of 1898, when Reedy's vigorously independent commentary on the issues leading up to the Spanish-American war won him a national following. In the interim his actions were erratic, often verging on the suicidal.

On November 2, 1893, in the course of a prolonged debauch, he was married to Agnes, or Addie, Baldwin, who ran a notorious St. Louis pleasure resort known as the White Castle. His bride is said to have paid for his visit to the institute of Dr. Leslie Keeley, where he underwent the much-advertised Keeley Cure for alcoholism. This treatment must have started soon after the wedding was performed by an obliging priest. The first extant volume of the *Mirror* begins less than four months later, with the issue of February 25, 1894, and there are no breaks in the magazine's continuity thereafter. Every volume for the following twenty-seven years bears the unmistakable mark of Reedy's hand.[2]

After his disreputable marriage Reedy's address was listed in the directory as 1324 North 24th Street, a few blocks from his father's, but he lived with his wife less than three months, if at all. Instead of returning to the new home she had prepared, he went to live with his friend George Tansey, a graduate of Cornell and a law student, who soon afterwards succeeded his father as head of a thriving transfer company and became president of the Merchants Exchange.

Mrs. Reedy tried in vain to communicate with her husband through his friends. "Tell her to go back where she belongs," he told his business manager, John J. Sullivan. In February 1896 she obtained a divorce on grounds of desertion and nonsupport, testifying that she and Reedy had lived apart for more than a year. During this period the vehemence with which Reedy attacked the "social evil" in his columns seemed a measure of his disgust with himself.[3]

Reedy's indiscretions became the core of a local mythology. It has been written—though the story is apocryphal—that his marriage to Addie Baldwin was in fact his second; that he had been married at eighteen to a woman twice his age, and that the Church had refused to consider that marriage null after the courts granted a divorce.[4] The very number of such unsupported tales makes them all suspect, and Reedy enhanced them with cheerful indifference. When a rival editor sent him the proofs of a scurrilous article about himself, probably intending blackmail, Reedy offered to fill in the scandals that had been omitted. Yet during these black years he was on terms of familiarity with men who were becoming prominent in every sphere of community life—lawyers, engineers, several leading financiers, two or three librarians, and many journalists. All his close friends were men of integrity and standing. Almost all remained loyal to him then and thereafter.

Whatever the facts of his first marriage (to Addie Baldwin) may have been, Reedy seems to have blamed the Church for solemnizing it and refusing to annul it. He had been a warm admirer of old Archbishop Peter Kenrick, who might have been the first American cardinal, Reedy said, but for his opposition to the doctrine of papal infallibility. He detested Kenrick's successor, Archbishop John Joseph Kain, a zealous opponent of divorce. Reedy seems to have felt that the Church would have done better to oppose hasty marriages like his own. The priest who had joined him in holy wedlock to a bawd later became an archbishop himself.[5]

But for all his bitterness against the hierarchy, unjust as it may have been, Reedy never lost the cast of mind imparted by his Catholic training as a boy and especially by his years at St. Louis University. This tutelage not only affected his thinking on philosophical and moral questions, giving a theological turn to his language, but showed itself in occasional eccentricities of behavior. Once when he and some companions had sat down to a steak supper late Thursday evening in Holy Week, Reedy at midnight suddenly stood up and overturned the table, declaring he could not bring himself to eat meat on Good Friday. Despite his strictures against Archbishop Kain, his rebellious attitude in the matter of divorce, and his hetero-

THE MAN IN THE MIRROR

dox comments about many questions on which the Church took a strict stand, he was often jokingly accused of being a Jesuit in disguise.

Apart from his lack of restraint in matters that affected him personally, Reedy's writing generally retained its light, ironic tone through his darkest years. Much of his satire was directed against the daily journalism of Joseph Pulitzer and of William Randolph Hearst, who bought the *New York Journal* in 1895 and was using the rebellion in Cuba as a theme to wrest circulation away from Pulitzer's *New York World*. Early in January 1896 that rebellion entered its second stage, when Spain sent out General Valeriano Weyler to curb the Cubans' stubborn two-year struggle for freedom. Reedy pretended to regard the long and bitter fight as no more than a subtle plot to cut off his cigar supply. "We may not care three thraunee's eggs for the principle of liberty," he wrote, "but we have got to protect our pockets and, therefore, Cuba must be free. If the war continues much longer the price of cigars will go up so high that we shall have to go after them on extension ladders." [6] When Weyler was accused of beheading an American correspondent, Reedy was happy to know that any American correspondent in Cuba had a head to lose.[7] He resented the efforts of Pulitzer and Hearst to exploit the sympathies of readers with their lurid accounts of the sufferings of Cuban patriots. He condemned the economic policies of the United States which had helped bring about Cuba's eleventh uprising in the interests of tariff-manipulating financiers with a stake in sugar. By 1896 the wild chauvinism of the two New York papers was infecting the whole country, and even the sober *St. Louis Globe-Democrat* ran headlines proclaiming "Spain's Hatred of Americans." [8]

However reluctant to heed such alarums, Reedy welcomed the air of expectancy and excitement the papers were generating. It was a good thing, he said, to see the American people

THE *MIRROR'S* "WAR BOOM"

begin to take an interest in the world at large. The spirit of America had seemed as decadent as the waning century. "Manhood," he said, "was getting rusty everywhere. It is limbered up by the anticipated throb of the war drum and the unfurling of battle flags." But he was convinced that there was no danger of our being drawn into the wave of imperialist adventures that was running riot in the world. He could not believe we should go to war over Cuba.[9]

Beneath his badinage he was nevertheless sometimes apprehensive. The prophets of America's manifest destiny to expand and conquer far-off colonies were making progress. He called Alfred Thayer Mahan's *Influence of Sea Power upon History* "the most remarkable and influential book" of the decade. Yet when Admiral Mahan spoke in St. Louis Reedy derided his preachment that Christian democracy needed a big navy for its evangelist.[10] Reedy opposed our involvement in the boundary dispute between British Guiana and Venezuela. He was troubled by the unrest in South Africa, disgusted by the Italians' adventure in Ethiopia, opposed to our annexation of Hawaii, and against meddling in Cuba.

Although a consistent defender of big business, Reedy spoke out against business intervention in national politics. When the Republicans held their convention in St. Louis in the spring of 1896 he regarded their candidate as a mere puppet in the hands of business leaders. "*Is* there any such person as Bill McKinley?" he asked, for the Governor of Ohio had seen fit to stay home for the duration of the presidential campaign. Reedy spoke of Governor McKinley as a mere figment of Mark Hanna's imagination, a myth like the sea serpent. "I read that men have gone to a place called Canton, Ohio, and have seen Bill McKinley. But men have written of voyages to the Moon and Mars and to Bohemia and the Land of Nod, and neither I nor the world believe these romancers." [11]

It was unfortunate for the *Mirror's* circulation that he was even more unfavorably impressed by the Democratic candidate. He was fearful and contemptuous of the "free silver" platform drafted by his old friends from the *Republican*, William Vincent Byars and Charles H. Jones. He went to Chicago and heard William Jennings Bryan deliver his "Cross of Gold" speech, but while admitting its power, called it "the cheap coin of stump sentimentalism." "Its meretriciousness was forgotten in the peculiarly vibrant quality of his voice," Reedy wrote. "There was a twilight plaintiveness in his tone most of the time, and then flashes of color and warmth that affected one like some of the deeper organ notes that one hears with his spine." Reedy denied that the speech was magnificent as some declared it. He returned to St. Louis to give reluctant support to the supposedly nonexistent McKinley. His friend Jones forcibly seized the *St. Louis Post-Dispatch* from Pulitzer and turned it for the time being into an organ of Bryanism and silver inflation. That was the popular tack.[12]

Reedy took the line pursued by his friends in the business world, most of whom were "Gold Bugs"—Democrats of a Southern complexion who bolted to McKinley's side.[13] He argued that abandonment of the gold standard would ruin the nation's credit and destroy its foreign trade. He accused the Bryan faction of socialistic leanings. But all the arguments Reedy could muster in favor of McKinley were singularly unconvincing, and his tepid stand rapidly cost him circulation and advertising revenue. The scandal attending his divorce that spring cannot have enhanced the magazine's popularity either. A month before the election, the *Mirror* was forced into bankruptcy.

"The paper had no business," Reedy said. "Its subscription list had fallen off." [14]

When the magazine failed and was put up for auction to satisfy its creditors, it was Reedy's friend James Campbell who

THE *MIRROR'S* "WAR BOOM"

saved the day. He bought it in, went over its financial position, and three weeks later gave the *Mirror* to Reedy with enough working capital to keep it in business. Campbell played a discreet but important role in Reedy's life during the next fifteen years.[15]

He was a short, solid Irishman with a tuft under his jutting lower lip that accented a firm chin. The high-buttoned tweed coat he wore over high-buttoned waistcoats gave him the look of a country land agent, but his air of pugnacious skepticism often softened into amusement, and his silvery laugh was famous. Reedy saw to that. He said that Campbell's laughter had been known to set off the time lock on a safe. Born in Mullrick, county Galway, on a twelve-acre patch of a tenant farm, Campbell had served during the Civil War as messenger boy to General John C. Frémont. The general took Campbell with him when his stormy exit from the Union Army left him free to return to the lucrative financial activities for which his earlier career as a presidential candidate and an explorer had fitted him. Later Frémont sent Campbell out to St. Louis to take over the little mule-drawn streetcar line that served the Fairgrounds. After putting that company on a sound financial footing, electrifying the line, and being trained as a civil engineer, Campbell rose rapidly as a financier in his own right.

Through his influence the *Mirror* came to enjoy advertising revenue from most of the great Western railroads (Campbell controlled the Frisco Lines, for example) and the banks (Campbell was a power in the two largest banks in St. Louis as well as being head of the North American Securities Company). And Campbell seemed to expect nothing from Reedy, who said that buying the *Mirror* in a fit of absent-mindedness was Campbell's only bad investment, and later remarked that even though the magazine seemed to have stood for everything that menaced his position, Campbell "never in sixteen years said a word" to influence the editor's policy.[16] Campbell

THE MAN IN THE MIRROR

always made a secret of his philanthropies. He supported General Frémont's widow (the daughter of Senator Thomas Hart Benton) for some years after the general's death; and at least once handed Reedy a large check unasked, when the *Mirror's* finances again became desperate.[17] As the owner of vast land tracts, mines, railways, and other utilities, Campbell was said to be worth $60 million. But in 1896 and for some years thereafter he had no reason to influence the *Mirror's* policies, for it was a defender of wealth and individualism.

Like other leading St. Louis financiers Campbell was also against intervention in Cuba. It may even have been he who convinced Reedy by the November of McKinley's election that a sinister force was building up the war sentiment by suggesting propaganda to Hearst and Pulitzer. For Reedy noted that "the more misinformation one gets about the state of affairs in Cuba the more the conviction grows that the 'war' is a sort of bluff, kept up by the Sugar Trust for the purpose of bolstering up prices." The dollar value of Cuban sugar imports had now fallen from a high of $69 million to a low of $13 million. And by Reedy's own count the casualties reported by the yellow press already exceeded the number of troops engaged on both sides. By January, however, Reedy had concluded that the war talk would lead nowhere, since the country was "in no shape to go to war with anybody." He called the hectic news a "fake" and the Weyler atrocities mere fabrications.[18]

The following summer, when the Hawaiian issue came up again, and President McKinley asked Congress to approve a treaty annexing the islands, Reedy called the request "national quixotism" and said McKinley's proposal was "a departure from the traditions and practices of the United States Government." He still opposed the large navy that would be needed to defend the territory, and the cost of assuming the islanders' debts. The expansionists' argument that we needed new lands for settlement he flatly denied: "There is no pressure of popu-

THE *MIRROR'S* "WAR BOOM"

lation here that needs an outlet. The people are drifting into our cities. The country is becoming uninhabited."[19] He grew sarcastic as he recalled the claims of Admiral Mahan and McKinley's ardent young Assistant Secretary of the Navy, Theodore Roosevelt.

But, the President's friends tell us, the glory, the greater national glory of it! We extend the benefits of the democratic form of government over a wider area of the earth and spread the light of liberty . . . We have difficulty enough in adjusting political conditions at home to the production of more good to the majority . . . We are not in shape to evangelize for liberty and freedom for the denizens on the outskirts of civilization. Our own house is not in order.[20]

So when Theodore Roosevelt succeeded in sending a fleet to Hawaii, Reedy sardonically called it "a fine fashion" in which to introduce free government. As to war with Spain, if it came it would cost us "more than the worth of twenty Cubas."[21]

That was in the fall of 1897. The Cuban revolution had now reached its third stage. For during the summer Spain's absolutist premier had been assassinated. The new liberal government that succeeded him recalled General Weyler and repudiated his brutal policies. Reedy's opposition to intervention may have been heightened by his second marriage, which had occurred that spring. His new wife's father had been born in Cuba.

How this marriage to the respectable daughter of a proud Creole family came about, only a year after Reedy's divorce, remains a mystery. Miss Eulalie Bauduy, familiarly known as Lalite, was the fourth of the eight children of Dr. Jerome Keating Bauduy, who had married a Miss Caroline Bankhead of Tennessee. One of the young lady's ancestors had come to America after the Revolution with a letter to George Washington. Another had been a partner of the Duponts of Delaware. Several had distinguished themselves in medicine; and Dr. Bauduy, who had served in the Civil War under General Rosecrans, had become the town's leading neurologist since settling in St. Louis. For a quarter of a century he had been professor of nervous and mental diseases at the Missouri Medical College, where Dr. Bernays taught anatomy. He had served as president of the St. Louis Medical Society and was author of a standard treatise on neurology.[22]

But Miss Eulalie was a young woman with a mind of her own. By Dr. Wolf's account she did not wait to let Reedy be introduced by friends but sought a meeting with him, telling him in a series of notes that she was an admirer of his writing. Again the fable is not convincing, but it is certain that Reedy soon succumbed to her charm and that they were married before a justice of the peace in March 1897. From the first they seem to have been very happy in their marriage. Mrs. Reedy's pious family can hardly have been equally happy about it, especially since their new son-in-law was in the thick of his feud with Archbishop Kain and did not scruple to proclaim that prelate a "Tittlebat Titmouse Torquemada" whose reforming zeal was "sufficient to cause the five wounds of Christ daily to bleed afresh."[23]

That was the climax in a series of attacks which may well have reflected Reedy's frustration on being denied a dispensation to remarry, on the plea that his previous alliance to Addie Baldwin had been no true marriage. Only a month before marrying Eulalie Bauduy, Reedy had publicly expostulated against the "unqualified submission to authority" which the Church demanded. "There is no use arguing about it. If two people love and want to be married, and the Church says 'Nay,' they will marry. Excommunication will not worry them."[24] It certainly did worry the Bauduys, as did his further remark that ladies and gentlemen who "dared obey their own hearts and defy the archepiscopal regulations" were liable

THE *MIRROR'S* "WAR BOOM"

to be "crushed by the curse of Rome." Having defied Rome's curse himself, Reedy tried to convince his readers that Archbishop Kain was even then being called to the Vatican to be disciplined, though the prelate pretended to expect a cardinal's biretta for his zeal.[25]

However violent the circumstances surrounding his wedding may have been, Reedy's felicity was soon reflected in hard work and success. After the bankruptcy the previous fall he had cut his magazine's price from a dime to a nickel, and by May he could claim 13,000 paid-up subscribers. The rise in circulation that followed showed there were "thinking people" both in St. Louis and elsewhere in America who shared a view like Reedy's, which was in frontal opposition to the propaganda later supposed to have made our attack on Spain inevitable. Long after the sinking of the *Maine*, in the spring of 1898, Reedy maintained his caustic resistance to the "zanies" who "howled for war."[26]

The result in terms of circulation was dramatic. Soon he could boast that local subscriptions had quintupled within a year, while those from out of town had increased tenfold in only six months. When the war crisis reached its height he began printing circulation figures under his masthead and talked archly of the *Mirror's* war boom. Six weeks after the *Maine* went down sales reached a peak of 32,250, which put the *Mirror* far head of the *Nation,* the *Atlantic,* and most of the established journals of opinion.[27]

To Reedy our unprovoked attack on Spain was not the "very pretty fight" Theodore Roosevelt and his friends had yearned for. It was a breach with tradition that was bound to alter the fabric of our national life for all time. Neither the sinking of the *Maine* nor the personal letter of Spanish Minister Dupuy de Lôme, which was pilfered from the Havana post office and spread on the front page of the *New York Journal,* seemed to him any sign that Spain wanted war. Reedy said Spain had nothing to gain "from the treacherous murder of sleeping men." She had no money to prosecute a war and might well lose her monarchy if forced into a defensive one. As to the de Lôme letter, giving the Minister's private opinion of William McKinley, it was shocking only because de Lôme had been telling the truth—something no diplomat must ever do. If we were to blow Spain's navy out of the ocean as a result, it would merely prove the accuracy of de Lôme's charges.[28]

During the six weeks the nation had to wait for the inconclusive findings of a naval court of inquiry investigating the *Maine* disaster, Reedy kept on decrying the war talk, and his circulation kept going up, until he was getting new out-of-town subscribers at the rate of two thousand a week. At the end of this period it was clear to him that Spain had surrendered to every demand the United States had made over a period of two years. Her new liberal government had acted with all the speed that could be expected, and would probably grant Cuba even the independence we had not yet asked for (though Reedy thought we had). Even if McKinley concealed from Congress all the concessions Spain had made and said that his "last overture in the direction of immediate peace" had had a disappointing reception, Reedy could agree with E. L. Godkin, who said in the *Nation* that McKinley's minister to Madrid had gained "one of the most brilliant diplomatic victories ever won." Not knowing what was in the President's mind, Reedy still hoped for peace. "Until the shooting actually begins I shall have hope of a peaceful ending of our difficulties with Spain . . . Premier Sagasta has acceded to all our demands but independence. He has been very prompt in his concessions . . ."[29]

By this time, however, Americans had salved their conscience by disclaiming any ambition to possess Cuba's 40,000 square miles of territory. Then, within a matter of hours, we had come into strategic control of 120,000 square miles of Philippine territory, on the other side of the globe. Reedy was quick to see other absurdities. We were going to war "for humanity's sake," to save those already freed from concentration camps. Soon we would be burning and ravaging their fields, and peaceful Cubans would be ground between the millstones of opposing armies. Our intervention was bound to "make their last state worse than their first." [30]

But once Admiral Dewey had astonished the world with his sudden conquest in Manila Bay, Reedy became convinced that further resistance to the government's policy would be futile. "There has been a Revolution," he declared. "We do not exactly realize it just now, but we will in a short time." We have become imperialists, he told his readers, "because we can't help it." [31]

As an imperial republic we would soon find our form of government materially changed. Basic American traditions were now doomed. We would need other strategic bases to protect those unexpectedly acquired; also an isthmian canal, a system of foreign alliances, and a centralized government—even though the 1896 elections had seemed "almost an insurrection against centralization." Reedy's further predictions were to prove uncannily correct. The South Pacific Dewey had invaded would become a tremendous battle ground in the twentieth century. Our next war would be with Germany. There would have to be a standing army and navy, an income tax, an enlarged diplomatic corps, and a fixed alliance with Britain.

"No one knows how it has all come about," he went on glumly. "Only this we know, that we do not shape events, but are shaped by them." He summed it up in one prophetic sentence: "The country into which you and I were born, brethren, is as dead as Carthage." [32]

THE MAN IN THE MIRROR

"The *Mirror* has not tried to be popular," Reedy had said early in his "war boom" period. He had assumed he was combating the prevalent sentiment of the country, but within a year it had become plain that there was far more widespread sympathy for his heterodox views than he had anticipated. Later, reflecting on the very agreeable circulation figures he was flaunting, he admitted that war had not hurt the *Mirror*.[33]

However reluctantly, he was now quick to accept the *fait accompli*, and in so doing he parted company with E. L. Godkin, Carl Schurz, William Dean Howells, Mark Twain, and other writers he respected who were determined to make a last-ditch stand against imperialist adventure. "Imperialism," said Reedy, "is a word of ugly memories, and the thing itself is about equally compact of glory and of foulness. The American people, in their hearts, believe that the Filipinos and the Cubans are entitled to liberty, and that we can help them to that goal."

Like most Americans, he was unprepared to foresee the bitter and disgraceful role we were to play in the Philippines and the long war we must wage to suppress the democratic aspirations of their leader Emilio Aguinaldo. It seemed to Reedy that the first step we must take as an imperial democracy was to cleanse democracy in America of the corruption which had overtaken it after the Civil War. "We cannot begin too soon," he wrote, "to strive for that decency in world politics which has been the hope and the despair of Americans in politics at home."[34] Dreaming of a "Republic of the World," he now saw that it must be his function to reverse the process of corruption that nullified democracy in St. Louis.

Confused and frustrated by the swift changes in the foreign scene, he was also misinformed by censored reports and hoped Aguinaldo would soon be caught and shot. With better reason he was contemptuous of Bryan, who resigned his colonel's commission in protest against the use of volunteers to subjugate the Filipino. For Bryan thereupon persuaded the Senate to ratify the treaty whereby we bought the mutinous islands from Spain, explaining that he would oppose imperialism later. The logic of Bryan's final act was totally incomprehensible to Reedy, who said: "We were all wrong in going to war in the beginning. Mr. Bryan advocated war. Therefore Mr. Bryan has tied himself in a knot. He has committed his followers to a struggle against the consequences of their own demand for war." [35]

For his part Reedy saw that we had assumed a responsibility toward the peoples we had aided in their rebellion against Spain. Some of them might not be ready for self-government, and we should have to teach them. He predicted a long struggle before democracy was achieved at home or abroad. "There will be terrible blunders," he said; "there will be clashes and suffering and woe and seeming failure, but the right of man to rule himself and his capacity therefor will be demonstrated." [36]

In reversing his stand to this extent, and particularly in shifting his emphasis from foreign affairs back to local matters, Reedy lost many of his new subscribers and stopped the magazine's sudden burst of growth. No circulation figures were ever printed under its masthead after the end of May 1898.

CHAPTER 8

STREETCARS AND CORRUPTION

When Reedy turned back to local concerns after the treaty with Spain had been ratified early in 1899, it was on the languishing plans for a World's Fair that he centered his attention. While the choice of such an objective may baffle outsiders, to St. Louisans it seemed natural enough.

Even in the hazy days before the Civil War the October Fair had been the cynosure of St. Louis pride. Abraham Lincoln, Edward Prince of Wales, and P. T. Barnum had all been ferried across the river to see it. In time the primordial river had been spanned and prehistoric mounds on its bank had given way to soot-blackened warehouses. But the Fair went on, reliable as the season of cool mists and floating gossamer after September's breathless heat. The Fairgrounds remained a favorite resort, a place to walk beside graceful lagoons under crimson oaks and ink-black cypresses, and pennants flying from high pergolas over race track and parade ground, side shows and bear pits and beer gardens.[1]

James Campbell's old streetcar line brought the holiday crowds to the Fairgrounds, setting them down within elegant fretwork pavilions spanning the Grand Entrance. Like every symbol of progress and civic greatness, the famous Veiled Prophet's parade that opened the Fair moved on car tracks. The Prophet is a romantic figure out of *Lalla Rookh*, but his floats are flatcars.

During the nineties the Fair had begun to fail, though its

STREETCARS AND CORRUPTION

president, Rolla Wells, whose father had started the town's streetcar system (driving his own horsedrawn omnibus, collecting his own fares) did what he could to revive it. Soon pleasure domes were left to crack and peel, and the once elegant Jockey Club was given over to bookies, touts, and auto racers. But while the antique magnificence of the Fairgrounds faded and sagged, St. Louis dreamed of a fair to end all fairs—a World's Fair to celebrate the centenary of Jefferson's purchase of the Mississippi Valley from Napoleon in 1803.

A series of articles in the *Globe-Democrat* in 1893, the year of the Columbian Exposition in Chicago, had set the grand scheme in motion. But with depression and wars and the bitter campaign of 1896, interest had flagged. One of Reedy's themes had always been the niggardly ways of the rich. They seemed to take more pride in abstaining from sins of the flesh than in any gesture toward generous living, and the Fair needed money. It required an initial outlay of five million dollars. So when he turned his attention back to local matters it was to the lack of support for the Fair that he pointed. The town's leaders were smug and indifferent, he said. What kept the Fair from becoming a reality was "the terrible, the deadly, mean envy of a lot of snarling rivals in business."[2]

He launched his campaign with a ferocious diatribe which he entitled, with apologies to William Allen White, "What's the Matter with St. Louis?" Lack of pride, especially among the wealthy leaders, had left St. Louis a "bloated village," "an execrably governed city, with public buildings that are disgraceful, with streets that are frightful, with every evidence that there is no strong power working here for the day of better things." Summing up, he hoped the World's Fair would at last "awaken this city's anaemic soul" to action. "The matter with St. Louis, then, is too much matter, too little mind. The people who predominate lack vision." There had been no "community of affectionate desire" to make it beautiful, but there was still time to show the world a metropolis whose people had hearts "responsive to beauty and all exalted things."[3]

Despite the resentment such an indictment aroused, it succeeded in its purpose. The response filled bushel baskets; the magazine was sold out at once. When the article was reprinted in a new pamphlet series, the pamphlet was sold out in turn. Afterward, Reedy dated the success of the St. Louis World's Fair and the civic reform movement that paved the way for it to the day his article appeared, in November 1899.[4]

Meanwhile the town's business proceeded as usual. That same month James Campbell handed the Democratic boss of St. Louis his check for $47,500 to buy a ten-year contract for his Welsbach Gas-lighting Company. That was the way business was done—through Ed Butler, an illiterate blacksmith who had made a fortune selling horseshoes to the street railway companies and now did a thriving business selling city contracts and franchises to the utilities. Ambitious to found a dynasty, Butler had sent his son to the university Reedy attended, then made him a member of the school board Reedy covered as a reporter. Now he was running him for Congress.

A gas company case had precipitated the slaying of Colonel Slayback, but it was the streetcar lines that dominated the economy of the spreading city. The individual streetcar companies had borrowed money to electrify their lines. Now, by devious means, they had been consolidated into one great trust, so overcapitalized that it could not afford to pay both its bondholders and its motormen. The mismanagement of the new Central Traction Company educated Reedy in what was basically the matter with St. Louis—and the nation.[5]

Early in 1900 the discontent of street railway workers was obvious to every passenger. Reedy noted that the company's management wielded such political power, had "such a death grip on the community," that the union labor people talked of

STREETCARS AND CORRUPTION

the necessity of a general strike to bring management to terms.[6] When the strike of streetcar workers broke that spring, however, there was an air of unconcern, almost of gaiety, in the air. At first Reedy went so far as to blame the whole affair on spring fever. Its seriousness soon became clear, however, as the national head of the union came to St. Louis to take charge. By summer, violence on both sides had become a national scandal. Samuel Gompers, head of the American Federation of Labor, entered the fray. Scab labor was being housed in car barns and fed from federally protected mail cars. Cars were being dynamited at night. Women passengers were hauled into the streets, stripped naked, and painted green. Patrons of scab-operated streetcars were refused groceries in neighborhood stores. Timid citizens left town, knowing the police had been taken over by the state Democratic party while the Republican mayor begged in vain for the militia. Business was in shambles.

But there was an *esprit de corps* among the patrician rulers of the city's economy, and they now proceeded to take matters into their own hands. They organized a posse of fifteen hundred gentlemen, set up barracks in the heart of the downtown wholesale district, and assured their wives they would soon bring the strikers to terms. Reedy could no longer write of workers suffering from spring fever. "All the rottenness of our system is exposed in this strike," he now wrote; "bribery in legislation, corruption in politics, bestowal of monopoly without compensation, concentration of power into irresponsible and incompetent hands . . ."[7] And what seemed most terrifying of all was the failure of the daily press to make clear what issues were at stake. Each paper was inhibited by its own political or financial affiliations. So Reedy decided to publish a comprehensive account of the origins and conduct of the strike, dealing out blame wherever it was deserved. His detailed narrative was gathered into another pamphlet, which had to be reprinted again and again.

THE MAN IN THE MIRROR

"As soon as all the street railways were consolidated into a Trust it was inevitable that there would be a strike. The Trust threatened the usual economies. The employes began to organize . . . If the capitalists could tie up the whole city in unescapable coils of rail and prevent construction of competing lines, why could not the employes . . . tie up the capitalists?"[8] He went on to give details of the managerial and political transactions that had taken place and to blame the union for its clumsy strategy and extravagant demands. Immediately after getting himself elected on a promise to curb the "insolence" of the trusts, the governor of Missouri had accepted a $50,000 bribe for signing a bill sanctioning the formation of a street railway monopoly in St. Louis. That intricate piece of legislation had been linked, Reedy said, to another scheme; it put the St. Louis police department in the hands of a Democratic jobber, Harry B. Hawes. The police in a body were then taken into the Democratic party's Jefferson Club, of which Hawes was president. Hawes had withdrawn police guards from trolley cars so they could help his candidates carry the Democratic primaries.

Then the posse had been formed, ostensibly to restore law and order. Reedy told of calling at its barracks on a grim Sunday afternoon, as striking union men paraded home from a rain-drenched picnic, right past the barracks. A streetcar approached. The striking marchers jeered. Some of them jumped aboard to pull the scab motorman into the street. Now shots rang out. "The way the *posse* rushed to its guns, the sharp, metallic clattering chorus of filling magazines, the dash for the street of those ready armed . . . showed that the *posse* men were more than half glad 'the music had begun.'" It was hard to believe how eager these impatient warriors were to kill, and yet they were no thugs but leading business and professional men, vestrymen in churches. If it had not been for the coolness of their leaders they might have shot

STREETCARS AND CORRUPTION

down a hundred strikers instead of the four who were hit. And the strikers were not entirely innocent; some carried pistols and brass knuckles. But Reedy could not repress a surge of pity for the poor fellows hauled into the barracks, "soaked in rain, pale and trembling, in their railway uniforms." These were no criminals, either, but humble men defending their rights. Not one would ever get his job back, though his family might starve for it. And their dead bore "ghastly testimony" to the folly of their leaders, who had brought them to the barracks, and to the stupidity of the mayor and the police, who had allowed them to bait the bloodthirsty sportsmen beside whom Reedy had stood, as if in a duck blind.[9]

One man who had made a fortune building up the St. Louis street railways seemed to have a solution for the complex of problems underlying the strike. He was Tom L. Johnson, one of the former owners whose lines had been consolidated by the Central Traction Company. Some years before, Johnson had read a copy of Henry George's *Progress and Poverty,* one of the books Reedy had given Fanning as a cub reporter. Deeply impressed, Johnson had retired from business to devote the rest of his life to promoting George's single-tax plan, a program for wresting the control of public resources and utilities from the hands of enterprisers who were misusing them and corrupting the political system. Tom Johnson had served as campaign manager when Henry George ran for mayor of New York. Then he had gone to Cleveland, been elected to Congress, and finally given up his seat to work as mayor for municipal reform. After serving Governor Francis, who was now president of the St. Louis World's Fair corporation, Fanning had followed Johnson to Cleveland and become prominent in the reform movement.

Reedy, who despised George's "socialism," had attacked Henry George bitterly during his campaign for mayor of New

York, vilified him when he collapsed and died during the campaign, and gone on ridiculing his theories after he lay dead. But Reedy had heard Johnson speak and been impressed by his humor and self-sacrifice.[10] Shaken by events in St. Louis, six months after the strike had been broken, Reedy published Henry George's short résumé of *Progress and Poverty* in the *Mirror*. Two years later he announced that he had signed an agreement with the typographers' union "in accordance with the principles of the paper on economic subjects generally." It was at this time that he let it be known that he had become a single-taxer, a position he maintained, half jokingly, as if indulging a personal foible, for the rest of his life.[11]

Meanwhile he continued to lunch with Campbell and his friends in a paneled private dining room at the Noonday Club, atop a downtown skyscraper. Several of this chosen group of rising young lawyers and executives were intimately concerned with the World's Fair and had been involved in the streetcar strike as well. Harry B. Hawes, president of the Jefferson Club and the police board, was one member of the group. Frederick W. Lehmann, attorney for the Central Traction Company and a close friend of Reedy and Campbell, was another. A third was James Blair, general counsel of the World's Fair corporation, a wealthy and idealistic reformer; his father, Francis Preston Blair, had saved Missouri for the Union and died poor for his pains—a course young Blair had no intention of emulating. A fourth member was Reedy's old friend George Tansey, now president of the St. Louis Transfer Company.

These and some others debated all that summer of the strike, agreeing that St. Louis must be cleansed of the paralyzing corruption that had overtaken its politics and that representative citizens must be drafted into the municipal government before the World's Fair could become a reality. What they could not agree on was a method of belling that particular cat. All summer and fall the *Mirror* echoed their debates. It published an article from Fanning showing how partial reform had been achieved in Cleveland by a unified effort to nominate business leaders at the primaries of the two major parties. It printed Reedy's conflicting plea for a third party that would inaugurate "a veritable cyclone of reform" in St. Louis. It printed James Blair's lofty rhetoric, preaching new political idealism and a return to old principles.[12]

Lunching at the Noonday Club, Campbell heard the debate wear on, listening with his customary patience and occasional bursts of his famous laughter. Then he decided that the time had come to act. His own plan was simple and forthright, characteristic of a man reputed to be worth $60 million and used to having his own way. He would buy up both parties, pay for their campaigns, and demand the right to pick a decent slate for each.[13]

He sent Harry Hawes to call on Ed Butler, the Democratic boss, and arrange the details. Apparently the first concession that had to be made was to send Butler's son Jim to Congress. Congressional elections were taking place that fall, and Campbell was to pick the municipal slate that would run on the Democratic ticket the following spring. Rolla Wells, son of the founder of the earliest streetcar lines and now president of the American Steel Foundry Company, told Campbell's emissary, James Blair, that he would run for mayor. Butler had already picked a candidate for circuit attorney when Harry Hawes called on him, but Hawes persuaded the Democratic boss to have his candidate give up the nomination. As Butler himself tells it: "So the next time I seen Harry I says, 'bring your little man around,' and he done it and I looked him over, and there didn't seem to be anything the matter of him, so I says all right and he was nominated." [14]

THE MAN IN THE MIRROR

The little man was Joseph W. Folk, a newcomer from Tennessee, a solemn, very young lawyer in black frock coat with black eyes behind shiny pince-nez. Folk was a lover of good round platitudes about good government, which nobody took literally. Although he had been Hawes's predecessor as head of the Jefferson Club, he had first come to general prominence as one of the attorneys for the labor union in the streetcar strike. Reedy mistrusted him as he did all declared reformers.[15]

Reedy nevertheless gave up without ado his plea for a third party and reconciled himself to Campbell's plan for municipal reform by bribery. It appealed to his sense of the absurd, and he printed a rollicking satirical ballad about the luncheon group at the Noonday Club, lampooning the incongruous alliance between Campbell's earthy practicality and Blair's high-flown idealism. The combination struck him as irresistibly funny—and harmless enough, since Campbell had now succeeded in getting as good a ticket for the Republican party as for the Democratic.

What Reedy found less easy to treat in a comic vein was the fact that a third party had been launched without the approval of the Noonday Club. Lee Meriwether, an able and practical advocate of reform and of public ownership of municipal utilities, split the Democratic ticket by filing as a public-ownership candidate. It was his second campaign for mayor. William Jennings Bryan supported Meriwether by attacking Rolla Wells in his new weekly, the *Commoner*. Old Governor Altgeld came across the river to speak for Meriwether, and was astonished by the massiveness of his following, which consisted of unpaid volunteers with no machine affiliation. Butler offered Meriwether $50,000 of Campbell's money to withdraw from the race, and was prepared to double that sum. When the bribe was turned down flatly, three gunmen were hired to put Meriwether out of the race, but he refused to be intimidated. He finished up the campaign guarded by six burly members of his campaign organization, each carrying a revolver. Although Wells was declared the winner in the unusually bloody elections of April 1901, there can be little doubt that Meriwether actually won a plurality over both machine candidates. As a prominent Republican told a conference on good government, however, no one could be sure. "No one knows and for that matter, few enough care." The state supreme court issued an injunction preventing a recount, saying that the sanctity of the ballot box must be upheld. But Ed Butler's son was refused his seat in Congress owing to the obvious fraudulence of the polling the previous fall.[16]

"The cry of fraud is rot," Reedy retorted in the *Mirror*. He claimed a share in the successful election of Wells and Folk, saying he had "reasoned out the situation" for a year and kept the public informed, which was more or less true. "It was Mr. James Campbell who found the way to reform," he went on shamelessly. "It was he who united the Democratic party . . ." There was no shred of truth in that claim, since the party had been irretrievably split. Reedy did not make the mistake of adding, as he had after the mayoralty campaign of 1897, that Meriwether had been secretly working for Ed Butler all along.[17]

When the *St. Louis Republic* did make that accusation Meriwether brought suit for libel. The jury hearing the case asked the judge if it might award him *more* than the $10,000 he was asking in damages. So there was a retrial, which Meriwether won, trying the case himself against Frederick Lehmann, the friend of Reedy and Campbell, who had taken part in the lunches at the Noonday Club and in the whole plan for reform by bribery. Meriwether won one libel case after another. In one criminal action he sent a Lehmann client to jail for two years for saying that Meriwether was secretly on Butler's side.[18]

Although the Campbell scheme had succeeded by sheer

force and could hardly be called a moral victory, Blair was as outspoken as Reedy in his satisfaction. He wrote a fairly detailed account of the proceedings for *Harper's Weekly*, hinting that the plan might well be tried in other corrupt cities. Reedy contented himself with claiming that an honest city government had been achieved. He preferred not to reflect on the methods of violence, intimidation, and fraud that had been used, for his objective was to make the city great and beautiful, to arouse its self-consciousness and shape its pride. He said that there had never been a perfect government and never would be while men remained imperfect. Meanwhile it was at least possible to put the best men in office.

The impression Reedy managed to convey was summed up in a flattering editorial by Sir Hubert Stanley in *Current Literature*. No magazine in the country, it said, had so consistently led sentiment "toward civic beauty" as had the *Mirror*. "While in its literary function the *Mirror* has contributed to the delight of readers everywhere, it has been especially admirable in its work for what it calls a 'new St. Louis' and 'a better St. Louis,' striving to impress citizens with a sense of corporate being." [19]

But for Reedy it was a Pyrrhic victory. Publicly he could take pride in having helped promote a better town and in keeping the plan for a World's Fair alive. His private misgivings were expressed in constant allusions to the *alleged* election of Wells and Folk. Publicly he could reprint with a touch of vanity Sir Hubert's praise and other evidence of growing recognition, for he was conceded to be a successful man and was not yet forty years old. Privately he was consumed by grief over the sudden death of his young wife.

Soon after they were married the Reedys had moved to a modest house on Spring Street in the West End, not far from

STREETCARS AND CORRUPTION

Lindell Boulevard. A younger sister of Mrs. Reedy had been divorced, so they had a nursery furnished for her baby daughter, Carol Ralston, who spent half her time with them, half with her grandparents, the Bauduys. That they would have welcomed children of their own was apparent from the affection they showed this child, who still recalls the lavish presents showered on her by her Uncle Billy. But Mrs. Reedy fell ill of a thyroid condition, then contracted an incurable heart disease. Carol was taken home by her grandmother, who brought her for one last visit to the house where her aunt lay dying. The old lady and the little girl stood in the hall, and the child looked up the long flight of stairs to the bedroom door where her uncle stood with his head in his hands, sobbing.

Lalite Reedy died in agony early that November before reaching her thirtieth birthday. George Tansey, the friend who had taken Reedy in after his disastrous first marriage, wrote her obituary for the *Mirror*.[20] Reedy at first wrote nothing to give any hint of his feelings, and his friends feared that the black mood he was in might lead to suicide. In his Thanksgiving issue were poems from friends like Bliss Carman, arguing against his despair; anonymous tales of lovers' quarrels happily mended, and an anecdote about some poignant incident when Lalite Reedy had met Addie Baldwin on a streetcar. In his editorial for that issue Reedy wondered what there was to be thankful for that Thanksgiving Day, and answered: "even for sorrow, even for death that comes at the end of a full draught of life to give it the last fine flavor and then—rest. *Deo gratias.*"[21]

CHAPTER 9

AT THE FAIR

WITH Rolla Wells installed as mayor, Reedy had become a prophet not without honor in his home town. He was reputed to be an insider, close to the group that had put over the election. And he looked the part, having gained in more than prestige. He weighed two hundred forty pounds now, and his rolling progress down the street was like a procession, punctuated by shouted greetings and guffaws. Everyone knew him—the paper boy, the bootblack, and the banker. He looked up to them all, as his friend Alexander Harvey of the *Literary Digest* once said; and they looked up to him. His great girth seemed a token of the good life and a promise of laughter. He had a way of puncturing each private vanity with a teasing wisecrack, and all enjoyed his familiarity, sensing the quick sympathy that lurked just below its surface.

Reedy's generosity was becoming both a legend and a threat to the magazine's solvency. He would take a week finding a job for an unemployed bartender or hand all the cash in the office to a newly discharged reporter. If there was no cash to lend he would go out and borrow some. He seemed bent on smothering bereavement under a tide of activity, and it was hard to see how he got through his vast stint of reading and writing. His work for the *Mirror* was always postponed until the last possible moment, when printers were rending

AT THE FAIR

their aprons and assistants were all but in tears.[1] Yet now he managed to attend World's Fair committee meetings and to start a new periodical, the *Valley Magazine*, a slick-paper literary counterpart of the *Mirror*, intended to replace the Mirror Pamphlets still selling ten thousand copies an issue. The *Valley* always lacked the spice and daring of the *Mirror* and lasted less than two years.

It was at this time, too, that Reedy won his reputation as the town's favorite toastmaster and after-dinner speaker. His infectious laughter, his earthy wit and believable modesty, were irresistible to well-fed banquet guests. Some still recall his presenting Elbert Hubbard with a limp suede-bound copy of the city directory in retaliation for Hubbard's publishing a similarly bound pirated anthology of Reedy's essays. "It gives me great pleasure to find myself in this large and distinguished gathering," he would begin; "I am large and you are distinguished." Then the great brown eyes would shine, the belly quiver with submerged laughter, the small hands gesticulate to emphasize his bulk; and the diners would melt indulgently.[2]

Mayor Wells, who took Reedy's phrase "The New St. Louis" for his slogan, tells of one such banquet, which he himself gave to celebrate that theme and unite the incongruous elements of the body politic: Butler's illiterate aldermen, millionaires like Campbell, and idealists like Blair. Just before Reedy was called on, the notoriously corrupt speaker of the House of Delegates offered an ornate toast written for him by a waggish judge. One and all must strive, the politician read woodenly, to make the city not only great and beautiful but "peerless for its moral forces and intellectual elevation." The tipsy ward and precinct leaders, in their rented dress suits, cheered while he read on desperately. Years later Wells could still remember Reedy and Lehmann beside him at the head table, doubled up with laughter.[3]

THE MAN IN THE MIRROR

Eight months after that banquet, in January 1902, Reedy's old colleague, James M. Galvin, shambled into the office of the new circuit attorney to pass the time of day.[4] Still the connoisseur of underworld gossip, Red Galvin was now working for the *Star*, which Reedy had edited before he started the *Mirror* with Fanning and Galvin. Circuit Attorney Folk, with his pince-nez, his Prince Albert, his dimpled chin and ingenuous gaze, must have fascinated the hard-bitten reporter impudently perched on his desk. Folk was fascinated in his turn by the story Galvin had written for the *Star* that day and now proceeded to elucidate.[5]

It told of the dilemma of two members of the Municipal Assembly trying to collect their reward for getting a new franchise passed. Charles H. Turner, president of the suburban street railway line, had borrowed a large sum from members of his board of directors to bribe the two houses of the Assembly. He wanted his cars to be allowed to run to the downtown railroad terminal over the Traction Company's right of way. Pending final approval of such a franchise the bribe money had been locked in two safe deposit boxes, each with a pair of keys so that neither party could open a box except in the presence of the other. Each alderman had sworn that if he talked his life would be forfeit: "My throat may be cut, my tongue torn out, and my body cast into the Mississippi River." Now that the new reform administration had made it impossible for the deal to take effect, both Turner and the aldermen claimed the money, and neither could get it out.[6]

After Folk had called a hundred witnesses before his grand jury without getting any revealing evidence, he asked Turner and his professional lobbyist to call at his office. Without a shred of evidence, he convinced both men, as well as their expert criminal lawyer, that he could send Turner and his accomplices to the penitentiary unless they turned state's evidence. Unlike the aldermen, Turner had taken no oath of secrecy. This aristocratic neighbor of Mayor Wells of Wellston now proceeded to speak out. No sooner was his story told than Folk marched into the two banks where the bribe money was cached and, again by sheer bluff, demanded and was given the two safe deposit boxes and their packages of thousand-dollar bills—evidence sure to impress any jury.[7]

Reedy at first suspected that Butler himself had been responsible for the revelation. "Bribery was his special monopoly, and a few indictments of those who thought it wasn't would demonstrate that he was the only man to do the business." But the Suburban Railway case was only the first in a series that Folk now proceeded to bring to light. In the end Ed Butler himself was indicted; and though the daily papers tried to shield the respected businessmen who had done the bribing, one Suburban Railway director, Ellis Wainwright, owner of the world's first skyscraper, thought it prudent to spend the next ten years in Paris. Even James Campbell was at last called before Folk's grand jury, and only saved from indictment by the statute of limitations.[8]

It was not until the summer following Red Galvin's call on the circuit attorney that Lincoln Steffens came to St. Louis, not until September 1902 that *McClure's Magazine* made the corruption Folk had exposed a matter of national concern. Steffens' shrill tone of outrage contrasted with Reedy's philosophical irony, which had reminded St. Louisans that before giving way to joy "at having leaped to the very pinnacle of perjury, bribery and fraud in the eyes of the world" they must remember there might be disadvantages in this new eminence. They had a habit of shrugging off such scandals as part of the necessary reality of modern politics and business. They must remember that the Fair made it incumbent on them to put their house in order, for it would soon bring them under the scrutiny of the entire world. The real house-cleaning must take place in their hearts, however. "Men's minds must be purged of sympathy with successful dealings simply because they are successful." [9]

At first Reedy admired and aided Circuit Attorney Folk; but as it became clear that Folk was using his prominence to campaign for a higher office, Reedy's mistrust of his zeal revived. Folk seemed to care nothing for men and their feelings. He professed loyalty to no one. He was so bent on keeping the spotlight to himself that he would not even entrust his able assistants with a part in the courtroom proceedings. In the end this resulted in poor staff work and reversals on appeal, not all of them explainable by the bias and venality of the state supreme court.[10]

Folk's undertaking was on the heroic scale, but his final score was not impressive. Up to the day Red Galvin walked into his office with the Suburban Railway scandal, only thirty-four cases of bribery had been brought to trial in American courts in a hundred years. Folk brought sixty-one indictments, put forty defendants on trial, and won lower-court convictions in about half of the trials. But in the end Butler and all the prominent businessmen and politicians were exonerated. Only eight insignificant aldermen of the saloon-keeper and hostler class went to prison. When the circuit attorney ran for governor, Reedy opposed him.

Mocking Folk's "self-conscious unconsciousness" and his evasiveness on basic issues, Reedy said "He is as elusive as a half-suppressed smile, as evasive as a woman who hovers between liking and loving, but all the time he is moving towards his own ends as a glacier glides down a mountainside." [11] Yet Reedy was fascinated in spite of himself by one aspect of Folk's character, his ability to inspire confidence in those whose burden of guilt made them long to confess even to a public prosecutor. Reedy commissioned Claude Wetmore of the *Post-Dispatch*, who had written and co-signed Lincoln Steffens' first muckraking article for *McClure's*, to discuss this aspect in an article for the *Valley Magazine*. Where Reedy had accused Folk of misusing his office to satisfy private ambition, Wetmore found that the inspired prosecutor forgot even himself in his efforts. Where Reedy had charged that Folk betrayed the secrets of the grand jury to the papers, Wetmore pointed out that the confessions Folk gave out were those which had been freely uttered in his office.[12]

It was characteristic of Reedy to give another writer the opportunity to disagree with him in his own columns. In the same issue he ran an article by James Blair stating another position remote from his own. Blair was replying to Henry Watterson of the *Louisville Courier-Journal*, who had said that idealistic statesmen had no place in modern politics, "not even standing room." Blair had been politically realistic enough to defend Campbell's reform-by-bribery plan, but he was outraged by such apparent cynicism.

Blair had become more and more loquacious as the spokesman of reform. He had traveled to Detroit in the spring of 1903, some six months after Steffens' first article in *McClure's* and soon after the appearance of another, entitled "The Shame of St. Louis," in order to tell the National Municipal League the significance of Folk's work in Missouri. And now he lashed out at old Henry Watterson. Speaking of the ignoble part America was playing both at home and in world affairs, he said that every true American "must and will cast down these false gods; and in the fulness of time, though it may be in the dust and ashes of repentance, he will acknowledge his error and then, with a generosity absolutely without limit, he will restore to each man that which is his . . ." Blair spoke with the authority of a man whose family stands beside the Adamses in American history and whose homestead fronts the White House. His voice had the sonorous ring of oratory heard in the day of Jackson and Webster and of his own grandfather, Francis Preston Blair, Senior.[13]

THE MAN IN THE MIRROR

But a few weeks later a former law clerk of his told a reporter of irregularities in Blair's own practice. As trustee for the family of a man who had been his father's and Lincoln's trusted counsellor, Blair had apparently misappropriated over $400,000. He now borrowed a large sum from Campbell, explaining that he must cover up for a black-sheep brother, and Campbell took a deed of trust on Stancote, Blair's great country house, advising his friend to resign as general counsel of the World's Fair corporation. The lawyer's ruin followed swiftly.[14]

Circuit Attorney Folk himself conducted a grand jury investigation of Blair. And as Blair was telling reporters he would infallibly vindicate himself, he was stricken as if by a bolt from above and fell backward down a stone stair in his garden. His physician told the papers the fall had rendered Blair "perhaps permanently insane." Even as he spoke, Blair's own client, the Mutual Insurance Company of New York, brought suit for cancellation of his life insurance policy, alleging that he meant to commit suicide. The next day the Blairs moved out of Stancote, and Campbell took over the estate and advertised it for sale. Some months later, soon after Folk's grand jury brought in an indictment for forgery, Blair died in Florida.

To Reedy it seemed unconscionable that the press should make Blair everybody's scapegoat. "It is a heart-breaking story," he wrote, and went on to claim his own share in Blair's transgressions: "Mr. Blair was a friend of mine. I believed in him even though it was seldom that we ever agreed on any point of policy. I knew him as a man of culture, a man of gentle affections, as a champion of an hundred causes that were good, as a champion of the idealities. However it may be with others, it is not for me to pounce upon him, and by attacking his deeds, inferentially exalt my own virtue." It was hard to say who was not in some degree guilty of the same inconsistency between aim and attainment.

"What punishment could be greater," Reedy concluded, "than the unmasking of a man to himself, the revelation of the complete overwhelming of light by darkness in his own soul?" [15]

Folk was elected governor on the Democratic ticket the following November. Theodore Roosevelt, who had succeeded to the presidency after McKinley's assassination, was running for re-election on the Republican ticket the same year, but he refused to "say anything in disparagement of Mr. Folk." Hawes had led the opposition to Folk's nomination as long as he could, and he had Reedy's support, for what it was worth. Folk carried St. Louis by a plurality twice as large as Roosevelt's. By now the rippling brook of clear water that Campbell, Blair, and their friends at the Noonday Club had set free just three years before, intending to wash up St. Louis for the Fair, had turned into a muddy torrent, sweeping men and houses on its crest.

Rolla Wells, the Noonday lunchers' choice for mayor, surprised Reedy by becoming far more successful in his more limited sphere than Folk turned out to be now that he was being widely considered as Roosevelt's probable opponent in the next presidential election. Wells declined a third term soon afterwards, satisfied to be known as the World's Fair mayor of St. Louis.

Though it started a year late and lasted only six months, the Fair surpassed the most flamboyant hopes of its creators. It vied with Queen Victoria's Diamond Jubilee as an expression of the spiral dreams of an age dedicated to material progress and world civilization based on private enterprise. The overseas territories of the United States, as well as the states themselves, participated; Asiatic empires and kingdoms, as well as European republics and African colonies, took part. Each showed the way of life it esteemed, parading its customs as it wanted them to be seen. Thirty-five acres were devoted to life in the Philippines alone, while Switzerland and the Tyrol tried to build facsimiles of the Alps on the ground allotted them. One might visit African kraals, Alaskan igloos, replicas of the bazaars of Stamboul and the streets of Cairo. One might meet tribesmen from seventy American Indian communities, Japanese villagers, Moros, pygmies, and twenty thousand others, all living on the fairgrounds. White plaster palaces stretched off in geometric vistas, punctuated by soaring fountains and interlaced with lagoons bearing craft of every sort: gondolas and junks, canoes and submarines. Twenty million travelers saw the varied life of the planet with eyes more innocent and awed than those that generally greet such exhibitions. A bonhommie captured in songs evoked by the occasion spread over the world, so that fifty years later in a Copenhagen brewery or a Moroccan bistro one might be asked to repeat the words of "Under the Anheuser Bush" or "Meet Me in St. Louis, Louis." Princes and prime ministers, savage tribesmen and carnival vagabonds, thronged the famous Pike and sauntered beside the Serpentine or along Art Hill. In an age still intoxicated with man-made wonders there were new thrills in witnessing for the first time such marvels as wireless telegraphy, aeroplane flights, and milking machines.

"This Exposition grew upon the world as a discovery, a matter of marvel," wrote the official historian, boasting that it surpassed Chicago in 1893 and Paris in 1900. London in 1896 was too provincial an affair to mention.[16]

For Mayor Wells, who assisted Governor Francis in the enormous task of entertaining celebrities and princely guests from every nation, the Fair was at once a climax and an his-

AT THE FAIR

toric dividing line. "The marvellous exhibits!" he exclaims in his memoirs. "The wonders and amusements of the Pike! The grandeur of the general ceremonies, with their military pomp and bands of music! . . . The World's Fair was, in many respects, the dividing line between the Old St. Louis and the New St. Louis. A new economic order was developing, and the modes of business and living were changing." [17]

For Reedy the Fair ended an era, too. As it came to a close he walked down the famous Pike alone, in October, the month the Veiled Prophet opened the old fairs. He had been a widower for three years now. His brother Frank had just died. Twice, Reedy had risen to modest success, first in national and now in local affairs. Twice he had tasted the gall of disillusionment and loss. The world had not changed so much as a man like Wells might imagine.

In the broad avenue that chilly night he passed Igorrote warriors from the Philippines wearing hideous store-bought togs still embellished with price tags, and blanketed Indians whose noses seemed to have turned blue with the cold, and plaster-of-Paris goddesses with a finger or an ear eaten away by the weather. Like Henry Adams, who had been there that summer, he listened to the hum of the great dynamo that lighted the displays, and mused on the passing scene and the passing of an era wrought in fragile plaster.

He heard the Boer War fusillades and thought of nations crushed by the ruthless ambitions of the great. As the air grew sharper he sought the crowds and the cheer of fragrant, noisy restaurants. Walking he mused:

> The sun goes down and the warmth passes. The night wind rises, and with it the chill of night. The lights gleam out, but they, too, seem as if the mighty hand of death were stretched over the great dynamo-heart . . . The din from the Pike comes clear and distinct to shatter one's dreams with a suggestion—well, of the laboriousness of our follies.[18]

CHAPTER 10

ROOSEVELT AND THE FREE PRESS

BRIBERY is, after all . . . a conventional offense, and in many advanced communities it is regarded as a trifling offense, a mere perversion of justice." [1]

There in a nutshell is the order under which Reedy had grown up. The occasion was one of Folk's celebrated trials; the speaker, defense attorney Judge H. Sam Priest, Reedy's friend and Frederick Lehmann's partner. Listening to the husky resonance of his voice one can all but catch the scent of julep. Yet one knows that his client (who sold a franchise at a profit of a million dollars) will never suffer from a "mere" perversion of justice.

The lawyer's words do not seem to have caused a single eyebrow to be raised, even from the bench, which may explain how Reedy could praise Campbell as first to abandon an "obsolescent" economic system, why he could defend Blair with such warmth, and what he meant by accusing Folk of "moral coprolalia." Campbell had sickened and Blair had died on a surfeit of the corrupt fare upon which Folk grew fat. The sudden spate of publicity Folk and Steffens had brought upon the town ignored the causes of its moral paralysis and did nothing to remove them. Their preachments, like Garland's essays in praise of veritism, merely replaced the tinkling prettiness of a Victorian fiction with the bombast and distortions of journalism. Though he still called himself a newspaperman, Reedy could not believe such methods would restore freedoms lost to abuse, nor enlighten those who sat in darkness. Men's minds must be purged of sympathy with success for its own sake, he had written, and that Augean task demanded a more penetrating form of criticism than the muckrakers'. Perhaps fiction could clarify what facts failed to make clear.

Meanwhile one political leader who knew how to write went a long way to leaven Reedy's pessimism during the years following Lalite Reedy's death. Earlier, Theodore Roosevelt had seemed to have "much of the Kipling spirit." Now Reedy gave the President his boundless allegiance and forgot his earlier misgivings about the Roughrider's tactics and imperial ambitions.

Even in July 1898, when the Spanish War was young, Reedy had picked Roosevelt as a likely man for the presidency.[2] When the campaign of 1900 came around he had regretted that Roosevelt had second place on the ticket, and that President McKinley ignored his young colleague's stand against the trusts. Reedy himself had been slow to accept the program for curbing trusts, saying there was only one dangerous trust in America, the Associated Press—a monopolistic conspiracy for the control of men's minds. In 1901, a month after Reedy had praised Vice-President Roosevelt's patience in the face of Mark Hanna's and McKinley's snubs,[3] the President was shot by the mad Czolgosz. Reedy wrote of Roosevelt's disappointment at having attained the highest office without a fair fight for public acceptance of his ideas and his program of economic reform. Apparently he already knew Roosevelt, who loved literary talk and indulged his taste for it when he was in New York, for Reedy wrote of the President now as a personal friend— "an American citizen without a single frill . . . full of sense and sentiment, each regulating the other.

"Mr. Roosevelt's politics are simple," he said. "He believes in American destiny as a republic. He believes that Americanism is individualism. He holds that man is the great thing, issues only the expression of man . . . He is not commercialist, not imperialist. He is for the happiness of all the people under representative government."[4] Reedy clearly considered the young president his ally against "sordid materialism," one who would never consider bribery "a mere perversion of justice," though the President laughed at wishful advocates of good government and called them "goo-goo" reformers. Moreover, astonishingly enough, Roosevelt was a successful writer. The month after he succeeded to the presidency Reedy reprinted a *New York Times* account of his writing career.

About the same time, Reedy defended the President against angry Southerners. He had grown up sharing the racial prejudices of the South, but when Roosevelt invited Booker T. Washington of Tuskegee to dine at the White House, Reedy showed that he had outgrown all trace of racial bias. "If the South is insulted because a man of brains and character and philanthropic educational achievement is shown the respect due these high things, then the South prefers barbarism to civilization."[5]

He expressed this conviction a few days before Lalite's death threw him into a state of demoralization, from which he sought to extricate himself soon afterwards by taking a trip to Washington. His articles from the capital show that he partly achieved the absorption he had hoped for; they do not read like the observations of a traveler or a neophyte. He seemed to know everyone and to go everywhere. On his return home he received from a Captain Asbury of Higginsville, Missouri, an angry letter canceling his subscription because the *Mirror* had defended the President for entertaining a Negro at his table. Reedy printed the letter with his reply, admitting that he himself had had a very pleasant luncheon at the White House, and adding that the captain might be interested to know that there had been a dog present at the presidential board. Reedy said he believed, though he could not be quite sure, that it had received some scraps from the table. "Anyhow the animal was present." [6]

Reedy saw the President several times while he was in Washington. Whether or not the President sought his advice on the political situation in Missouri, and continued to seek it thereafter as some have thought, Reedy continued to give Roosevelt friendly counsel and staunch support in his columns. Throughout the second term, while business leaders with whom Reedy associated in St. Louis grew more violent in their opposition to the President's antitrust policy and his efforts to regulate the railroads and the banks, Reedy defended him. He insisted that these were the same businessmen who had thought Folk had "gone far enough when he landed a few members of the House of Delegates behind the bars." [7] Reedy was even becoming more tolerant of Folk, impressed by the governor's courageous conduct of his office. He was drawn to Folk, too, by the mounting opposition of the press, which Folk shared with Roosevelt. While the newspapers had not prevented Roosevelt from winning the biggest popular majority ever accorded a presidential candidate nor kept Folk from topping Roosevelt's record in St. Louis, the unfavorable publicity increased in venom as opponents came to fear that Roosevelt might run again and that Folk might be his Democratic opponent.

In the spring of 1908, when this possibility was still being discussed, and the attack on Roosevelt was at its height, Reedy had an opportunity to answer the sniping press lords to their faces. At the Missouri Press Association's meeting in Excelsior Springs, Walter Williams outlined his plans for the state university's new school of journalism, of which he was to be dean. Reedy followed the veteran editor with an address that has gone down in the history of journalism as something of a classic.[8]

He saw the metropolitan newspapers of America as the last

beneficiaries of *laissez faire* and the greatest menace to the survival of democracy. Their owners claimed a constitutional freedom they dared not exercise for fear of antagonizing those to whom they were beholden for loans and advertising revenue. Money had corrupted the freedom of the press quite as much as it had taken away the citizen's freedom to vote for candidates of his own choice. The individualism that had seemed an essential aspect of American society was on the verge of disappearing. Reedy could think of only one editor, "dear old Henry Watterson," who still controlled his own paper. He could think of only one publisher who had ever known how to write —Joseph Pulitzer. But even if Pulitzer had once been independent, he was so no longer. He was now restricted by the very considerations of financial self-interest his papers pretended to attack. When Roosevelt had asked Pulitzer what railroad investments he held, Pulitzer could not afford to reply. It was loyalty like his toward the companies in which publishers invested that made it impossible for the papers to support the President in his attempt to control the railroads.

All the papers had either supported Roosevelt at first, Reedy continued, or recognized his popularity by refraining from attacking him. It was only "when it seemed probable that Roosevelt was likely to accomplish something" that the papers began to discredit him. One group of journals called him sincere but erratic, another charging him with insincerity. The *New York Times* had at first been an idealistic supporter of the President, but when he began to put his stated principles into operation, it turned on him with the rest. Reedy hinted that its change of front was the result of a libel suit the publisher of the *Times* brought against William Randolph Hearst. The suit was speedily dropped when Hearst's attorney threatened to call the *Times's* financial backers as witnesses.

But Roosevelt was by no means the only political advocate of basic reforms who had been supported by the papers until his policies became disturbing to their financial backers. Folk had been attacked in Missouri, Francis Joseph Heney in San Francisco, Robert La Follette in Wisconsin, and Tom L. Johnson in Cleveland—all for the same reason. "There is not a man in the United States to-day who has tried honestly to do anything to change the fundamental conditions that make for poverty, disease, vice and crime in our cities, our courts, and in our legislatures, who, at the very moment at which his efforts seemed most likely to succeed, has not suddenly been turned upon and rent by the great newspaper publications." [9]

Reedy's indictment of the press would be of sufficient interest to students of journalism to be worth reprinting. Unfortunately, it appears to have been delivered extemporaneously and never edited. He concluded it by expressing the hope that private pamphleteers might exercise the freedom which newspaper publishers had made a mockery. But in his heart Reedy no longer hoped that any form of journalism would serve to enlighten an America convinced that bribery is a "trifling offense, a mere perversion of justice," that nothing succeeds like success, and that business is business. Himself a pamphleteer, he published his address as a pamphlet, but he had little hope that it would effect any change in the situation. Reedy had come to look to the literary artist, the writer of fiction or poetry, to accomplish what he and his kind never could.

CHAPTER 11

THEODORE DREISER

In the *Republican's* city room, as Reedy said, literature had been the common dream. To leap the chasm between disgruntled journalism and a more durable literature is the fantasy of many a hopeful cub reporter. Theodore Dreiser was one of the rare dreamers who did leap it, and Reedy was there to help him to his feet when he scrambled up the other side. F. O. Matthiessen calls him Dreiser's first real champion.[1]

At twenty-two Dreiser had looked on the editor of the *Mirror*, nine years his senior, as one of the brilliant journalists who had graduated into the world of letters. It is unlikely that they met during Dreiser's sixteen months in St. Louis in the early nineties. In those days Dreiser, a gangling, self-conscious cub with a flair for bizarre dandyism, was far too shy to approach Reedy at the *Globe-Democrat*, for Reedy was a feature writer, a legendary and privileged personage. Dreiser was given to hero worship, and Reedy was among his idols, along with Joseph B. McCullagh, the *Globe's* great editor, and Eugene Field and Mark Twain, journalists who had left Missouri to find world fame.[2]

Sixteen months may seem a brief stretch, but Dreiser magnified his days. For him the town was radiant and golden with expectation. He saw intensely and stored up each impression: the furniture of his friends' bohemian flat, a gleaming white mansion like James Campbell's, girls in their bustled silks, and the Veiled Prophet's ball in its purple elegance; Ed Butler's thousand-dollar diamond and the dingy half-world where a Negro knifing spattered the gutter scarlet. Each memory was dyed with its vivid love or hate. He despised Reedy's partner, Red Galvin, and loved a Missouri-prairie school teacher, Sara White. They became engaged after an excursion to the Chicago World's Fair, paid for by the *Republic*, his second paper. (As the *Republican* it had been Reedy's first.) The betrothal to Miss White lasted six years, during which Dreiser returned to St. Louis for several fleeting visits to confirm his enchantment, meanwhile producing an imitation Elizabethan sonnet cycle to celebrate his love.[3]

After he resigned from the *Republic* in the spring of 1894, his newspaper career was brief. It filled only a year, during which he worked in Toledo, Cleveland, Buffalo, Pittsburgh, and New York. Though he spent no more than a few days in Toledo covering a streetcar strike, his friendship with Arthur Henry, his city editor on the *Toledo Blade*, was of lasting consequence, for though his editor on the *Republic* had urged him to emulate Zola and Balzac in his reporting, it was Henry who persuaded him to try his hand at prose fiction. Dreiser's months on Pulitzer's *New York World* persuaded him to leave newspaper life for good. Frightened and insecure in a craft he had only half learned, he was humiliated as well at having to turn his stories over to rewrite men. So he resigned.[4]

In the fall of 1895, after a summer of unemployment in New York, he induced the firm that published his brother Paul's songs to let him start a magazine, which he called *Ev'ry Month*. It was to be a vehicle for sheet music. His subscribers were ladies who could play or sing. Paul had written "The Bowery," and Theodore had supplied the lyric for another of Paul's better-known songs, "On the Banks of the Wabash." But he considered such work frivolous and sought to pattern his magazine after Reedy's, as he showed when he entitled his editorial paragraphs "Reflections" and signed them with a pseudonym.

THE MAN IN THE MIRROR

There the resemblance ended, for Dreiser altogether lacked Reedy's light touch. Where Reedy signed his "Reflections," with scatographic intent, "Uncle Fuller," Dreiser signed his "The Prophet."

His paragraphs always verged on the lugubrious. "The language of patriotism has been usurped by fraud and greed," he told his voteless lady readers during McKinley's front-porch campaign against Bryan. "Do you know that human beings are innately greedy . . . that they dream of fine clothes and fine houses and of rolling about luxuriously in carriages while others beg along their pathway? . . . And will you let the affairs of your country fall into the hands of those who will not stop at aught to gain their shameless ends?"[5] Yet even while railing against malefactors of great wealth, he himself longed for money and power. "How to be successful—what a burning question that is to one trying to succeed!" he wrote.[6] He urged the ladies to improve themselves, and confided his own formula. One reads novels to be improved; why not more serious books—Spencer, Darwin, and Huxley? Pondering the accidents of fate after the St. Louis tornado, which had spared his fiancée, Dreiser mused that "man is the sport of the elements; the necessary but worthless dust of changing conditions, and that all the fourteen hundred million human beings who swarm the earth after the manner of contentious vermin" are no more than "a form of heat dissipation."[7]

Caught between determinism and a raging thirst for justice, between concern for the common man and for Theodore Dreiser, this bemused philosopher infected the magazine with his own ambivalence. America must develop ideas and tastes of its own, he would demand in one issue. The next would be given over to Queen Victoria's household with its thousand retainers and acres of rich apartments. His feature writers would describe the British Queen's palace as they did the homes of American millionaires—with transparent envy. Dreiser compounded their snobbery (gaping at the sandpapered oysters on the royal table) in his editorial. There he praised Victoria's "motherly guidance" of her realm, which had proven "vastly beneficial to the entire world," hinting that America could do with a bit of motherly guidance, too.[8]

In the course of his editorship Dreiser printed dozens of such features and paragraphs, an article by his Toledo city editor Arthur Henry, a story by Stephen Crane, and at least two of Reedy's essays from the *Mirror:* his scathing attack on the popular novelist, Hall Caine, and his obituary for McCullagh. Reedy showed that he was at least aware of Dreiser by reprinting one article from *Ev'ry Month,* in 1897.[9]

By the end of that year Dreiser gave up his magazine to become a free lance and started writing "Life Stories of Successful Men" for a new periodical called *Success.* By December 1898, just a year later, he had made enough money to send for Sara White, whom he married in Washington and brought home to New York. The next summer Arthur Henry persuaded him to bring his bride to Maumee, outside Toledo, and embark on the adventure of writing short stories. While these proved harder to sell and far less remunerative than his feature articles, Henry managed to goad him into starting his first novel that fall of 1899, when he accompanied the Dreisers back to New York. Interrupted by spells of depression but cajoled and nudged along by Henry, Dreiser brought *Sister Carrie* to a conclusion in May 1900—still harassed by a nagging feeling that he should have been writing salable articles instead.[10]

The story of *Sister Carrie's* unhappy beginnings is common knowledge: how it was handed to Frank Doubleday just before he sailed for Europe; jubilantly received as a masterpiece by Frank Norris, then an editor for Doubleday, Page & Company; accepted under contract by Walter Hines Page; and then buried in an unsold cheap edition of a thousand copies after someone had read it in proof and was shocked. Soon after the manuscript was out of his hands, Dreiser went to Missouri for the summer. It was on this trip, presumably, that he first met Reedy.[11]

One has the impression that Dreiser was in a state of rapidly alternating elation and melancholy that summer. He was filled with self-confidence even after Henry wrote that there was likely to be trouble with the publishers; even after receiving Page's chilly letter asking to be released from their contract because (as Page said) people like Dreiser's characters did not "interest" him or the public. Still elated, Dreiser told Page and Henry of the letters of congratulation he had received from the editor of the *Atlantic* and from newspaper friends. He had told "the boys" about his book in St. Louis, asked Page to consider the damage to his reputation if the novel should be suppressed; yet he wanted Henry to know that the "little delay" he envisaged could not distress him. He considered his career secure because those things which he felt were, as he said, "needed by society and will work for its improvement —the greater happiness of man." [12]

It was in no such exalted mood that he talked to Reedy, who later recalled his pessimism. It was late in December that Reedy received a copy of *Sister Carrie*, not one of the hundred-odd copies Frank Norris is supposed to have sent out for review, but one with a glum inscription from Dreiser himself. Reedy must have read it through on Christmas Day, for on the twenty-sixth he scribbled a note telling Dreiser, "It is damn good," and promising to say so "as emphatically as this" in the *Mirror*. He wished Dreiser a happy New Year a few days later but refrained from hoping that it would also be a prosperous one, for he considered Dreiser "no prosperity friend." [13]

What Reedy did say in the *Mirror* on January 3, 1901, was

that he had read the book at a sitting and was fascinated. It had been neither "extensively advertised by its publishers" nor enthusiastically reviewed, if it had been reviewed at all, in literary journals. So he sought to pique his readers' curiosity and stir up a demand: "Now, it isn't at all a nice novel. Neither is it nasty, which is supposed to be the antonym of nice. It is a story on the seamy side. It deals with the 'fall' of a girl who goes to Chicago from a little Wisconsin town, and strange to say, though the situation is treated with calm frankness of tone, the fall is a fall upwards." [14] These opening remarks suggest that Reedy had to allow for a priggish reaction he did not share. He took issue with the prevalent view that depravity should be punished in novels as it seldom is in actual life. In the note he sent Dreiser the day after the review came out he apologized for appealing to his readers' pruriency: "I wrote the article with but one purpose in mind, to make people read [the book]. I repeat again, the book has grip. Good as it is, you can and will do better, but I sincerely hope you'll not be so concerned to remedy faults as to neglect the grip." [15]

Clearly, Reedy felt it was of the first importance that the actualities of life in America be presented just as Dreiser, with naïve astonishment, did present them. In his review he called *Sister Carrie* "a very serious production" and went on to show how it surpassed Garland in its style. "It is, in spite of veritism, very much restrained. It is photographically true, and yet there is an art about it that lifts it often above mere reporting. And there grows upon the reader the impression that there lies behind the mere story an intense, fierce resentment of the conditions glimpsed."

The shortcomings Reedy found in Dreiser seemed trivial by comparison with his accomplishments. He mentioned the bathos, the crudeness of diction and syntax. "At times the whole thing is impossible, and then again it is as absolute as life itself. The writer errs frequently in the selection of the material for his pictures, the incidents he portrays, but the story, as a whole, has a grip . . . You read it through with interest and a stirring of the emotions, and when you sit down to write a criticism of it, you find yourself trying, as it seems, to . . . analyze the charm away. But you cannot. The charm, despite violence to taste and hovering intimations even of absurdity, remains superior to and defiant of analysis." [16]

Disregarding the press of other business, Reedy took pains to reassure Dreiser about the eventual success of his work. In a note sending off copies of the review he acknowledged another despairing letter in which Dreiser must have referred to Reedy's matter-of-fact reception at the time of their meeting. It now seemed hopeless that the publishers would relent and make any effort to distribute the book. "My un-idealism in our little talk seems to have hit you hard," Reedy replied, "judging by the inscription of the volume and your note to hand to-day. Well, I *have* an ideal: it is, to be cheerful and —between you 'n me—it isn't always easy in the face of the facts." [17] When Dreiser persisted in taking a hopeless view of *Sister Carrie's* prospects, Reedy answered that the book was being discussed. He knew of at least fifteen persons in St. Louis who agreed that it was "a tip-top novel." An elderly lady had denounced it at a dinner party, saying she had seen "just such drummers . . . doing just such things" on trains.[18] This Reedy took to be better than a compliment. He advised Dreiser to use all his newspaper connections to create a demand the publishers must recognize, and gave him the name of a friend in Chicago who would review it sympathetically. He was still sure the book would be a "go." At Dreiser's request he then sent the book to his Chicago friend himself.[19]

By autumn the English edition was out, and Dreiser had some hopes of finding an American publisher who would give the book a fair chance. Reedy wrote that he was "much gratified to read in the London *Saturday Review* a very appreciative notice." He noted that the Chicago *Record-Herald* seemed much impressed by the *Saturday Review's* discovery—"all of which ought to do you considerable good." Once more he offered to help wherever he could. The next issue of the *Mirror* boasted of having been right as usual in its initial estimate of *Sister Carrie*. The novel was winning fame abroad.[20]

Dreiser responded by sending him the manuscripts of some short stories accompanied by another morose note. "If life wears the aspect you endeavor to reflect in your letter," Reedy answered, ". . . the whole thing is hardly of enough importance to worry about it. Everything is for the best, as we come to find out as we grow a little older. At least I am not able to look at the matter in any other way." [21]

Reedy's wife died three weeks later, and by this time he must have feared that the end was not far off. Far from putting Dreiser out of his mind, however, Reedy had a New York correspondent look into the story of how Doubleday, Page managed to suppress a book they were under contract to publish. Later, while Reedy was in Washington visiting President Roosevelt, he brought out the correspondent's detailed report, and the following week he published one of the stories Dreiser had sent. It was one of those Dreiser had written at Maumee and been unable to sell; it was based on an incident in the old Bloody Third police station. The story, "Butcher Rogaum's Door," appeared in the Christmas number of the *Mirror,* one of the few issues each year for which Reedy could afford to buy fiction." [22]

During the next five years Dreiser had no further direct contact with Reedy. The "good luck and good health and good spirits" Reedy had wished him at New Year's proved a vain hope. The depression from which Dreiser had been suffering worsened, leading him to the verge of suicide. He suffered much as Hurstwood had in his novel, and perhaps it was the insights he had gained in creating Hurstwood that saved him. It was not until 1903 that he was well enough to take another editorial job.

In the long interim of silence, however, another bond between Reedy and Dreiser was unknowingly formed when a young man, burning to become a writer, called on Reedy, later going to see Dreiser to ask for work. Harris Merton Lyon had been a reader of the *Mirror* while a student at the University of Missouri, and now came to ask Reedy's advice as he set out on his career. "He was crazy about the *fin de siècle* stuff," as Reedy subsequently told Dreiser: "I hope the recording angel will put it to my credit that I steered him off that." [23]

Lyon went to New York and put himself through a rigorous schooling, living in a hall bedroom, eating at shabby quick-lunch counters where one might study the customers and forget the fare. It was in 1906 that he came to see Dreiser, who had just taken over as editor of the *Broadway* magazine, and Dreiser hired him as an editorial assistant. For the time being Dreiser had given up hope for *Sister Carrie* and for the second novel that had been interrupted by his breakdown. Frustrated in his own ambitions, he became absorbed in observing Lyon's. It was like reliving his St. Louis days, watching Lyon strike so many of the attitudes he himself had struck. He was enchanted by the young man's arrogance and disdain for literary commercialism; Lyon was "so intensely avid of life, so intolerant," that the older man found it no easy matter to win his confidence or stand up to his rebuffs. That youthful zest was nevertheless a splendid thing to behold. "Once he said to me quite excitedly, walking up Eighth Avenue at two in the morning . . . 'God, how I hate to go to bed in this town! I'm afraid something will happen while I'm asleep and I won't see it.'" [*] [24]

[*] Reprinted by permission of The World Publishing Company from *Twelve Men* by Theodore Dreiser. Copyright 1919 by Boni & Liveright, Inc. Copyright 1946 by Helen Dreiser.

THEODORE DREISER

Still childless at thirty-five, Dreiser expressed some of his own yearnings for a son in his relation with Lyon. Perhaps he unconsciously gave away some of his dissatisfaction with his own father, too, when he came to write of their friendship. He said the young man did not appear to know who his father was or be greatly concerned whether his mother had married him or not. Though thinking of Lyon as his own son, he admitted that the youngster's bravado sometimes palled. "At times I thought he ought to be killed—like a father meditating on an unruly son—but the mood soon passed and his literary ability made amends for everything." * [25]

Then, in 1907, Dreiser's luck changed. In March he wrote Reedy that he had at last found an American publisher for *Sister Carrie,* which had been "offered to every first class publishing house in New York, barring none, and then turned down." He added that he saw the *Mirror* almost every week in the hands of some author calling at the *Broadway.*[26] In June he became editor of the *Delineator* and was established as a success—at least commercially. But he left Lyon behind on the *Broadway,* to be spoiled, as he thought, by its publisher's too lavish encouragement. When the young man wrote a story with a happy ending, Dreiser could not forgive the compromise, and when Lyon became a friend of O. Henry, Dreiser accused him of imitating the popular author's style.

Sister Carrie was republished as one of the first offerings of B. W. Dodge's new firm, and Dreiser showed Dodge the happy letter of congratulations he received from Reedy.[27] The novel was promoted with excerpts from the 1901 reviews by Reedy, Hamlin Garland, and Brand Whitlock. Soon afterwards, Reedy took up Lyon, printing one of his stories in his 1907 Christmas issue and several essays, poems, and short stories thereafter.[28]

* Reprinted by permission of The World Publishing Company from *Twelve Men* by Theodore Dreiser. Copyright 1919 by Boni & Liveright, Inc. Copyright 1946 by Helen Dreiser.

THE MAN IN THE MIRROR

In 1908 Dodge's publishing house brought out Lyon's first book, *Sardonics,* a collection of short stories which might have been a success if the firm had not failed immediately afterwards.

The letters that passed between Reedy and Dreiser in the ensuing years were the routine exchanges between an author pushing his own work and a friendly critic who reserves the right to praise or damn. Reedy was lukewarm in his reception of *Jennie Gerhardt,* enthusiastic about *The Financier,* and almost convinced of Dreiser's greatness when its sequel *The Titan* appeared.[29] Dreiser, he said, writing of *The Titan* in 1914, "is big because he has no philosophy, no economics, no sociology, no tradition, no background, no learning to stop him from boldly picturing and saying things so obvious no cognoscenti of letters would venture upon them for fear of being accused of banality." [30]

In Cowperwood the financial genius, hero of *Financier* and *Titan,* Reedy could recognize not only Dreiser's model, Charles T. Yerkes, but all the arrogant financial giants who had dominated America up to the time of the scandals Reedy and Folk and Lincoln Steffens had helped expose in St. Louis. Here was the pathos of genius perverted to the ends of a corrupt system. Here was tragedy like James Blair's and empty triumph like James Campbell's. Cowperwood was "Yerkes plus," Reedy told Dreiser, implying that his hero transcended Cowperwood's original. And he added, with a familiarity meant to inform Dreiser that he had at last arrived: "You are the goods, me boy, and I'm proud of you." [31]

Reedy had had to struggle over his review of *The Financier* as he had not struggled over *Sister Carrie.* But though the notice did not appear for over two months, he was unusually pleased with the result, as he indicated by sending to Dreiser Thomas Bird Mosher's enthusiastic remarks about both the book and the review, in January 1913. The Portland publisher had called Reedy "the only man in this country who could possibly have written such a review," adding: "Old man, your head for once is bigger than your heart, and it would be hard to chase that fat fantastic heart of yours into all the holes and corners it has probably crept into since the days when you were a news-paper boy and I was a poor damned book clerk in St. Louis in '79." "My approval is not worth much," Reedy told Dreiser, "but Mosher is a High Priest of Letters." [32]

Yet Reedy's review of *The Financier* did justify Mosher's approval by its penetrating humanism and moral intuitions. "I cannot convey to you that smouldering glow in the story that shows through the texture of Dreiser's words like the absinthean, opalescent color in favrile glass, but often and again flames up in diamond brightness. The whole story is so fused and fluid that it's not like a story at all. It's like nothing in the world but life."

He called the novel's theme selfishness—"Self bent on Self's ends to the end of everything." One was only dimly aware of the writer, he said, except as a voice guiding us through "this hell which is only the life of Self." Crowded and passionate as it was, the book depicted heroic agony. Such inklings of happiness as it contained reminded him of Shelley's words: "Hell is a city very much like London"; only he would have said Philadelphia—or St. Louis.

"Finally," he concluded, the novel had an odd effect, stamping it with "something like greatness." "You close the book hating no one, but sorry for everyone in it. Yes, Dreiser's like Clarence Mangan: 'He too has tears for all souls in trouble, here and in Hell.'" [33]

PART THREE
THE *MIRROR* AND THE POETS

CHAPTER 12

REAL WOMEN AND LOVE LYRICS

Shortly after the World's Fair the *Mirror* had begun two series of portraits of St. Louis people, showing that William Marion Reedy had not forgotten its function as a society magazine.

The first of these "departments" he did in collaboration with a gifted young painter, Albert Bloch. Entitled "Kindly Caricatures," it eventually came to more than two hundred familiar thumbnail sketches of local celebrities as various as Taft's Secretary of Labor and Commerce, Charles Nagel; Frederick Lehmann, president of the American Bar Association; "Col." Abe Slupsky, a character well known around the Four Courts and at the track; Denton J. Snider and William Schuyler of the old St. Louis Movement; Dr. A. C. Bernays, the brilliant innovator in surgery; and Henry Blossom, a literate insurance man whose opera, *The Red Mill*, was destined to play in Forest Park during some fifty summer seasons.

Illustrated by Bloch's trenchant cartoons, the vignettes were often gently satiric, sometimes biting, yet occasionally kind to men like Ed Butler with whom the magazine had dealt harshly in the past. Bloch's keen intelligence and wide-ranging interests made him a valued contributor of articles as well as drawings, even after Reedy sent him off to Munich on a monthly allowance, to complete his education.

The second department was entitled "Blue Jay's Chatter" and purported to be the personal letters of a St. Louis society

THE MAN IN THE MIRROR

woman to a friend traveling abroad. Blue Jay's colloquial, slovenly style was a satire on the mentality of polite society. She commented tartly on the manners and doings of actual persons—their intrigues and love affairs, their political and business alliances, their battles, their entertainments, the confidences they exchanged at the Country Club or in a Turkish bath, their reading. Like her creator, Blue Jay was a great reader; her taste ran mainly to novels about smart society, notably those of Henry James and Edith Wharton. When Mrs. Wharton scored her first great success with *The House of Mirth*, Blue Jay told her friend that its depiction of life was as characteristic of St. Louis as of New York. "And it's done with a touch that simply reveals one to oneself." [1]

Blue Jay was not above commenting on the foibles and misadventures of the editor of the *Mirror* himself, his divorce and remarriage, and the disfavor with which he was regarded in respectable circles. ("I'm not 'in good' here at all," Reedy confided to Mosher. "They don't like the girl I like . . . They think I'm hopelessly depraved because I don't marry . . .") [2] It was reliably rumored that Reedy had a room of his own in the well-known house of pleasure set up by a Mrs. Margie Rhodes to accommodate distinguished visitors to the World's Fair. But this Blue Jay did not mention.

At the end of February 1905, while he was away in Washington attending President Roosevelt's second inauguration, that prominent Republican, Thomas J. Akins, must have been startled when he saw Blue Jay's paragraph about his debutante daughter's taking to the stage:

There's a new girl in the Odeon stock who excites much interest, Zoë Akins. She's the daughter of Chairman Akins of the Republican State Central Committee, United States Sub-Treasurer . . . He's a banker, a friend of the President, and he is to be in the head-set at the inauguration. Well, this Zoë Akins is the weirdest girl. She

136

affects dresses very simple and severe, and won't wear plumes in her hats. She is preternaturally bright . . . She writes exquisite impressionistic verse, and has the oddest views upon things. She's very young but is as wise as a centenarian, and very girlish withal. She's up on music and art, and is in brief an Admirable Chrichton-ness. I haven't said that she is beautiful, but she is, at times, and is always interesting, with a slight suggestion of pose.[3]

This item was calculated to put down any suspicion that Miss Akins, like young Bloch, was a collaborator of Reedy's. But if not Blue Jay herself, Miss Akins was certainly the most indefatigable collector of items for the column Reedy was writing under the name of that noisy and predatory bird.[4]

Her career on the stage was short-lived, amounting to little more than a bit part in *Romeo and Juliet*, but Miss Akins' taste for the theater was more than a passing whim. It led to her becoming first a play reviewer for the *Mirror* and finally one of New York's leading playwrights. It was no accident, when she won a Pulitzer Prize, that the play was adapted from Blue Jay's favorite, Edith Wharton.

Born in the Ozarks but reared in St. Louis, Zoë Akins claimed descent from "Shakespeare's friend the Earl of Pembroke" and said another "literary" ancestor had been a newspaper editor in Jackson's time. Such data she was happy to confide to interviewers, when given the chance.[5] As Blue Jay soon remarked, the young woman had a genius for publicity. "She writes good poetry, has two plays nearly accepted, has been on the stage as recitationist and actress, teaches classes in Self Culture Hall, writes theatrical criticism, is collaborating with Freddie Robyn on an opera or musical comedy, rides horseback, hunts, fishes, sings, paints, goes to the Baptist Church, wears pretty gowns gracefully, but occasionally atrocious hats, talks like Mme. de Staël and has her share of good looks . . . And she sure does get the headlines and pictures in the papers."[6]

Reedy was captivated by the gusto and daring with which

she greeted life, amused by her consuming ambition, and fascinated by the stratagems she found to woo fame in any field that seemed to invite her at any moment. He was also a man afflicted by insatiable loneliness. Though far from pretty, Miss Akins was not without physical charm. By the spring of 1905 he had fallen helplessly in love with her, and his passion quickly led to fevered offers of marriage.

"Oh, Zoë, the youth of you, the dawn-spirit of you, the fresh, free, poetry of you," he wrote her. And again, "I want to let go of [the] life of the pen, of all the things that prison and chain me. They're all so mean and small and contemptible when seen in the light that you shed on things for me." And he confessed to her again and again that sense of fraudulence his work aroused in him—"telling the people about things on which I'm less informed than they are." [7]

In March Miss Akins wrote her first review for the *Mirror*, a flattering account of E. H. Sothern and Julia Marlowe's production of *Much Ado About Nothing*. That in turn brought about a meeting with Miss Marlowe, doubtless arranged by Reedy, who enlisted the great actress's aid in his suit. "Miss Marlowe loves you[,] and she'll tell you what I tell you—if she hasn't already. I think she wants me to have you—didn't she say so, delicately, deliciously, in her note[?]" In the same letter he plunged into the problem of winning her parents' consent to their marriage, sure that if her father would "inquire in the right way he'll learn as much or more *good* than *bad* about me. I mean that he'll find that my badness has not been of the kind that a man can't condone, and that none of it involves anything dishonest . . . My faults and follies have a glare of course, but they are at least or have been rather on the generous . . . order." [8]

Unfortunately the young lady was only eighteen. Their meetings were secret, and when Frances Porcher got wind of the romance she threatened to inform Miss Akins' father. Having been Reedy's assistant even before the *Mirror* was born, Mrs. Porcher enjoyed the privilege of an old nurse. Her threat may have inspired Reedy to suggest to President Roosevelt that summer that he might well consider appointing Akins his minister to a foreign capital. But it was neither Mrs. Porcher nor Chairman Akins who put an end to the suit. It died of attrition within a few months. Miss Zoë had time for only one absorbing interest: what she affected to call her Career.[9]

Miss Marlowe had urged her to read more, and especially the modern European dramatists. Reedy gave her James Gibbons Huneker's *Iconoclasts* to review. She rushed to the defense of the modern stage and was gravely judicious in her appraisal of the veteran critic who knew as much about Continental drama as any American alive. Miss Akins chided Huneker for ignoring American playwrights, praised his erudition, and concluded that besides being enthusiastic in his defense of literary trouble-makers, Huneker looked "yearningly for trouble on his own account." [10]

This charming impudence she promptly followed up with a plea that Reedy ask Huneker to obtain an interview for her with Charles Frohman, the producer, for she still longed for a career on the stage. Huneker replied at once: "Your young friend—whose brilliantly written critique made me blush—may not take my advice but I'll tender it just the same; tell her—don't. [The stage is] a hell, morally and physically (mentality is an absent quantity). She uses her pen like a veteran. Write novels but—the stage, never!" [11]

A good deal of Miss Akins' knowing talk of the European theater had probably come from her friend Sara Teasdale, who had been living abroad with her mother that year. Zoë and Sara had attended the same small, select girls' school as children, though afterwards Miss Akins was sent to Monticello Academy across the river, and Miss Teasdale to Mary Institute, whence she had gone on to Washington University. The spiritual guardian of the Institute and the University had been T. S. Eliot's grandfather, who founded both before he joined Blair and Brokmeyer in the Civil War. Dr. William Greenleaf Eliot would not have approved of their friendship, for he had warned his charges that a lady must not seek fame "independently of those qualities which adorn her moral character." Those who did, he said, "fail to excite admiration." [12]

Sara Teasdale was content to abide by his doctrine. She was as retiring and slow to bloom as Zoë Akins was daring and precocious, and she never shook off the demure airs of the Institute. That spring Blue Jay reported her return from Europe: "Sarah will make her social debut this winter, I suppose . . . But it's a shame that Sarah's got to keep up the family tradition and do the social act; for she's the cleverest girl in a family of clever women . . . I think it's a shame that she isn't poor because she'd *have* to use her brains then. Perhaps she will . . . anyway." [13]

The youngest by many years in a lively family of four children, Sara was brought up to consider herself delicate, was held back in school, and was still being effectually discouraged from growing up. The company she loved was that of six school friends, talented girls calling themselves the Potters, whose club was a play house. Mrs. Porcher wrote of their activities in 1906, telling of the very little magazine of which they circulated a single copy each month. The girlish tone of Sara Teasdale's lyrics attested her hothouse fragility. While her old friend Zoë Akins was throwing herself into the affairs of the world—helping Reedy while holding him off with one arm, serving as her father's secretary while pretending she had scarcely heard of the *Mirror*, telling her friends all about her passionate affairs of the heart—Miss Sara stayed home, "always on the verge of a poetic but carefully controlled passion," as one friend put it.[14]

WOMEN AND LOVE LYRICS

One of Sara Teasdale's earliest admirers was Orrick Johns, recently back from the University of Missouri, where he had been a friend of Dreiser's protégé, Harris Merton Lyon. Handicapped by the loss of a leg, he was the aesthetic, self-conscious son of one of Pulitzer's most robust and capable journalistic fighting men. Young Johns presently succeeded Zoë Akins as the *Mirror's* play reviewer.

The world in which Sara Teasdale lived was comfortably set apart from the world of journalism and even from the sedate, walnut-paneled solidity of the Merchants Exchange, where her father dealt in commodities. He was an imposing man with white beard, his wife a small and dynamic matriarch. Soon after the return from Europe Mrs. Teasdale moved her husband, her youngest daughter, and her collection of Oriental rugs into a commodious house near Forest Park, in Kingsbury Place—one of those private streets unique in St. Louis, a white marble gate at either end, islands of shrubbery separating the two lanes of pavement, the mansions hidden by great trees, and the main gate embellished with a sculptured nude. There Mr. Teasdale could escape the company of loquacious women and walk out to the stable after dinner to commune with his fine horses. In the afternoons Orrick Johns would come out on the streetcar to talk about poetry and ask Miss Sara's opinion of his verse, or take her driving in her own trap. Once when he drove rashly over a snowbank and the vehicle tipped and caromed off a streetcar, she sat perfectly still while he struggled with the plunging horse. That kind of restraint was audible in some of the earliest lyrics of hers that Reedy printed.[15]

Even the first of these, entitled "The Little Love," had that simplicity and delicacy of cadence which became her hallmark. Like an earlier contribution to the *Mirror*, a prose parable written in imitation of "Fiona McLeod," whose writing Reedy and Mosher had been publishing since 1900, the lyric had a cryptic symbolism. This she soon cast off, but as Reedy pointed out after printing only two of her lyrics, they had simplicity and transparent clarity, which set her off from the ornate sentimentalism that prevailed in 1907. He printed another in his Christmas number that year: "I ceased to love him long ago."[16] One did not have to believe Miss Teasdale's passions had a historical basis; they had the reality of powerful feeling held down by an overmastering and perhaps self-punitive discipline. That her lyric manner made a strong impression on Zoë Akins is shown in the latter's "Vilanelle of Memory," printed on the facing page. It may well have been an allusion to her earlier love for Reedy:

> Time, my dear, has made us sane,
>   Yet there shudders—who knows why?—
> In my heart a little pain
> As I touch your hand again.[17]

This is an effort at a straightforward effect like Miss Teasdale's, even if the syntax, the tone, and the shudder are Miss Akins'.

For a time Sara Teasdale must have been more strongly influenced than Zoë Akins by their friendship. It may well have led to her writing dramatic monologues, some of them sent to the *Mirror* and later included in the collection, *Helen of Troy*.[18] But she put herself through a rigorous apprenticeship to Keats, and though Miss Akins may have suggested the subject of her *Sonnets to Duse*, it was his flowery imagery that made "vanished Grecian beauty" live again in her verse; it was his sonority, his inner rimes and suspensions, she was after. These devices also set the tone for her sonnet "For the Anniversary of John Keats' Death," which appeared in the *Mirror* of March 12, 1908. Year after year she went on refining a craftsmanship which won respect even from a generation of poets who were seeking quite dissimilar effects.

Zoë Akins lacked such discipline. When Grant Richards brought out in London (on Miss Marlowe's recommendation) her *Interpretations: A Book of First Poems*, it revealed what

WOMEN AND LOVE LYRICS

Reedy had already determined for himself, that a potential poet would be lost when Miss Akins had her first Broadway success. She had already demonstrated poetic talent in her tribute to Sara Teasdale, "Sappho to a Swallow on the Ground." This was the best of ten lyrics she published in the *Mirror* during the first five years of her friendship with Reedy.[19]

During these same years Reedy and his magazine went through a crisis almost as shattering as that of 1896, when the *Mirror* was bankrupt. The panic of 1907 brought about the downfall of many business houses far more stable than the *Mirror*. Nearly forty years later, William Allen White could recall no time when he had seen the country "droop and wilt" as it did now. When the *Mirror* seemed certain to go under and Reedy was turning down James Campbell's offers of aid and seeking to escape despair in bouts of hard drinking, Reedy's mistress, Margie Rhodes, conspired with Jack Sullivan, his business manager, to save the magazine. She made the company a loan of $5,000 at the critical moment, without Reedy's knowledge. Later, Campbell walked into Reedy's apartment one night and persuaded him to accept a gift of another thousand, saying he still considered him "a pretty good fellow" and knew he was in trouble.[20]

The depression was to last well into the years of the first World War. Meanwhile, year after year Reedy was supporting Albert Bloch in Munich, receiving in return an occasional cover drawing or article. He followed Bloch with a constant stream of scolding, loving, pleading, irate letters urging him to find a teacher and learn the rudiments of his craft. "I tell you, my boy, that you can't go it alone. You *must* ground yourself in the traditions, the conventions of execution."[21] Yet Bloch, though Reedy hammered at his egoism with heavy sarcasm, refused to put himself under a master. He fell in with that brilliant group led by Wassily Kandinsky and Franz Marc, who were bent on forging a "great synthesis of the arts to reunite man in his apprehension of nature." Bloch was one of the fourteen painters contributing to the group's first exhibit, named for one of Kandinsky's paintings, *Der Blaue Reiter*. The others included Arnold Schoenberg, August Macke, and Henri Rousseau—Paul Klee joining them soon afterward. "I know very well Pater's dictum that 'all art is striving constantly towards the condition of music,'" Reedy commented, "but that is an extravagant assertion of a commonplace. All art strives to connect with the feelings as directly as possible, and with as little intermediary obstruction as possible, but the arts are not convertible; they are strictly separate compartments, and the attempt to paint music or sing color is simply a metaphor, and cannot be made a fact."[22]

Despite aesthetic disagreements, Bloch continued to contribute to "Kindly Caricatures" and kept Reedy up to date on movements of which even Percival Pollard and James Huneker were scarcely yet aware. His filial friendship was a moral support Reedy badly needed, and Reedy told him in long confidential letters of problems he could share with no one else. Invariably he would end up with a scolding, and Bloch would reply in kind.

Another friend who had to tolerate Reedy's moods during this trying time was that extraordinary bluestocking, Thekla Bernays. Most of her adult life had been spent as companion and housekeeper for her brother. Doctor Bernays died in 1907, and she set to work recounting his career in a memoir, quoting Reedy frequently, along with medical authorities who explained the significance of the doctor's work and supplied a bibliography of his contributions to general surgery.[23]

Reedy always said Thekla Bernays had the greatest woman's mind he had ever known. He found her both wise and innocent, discerning and gentle.[24] She knew all about Reedy's personal life, too, though she did not meet Miss Akins until the end of 1908, when Reedy introduced them. At that time he was recovering from a leg fracture he had suffered one late night getting out of a friend's automobile. "I shan't write you about Miss Akins," he told her. "She will develop herself before you in brief time." But he added a few comments just the same. "She is bright, quick, precocious, generous—all that and more, but she doesn't 'stick' and her sincerity is evanescent." Her liking for celebrities and publicity he could condone as the mark of youth, but by now Reedy was impatient with her assumption of "an association with me in literary matters for which there is no justification." [25] Zoë Akins and Thekla Bernays became lifelong friends. "She *does* love you," Reedy told Miss Bernays a few weeks later, "but then—who doesn't[?]" [26]

Miss Bernays showed him thoughtful attentions while his leg was mending, and began contributing to the *Mirror*, once it was understood that Reedy might accept her articles without paying for them—a step he balked at. When he could get about again she asked him to a dinner party; he must come because she had taken special care in her choice of guests. "Why?" he asked. "What's the use of being careful *after* you've invited *me*?" There was always that gulf between her impeccable standing in the community and his notoriety. In private there were no gulfs, and Reedy could unburden his innermost thoughts. "I begin to hate myself for not being better grounded," he would tell her, unconsciously repeating the phrase he used in scolding Bloch. Or, discussing Jean-Jacques Rousseau and Stendhal, "What a sordid story these lives of wholesale lovers make." [27] There was hardly a topic they could not discuss, and Miss Bernays had too much *savoir faire* to mind the gossip that soon linked their names as a likely couple, a good match. Hostesses began asking them to the same dinners. And what conversational feasts those were!

It must have been at one such party, shortly after his leg

was healed, that Reedy held forth on his old enthusiasm for Hawthorne, and Miss Bernays made the remark that there was no "real woman" save Hester Prynne in any American novel. Real as Carrie Meeber had once seemed, Reedy laughed off the objections of other guests and agreed with Miss Bernays. A few days later, lecturing at an intellectual ladies' club, she made the same claim. Then Reedy ran across an essay by G. Lowes Dickinson declaring that there was not even one great love lyric in American literature. Putting the two thoughts together Reedy found them a disgraceful commentary on American letters or American women. He was not sure which.

The dogmatic charge was only partly facetious as he developed it in an essay, "Women and Love Songs." His disgust with American writing was genuine. He would send Bloch no American books and told him he was missing nothing. "Nothing whatsoever." [28] What was wrong with our literature reflected something the matter with our lives, he said in his essay. Americans feared all feelings. "That's why we have so many jokes about poets and poetry. Then, when we do poetize, we are afraid of the one thing a truly great love song must have —simplicity. Even Poe's exquisite 'To Helen' is not, properly speaking, a love lyric. The intellectuality of it is too dominant . . ." [29]

One young reader, annoyed by Reedy's charge that America had achieved "mighty little literature, in more than one hundred and thirty years of nationality, writing, and love-making," spoke up hotly for his contemporaries. He lauded the heroines of Frank Norris and David Graham Phillips, and recalled a love lyric of Bliss Carman's which he had considered perfect when he clipped it from the *Mirror* itself. "But go ahead, Brother," the letter writer concluded. "The pages of the *Mirror* are as full of errors as the flowing talk of a healthy, normal, aspiring man. You lack the damnable gift of spinning delicate

WOMEN AND LOVE LYRICS

distinctions that lead a winding route to nowhere." [30] The letter was signed by an unknown Chicago newspaper reporter, "Yours always, Charles Sandburg."

Reedy told Miss Bernays that neither Sandburg's letter nor any of the others his essay called forth had succeeded in disproving her claim. Of Norris and Phillips he added, however, "I do not know those writers at all." It was a rare lapse forgetting Norris, whom the *Mirror* had praised seven years before. But Reedy was less concerned to win an argument than to win respect for Hawthorne. Above all he wanted to improve the quality of poetry.

In 1909, at the time of this incident, Reedy was going through another crisis that partly explains the careless writing of which Sandburg had complained. The *Mirror* had been saved by Campbell and Mrs. Rhodes. Reedy's morale was being looked after by Miss Bernays. But that March of 1909 his father died. Because they had been estranged for years and Reedy blamed himself for being unable to assuage the old man's loneliness, he found the loss both meaningless and shocking. He could not acknowledge Miss Bernays' note of condolence, forgot to come to one of her dinners, became physically ill on realizing the enormity of his rudeness, and addressed his effusive apologies not to her but to *Dr.* Bernays.[31]

In the meantime Mrs. Rhodes had taken note of his distraction and of the gossip which linked his name first to Miss Akins', then to Miss Bernays'. It seemed only a question of time before Reedy (now forty-six) would take a wife. She moved suddenly to make known her candidacy for the title. She closed her notorious house, bought a farm in the county, and sent the packers to Reedy's rooms after they had crated her own belongings. Thinking back over the lonely years since Lalite's death and remembering the gallant help Mrs.

147

Rhodes had given to stave off bankruptcy without his knowledge, Reedy decided to move to the farm. Doing so would necessitate marrying. He wrote Bloch cheerfully of the news. "She's made herself calico wrappers, sun bonnets, wears a towel around her head, and she's boring people for knowledge about chickens and cows and hogs. Damned if her delight isn't the best thing I've seen for a coon's age. I suppose there'll be talk about me, but to hell with it. There's been talk for eight years." [32]

Three months later the marriage took place, and shocked readers wrote in to cancel their subscriptions. Old newspaper friends and companions in even less respectable walks of life were shocked, too. One reporter and occasional contributor to the *Mirror* simply left town, and Reedy did not hear from him again. But Miss Bernays wrote an understanding letter of congratulation. A prominent judge sent his check for $20 to renew his subscription for ten years, adding a box of cigars and a note saying he had heard some subscribers had been lost. Frederick Lehmann, now Solicitor General of the United States, continued to contribute articles. And President Roosevelt included Mrs. Reedy in an invitation to a house party—which she tactfully refused.[33]

The newspapers treated Reedy's career as a farmer with glee, and he himself found that cows made excellent copy. By August he could report that his most difficult battles were against inept farm hands and the perversities of nature. "The madam is a most ferocious gardener," he told Bloch, "and is out in the fields all the time." This, he added, helped her forget the pleasures of a "very lively life in town." A more astonishing development was Mrs. Reedy's burgeoning maternal impulse.

In order to protect herself from this loneliness she has taken to live with us a little girl of eight years, to watch whom is very interesting. I have known very little about children, but I find

WOMEN AND LOVE LYRICS

from my observation of this little girl that they are very much like mules, strangely perverse, and with the most wonderful hints of wisdom in their ignorance. I don't know that I have come across anything more interesting than to follow this kid in her mental and other wanderings. The madam is thinking very seriously of adopting her, and I don't know but it would be a good thing. She is a bright child and very affectionate . . .[34]

The adoption did not take place. The newspapers had their fun, and Reedy's own amiable accounts of farm life continued. Two years later the farm house burned to the ground, and the adventure came to a temporary halt. The marriage survived.

CHAPTER 13

THREE CRITICS
IN SEARCH OF AN ART

UNTIL 1909, when he started his column "What I've Been Reading,"[1] Reedy could not have called the *Mirror* a critical journal. Yet with Pollard and Huneker among its regular contributors the magazine mustered three of the most vigorous critical minds in America. It was a case of three critics looking for something to criticize. Impatiently surveying the poverty of the native scene, they were always in danger of lighting on one another.

All were convinced of the superiority of European over American writers at the time. All were seeking writers who might redress the balance. And all blamed the genteel fussiness of university critics for the creative poverty. Reedy was perhaps more stridently anti-academic than the other two. He was fiercely intolerant of the pedantry of schoolmen out of touch with life as he knew it.

He sneered at Charles Eliot Norton of Harvard for the coldness of his dissection of Renaissance poetry and called his arguments against imperialism sentimental. He ridiculed Harry Thurston Peck of Columbia for bowdlerizing Petronius in his well-known translation and for an article he wrote for his magazine the *Bookman*, "How to Tell Vulgar People." (The way to tell them, Reedy answered, was by noting any resemblance they might have to Professor Peck.) He hooted at William Lyon Phelps for saying that Rudyard Kipling took delight in scenes of drunkenness and in profanity and bad smells; and especially for calling Kipling ill-read. "Kipling is not well-read, eh? But Kipling is well-written. Beastly details offend Professor Phelps, do they? Does he hold his nose when he reads Fielding, Shakespeare, Montaigne, Dickens?" Literature for Reedy had to be in touch with life, and life was not all "prim and puritanical, New Havenesque." [2]

There were, of course, university men, some of them distinguished, who enjoyed the freedom of the *Mirror's* columns, even if Reedy sometimes took issue with what they said there. His close friend, Dean Otto Heller at Washington University, made the magazine a focus for information and discussion of Ibsen. His *Henrik Ibsen: Plays and Problems*, was published after several articles on the Norwegian dramatist were tried out on *Mirror* readers. Reedy also sought and published articles by Kuno Meyer, Walter Raleigh, Arthur Quiller-Couch, and Thomas R. Lounsbury. In time, some of the younger men, among them Lascelles Abercrombie, sent him poems as well as critical essays. Howard Mumford Jones also contributed. But when Reedy would praise a scholar like Brander Matthews as the best literary essayist in America (after the Emersonian John Jay Chapman), Pollard would presently attack Matthews.

Pollard denied that it was the function of criticism to expound rather than to judge, as Professor Matthews had said. He called Matthews "hopelessly invertebrate"; if expounding were the function of criticism, Matthews' earlier judgments were worth nothing at all. Pollard then characterized Matthews as merely a feeble imitation of Andrew Lang. Earlier, Reedy had proclaimed Lang "the champion long-distance, fifteen years, go-as-you-please, literary hack who can write with four pens between the fingers of each hand." [3]

Pollard, a resident of Baltimore and Connecticut, was born in Pomerania and educated in the east of England. Working for a New York review—though using the *Mirror* as his permanent address—he imparted to readers his exhaustive familiarity with every literature in every Western land. He was determined to vindicate American writers of a provinciality no one could accuse him of sharing. In an essay on Shaw's prefaces, for example, he would not only point to their critical virtues, their wit and ideas, and their relation to the plays; he would relate Shaw to the convention of critical prefaces since Dryden and show Shaw's debt to his forerunner, Oscar Wilde, and his contemporaries, Max Beerbohm, George Moore, and Kipling. As his friend H. L. Mencken said of him, Pollard seemed to know everything and everyone; and lest his foreign background prove a handicap, he made it his business to know more about American literature and history than most educated Americans. If British readers were looking to America for "the red shirt and top boots of Joaquin Miller, the disheveled exuberance of Walt Whitman," he could tell them of Miller's and Whitman's literary descendants, however obscure they might be. If Gertrude Atherton romanticized Alexander Hamilton in a biography, Pollard knew all about the real Hamilton. In 1904, discussing James Branch Cabell's novel, *The Eagle's Shadow*, he had remarked that its heroine could swear as round an oath as any Viennese countess or baroness he had ever listened to, "dear old ladies in white caps"—he knew them, too.[4]

Pollard often contributed satiric fiction to the *Mirror*. Reedy had published his very bad satiric novel, *The Imitator*, which appeared anonymously and was often—perhaps maliciously—ascribed to Reedy himself.

Huneker, too, used the *Mirror* as a testing ground for short stories. Many of his sketches were printed there before appearing in book form. Reedy liked to tease the erudite and dignified critic of the *New York Sun* (a most decorous paper) for his intimacy with the "crazy artists" and musicians he satirized. Reedy wanted to know where the satire came in, since Huneker "wound up worshipping the vagaries" of his own characters. "He is like all keepers of madmen," said Reedy, "tainted with the madness of his own charges." [5]

Perhaps it was precisely this capacity for getting involved in a fiction that made Huneker the critic he was and kept him from succeeding at fiction—satiric or otherwise. As Mencken remarked, all the other critics, including Howells, were pedants lecturing. "But Huneker, like Pollard, makes a joyous story of it: his exposition, transcending the merely expository, takes on the quality of an adventure freely shared." [6] Most of Huneker's sketches in the *Mirror* had European settings, whereas Pollard tried to translate the exquisite and dégagé atmosphere of Wilde or Gautier into an American bohemia. It was inevitable that these two critics, both somewhat vain and opinionated, both overworked since their early days writing for *Town Topics*, should at last collide with one another and turn the *Mirror* into a battleground.

Pollard, the born European, thought that Huneker, the native Philadelphian educated abroad, was indifferent to the American achievements that he, Pollard, was trying to magnify. Though he himself knew every novelty in European decadent literature, he blamed critics who preferred the Europeans for the failure of an American literature "rank and rotten with prosperity." Having first charged Huneker with being one such critic, he sharpened the sting in a little ballad addressed "To Our Canniest Critic on Gautier's Birthday." He sent this to the *Mirror*, perhaps guessing that Reedy, with his affection for Huneker, would welcome the storm of protest such an attack would arouse among the artists and writers Huneker had helped. Reedy printed it.

> High though his shrewdness carried him
> In his own native land,
> To not one fellow-countryman
> He lent a helping hand.

> His was the genius of the Jew
> > With Jesuit craft combined;
> A dexterous skill in juggling words,
> > A grasping, copious mind.
>
> He will go down to fame as one
> > On foreign fodder grown,
> Who never wrote a stupid word
> > Nor—any of his own.[7]

Reedy quickly realized it had been a mistake to publish such a cruel diatribe. Much as he loved a fight, he seems to have been embarrassed at the ferocity of this one, especially since the victim of an unprovoked attack had been ambushed rather than challenged. Reedy identified Huneker as its target, apologized, and came to his defense. It was true, he said, that Huneker was mainly interested in European art and letters, but Americans must be grateful for what his discoveries could teach them. For there was little to discover in this country, "with its literature and art, in the main, wholly derivative, utterly proper, and inanely conservative." The ferment abroad was certainly preferable to the stagnation at home. In any case, he regretted that the two most competent critics in America could find nothing more suitable to attack than one another. It was their business to be fighting bad art.[8]

Reedy himself had been making a one-man stand against several native successes he considered unjustified. He admired Whitman but despised the "Whitmaniacs," servile and puny imitators of the good, gray poet. He enjoyed Eugene Field's *Sharps and Flats* but charged the author with being puerile and insincere; he was especially disgusted when the St. Louis Board of Education decided to name a public school for him. For twelve years Reedy had stood out almost alone against the flood of adulation that had continued to mount ever since

CRITICS IN SEARCH OF AN ART

Edwin Markham's "Man with the Hoe" appeared in the *San Francisco Examiner* in 1899.

The success of that poem showed how eagerly America awaited a poet who reflected its own political climate. It had attracted five thousand comments, mostly favorable, and the newspaper had run a page of letters and parodies every day for six months. Markham's reputation continued to grow, and a society was formed to enhance it further and to collect favorable notices of his masterpiece. Joaquin Miller called it "big as the whole Yosemite." William James said it "reeks with humanity." H. L. Mencken found it "the greatest poem ever written in America." Ambrose Bierce did not question Markham's "primacy among American poets," to which Howells agreed—"always excepting my dear Whitcomb Riley." Yet when Markham came to St. Louis on a triumphal tour, Reedy denied that what he had written was a poem. Passionate as its protest against the subjugation of the common man may have been, Reedy called it meretricious. He resented the falsity of a symbol which, though capable of stirring men to action, would point them in the wrong direction. "There is no man with a hoe, as Millet painted him, in this country. There is no oppressor bending the back, flattening the brow, dulling the eye, of the American laborer, or any other laborer, while in France 'tis not the weight of centuries that gives him his stoop, but the very simple fact that the hoe handle is short." Reedy held to this jaundiced view later, when Professor Phelps and Van Wyck Brooks joined the cheering section.[9]

What Reedy and Pollard and Huneker were all looking for was not a poet but a native poetic tradition. Huneker, for example, had begun as an admirer of Poe in the seventies, when most of Poe's admirers were in Paris. He knew Whitman in Philadelphia and tried to teach him the elements of music, taking him to concerts at the Academy of Music before he himself went to Paris to continue his studies. Paris taught him that Poe was the true classic American, the founder of a living tradition, Whitman merely a "muddled echo" of transcendentalism, itself a pale dilution of Hegelian idealism.[10]

But now Reedy became aware that Whitman belonged in the line of another and more important tradition. One of the first books discussed in "What I've Been Reading" was George Rice Carpenter's life of Whitman, recently added to the American Men of Letters Series. What impressed Reedy was Carpenter's contention that venerable conventions in American oratory and a high regard for Emerson had helped shape Whitman's art. Far from being formless, as Reedy had hitherto maintained, Whitman's verse obeyed "a rhythm system of its own, one discoverable to whomsoever reads intelligently." What Reedy had to say about this book would be sure to make a strong impression on a St. Louisan like Orrick Johns, or Chicagoans like Carl Sandburg and Harriet Monroe. "Professor Carpenter sees in Whitman the one poet of the people who was not a renegade, who did not hark back to the aristocratic forms." After learning from Carpenter's insights, he went back to Whitman with "illimitably enlarged heart-capacity." [11]

It was one thing to begin to place Whitman in the stream of nineteenth-century literary evolution, another to assimilate him as an influence wholesome and seminal for the twentieth century. In 1907 after visiting Mosher in Maine, Reedy had gone out of his way to meet Horace Traubel in Boston on his way home. He admired Traubel's zeal in promoting the reputation of Whitman and publishing his works, especially the fine *Camden Diaries,* but he had no use for Traubel's poetry or for the swarm of free verse echoing the cadence of *Leaves of Grass,* of which it formed a part. Traubel had turned the propagation of Whitman's influence into a native industry. And if there was one class of poetry Reedy found utterly hopeless it was the "Whitmaniac." [12]

But a poem he encountered in the *Atlantic* and reprinted the month he commented on Carpenter's book appealed to Reedy as an exception. It was by Harriet Monroe, who had made her debut as laureate of the Chicago World's Fair. Reedy had paid no attention to her since reprinting one of her articles in 1898. Though he found her new poem, "The Hotel," reminiscent of Whitman, he called it the best thing of its kind. "It has all the good gray poet's particularization and leads up to something like his large generalization," he remarked in a headnote when he copied it.

In retrospect it is hard to see the parallel. Miss Monroe's poem is in a free style of her own, far removed from Whitman's. But it is a metaphysical airship with a rich symbolic cargo. It soars above the Waldorf-Astoria in New York, where Miss Monroe conceived it while waiting for train time. It echoes Christ's words in St. Mark, "Unto them that are without, all these things are done in parables: that seeing they may see and not perceive . . ."(4:12) Miss Monroe translates this into a modern context. She seems to have had no idea to what extent this poem surpassed her usual work, but after it had been reprinted in the *Mirror* she chose it to head her collection, *You and I*. Reedy had seen in it elements of which she herself seems never to have become aware.[13]

But home-bred poets he could admire without restraint were few. He continued to encourage Sara Teasdale, and when her "Helen of Troy" seemed to show that she was ready for a larger audience, he returned it to her and persuaded her to send the poem to *Scribner's*, "which could pay more nearly what it was worth." [14] He reprinted it, as he reprinted Edwin Arlington Robinson's "The Man Who Came," about the same time. But Robinson, like Emily Dickinson, whom Reedy was now actively recommending to younger poets as an inspiration and a model, seemed to belong to the nineteenth century, whose close was still being chronicled in the obituary columns.

Swinburne, Henley, Francis Thompson, Lionel Johnson, and J. M. Synge had all died recently; and Arthur Symons, a score of whose poems and essays Reedy had published since the middle nineties, was reported to be in a state of senility and decline.

Even so, Britain seemed infinitely better off than America. Offhand, Reedy could name sixteen British men of letters still in their prime—Kipling, Galsworthy, Hardy, Yeats, and Shaw among them. He could think of only four Americans in that class—Howells, Twain, James, and Huneker. "For the rest," he sighed, "nothing." We've no poet but Markham—a Bryant returned . . . Plenty of books we have, but literature?" The last serious American novel he could recall dated back to 1890—Fuller's *Chevalier of Pensieri-Vani*. Americans, he was sorry to say, had not yet proved that they could produce a single work of art reflecting modern life. They were afraid of life, hence of art.[15]

And what was he looking for? Where did all these fumblings and grumblings, these ribald shouts and scathing rejections lead?

It is never possible to say what a critic is looking for until he has found it, but Reedy had by now established a critical standard of his own. It was clear that he was seeking something very different in poetry from what he liked in prose, and that poetry for him was of transcending importance. The years of seemingly revolutionary change in the political life around him had altered his criteria for fiction, but not for poetry.

What Reedy found in Thomas Hardy or Theodore Dreiser was a recognizable, objective statement about life as he knew it; one informed with awareness of human imperfection and aspiration. Such a statement must reflect a critical, analytical organization of human experience in terms of values. It must be the result of honest observation, not of dogma or theory. Reedy could write sympathetically of Upton Sinclair, while condemning *The Jungle* because its socialism did not meet facts "as a fact itself." [16] A novel must conceal no unpleasant truth in the interest of some lofty didactic purpose conceived to be a higher truth. Reedy asked a prose writer also to observe a decent proportion between "sense" and "sentiment." The novelist must suggest the need for action without advocating specific action. He must see with a proper mixture of involvement and detachment. He must be a realist.

And what was realism? In 1901 a *Mirror* reviewer called Jane Austen a realist for her day, but added that "to-day realism means pessimism." In Reedy's discussion of Hardy there is sometimes the same implication, that whatever reality may be, it is grimly unpleasant. Yet this widely held belief ran counter to Reedy's fundamental philosophic position and was one he never shared more than fleetingly. In 1909 Reedy says that Galsworthy's *Power of a Lie* is realistic, for while one resents seeing triumphant wrong "laurelled Right," one knows that such injustice does occur. Privately he tells young Bloch that Galsworthy is a realist all right and makes no apologies for life—"sorry enough for it, but [he doesn't] see how he can help it." Six months later he adds, "Galsworthy is very good, but I must confess that he is terribly distressing. I don't know that any man so hopelessly content with seeing things and devoid of any symptom of a purpose to change them can be lastingly effective or valuable in literature." [17] About the same time he marks down Upton Sinclair as a propagandist.

While Reedy could not tolerate the didactic in fiction he was not satisfied with pragmatism either. He demanded moral wisdom, and castigated political immorality as "pragmatic," to the annoyance of one attentive reader: Walter Lippmann objected that pragmatism is not a moral theory at all. "It has no more to do with right and wrong than I have with the life of the angels." But Reedy disagreed, denying that William James and John Dewey had a patent on the word.

These were matters he could discuss with reference to prose but not to poetry. For Reedy, a poem was an emotional equation between man and reality, not a philosophical one. Prose might well observe changing concerns, conditions, and assumptions; poetry must confront the unchanging void in which man acts out his essentially changeless repertory of experiences. That fiction must cope with the growth of knowledge, while the poet's intuitions must anticipate knowledge, was a basic tenet; Reedy had said in one of his earliest critical essays that man's poetic insights outrun his reason. "His poetry has led his science everywhere." [18]

It is this factor to which Reedy doubtless refers when he calls William Ernest Henley a competent, manly poet because he combines realism with impressionism. Impressionism, in Reedy's meaning, is the undefinable apprehension, the unsought revelation. It is also the whetted sensitivity of the poet, whose heightened perceptions are all-embracing and defy the erosion of time. In poetry realism may be tragic, but can never be pessimistic. Poetic realism is unlike the realism of philosophy, of politics, or of prose. It is the recognition of ultimate or anagogic realities in a universe where matter and spirit are equally exponents of force, and force is the power of overwhelming love or attraction or desire for the good.

Force, Reedy asserted, may be material or spiritual, human or divine; it is all one. It is also the dynamic element in a poem, what gives it simplicity, density, and tension. A poem is necessarily a concentrated expression, and, like a force in physics, it must confront the stubbornness of matter, the hardness of reality. It represents man's feelings about a universe in which his weakness is supported and sustained by the sum of all power that overwhelms and orders chaos. A poem for

Reedy, then, is an ordered, dynamic statement about reality, based on vivid sense apprehensions. It is a metaphor relating personal experience to forces that exist (as he constantly says) "beyond the flaming ramparts of the world." [19]

Thus Reedy contends, one need not expect to find anything new in poetry. Its freshness derives from the poet's perpetual astonishment with what has been seen and said often enough —but not by him. Prose may be a part of life. Poetry has a life of its own. The poet must learn his craft by long apprenticeship to the masters of its conventions. Hence it is important to place Poe and Whitman in a living tradition, to show that Whitman (as Wilde had agreed) possesses something in common with Homer. This leads to the hope that other poets will come along and put America in touch with the viable seed of their own past. The Word like seed may fall on desert places and be eaten by the fowls of the air. American seed may sprout in Europe. Americans may have to seek their own strain there.

CHAPTER 14

EZRA POUND, POET IN EXILE

SOME of the verse William Marion Reedy published in the final third of the *Mirror's* life and the last decade of his own tested the very nature of poetry. Whatever critics may decide about it in the future, it will remain important for having called in question the essentials of the art. Such basic questioning can occur only at rare intervals and has sometimes marked the periods of great achievement. Of all the poets who undertook the job of testing, trying, legislating, and probing that now began, none was more challenging than Ezra Pound.

After a brief bout with academic life in America, Pound had gone to Italy and then London in 1908. Elkin Mathews published his first two considerable collections in 1909. The *Mirror* printed two lyrics in 1910, and only one other before 1915. But there were also some reviews and early discussions; and because of Pound's so-called "instigations" of other poets, it is worth taking a close look at the few scraps of evidence, wherever found.

One would expect that T. S. Eliot, a St. Louisan, would figure in the *Mirror* or that it would figure in *his* development before he encountered Pound. But the magazine merely noted his Harvard class ode when he graduated in 1910—and had scarcely anything to say about him thereafter. Mr. Eliot, on his side, is afflicted with a strange amnesia about his St. Louis beginnings. In his early days of lecturing he gave himself out to be a New Englander. Much later, he spoke at Mary Institute

EZRA POUND

and, recalling his boyhood afternoons on its playground, called himself its only living alumnus. But he told the curator of a Sara Teasdale collection at Yale that he did not recall ever having heard of Miss Teasdale. Queried about his early reading of the *Mirror*, he could not remember ever having seen a copy. As Sean O'Faoláin remarked in 1960, after a trip to St. Louis, Mr. Eliot must have run across the name "Prufrock" there. It could have been in the *Mirror's* regular advertisements of the "New Furniture House of Prufrock." One supposes he likewise encountered the name "Sosostris" or "Sesostris" in Reedy's frequently reprinted poem, "The Conquerors."[1]

What is clear is that Mr. Eliot was not aware of Mr. Pound at the time of Pound's coming to England, either; for in his first study of his friend's work he found him influenced almost exclusively by Browning and Yeats and not at all by Whitman. He did not realize that in 1909, and thereabouts, Pound felt that his own career had been foretold by Whitman—who had known all along what Pound's function was to be, something (Pound adds) "of which Ezra Pound was not quite sure himself at the time."[2] Later, Pound was as reticent about his Whitman phase as Eliot was about St. Louis. In 1909 Whitman's admirers were a drug on the market, and each was probably sure in his heart that the bard had predicted *him*.

What Pound learned from Whitman was not the ebullience they shared, for that could not be learned. But it may have been freedom and the indifference to hostile criticism. The extreme toughness of a Whitman or a Pound, able to shrug off the scorn of friends and enemies alike, does not always go with poetic sensitiveness. What Pound learned from Yeats was ardent craftsmanship founded on the study of an ancient literature in another language. To Reedy and Eliot (though Reedy had begun to change his tune) Yeats still seemed a "minor survivor" of the nineties, until Pound began to praise him.[3]

THE MAN IN THE MIRROR

Browning has often been called Pound's direct ancestor, and Reedy read him in the same spirit Pound did—one very different from that of the plague of ladylike Browning societies that flourished everywhere. To a subscriber who asked for an interpretation of "Rabbi Ben Ezra" in 1898 Reedy said, "It seems to me that Browning means what he says in the poem." He poked fun at Thomas Wentworth Higginson's "solemncholy" disquisition on "Childe Roland," which the old man had called Browning's profoundest work. But fearing he might have sounded disrespectful toward the poem, Reedy reprinted it the following week, saying he had not meant to deny its significance—"for, evidently, it must mean something." He was as sure as Browning had been that *explication de texte* is vain. "For poetry that does not explain itself," Reedy once remarked, "must be something else, but it is not poetry." [4]

Reedy also took issue with the Browning Society assumption that their poet had been inanely optimistic. What optimism Browning had was hard bought. He had gone to "the obscure places of the human heart and soul . . . to the extreme of pessimism to find optimism," Reedy insisted, adding that "for all his knobbiness and thorniness and intricacy" he was a virile poet, the best "exponent of the dramatic conflict in the soul of modern man." Later, Reedy repeatedly refers to Pound as "knobby" and "thorny," terms he never uses for any other poet.[5]

With this attitude toward Browning it is not surprising that Reedy chose Pound's "Mesmerism," a parody and reply to Browning's dramatic monologue of the same name, as the first of his poems to appear in the *Mirror*. Though he published it, and (a month later) "A Ballad for Gloom," without a credit line, they were probably not contributed by the poet. More likely Reedy copied them from *Provença*, the first American collection of Pound's work, which Small, Maynard must have sent him for review. Pound's "Mesmerism" is like a private and intimate conversation between master and apprentice on a topic of common interest—a shared joke and a subtle one.[6]

Browning had objected to Mesmer's new hypnotic technique. Like spiritualism and his own dramatic lyrics, hypnosis depended on the willing suspension of disbelief. Considering mesmerists to be charlatans, perhaps he feared they showed up a touch of charlatanic make-believe in his own poetic method. At least that is what Pound implies.

Into the counterfeit Gothic setting of Browning's "Mesmerism"—with its guttering torches and ominous deathticks—Browning throws the incongruous line,

> And a cat's in the water-butt—

which Pound takes for the epigraph of his parody. Pound then begins:

> Aye you're a man that! ye old mesmerizer
> Tyin' your meanin' in seventy swadelin's,
> One must of needs be a hang'd early riser
> To catch you at worm turning. Holy Odd's bodykins! [7]

He takes delight in penetrating Browning's *swaddling* of his meaning and chortles with glee at finding him out for the "old mesmerizer" he is. He has caught him at "worm turning," the act of identifying himself with the victim of his own satire. "I'm on to you," he is saying, relishing the sense of complicity and chuckling over it. For both are unmasking mesmerists in public, and each knows himself to be a mesmerist, too.

Beyond the joke, Pound is showing that he has caught the peculiar "absolute rhythm" he learned from Browning, with its subtle conveyance of a precise shade of mood. Without borrowing Browning's meter, he produces an admirable imitation of the rhythm, and revels in this ability, calling his master "Old Hippety-Hop o' the accents." This irreverence betokens sincere admiration. It is as if to say he knows Browning is still alive and (whatever anyone in the audience may think) still capable of enjoying a joke.

As usual when he introduced a new poet, Reedy had nothing to say about these first poems. It is surprising, nevertheless, that he should have said nothing about Pound's early adaptations of Villon, one of his favorites. Perhaps uncertain of his own scholarship, he was unwilling to accept the young poet's hardness; it was in such contrast to the accepted pre-Raphaelite versions of Villon. That was certainly in his mind when he asked his friend William Schuyler, the old Hegelian, to review Pound's *Sonnets and Ballate of Guido Cavalcante*. There was a certain logic in the assignment, for the critics of the St. Louis Movement were devotees of Dante, Guido's closest friend, and Reedy was not. But Schuyler was entirely unprepared for Pound, a phenomenon not dreamt of in his philosophy. He took him to be an Englishman and a serious Romanic scholar. It did not occur to him that Pound was a poet. Considering how slipshod was Pound's scholarship and how inspired his feeling for verbal nuances, it is ironic that Schuyler commended him for pedantic virtues and condemned his "very crabbed literality." [8]

Pound, of course, studied Guido and the troubadours much as Browning had studied the Italian painters. He was looking for poetic matter, splendor, and caught what scholars fail to grasp with their more methodical processes. He heard the roughness and vigor, the rasp of irony in the troubador songs. Instinctively he knew that the soft, langorous, gauzy texture that Gabriel Rossetti, John Addington Symmonds, and Andrew Lang had tried for in their translating was yard goods, not samite. Pound's problem was that of the Elizabethans when they went to Italian models, his solution much like Sidney's. He must grasp and wrench the English, bend it to new forms, use force, and leave the grammarians and dictionary makers to their fuss. He was nevertheless an indefatigable student of technique.

No wonder he became irritable when a critic like Schuyler printed one of Rossetti's translations beside his, "to show how a real poet can transfer the work of another poet into another language, and make not such a 'bad poem' out of it, after all." Somehow that condescending tone, that heavily bearded avuncular manner reverberates with echoes of the St. Louis Movement, praising virtue from the dais of high school assembly halls or spirituality in the columns of the *Journal of Speculative Philosophy*.

Reedy grew more interested as the young poet's work became more obscure, admitting, after a while, that he didn't "get" Pound's poetry but that he did get a strong impression of "his value in a good fight he is making for stark seeing and saying." His admiration grew with the number of Pound's opponents. Afterwards, advising Babette Deutsch how to handle Pound in a critical article she was doing for the *Mirror*, he hoped she would go out of her way to "get in something violently katachretical, something that will make him grind his teeth, pull out his hair and turn handsprings. Pound in a rage is most delightful," he explained. "Really, though, there is much good stuff in him, despite his choleric eccentricities." [9]

In another letter he told Miss Deutsch of their years of happy feuding: "I've had correspondence with Ezra and have reveled in his ingenuity of insult, which same I met with ribald joshing. He desisted because he couldn't make me as mad as he got himself. He is a most thorny and knobby person but there is some substance to him." [10] These letters were written later. Meanwhile, literary events in America went forward tumultuously, and the *Mirror* had become a focal point in areas of controversy from which Pound excluded himself by his decision to remain abroad.

CHAPTER 15

POETS IN THE MARKET

During the years when Pound and Eliot were striving to alarm London into noticing their work the tiny literary group that centered around Reedy in St. Louis grew larger and more restive. It became apparent to one after another that success could be won only in New York or abroad. But what kind of success? That was the question.

Some (like Fannie Hurst, a Washington University undergraduate when she first appeared in the *Mirror* in 1909) took off almost at once.[1] Others, like Sara Teasdale, made regular visits to New York and came back to resume their painstaking filing and polishing. A few, like Zoë Akins, stayed home mostly, eating their hearts out with vague longings and ambitions.

"I wonder what waits for me in New York," she told Miss Bernays. "Nothing, I hope, that will wreck my faith in the honesty and beauty of my work."[2]

The outlook for writing that was not ground to a precise formula was disheartening. The stage was in the doldrums, even if William Vaughn Moody, Clyde Fitch, and Percy Mackaye did still get their plays produced. The magazines paid a penny a line for fiction and five or ten dollars for a lyric poem to use as filler. Though 13,470 books were published in 1910—a record that would stand for over forty years—publishing was in the hands of a few old-line houses untroubled either by challenging new ideas or by the rivalry of any considerable number of adventurous newcomers.[3]

POETS IN THE MARKET

It might have been read as a hopeful sign that the great popular magazines which had reached a peak of prosperity in the nineties were now in a state of decline. The *Century* had lost half its circulation. *Harper's Monthly* and *Scribner's* were falling off. The muckraking magazines had had their day, and *McClure's*, their sensational leader, experienced a rift in ownership that gave *American Magazine* (formerly *Leslie's Monthly*) a new staff and a new lease on life. But the long trend was better indicated by George Horace Lorimer's accomplishment in building an unheard-of circulation of two million for his *Saturday Evening Post,* which for ten years had stuck doggedly to the most rigid of formulas: the romance of financial success. Its own success was to have a deadening effect on other magazines for years to come.[4]

Even if it had been true that the general downward trend put talent-hunting editors of popular monthlies on their mettle, the outlets for new talent were diminishing. For almost all the bright little magazines of ten and fifteen years before were dying or dead. The *Chap-Book* and its hundred imitators were long since forgotten. Gelett Burgess' *Lark* and John S. Cowley-Brown's *Goose-Quill* died young and left no offspring. B. Russell Herts's *Moods* was short-lived, and Michael Monahan's *Papyrus* sporadic. William C. Edwin's *Bellman* and Elbert Hubbard's *Philistine* had lost what little savor they had ever had and with it much of their following. The *Bookman's* erudite, genteel editor, Harry Thurston Peck, once the target of Reedy's banter, committed suicide. A few established literary journals of solid worth managed to hold to their appointed course, among them the *Atlantic,* the *Dial,* the *Bibelot,* and *Sewanee Review.* But like some more popular magazines on about the same plane, these were only holding their own. One of the few exceptions to the general plodding trend was *Current Literature,* which doubled a circulation of 50,000 between 1908 and 1910. Reedy was friendly with three of its four editors—Edward J. Wheeler, Alexander Harvey, and George Sylvester Viereck. He now began to borrow more and more material from them, evidently by agreement.[5]

It was Reedy's association with another New Yorker who was primarily a book publisher that began to open up opportunities for his writers during this slow time. In 1910, when Mitchell Kennerley bought the *Forum* (a distinguished contemporary of the *North American Review* and the *Arena*), Reedy began actively to collaborate with him.

Kennerley had begun life as an office boy working for John Lane and Elkin Mathews in London, and had come to New York as Lane's agent, in 1896, when he was a boy of eighteen. The following year he had had the shrewdness to buy the rights to a successful book from the dying Chicago firm of Stone & Kimball (publishers of the *Chap-Book*) and the good fortune to fall in love with Reedy's New York correspondent and French translator, Aimee Lenalie. He seems to have met her through Mosher, who was his oldest friend in the United States. But Kennerley was also close to Michael Monahan, Richard Le Gallienne, Bliss Carman, and other poet friends of Reedy's. His name first appeared in the *Mirror* in 1905, the year he sold his magazine, the *Reader,* intending to devote full time to publishing books on his own.[6]

In his history of American book-publishing, Helmut Lehmann-Haupt calls Kennerley not only one of the most colorful figures in the field but, with Benjamin W. Huebsch, one of the two men who altered the literary scene before World War I by catering to the tastes of an educated, cosmopolitan reading public then just emerging. The list of authors Kennerley built up under his own name in the next five years is of great interest. Besides such names as Carman and Le Gallienne, already prominent in the *Mirror,* the *Chap-Book,* and the *Bibelot,* it includes others who rapidly became as well or better known. Before 1910 Kennerley had published works by Pound's friend,

POETS IN THE MARKET

Allen Upward, and by A. E. Housman, Frank Harris, Yone Noguchi, John G. Neihardt, John Masefield, Ferenc Molnar, Granville Barker, and Edwin Björkman. One very popular novelist (whom the *Mirror* pronounced "putrescently prurient"), Victoria Cross, helped pay the deficits incurred by the belles-lettres.[7]

Kennerley's ground-floor office in 58th Street soon became a literary gathering place, as his little Fifth Avenue bookshop had previously been. Reedy used it as his headquarters on the annual trips to New York he made late every summer. On weekends his visits to the publisher's Mamaroneck home were memorable events for the Kennerley children; and on one of the rare occasions when she accompanied her husband to New York, Mrs. Reedy became a fast friend of Kennerley, whose amatory adventures were as notorious as her own. He was one of Reedy's few friends who seems to have found her former profession no barrier to the full enjoyment of her gaiety and robust humor.

Later, Kennerley moved his center of activity to the Anderson Galleries on Park Avenue and proceeded to establish an auction market for rare books that became so high priced a competitor complained he drove the "moderate collector" out of the market for twenty years. The injured rival could not help adding that Kennerley was able to do this because he was "the most accomplished, the most brilliant" entrepreneur in the trade.[8]

For all his gifts—and they included friendly warmth and generosity—Kennerley was as erratic a businessman as Reedy himself. There was a touch of perversity almost bordering on sadism in his repeated failure to pay impecunious writers when he had money, or paying them with bad checks when he had none. He was as dear a friend as Reedy had, but caused him acute embarrassment when he made a flying visit to St. Louis, borrowed $30,000 from the book collector, W. K. Bixby, to whom Reedy had introduced him, and departed by the next train.[9]

Kennerley's ability to part American millionaires and their money approached the genius of Lord Duveen. A single auction brought in nearly two million dollars. Yet this plunger and spender left an estate amounting to no more than a month's room rent in the modest hotel where, having outlived Reedy, Mosher, and his own fame, he finally hanged himself.[10]

After 1910 hardly an issue of the *Mirror* failed to mention Kennerley's books, though from the first the reviews were by no means always favorable. Reedy had brought out serially George Sylvester Viereck's *Confessions of a Barbarian.* When Kennerley published it as a book Reedy remarked to Miss Bernays that Viereck was now one of the leading spirits in the group that was rejuvenating Kennerley's *Forum* magazine. St. Louis had become a nest of singing birds, he added, now that the *Forum* was publishing Sara Teasdale, Zoë Akins, and Orrick Johns.[11]

Through his work as an editor of *Current Literature* and a contributor to the *Forum* and the *Mirror,* Viereck was rapidly establishing himself as the last voice of the decadence in America. He seemed bent on reliving the critical career of Percival Pollard, now rapidly drawing to a close. Like Pollard, he was born in Germany and knew its language. His father had been a member of the German Diet. But he himself grew up in New York and was graduated from its City College in 1906, a year after the *Critic* published his essay "Is Oscar Wilde Alive?"—which the *Mirror* reprinted. Bloch interviewed him two years later and was adversely impressed by his "pimply puberty"; but Reedy continued to encourage Viereck and defend him against the scathing attacks of his friends, his readers, and even himself—for Viereck turned in a bitter lampoon on his own style.[12]

POETS IN THE MARKET

Like Pollard—and Whistler—Viereck had a positive genius for making enemies. He could make himself disliked in several countries at once, lecturing on American poets in Hamburg and Berlin, managing to get his sharp judgments reported in England and America. "I have already admitted that I perish in my conceit," he said in defending himself against an attack in the London *Academy*. "No one has ever criticised American institutions more savagely than I have done . . . The ready acceptance of my book by American critics was the most hopeful sign in the history of American culture." [13] Viereck's vanity soon became wearisome but Reedy kept up the play of attention, explaining to objectors that his contributions helped circulation. Within two years, though, even Reedy was worn out. When he came to review *The Candle and the Flame* and heard that the young man had said he would write no more poetry, he took Viereck down: "The kind of poetry he writes suffers from having been done before, notably by Mr. Swinburne, Mr. Wilde, and Mr. Rossetti." Reedy called it "a singing gospel of homosexuality," and had no more to say on the subject.[14]

Another writer for the *Mirror* did. Viereck was one of the twenty-eight charter members of the Poetry Society of America when it was formed in 1910. This was one of the grounds on which Orrick Johns attacked both him and the Society soon after replacing Zoë Akins on the staff. He belittled Viereck's "militant naughtiness," feared that the society would soon become an exclusive legislature of taste, and declared that the lyric genius of young America would beg entrance at its doors in vain—unless that genius "turns out to be George Sylvester Viereck."

Young Johns had been hired as the *Mirror's* play reviewer and occasional essayist partly because Reedy said his own girth made it no longer possible for him to be comfortable in a theater seat, partly as reward for a facetious article hailing

Pollard and Viereck as first fruits of a "*Mirror* school of literature." Referring to Viereck's *Confessions of a Barbarian*, he had said the school began "as men usually end, with confessions." He called Viereck's vaunted style "mere Reedyese" and taunted Pollard for having alienated so many publishers that no one but Reedy would print him any longer.[15]

Johns wrote another article for the *Mirror* soon afterwards which inadvertently won him a niche in that pantheon, the *Literary History of the United States*. There was in the winning of this distinction an element of the ridiculous which literary historians have seen fit to pass over.

Orrick Johns was a confused young man forever toying with radicalism. This preoccupation seemed to compensate for the feelings of inadequacy brought on by bickering with his father, George Sibley Johns, who was Reedy's companion, Pulitzer's sometime favorite, and one of Woodrow Wilson's Princeton classmates and confidential advisors. Much influenced by the communistic leanings of a brilliant young friend on the *Post-Dispatch*, Orrick wrote, with a kind of desperate cleverness, in favor of a vigor and social significance in poetry, which neither his verse nor his critical writing exemplified.[16]

In 1911 Kennerley brought out a book of sonnets by Ferdinand Pinney Earle, a wealthy dilettante whose marital indiscretions and extramarital "affinities" had made his name a by-word. Reedy had once called him a "vain and eccentric ass." Johns praised Earle's sonnets in an unctuous review that went so far as to hail the improvements he had made on the sonnet form: "Abomination upon forms and formulas. Let us have poetry!" [17]

Soon afterward Johns resigned from the *Mirror* and went to New York, where Sara Teasdale was spending the winter and was happy to introduce him at the Poetry Society he had traduced. At its February 1912 meeting Edwin Markham read his own poems, and members discussed the effects of modern urban life on poetry. Johns heeded the drift of the discussion and worked it into his poem "Second Avenue." Its theme, as he later said—"economic equality, more leisure, high-thinking —[was] all very romantic and confused, of course"; but with assistance from Miss Teasdale and her friend Louis Untermeyer it was sold to the *Forum*.[18]

Ferdinand Pinney Earle had just offered Kennerley $5,000 to bring out a book to contain the hundred best poems submitted in a contest for which he put up $1,000 in prize money. He himself would be one of the judges, the others being Reedy's friend, Edward J. Wheeler of *Current Literature*, and William Stanley Braithwaite of the *Boston Transcript*. At Kennerley's suggestion Johns submitted "Second Avenue." As president of the Poetry Society, Wheeler had attended the same meeting that had affected Johns, and was pleased with the poem's "social content." Earle himself later claimed he had voted for Edna St. Vincent Millay's "Renascence." But he cannot have protested too vigorously when Johns, an admirer of his sonnets, was awarded the first prize.[19] The Lyric Year was advertised as an annual event intended to honor poems charged with the "Time Spirit." That Earle presently became involved in another divorce, a kidnapping, and an extradition proceeding that eventuated in his being declared insane—all prevented a second poetry contest. The book containing the hundred poems selected by the three contest judges enjoyed the patronage of a captive public: the ten thousand poets who had hopefully contributed entries. So the third judge, William Stanley Braithwaite, decided to bring out an annual *Anthology of Magazine Verse* as a successor to the *Lyric Year*. This was published for some years by Kennerley's associate, Laurence Gomme, the bookseller.[20]

Reedy's comment on the news of Johns's success was a masterpiece of ambiguity. Of "Second Avenue" he wrote:

"how splendid a poem it is, no one can say who has not seen the one hundred of which it was voted first in the *Lyric Year*." The mere selection of a hundred poems proved that Earle was a poet, he said, implying that it certainly did not prove him a critic. He spoke with satisfaction, however, of Miss Akins' and Miss Teasdale's offerings, and commended the "wonderful poignancy" of Miss Millay's "Renascence," which he later reprinted. But he left the reviewing of the anthology to an assistant, Elizabeth Waddell.[21]

Though she found in it some encouragement for believing in the future of American poetry, Miss Waddell felt the collection contained too many imitations of Whitman and Browning. She objected to Earle's limited objective: poems "informed with the Time Spirit," as he demanded, seemed to her evanescent by definition. Echoing Reedy, she asserted that poetry should be "of and for all times." [22]

Reedy himself might have taken satisfaction in the large representation the judges of the Lyric Year had given to poets previously published or sponsored in the *Mirror:* twenty of the hundred. But after Miss Millay, the twenty-year-old wonder who was for the time being everybody's favorite, his interest centered on Nicholas Vachel Lindsay.

CHAPTER 16

VACHEL LINDSAY, POET ON NATIVE GROUND

A FORMER feature editor of *McClure's Magazine* had called Vachel Lindsay to Reedy's attention in 1910. "What does he do and how does he do it?" Reedy had replied indifferently, adding that poetry was a luxury he could not just then afford. "Times are so hard out here I find it rather difficult to raise money to buy beer." [1]

Himself a poet, Lindsay's promoter, Witter Bynner, pushed his find with energy. He told Lindsay to send Reedy a copy of his single-issue *Village Magazine* and called it to the attention of other friends—his Harvard classmate Arthur Davison Ficke, Edward J. Wheeler and Jessie B. Rittenhouse of the Poetry Society, Hamlin Garland, and Ezra Pound. Wheeler printed a poem from the *Village Magazine* in *Current Literature* with a four-page illustrated discussion of the poet.[2] Garland, who had been impressed with Lindsay's tribute to Poe, invited Lindsay to Chicago to address his club, introduced him to his friend, the novelist Henry B. Fuller, and visited Lindsay's parents in Springfield, Illinois, to tell them their son was a genius.[3] Bynner's old associates on the *American Magazine* (offshoot of *McClure's*) took up Lindsay in 1911 and began to feature his work. The poem that broke down Reedy's apathy first appeared there, then in *Lyric Year*. When Kennerley reprinted it in the *Forum* Reedy copied it in the *Mirror*. "The Knight in Disguise" was an odd, courtly tribute to

THE MAN IN THE MIRROR

William Sydney Porter—O. Henry—whose premature death, as Reedy told Bloch, had "touched the people of the United States much more deeply than the death of anybody, with the possible exception of Mark Twain." [4]

Lindsay had sensed the universal bereavement and written of Sydney Porter as a modern knight whose loss was mourned as widely as that of an earlier Sidney:

> Is this Sir Philip Sidney, this loud clown,
> The darling of the glad and gaping town?

Porter, too, came of a proud family, yet won fame under a pseudonym. He had appealed to the masses as well as to his peers. To Lindsay he seemed to have the innate gallantry of the Elizabethan knight, and there was an aptness to the parallel, for both Sidneys were exemplars of obsolete codes of chivalry, each won the popular affection by his discreet sympathy with human suffering, and each was cut off in his prime. Lindsay's concluding couplet was almost as deft and elliptic as one of Astrophel's:

> Yea, ere we knew, Sir Philip's sword was drawn
> With valiant cut and thrust, and he was gone.[*][5]

Ezra Pound, to whom Bynner had also sent samples of Lindsay's work, could appreciate this appeal to the chivalric tradition. Though he now called himself the overseas correspondent of Harriet Monroe's newly launched *Poetry: A Magazine of Verse*, he was still seeking to infuse modern poetry with the glamor of ancient knighthood. Both Pound and Lindsay were also seeking to align themselves with American forerunners—Pound with Whitman, Lindsay with Poe.

Yet Pound and Lindsay soon came to represent opposite poles in the poetic movement that was snowballing in America by 1912. Lindsay called himself an "autochthon," declaring for the

---

[*] Reprinted with permission of the publisher from *Collected Poems* by Vachel Lindsay. Copyright 1923 by The Macmillan Company; copyright 1951 by Elizabeth C. Lindsay.

responsibilities of the poet to his native ground, while Pound was contemptuous of small-town culture. Lindsay was a collector of ballads, vaudeville songs and revival hymns, while Pound was the connoisseur of Provençal lays and rondels. Pound could not accept for long Lindsay's treatment of chivalry or any topic. He wanted to assert the courtly tradition by appeal to recondite scholarship and by casting off from the common life to which Lindsay's bark remained fast moored. Moreover, Pound was a disciple of Yeats, and when Yeats went to Chicago to receive a *Poetry* magazine prize at the same time Lindsay received one, there was cause for jealousy—more especially so since Yeats took occasion to praise the "strange beauty" of Lindsay's work. Pound called the award to Lindsay "peculiarly filthy and disgusting." [6]

So, if Pound and Lindsay both sought to revive the luster of poetry and knighthood, they had very different ways of doing it. They were two ungentle knights pricking on very different plains. "I wish Lindsay all possible luck," Pound had told Miss Monroe before she enraged him by her award, "but we're not pulling the same way, though we both pull against entrenched senility." [7] For better or for worse, the *Mirror* pulled Lindsay's way, not Pound's.

Lindsay was thirty-two when Reedy reprinted his poem for O. Henry in June 1912. He was a disappointed commercial artist returned to Springfield, the center of his world, where he was born in a spacious, plain house Lincoln had sometimes visited. "Everything begins and ends there for me," Lindsay once wrote.[8] But he traveled much, and in another way he led an unbounded life, a mystic who walked in heaven "upon the sacred cliffs above the sky" and drew angelic maps of the universe in the style of cheap magazine engravings.

If he was another Blake, as Reedy suggested, he had been to the wrong schools and admired all the wrong masters. He had

THE MAN IN THE MIRROR

written his first poem while at Hiram College, and chanted it to his friends "literally hundreds of times." Hiram, outside Cleveland, is one of the many colleges and seminaries founded in the Ohio Valley by the Disciples of Christ, a sect led by Alexander Campbell,[9] who was confident the millennium would occur in 1866, which turned out to be the year of his death. Lindsay wrote a trilogy on the life of this prophet, prefacing it with Campbell's words: "The present material universe, yet unreveled in all its area, in all its tenantries, in all its riches, beauty and grandeur, will be wholly regenerated. Of this fact we have full assurance, since He that now sits upon the throne of the Universe has pledged His word for it, saying: 'Behold I will create all things new,' consequently . . . new pleasures, new joys, new ecstacies."[10] This impassioned sense of impending joy, of such access of delight as the most voluptuous pleasure can give no hint of, suffuses Lindsay's best poetry.

Hiram College, which he left without a degree in 1900, struck Lindsay as "astringent." But when he went on to study art in Chicago and New York, he took with him a profound confidence in the unity of all created things, a belief that man is "fundamentally educated by the phenomena of nature." He seemed never to care a rap for the manners and trappings of this world.[11]

In New York he served as a Y.M.C.A. lecturer while vainly peddling his quixotic pen-and-ink fantasies to the magazines. In Illinois he would address temperance and revival meetings, gratifying his mother, who was a thwarted missionary, and mystifying his father, an impecunious family doctor. On several occasions he had tramped more than a thousand miles across the country, chanting his poems in return for a night's lodging on a farm or putting up at a Salvation Army shelter in a city. He had frequent visions. In 1906, returning home after a tramp from Florida to Indiana and a summer trip to

VACHEL LINDSAY

Europe with his parents, he saw Christ in his stateroom, and began a poem, "I Heard Immanuel Singing." He included it in one of the little illustrated books of verse that he entrusted to a job printer in Springfield and circulated among his friends. One of these was entitled *Rhymes to Be Traded for Bread*.

In 1912, when Reedy encountered his O. Henry poem in the *American*, Lindsay was spending the night in a Negro cabin outside the town of Mexico in the Missouri saddle-horse country. The poet was on his way to California, trying to shake off the disappointment of a Springfield love affair, tramping and laboring in the fields, trading his rhymes for a night's lodging, chanting them in farmhouses and shanties, sleeping in wet rags and imagining himself another St. Francis. As he walked and labored he mused about the dying founder of the Salvation Army, an organization whose hospitality he had so valued in the past, humming to himself the hymns he had heard Salvation Army bands play in city streets. In Colorado he met his parents and the girl he had left behind in Springfield, stopping with them at his father's summer camp. Meanwhile his poems in the *American* were winning him a following. Harriet Monroe sent him a letter of appreciation and invited him to contribute to *Poetry*.

Despite his regard for ruggedness—of which he had a sizable fund—Lindsay lost his nerve after leaving Colorado to hike to the West Coast. He wired home for money and took a train to Los Angeles. Replying to Miss Monroe's letter, he told her he was still a citizen of Springfield and "horribly homesick." Afterward he sent her a poem written in Los Angeles and told her how he had come to write it. "General William Booth Enters into Heaven" was its title, and it grew out of his musing over the death of the Salvation Army general and out of the street-band hymns Lindsay had been humming. He had stayed with an uncle in Los Angeles. Twice he set out on foot for San Francisco, and returned to his uncle's demoralized. He had sat down and written the poem partly to recover the light-hearted state he remembered from his 1906 tramp. He told Miss Monroe that he hoped when she published it it would be quoted "even more than the O. Henry poem." [12]

Back in Springfield early in January 1913, the month "General Booth" appeared in *Poetry,* Lindsay wrote to Reedy of his plan for a somewhat modified hobo expedition the next summer. He sent a copy of *Rhymes to Be Traded for Bread,* explaining he still had half the issue left, "not making as long a trip as I had expected." Henceforth he would send the pamphlet on ahead so he could be sure of a handout and a bed in the hay.

Reedy's assistant, Miss Waddell, replied in an article, promising Lindsay all the delicacies of the Ozarks if he should pass through Missouri again. She had seen so much of his work in the *American Magazine* that she told readers of the *Mirror* he was already a "well known poet . . . lately of the staff of the *American.*" His *Rhymes* seemed to her "vivid, fanciful, sometimes playful, and full of quaint conceits." She admired his "wide-awake social conscience" and the optimism of

> 'Tis not too late to build our young land right,
>   Cleaner than Holland, courtlier than Japan,
>   Devout like early Rome . . .* [13]

Even more impressive she found Lindsay's tribute to John Peter Altgeld, the Illinois governor Reedy had attacked so scurrilously in the nineties, the "crouch-necked" Altgeld who had aided Bryan and Lee Meriwether. Older readers of the *Mirror* may have wondered at finding Altgeld canonized in its columns, but times had changed. Clarence Darrow and Edgar Lee Masters, successors to Governor Altgeld's law practice, were now frequent contributors to the magazine.

* Reprinted with permission of the publisher from *Collected Poems* by Vachel Lindsay. Copyright 1923 by The Macmillan Company; copyright 1951 by Elizabeth C. Lindsay.

VACHEL LINDSAY

For Lindsay the old governor who had defied and finally broken Grover Cleveland was a towering figure in a parade of home-town heroes headed by Lincoln. While Springfield, always intensely conservative, tried to live down Altgeld's memory, Lindsay celebrated it in an oracular ode, "The Eagle that is Forgotten"—one intended rather to be breathed in a husky whisper than chanted.

> Sleep softly . . . eagle forgotten . . . under the stone.
> Time has its way with you there, and the clay has its own.
> Sleep on, O brave-hearted, O wise man, that kindled the flame—
> To live in mankind is far more than to live in a name;
> To live in mankind, far, far more . . . than to live in a name.*

This, the bardic, was only one of Lindsay's moods; another came out in "A Net to Snare Moonlight," whimsical lines Reedy published early in the spring of 1913. Yet another, and perhaps the most characteristic, with its blend of dire prophecy and light fantasy, showed itself in "The City That Will Not Repent," which Reedy published in June. It grew out of Lindsay's visit to San Francisco the previous summer, and must have had a particular poignancy for Reedy, who had written one of his most popular and often reprinted essays about the earthquake and fire of seven years earlier. Now San Francisco was announcing plans for an international exposition to celebrate its recovery. In a fanciful vein, recalling the city's early reputation for waterfront revels and unbridled vice, Lindsay called the catastrophe its punishment and personified the revived city as an unrepentant strumpet:

> Sea-maid in purple dressed,
> Wearing a dancer's girdle
> All to inflame desire:
> Scorning her days of sackcloth,
> Scorning her cleansing fire.

* Reprinted with permission of the publisher from *Collected Poems* by Vachel Lindsay. Copyright 1923 by The Macmillan Company; copyright 1951 by Elizabeth C. Lindsay.

THE MAN IN THE MIRROR

The tone implies a moral judgment, as if the poet acquiesced with some enthusiasm in a well-deserved punishment. Yet he is carried away by the city's splendor and shares her excitement as she prepares for a new orgy. His voice becomes insouciant, then almost abandoned, as he foresees a dire ending to the coming carnival.

> Dance then, wild guests of 'Frisco,
> Yellow, bronze, white and red!
> Dance by the golden gateway—
> Dance, tho' he smites you dead.* [14]

The poem is eloquent testimony to a disorder Lindsay's brave show of independence vainly tried to mask. He had a deep affective dependence on his religious mother and was guiltily dependent for funds on his father, who was never prosperous. Lindsay's mischievous humor was like a child's. He could find no outlet save poetry for the sexual and aggressive impulses that seemed to conflict with his religion. He could not hold a job. Being penniless, he could hardly hope to marry. Yet his craving for woman's love was outspoken; he was anything but shy. His failing lay deeper, and that was revealed in his romance with Sara Teasdale, to whom he was introduced by letters from Miss Monroe soon after "The City That Will Not Repent" was published in the *Mirror*.

Lindsay burst on Miss Teasdale, the prim lady of his dreams, in a flood of letters, sometimes two and three a day, telling of his delight in her poetry, his unsatisfactory Springfield love affair, his hopes and his desires. He sang of her golden hair and eyes, and asked for a "sample of the goods" to see whether her hair were really as he imagined. He wished to come to St. Louis to meet her and tried to convert her to his doctrine of artistic duty to the home town, hoping she loved her "village" as he

---

* Reprinted with permission of the publisher from *Collected Poems* by Vachel Lindsay. Copyright 1923 by The Macmillan Company; copyright 1951 by Elizabeth C. Lindsay.

VACHEL LINDSAY

loved his. He wanted to meet her friends—Reedy and Johns and Zoë Akins—if she really cared for them. He discussed poetry at length, saying he did not consider Whitman to be in the great tradition of American letters as Emerson and Mark Twain were. Miss Teasdale was amused and interested, replying as often as she could to the letters that poured in all fall and into the winter.[15]

Meanwhile, in the autumn of 1913, Kennerley brought out Lindsay's first book, *General William Booth,* and started publishing his "Adventures While Preaching the Gospel of Beauty" in the *Forum.* When Reedy reprinted "The Kallyope Yell" from this series he prefaced it with a headnote, his first public comment on Lindsay.

The poem's theme is the coming day of the common man. Lindsay equates the American dream of equality with the ideals of democratic Rome and with Christian faith in a millennium when all shall be equal. It opens with a challenge to pride: *

> Proud men
> Eternally
> Go about,
> Slander me,
> Call me the "Calliope."

These are the meditations of a circus steam organ, demanding that its name be pronounced in common accents to rime with "hope," not in egoistic ones to rhyme with "me." There is powerful syncopation:

> Tooting joy, tooting hope,
> I am the Kallyope.
> Car called the Kallyope.

* Reprinted with permission of the publisher from *Collected Poems* by Vachel Lindsay. Copyright 1923 by The Macmillan Company; copyright 1951 by Elizabeth C. Lindsay.

THE MAN IN THE MIRROR

And much of the poem is couched in the gibberish of college yells, falsetto nonsense rimes imitating the calliope's music:

> Hoot toot, hoot, toot, hoot, toot, hoot, toot,
> Willy willy willy wah HOO!

These Reedy felt called on to defend: "Most *Mirror* readers . . . will start up, saying, 'This is not poetry; it is drivel; it is rot.' But read it again, and if you are not an indurated classicist you'll find it full of suggestions leaping out of the Steam Calliope in the Circus Parade dear to all children." [16]

Reedy's old reporter friend, the erudite William Vincent Byars, considered himself an "indurated classicist," but he was carried away by Lindsay's poem. Byars had contributed nothing to the *Mirror* for ten years, being occupied with running a little press bureau and with a vast project in Shakespearean scholarship. He was somewhat discouraged about the *Mirror*, too, Reedy having rejected some of his offerings as being "in advance of the outposts of average American culture." Lately Byars had been writing for the *Globe-Democrat* some articles in a whimsically pedantic vein, which he signed "Horace Flack." In the character of Flack he wrote an indignant letter to the *Mirror* protesting Reedy's headnote.

"Your approval of 'The Kalliope Yell' by Nicholas Vachel Lindsay shows that you know high art when you see it," Flack said. But he was "smitten and staggered" by the supposition that an indurated classicist would not understand Lindsay's art. Most classical scholars, he admitted, could no more appreciate Lindsay than they could Pindar, for the "Yell" was Pindaric, and Pindar would, like Lindsay, have rhymed "callyope" with "hope." Furthermore, he wanted to inform modern editors that the only hope they had of learning to read Pindar was "by beginning to learn from Lindsay, who, if he is not wholly Pindaric, is far more so than any editor of Pindar I have ever heard of." [17] Like Pound, Byars had a totally different notion of the tone of classic poetry from that taught in the schools or embodied in pre-Raphaelite translations. The rustic coarseness that gave vigor to Lindsay impressed Byars as being in the highest, most venerable tradition.

Unfortunately Lindsay had little confidence in the very qualities Byars and Reedy admired in his poems. They were too frankly charged with the joy of life. He felt he must explain himself. So he sent Reedy the poem he had written after seeing Christ in his stateroom on the ship coming home from Europe in 1906, together with an account of his conversion. He spoke of a gospel of beauty and of the conflict he felt between love of beauty and love of God.

"The Beauty-lovers of America . . . are plain pagans, worshiping neither Athena nor Mary, [while] the God-lovers are blind to beauty." This conflict, he went on, had occurred in his own flesh for years. "I Heard Immanuel Singing" expressed its resolution, but the poem, which Reedy printed along with extracts from Lindsay's letter, is as droning a piece of cant as any that Dwight Moody and Ira Sankey ever culled for their hymnals. One is not surprised to learn that Lindsay intended it to be sung to the tune of "The Holy City." What is hard to see is how one of the *Mirror's* readers caught in the letter an unconscious echo of Thoreau—though the echo is surely there.[18]

Miss Teasdale had meanwhile gone to New York. It was the winter of 1913–1914, when she introduced Orrick Johns to the Poetry Society. Lindsay's letters pursued her, and although she still fancied herself in love with a handsome young Harvard poet, John Hall Wheelock, who worked for Scribner's, she wanted Lindsay to join her and attend a meeting of the Society, to which she and Miss Rittenhouse had got Lindsay elected without telling him beforehand. But Lindsay could not go to New York unless Kennerley paid him his royalties, and Kennerley ignored his pleas. So he stayed home and dreamed of turning Springfield into another Dublin, saying all it needed was a Lady Gregory—and another Synge. He was also cheerfully productive. He wrote innumerable "Moon Songs" for Sara Teasdale and told her in January that he had finished his "Fireman's Ball." In February his "Flute of the Lonely" appeared in the *Forum* and the *Mirror*. He was working on "The Santa Fé Trail." On Lincoln's birthday he recited "The Congo" at a banquet, and his wild African gestures left the proper Springfield audience stunned with embarrassment. A week later Miss Teasdale was back home, and he visited her for the first time in St. Louis.[19]

It was a most public wooing, perhaps the best documented since the Brownings'. The *Mirror* carried constant testimony of the poets' feelings. First, Reedy printed Lindsay's "Two Easter Stanzas," lover's complaints addressed to the young lady Lindsay had loved and lost in Springfield. When Lindsay visited Sara Teasdale in St. Louis, Reedy accepted more of his love songs. Although rather overwhelmed by his exuberance, Miss Teasdale wrote her friend Louis Untermeyer in New York that Lindsay was "a real lover of mankind, with a humorous tenderness for its weaknesses." Listening to him recite, she said, "You forgive him the celluloid collar and the long craning neck that seems to grow unspeakably when he lifts his voice in recitation." [20] When Lindsay visited her again they attended Percy Mackaye's St. Louis masque in Forest Park and saw the vast pageant performed on a stage hung over the lagoon that had been the center of the World's Fair. The *Mirror* reported Lindsay's small, private performances more enthusiastically than the pageant and masque, which were attended by audiences of well over a hundred thousand each night.[21]

Meanwhile, another rival for Sara Teasdale's affections came on the scene, a young St. Louis businessman who had fallen in love with her for her verse and now persuaded Mrs. Eunice

VACHEL LINDSAY

Tietjens of *Poetry* magazine to arrange a meeting, which he said marked "an epoch" for him.[22]

Early that summer Lindsay followed Miss Teasdale to New York, where he was received as a lion. Mrs. William Vaughn Moody lent him her Washington Square apartment. All Miss Teasdale's friends—Bynner and John Hall Wheelock and Louis Untermeyer—wanted to entertain him. He met Dreiser, and they talked of Altgeld. Miss Teasdale took him to Staten Island to meet Edwin Markham. Upton Sinclair came in from the country to see him, and Percy Mackaye gave him a card to the Players. He and Sara Teasdale went everywhere together, riding on buses and ferries, discussing the war articles in the *Mirror*. Lindsay told her he would consent to be crucified if it would stop the war. He wore her out with his talk, and she caught cold walking in the dew in Central Park, and took to her bed. The young St. Louis businessman overwhelmed her with letters and flowers, and telegrams begging her to marry him. Soon sensing a change in her feelings, Lindsay gave up. He said he could see that her health would not permit her to marry and live with him. He proposed a "marriage of poets" in which they should live apart, only meeting when each had completed some major poem.[23] Later that summer at her family's home in Charlevoix, Michigan, Sara Teasdale announced her engagement to the businessman, Ernst Filsinger. She had been his Beatrice, Lindsay told Mrs. Moody: "We were just alike in many ways it would take Henry James to show."[24]

Some of the poems that grew out of this intense love rivalry were printed in the *Mirror*, among them Miss Teasdale's "Spring Night," which later headed the collection *Rivers to the Sea:*

> Oh, is it not enough to be
> Here with this beauty over me?
> My throat should ache with praise, and I
> Should kneel in joy beneath the sky.

THE MAN IN THE MIRROR

> Oh, beauty are you not enough?
> Why am I crying after love? *[25]

To which Lindsay replied in a "Moon Song" entitled "Gloriana: Poet of St. Louis:"

> Girl with the burning golden eyes
>   And red-bird song, and snowy throat:
> I bring you gold and silver moons
>   And diamond stars, and mists that float.
> I bring you moons and snowy clouds,
>   I bring you prairie skies to-night
> To feebly praise your golden eyes
>   And red-bird song, and throat so white.**[26]

Publishing twelve of the "Moon Songs" in a group, Reedy praised the poet's "word-sense" and his "plastic, changeable" rhythms, but seemed less convinced of his intellectual power, and perhaps just a little suspicious of his misty, starry imagery.

As to his ideas Mr. Lindsay is probably more akin to William Blake than any poet America has had. Implicit in his simplicity is a mystic attitude toward things. He sees the sun shouting "Holy, holy, holy!" The world of sense to him is fused with spirit—he is otherworldly when most observant of material things. His apprehensions and comprehensions are uncomplicated . . . In his singing there is a rural clarity. There is no city smoke in his pictures. And his utterance is always marked by something of spirituality; almost one would say it is disembodied. That he inherits from Wordsworth is plain. He is sib likewise to that piercingly effective, that vivid, swift, but oddly stammering poetess, Emily Dickinson, whose work is all too poorly known. Lindsay is a poet essentially of the man unpuzzled by the sophistications of civilization.

Reedy went on to mention the poet's concern for village life and art and his desire to dignify home-town life—what Lind-

---

* Reprinted with permission of the publisher from *Collected Poems* by Sara Teasdale. Copyright 1937 by The Macmillan Company.

** Reprinted with permission of the publisher from *Collected Poems* by Vachel Lindsay. Copyright 1923 by The Macmillan Company; copyright 1951 by Elizabeth C. Lindsay.

say called his New Localism. One might justifiably call it, said Reedy, "a refined and inspired yokelism."[27]

Thus he hedged his praise of Lindsay just at the time when New York was welcoming him with that effusive flattery that has ruined so many young writers. While Reedy's appreciation was genuine enough, it called attention to a "spirituality; almost . . . disembodied," which was the evidence of weakness rather than strength.

For the same tragic flaw that lost Lindsay his chance of marrying Sara Teasdale lost him his chance of producing great poetry. There was talent enough and Lindsay had a plain way of seeing and speaking that is a sign of greatness. His vision was incisive, his diction often brilliant, his feeling for sound and rhythm more natural than what Pound had showed. But these gifts are only the raw material of poetry. They needed to be formed, curbed by a critical self-knowledge that Lindsay lacked.

A close analysis of some of Lindsay's best lines makes the tragedy of his failure to produce more of them all the more painful. He had a natural gift for concision, great facility, a wonderful ear for tone. His energy and fluency were abundant; poetic ideas thronged in on him. The message he had for his countrymen was genuine and important, and he knew how to make them pay attention to it. But "gold and silver moons / And diamond stars" has the thinness of those swarming drawings of his that seem to belong in dusty magazine files or dog-eared Edwardian children's books. He is not offended by rhyme-bound phrases—"mists that float." Unconsciously he echoes the triteness of the schoolroom poets his best work so far surpasses.

After a time the thrilling strangeness of the voice that was heard so clear in 1914 became commonplace. Some of the booming sonority and husky intensity that delighted audiences as Lindsay barnstormed the country could still be heard, but too often the tone was marred by an unwillingness to prune away wild wood. At the same time Lindsay did much to revive faith in the vitality of poetry and was joyously successful in bursting the bonds of what Pound had called "entrenched senility," and what Reedy had said was "inanely derivative."

CHAPTER 17

CROSSING SPOON RIVER

REEDY's friend Edgar Lee Masters came from a country town near Springfield and became Lindsay's friend and biographer. But the contrast between the two could not have been more fundamental. Where Lindsay remained the pastoral innocent, Masters had been engrossed in the contentions of Chicago life even before becoming Clarence Darrow's partner in Governor Altgeld's old law firm. An avowed agnostic, a rake who boasted of his conquests, a fighter who generally quarreled at last with his friends—Masters had only one thing besides Illinois citizenship in common with Vachel Lindsay: a passion for poetry.

In this he was encouraged by a former St. Louis comrade of Reedy's, Ernest McGaffey, whom he had met on arriving in Chicago in 1891. Both Masters and McGaffey were reluctant lawyers who wished they were poets. Theodore Roosevelt and John Burroughs liked McGaffey's *Poems of Gun and Rod;* Reedy reprinted two or three of them in the nineties, and Edmund Clarence Stedman included five in his *American Anthology* in 1900. McGaffey found a publisher for Masters' maiden *Book of Verse* and shared his friend's grief when the firm failed right after printing it. So in 1901, when McGaffey achieved the distinction of having his "Sonnets to a Wife" accepted by Reedy for serial and then book publication, he wanted to share his success. He sent the *Mirror* five of Masters' poems with an essay puffing this "unappreciated poet." Masters' genius did not impress Reedy, nor would it have been apparent to anyone who did not love him as a friend.[1]

Reedy did not meet Masters until around 1907, when he came with a letter from McGaffey, now secretary to Mayor Carter Harrison of Chicago. Masters needed a Missouri associate in a libel suit he was defending for one of the Chicago papers, and Reedy introduced him to one. They met twice on that trip, and talked of books and politics. Afterwards they corresponded, sometimes as often as twice or three times a week.[2] "It was the outstanding friendship of my life, as it was of his," Masters wrote later. "No man was so close to him as I was; nor any so close to me as he was."[3] Reedy was one friend with whom he never fell out. Again and again Masters attempted to convey his admiration for Reedy—for his conversation, his omnivorous reading, his gusto, but chiefly for his vision. After another meeting he wrote of him:

> It's not so hard a thing to be wise
> In the lore of books.
> It's a different thing to be all eyes,
> Like a lighthouse which revolves and looks
> Over the land and out to sea:
> And a lighthouse is what he seems to me! [*]

It was Reedy's eyes his friend dwelt on in trying to evoke his peculiar magnetism. Reedy, he wrote,

> classifies
> Men and ages with his eyes
> With cool detachment . . .[4]

Fond as Reedy became of him, he took no interest in Masters as a poet in those early years. The busy lawyer found time to publish six plays and three more books of verse. Only two

[*] All quotations from the works of Edgar Lee Masters are reprinted here with the kind permission of The Macmillan Company, New York, and Ellen Coyne Masters.

of the plays seem to have been noticed in the *Mirror* at all. In 1902 it reviewed *Maximilian,* a blank verse tragedy, with chary praise and strict reservations.[5] In 1910 *Eileen* was labeled "Another Sex Play." As if aware that the shoddy adultery that comprised its plot was recent biography, the reviewer was acidulous: "Mr. Masters knows how to do things of this sort, but whether they are worth doing is another question." [6] Other critics were more generous. In 1911 Orrick Johns found some very kind things to say about Masters' third book of verse. Ezra Pound tentatively praised his fourth, finding in it a "sense of personality and out-and-outness." Reedy failed to see what either of them admired in the poems. He was interested in Masters' legal and political articles, especially on labor questions; he liked him and valued his learning. As to poetry, privately he told Masters, "For God's sake lay off." [7]

Discouraged in his literary hopes, Masters was in a receptive, almost a chastened mood, when he met Theodore Dreiser near the beginning of 1913 and Carl Sandburg at the end of that year. His fifteen-year marriage to the daughter of a street railway president had grown embittered when his mistress called on his wife. He had fallen out with Darrow and started a new law office, which was slow to attract clients. He had lost a long, difficult labor union case and been disappointed in a federal judgeship to which Bryan and Mayor Harrison had asked President Wilson to appoint him. His poetic idiom was hopelessly insufficient to express the anger and frustration, much less the sexual rage which pervaded his private letters. Nor did prose afford a better vent for his feelings.[8]

Reedy sent him two novels for review. Their author, Mary Fisher, had been Masters' teacher in Lewistown, where he grew up.[9] With awkward vehemence Masters opposed Miss Fisher's spinsterish belief that only renunciation can resolve the dilemma of illicit lovers. Without saying so he seemed to be contrasting her with Theodore Dreiser, blaming her for setting her novels in Italy, not America, wishing her heroine were a wage-earner, not a doctor's wife.[10]

Dreiser had become his paragon. Even before Reedy declared that *The Financier* had "something of greatness," Masters had written to praise the novelist for his "sceptical daring" and unmatched comprehension of American life. "Your treatment of evil, and sin, and such things is such an unmasking of the passing show." He offered to help with background if Dreiser should ever write a labor novel. He gave him free counsel on the laws of libel. There was a warmth and openness in his letters that the novelist found irresistible, sometimes underlining the passages that pleased him. So in December 1912, when he came to Chicago to gather material for *The Titan*, his second novel about Charles T. Yerkes, it was natural for Dreiser to ask if he might call, and inevitable that they should become close friends. Dreiser himself was a frustrated poet.[11]

A year later, just before Christmas in 1913, Sandburg called on Masters, carrying a copy of the *Mirror*. Perhaps moved by seasonal charity, Reedy had taken one of Masters' poems for his holiday number. Reporting a labor case Masters was trying, Sandburg used the magazine as his introduction. He had the look of a Swedish cobbler the lawyer had known back in Lewistown. At ensuing meetings Sandburg would pick up items of labor news and they would chat about books and politics. Sandburg showed Masters his own abortive first effort, a lyric collection printed in 1904. And although he had been in Chicago only just over a year, he opened up vistas of bohemian life to the veteran Chicagoan. Three months later he opened up other vistas, when Harriet Monroe brought out Sandburg's first nine "Chicago Poems" and Reedy reprinted the one with which Sandburg and Chicago have been identified ever since:

CROSSING SPOON RIVER

Hog Butcher for the World,
Tool Maker, Stacker of Wheat,
Player with Railroads and the Nation's Freight Handler;
Stormy, husky, brawling,
City of the Big Shoulders:
They tell me you are wicked, and I believe them . . .[12]

Masters' first plays had been a pastiche of Elizabethan blank verse, and he still signed his lyrics with a pen name borrowed from two Elizabethan dramatists, "Webster Ford." Seeing Sandburg's striking verses led him to consider changing his style. Reedy had given him a copy of the *Greek Anthology,* praising its "ironic, sardonic, epigraphic" qualities, and he was so enthusiastic about it that he urged Dreiser to go out and buy a copy at once. It had the rustic, realistic tone Masters had wanted to express in a novel of Illinois village life he had long considered writing. Now he tried out the epigram form in a free-verse compliment to Dreiser and sent it to him. In "Theodore the Poet" he imagined his friend to be a boy growing up along the Spoon River, where he himself had spent his spare time, sometimes watching the door of a crayfish burrow as a poet watches men and women, "Looking for the souls of them to come out . . ."[13]

Years before, in Lewistown, Masters had quarreled with his mother over a literary difference of opinion. He had left home for good when she ended the dispute by hitting him on the head with a rolled window shade.[14] In May 1914, the month after he wrote the epigram for Dreiser, she visited him in Chicago. Now they chatted amicably about friends he had lost track of and neighbors who had died or come to grief. He felt like some ghost traversing the lost years and mislaid lives that unrolled in his absence. When his mother left, on a Sunday afternoon, he returned alone from the railroad station to his room. Immediately he wrote several poems and sent them off to Reedy. Among them was "The Hill"—"Where are Elmer,

Herman, Bert, Tom and Charley . . . ?" The letter of acceptance he received by return mail astonished him, and he wondered whether Reedy's enthusiasm were ironic. "When I wrote these first pieces, and scrawled at the top of the page 'Spoon River Anthology,' I sat back and laughed at what seemed to me the most preposterous title known . . . When I saw that he really liked the work I wanted to change the title to 'Pleasant Plains Anthology,' but he dissented so earnestly that I yielded to his judgment." [15]

Reedy's recollection of the occasion differs slightly. "First, half piqued at my rejection of his efforts in accepted verse forms, he hurled at me three of the poems, with a satiric query that perhaps this was what I liked. I printed them. He was surprised, half suspecting I was guying him." [16] Reedy had actually printed five of the earlier, conventional poems. There were seven rather than three poems in the group he now published. But the essential fact is plain. The series of poems which grew out of that first experiment had more far-reaching effect than anything Reedy had ever printed before.

They were a work of sustained inspiration. Masters' recent reading of the *Greek Anthology* and his discussions with Dreiser and Sandburg had given him a new conception of form. His recent conversations with his mother had released a torrent of feeling and recollection. The inhibitions that had crippled his earlier work were washed away, and he was at last free to write from the heart. The final poem of the opening group, which should have been printed as the introduction, echoes those chats with his mother. There are two voices, one questioning, the other responding:

Where are Elmer, Herman, Bert, Tom and Charley,
The weak of will, the strong of arm, the clown, the boozer, the
    fighter?
All, all, are sleeping on the hill.

CROSSING SPOON RIVER

> One passed in a fever,
> One was burned in a mine,
> One was killed in a brawl,
> One died in a jail,
> One fell from a bridge toiling for children and wife—
> All, all are sleeping, sleeping, sleeping on the hill.

The seeker goes on to ask news of girls he once knew and is told that many of them, too, have come to pathetic ends:

> One died in shameful childbirth,
> One of a thwarted love . . .

Nor had their elders fared better after bringing home "dead sons from the war, / And daughters whom life had crushed . . ." Buried with these victims of life was an American epoch, a rural epoch once vibrant as a fiddle at a square dance, now broken, never to be heard again.

> Where is Old Fiddler Jones
> Who played with life all his ninety years,
> Braving the sleet with bared breast,
> Drinking, rioting, thinking neither of wife nor kin,
> Nor gold, nor love, nor heaven?
> Lo! he babbles of the fish-frys of long ago,
> Of the horse-races of long ago at Clary's Grove,
> Of what Abe Lincoln said
> One time at Springfield.[17]

It was the peculiarly American intonation and detail, an echo of prairie accents and a whiff of the fish-frys of long ago, that set the key for the other poems. All but one of those written and published in ensuing weeks voiced the loneliness and regrets of the dead, each in a distinctive tone of voice and manner of speaking. The exception was the Dreiser epigram, which appeared in a group of epitaphs a few weeks later. "Imagiste ventures into rural delineations of fate and sorrow," Masters called them, asking Dreiser's opinion two days after the first group appeared. And he went on to confess that in

THE MAN IN THE MIRROR

writing them a feeling like sorrow had come over him—"something of the terror and loneliness of life, the consciousness of the flying years." [18] That quality pervaded the poems.

Perhaps some premonition of doom in the air also gave poignancy to these voices from the grave. The United States had just invaded Mexico when the first poems appeared, on May 29, 1914, headed "Spoon River Anthology" and signed Webster Ford. The next group came out three weeks later, the third on July 26, two days before the Austrian archduke and archduchess were slain at Sarajevo. In the hush between calamities these poems from the tomb were portentous as the ripple of breeze that predicts a tornado. Excited readers were soon writing in to express their astonishment and approval. One was inspired to give his own vivid impression of the graveyard where "All, all, are sleeping on the hill."

> I seem to see the shunned God's acre, baking under an August sun, the parched grass crackling over and amid the marked, unmarked, and sunken graves[;] thirsty geraniums wilting on those remembered, obscene tinfoil shining through the wreaths of one of yesterday; the soldier's monument, bumptious, arresting, its *Pro Patria* newly illumined by Knowlt Hoheimer. It stands along the brow of a yellow claybank shelving down to the Spoon, a creek now, never a river but in freshet season . . . A desolate, lonely, uninviting city of the dead that calls peremptorily to the unlovely, dead-alive town in the distance . . .[19]

For Reedy personally it was also a time of abrupt change—from custom and the past. Instead of going to New York for his usual holiday he was going to Europe with Harry Hawes, who had been his political opponent in the days when they had both lunched with James Campbell at the Noonday Club. Campbell died suddenly just before they left, and the *Mirror* called his passing the end of an era. For the last time, Reedy defended his patron against the newspapers, which implied that Campbell had been the source and center of municipal corruption. Then, while Reedy and Hawes were abroad, Austria declared war on Serbia; Germany invaded France; Russia invaded Germany. And the Britannic peace under which Reedy and his magazine and most of its readers grew up had ended, as salvo on salvo rocked the ground. In St. Louis, far from the din of battle, Reedy's deputy editor announced that "Spoon River Anthology" was being acclaimed everywhere. The supply of magazines containing the poems was running low.[20]

Masters had thought of going abroad with Reedy and Hawes, but went instead to a Michigan resort. Week after week, while Reedy reported the upheaval in London and the Irish unrest, the epitaphs were being written and printed. Some ten or twenty lines in length, they were gathered in "garlands" such as flower peddlers might hang beside a cemetery—the general title "Anthology" suggesting a flower harvest. As time went on Masters came to think of the characters celebrated in his epitaphs as members of families and groups, their lives interlaced in curious patterns. This insight came to him only gradually.

Thus the second garland is headed by Benjamin Pantier, the unhappy lawyer whose wife has driven him to drink—or so he believes. Not until months later did readers hear her side of the story:

> I know that he told that I snared his soul
> With a snare which bled him to death.
> And all the men loved him,
> And most of the women pitied him.
> But suppose you are really a lady, and have delicate tastes,
> And loathe the smell of whiskey and onions.
> And the rhythm of Wordsworth's "Ode" runs in your ears,
> While he goes about from morning till night
> Repeating bits of that common thing;
> "Oh, why should the spirit of mortal be proud?"
> And then, suppose:
> You are a woman well endowed,
> And the only man with whom the law and morality

THE MAN IN THE MIRROR

> Permit you to have the marital relation
> Is the very man that fills you with disgust
> Every time you think of it—while you think of it
> Every time you see him?
> That's why I drove him from home
> To live with his dog in a dingy room
> Back of his office.[21]

"Our story is lost in silence," Benjamin had said in his epitaph. But the Pantiers' quarrel left its mark on all Spoon River. Other garlands kept referring to it. Trainor, the druggist, thinks he can understand their incompatability, "being a mixer of chemicals." Ironically, he was killed making an experiment. Emily Sparks, the schoolteacher, makes no pretense of understanding, but loves the Pantiers' son and prays that the fire set ablaze in his spirit by the friction between his parents may turn into the light of genius. Whatever impulse led Mrs. Pantier to drive her husband from her bed, it had ramifications throughout the community. For her reforming zeal made her president of the Social Purity Club, and the club joined forces with the revivalist church headed by a hypocritical banker. In the end there was a political battle between these forces of Prohibition and a new liberal party. The bank failed; the courthouse was burned down; and the town marshal, among others, was killed. New graves were dug on the hill, each headstone bearing its euphemistic inscription and guarding its secrets. "Our story is lost in silence. Go by, mad world!"[22]

It might be said that the poems were at their best as they poured out in the *Mirror* with no premeditated order. Their impetuosity had the conviction of unforeseen events and the spontaneous feelings they provoke. The community they portrayed was like a closely woven fabric. Its men and women moved like shuttles in a loom of cause and effect, tossed by forces incomprehensible to them all. Each epitaph had a moral design, yet none could read their moral. No one could be sure whether Pantier or his wife had been responsible for the broken marriage that wrecked the life of their son and had other, far-reaching consequences. After one views their problem from all sides the truth is still unknown.

Seen as a whole, the "Anthology" has three basic themes, and one of them is the vanity of human knowledge. Masters brings out this theme in the epitaph of Oaks Tutt, the idealist who returns from the fallen empires of the Mediterranean bent on reforming the world. Back in Spoon River he is frustrated by the cynicism of the poet Jonathan Swift Somers, who ridicules his pretensions as a prophet, saying:

> "Before you reform the world, Mr. Tutt,
> Please answer the question of Pontius Pilate:
> 'What is Truth?'"[23]

Like the pragmatic philosophers of his time, Masters denied that there is any purpose in searching for absolute truth. What man can hope for is only to find a hypothesis that will work. But for this insight the poet was not beholden to William James. Browning had explored the same poetic situation in *The Ring and the Book*, which, like Masters' epitaphs, views a human conflict from the vantage point of each participant and concludes that it is not given mankind to know anything. Moral knowledge, at least, remains elusive, "and human estimation words and wind."

A second theme of Masters' poems is freedom. Much of the larger story, gradually pieced out in separate epitaphs, revolves around the battle for freedom waged by John Cabanis and the liberals against Mrs. Pantier, the banker, the dishonest editor, and the other prohibitionists. That is the argument of "The Spooniad," fragment of an epic by Jonathan Swift Somers, published soon after Webster Ford's own epitaph, with a headnote saying that it had been found among Somers' papers by William Marion Reedy "and was for the first time published in *Reedy's Mirror*." Actually "The Spooniad" is no true fragment but a subtle parody of the first and sixth books of *Paradise Lost* (a fact which neither Reedy nor any other critic seems to have noticed), and it reveals the transcending unity of the many complex elements that went into the "Anthology." The politics of Spoon River are there likened ironically to those of the *Iliad* and the war between God and Satan in Milton. Masters' theme, like Milton's, is freedom of the will and man's perverse insistence on misusing it to bring about his own destruction. This realization haunts the souls of all those "sleeping on the hill." Their struggles for freedom and their failure to use it mock their rest. Freedom to love and enjoy is equated with justice, good, and ultimate truth; while the repressive zeal of Mrs. Pantier's Social Purity Club and the party of Prohibition is rooted in hypocrisy, greed, and evil—the effects of frustrated love.

Not all the lives chronicled in these brief histories were drab or warped, however. As the series progressed there were more and more epitaphs expressing nobility and a sense of purpose and fulfillment. Most of these belonged to an older generation; many of them portrayed historical figures. There was Anne Rutledge—

> Beloved in life of Abraham Lincoln,
> Wedded to him, not through union,
> But through separation.[24]

There was William H. Herndon, who had been the partner of Lincoln and of Masters' father. He had seen a great tragedy enacted, and its austere glory still burned in his words:

> O Lincoln, actor indeed, playing well your part,
> And Booth, who strode in a mimic play within the play,
> Often and often I saw you,
> As the cawing crows winged their way to the wood
> Over my housetop at solemn sunsets,
> There by my window,
> Alone.[25]

CROSSING SPOON RIVER

Most memorable of all was Lucinda Matlock, drawn from Masters' recollection of his grandmother. Like others of her time, she had nothing but contempt for the poet's generation.

> At ninety-six I had lived enough, that is all,
> And passed to a sweet repose.
> What is this I hear of sorrow and weariness,
> Anger, discontent, and drooping hopes?
> Degenerate sons and daughters,
> Life is too strong for you—
> It takes life to love Life.[26]

Here in a nutshell was the third motif of the "Anthology" —that living holds precious gifts for those who have the strength and the will to prize it. Only at the moment when life is snatched away, however, can one know with due intensity what it is worth.

When Reedy gave up hope of visiting the battlefront and returned from England that autumn, it was to Clonmel, his twenty-seven-acre farm on Manchester Road. Mrs. Reedy, still the devoted farmer, had insisted on rebuilding the house the year after it burned down. By now life was restored to its familiar cycle, and Reedy had accustomed himself to the commuter's routine. Apart from acquainting him with the endless rustic talk that is a perpetual hum in the Middle West, Reedy's years at Clonmel had prepared him to appreciate the subtleties of country politics that bulk so large in Masters' world. Reedy's account of an election day of the period shows how well his ear was attuned to its modulations—that mixed tonality of nasal humor and partisan rage, of droning gossip about land and sudden outbursts of defamation, that one hears only in the country.

His account reads like a comic eclogue in prose. He tells of hearing the Indian Runner ducks and rising early on a November day to assist at the calving of two cows; of haggling with a farmer who rides up in the rain to look over his shoats, and rides off incredulous that Reedy (a landowner) can think of voting for the single tax. He recalls the bitterness of the campaign just ended and the general anxiety over the farm vote that summer. Another neighbor, a rich man, comes along "with fire in his eye" and wants to know if Reedy needs money:

> If I do he'll lend it . . . so I can fix the fence between his place and mine and keep my heifers and shoats out. . . . He takes me to the polls in his automobile. When I tell him I'm going to vote the State Socialist ticket and for the Single Tax, he tells his chauffeur to speed up and whizzes me past the election booth for a mile and a half. . . . His parting shot as he speeds away . . . is that I ought to vote at the Insane Asylum.[27]

And Reedy goes on to recount with amusement how grimly believable had been the violent claims and charges and the ominous prophecies now receding like echoes down an empty corridor. But his equable mood is shattered that night. As he and Mrs. Reedy lie abed he confesses that he *may* have forgotten to vote for the single tax after all. Her wifely awe had dwindled earlier, when her lantern beam had discovered her lord and master struggling to extricate a cow's hind leg from a halter throatlatch, and she saw him kicked ignominiously into a wall. Now she consoles him with the acid reflection that at least women will be going to the polls next election day.

That same mixture of domestic and political tragi-comedy animates much of "Spoon River Anthology." There is John Cabanis, who left the Prohibitionists and started his liberal party, not in simple disgust, but partly for love of his free-living daughter Flossie, and partly in the conviction that freedom demands that men like him sacrifice themselves and eventually die—

> Like the coral insect, for the temple
> To stand on at the last.[28]

There is Adam Weirauch, the butcher, "crushed between Altgeld and Armour." And there is George Trimble, who had

CROSSING SPOON RIVER

stood on the steps
Of the Court House and talked free-silver,
And the single-tax of Henry George.[29]

Reedy was admirably equipped to interpret such men and such poems.

Back in St. Louis he found letters from all over Europe and America hailing the unknown poet of Spoon River. He hastily copyrighted the series, a detail lawyer Masters had overlooked, and set down his impressions of the greatness of the event. "Spoon River Anthology," he said, was the "most typically American work in untrammeled poetry" since Walt Whitman. If the *Mirror* were remembered for nothing else it would be remembered as the channel "through which Spoon River found its place in the world's geography of the mind and heart." [30] Then he had to go to Chicago to try to persuade Masters to let him reveal his identity. Though it had done no harm to be known as the author of bad poems, Masters was sure it would ruin his law practice to be identified with these successful ones. The argument went on for some time, and it was not until three months after Reedy's return home that he received permission to disclose Masters' name. Replying to the flood of increasingly insistent, "almost angry," queries, he simply reprinted Masters' paragraph from *Who's Who*.

In a long critical article Reedy went on to analyze the poetic device of using an epitaph collection to reveal the secret inner life of a people. He spoke of the sympathy and irony of the self-portraits and their "terrible truthfulness." Were these dead the victims of fate and environment, or had they somehow failed to live up to the possibilities of free will? "That the life stories here revealed adumbrate some scheme or plan of existence, to which they conformed or with which they were at odds, is undeniable," he asserted. But he was at a loss to define the theological point of view, unless it derived from the religion of Kant. Poetically he was on surer ground. In Masters' epitaphs Reedy saw constant paradox—fools displaying wisdom, property rights destroying human rights, and justice made the instrument of injustice. Only after life had ended for them could the men and women of Masters' world see the paltry causes that had led to great misfortunes. Often they could then see that they had been the victims not of fate but of their own pettiness.

What Reedy emphasized, though, was not the tragic attitude or the philosophical content of the work, so much as the uniquely American climate in which these lives had sprouted like field corn and grown up, straight or twisted. Each had bent to the same hot wind that had blown on "Lincoln and the democratic movement, from Greenbackism to the New Freedom, and the trust magnates, and women who made Paris turn to watch them as they passed." He implied that the world was turning to watch Masters with similar awe, hailing him as a new light and a new voice: "The light and the voice are American—American of the country's declining heroic age . . ." For Reedy the years he and Masters had lived were a time of "multiplying complications," when basic values and ideals and hopes went down to drab defeat, while materialism throve like swelling eruptions of smut on corn. But he was still optimistic. For at last a poet had come to redress the balance and restore some sense of the fundamentals of American faith.[31]

It would take profound insight to reach such a conclusion while the "Anthology" remained unfinished and most of the poems recalling nobility and high purpose were yet to be written. Perhaps Reedy's remarks even inspired such poems. To see the undoubted moral drift of the work at this stage was, in any event, an imaginative achievement. For many clever critics denied that it had any moral substance whatsoever.

One who did not deny it was Ezra Pound. While the series was still running in the *Mirror* the overseas correspondent of *Poetry: A Magazine of Verse* was urging Harriet Monroe in imperative block letters to "GET SOME OF WEBSTER FORD'S STUFF FOR 'POETRY.'"[32] Just before the series came to an end he wrote a jubilant article about Masters for the *Egoist*. "At last!" he told his British readers. "At last America has discovered a poet." Ever since Whitman any poet born within that "great land of hypothetical futures" had to come abroad for recognition. Now it had one editor (Reedy) "sane enough to print such straight writing in a 'common newspaper'" and one critic (Miss Monroe) sane enough to quote it in a literary review. Most of all he was pleased to find in Masters a poet so rugged he might endure the withering anti-aesthetic weather of the West; one capable of dealing with actual life direct and plain, not in the "murmurous" idiom of derivative poesy. Masters, he declared, used "the speech of a man in the process of getting something said."[33]

Although Miss Monroe reprinted three of the poems and praised Reedy's discrimination in having recognized Masters, privately she was vexed that a St. Louis editor should have "discovered" a Chicago poet. Chicago was her own preserve. When Masters had completed the series he sought to propitiate the angry muse with a libation—a flattering review of Miss Monroe's book *You and I* for the *Mirror*. Then he collapsed, had pneumonia, recovered, and went to work sorting his epitaphs for a book. A year and a half later Pound was still demanding in petulant letters to Miss Monroe, "When do we get some MASTERS? ? ?"[34]

Meanwhile Pound wrote a second essay about the Spoon River poems, enlarging on what he meant by good poetry. What he insisted on was realism—"a straight statement of life." "I want nothing beyond that, no circumlocutions, no side views. If the matter is splendid or tragical the reader will know it well enough without the author's adding descriptive adjectives and interjections of 'Ah, sad the day!' for the sake of the rhymes or the metre, or because he has not control enough to stick to plain statement." He went on to quote from Masters' less felicitous epitaphs, and to disparage the "clichés of political journalism" still hanging over from Masters' "poetic diction period." But he added that when Masters wrote forthrightly each poem had a "cause," a sort of "core of reality," and he quoted "The Hill" and "Doc Hill." Masters, he declared, knew how to recognize the "eternal poetic situations when they appear." For Pound the lasting enjoyment of a work of art consisted in the feeling that one had confronted such situations, since they alone contain the reality of life itself. He was thankful that Masters had this "confronting" quality, the lack of which is irremediable.

But now Pound qualified his praise with a warning:

If the author will spend certain hours in revision, a rather strenuous revision; if he will take a few months of meditation wherein to select from the rather too numerous poems . . . he should be able to make a book . . .

If, on the other hand, he grows facetious, or lets down the tone, relaxes his seriousness, grows careless of rhythm, does not develop it, allows his method to become mere machinery, "systematizes his production," then one will have to register another disappointment.[35]

An accident kept Masters from seeing this percipient comment at a time when he might still have been impressionable enough to heed its admonition. Pound had written the essay as one of his "Affirmations" that winter, while he was serving as W. B. Yeats's secretary and living with him in Sussex. He sent it to the leftist journal *New Age,* but its editor had a horror of free verse and refused to print anything favorable to it. When he returned to London Pound sent the article to Masters with a letter "full of strange oaths and firecrackers" and "many kinds of blasphemy on editors." [36] By the time he received it Masters had already finished reading proof on the book, which Macmillan published in April. Reedy did not print Pound's article until late in May, and then defended Masters, who had by now made some of the mistakes against which Pound had cautioned him, and presently proceeded to make nearly all the rest of them. The series had concluded in the *Mirror* only five months earlier, and already the atmosphere of controversy the poems engendered precluded the kind of meditation Pound recommended. There is some question, however, whether Masters had a capacity for that kind of soul searching.

Spoon River Anthology proved to be the most popular book of native poetry in the year 1915, when books of poems were among the most popular books. Its first edition ran through nineteen printings, and a revised and expanded second edition followed in only eighteen months. This was an unheard-of phenomenon in the book trade. *Publishers' Weekly* called the *Anthology* "the outstanding book—not only the outstanding book of poetry—" of that year and interpreted its success as pointing a new and incalculable trend threatening the preeminence of the novel. The controversy *Spoon River* aroused was largely responsible.[37]

Dreiser was among the first to be drawn into it, because his novels made him the foremost "realist" in America. Masters' realism, like Dreiser's, raised moral as well as stylistic questions. Like pragmatism in philosophy, the realism of both writers began with the premise that truth is relative, changing with man's perspective, and can never be finally determined. Every hypothesis must therefore be tested by the question, does it work? Masters was testing ethical assumptions by that question and finding that most of the assumptions by which Americans lived do not work out to an ethical desideratum.

Apart from ethical realities, Masters was investigating and describing psychological ones as well. Here he was accused of excessive realism; of depicting what some readers considered scientifically tenable but artistically inadmissible facts.

THE MAN IN THE MIRROR

This was the nub of disagreement in a debate Kennerley published in the *Forum* the following January. Bliss Carman and Willard Huntington Wright spoke of his realism with contempt, as a quality alien to the spirit of poetry. William Stanley Braithwaite and Sheamas O Sheel praised his irony and pathos, above all the accuracy of his vision.[38] A more clear-cut definition of the issue came out in a debate between Orvis B. Irwin and Roger Sherman Loomis, which ran in the *Dial* from March into June 1916. To Irwin the *Anthology* was not art, because it lacked "high idealism." While he did not deny that "things do happen as they happen in Spoon River," he felt that psychological irregularities like those depicted by Masters (witness the sexual aversion of Mrs. Pantier toward her husband) are the province of clinical research not of poetry. Masters, he said, "crept like a reptile through slime and evil." Loomis replied that truth could not be split; what was ideally so was really so. Writers committed to a higher idealism, "glossing over the black horrors of a chaotic universe, minimizing them, palliating them, denying them," had turned perceptive people away from all literature. A new and valid vision, he asserted, had been brought to literary art by Zola, Hardy, and Masters, writers who knew no distinction between scientific and poetic truth.[39]

Reading these debates and many others like them, from afar, Pound injected himself into them again and again. "Soft soap and leprosy" he called arguments like Irwin's. In New York the British novelist John Cowper Powys had seen the *Anthology* in proof; Dreiser had showed it to him at Masters' request. Powys' writing first appeared in the *Mirror* about the time the book came out, and Reedy hailed him as a "sweaty sort" of intellectual laborer, who "doesn't so much explain as explode."[40] Powys, barnstorming America, applauded Masters wherever he went. When Powys was contradicted by a critic who called Masters a cynic, Pound protested violently:

CROSSING SPOON RIVER

One might as well call the sayings of Christ cynical, he wrote Reedy. "If there ever was a writer who looked on the mildly nauseating spectacle of human imbecility with a sort of universal forgiveness," that writer was Edgar Lee Masters. And Pound talked of the "pink-talcum-for-the-baby's-skin" reviews written by gentlemen wearing little blue ribbons on their undershirts. If *they* stood for American literature, he was happy to say that at least they had nothing to do with life and talk in the United States as he had known them.[41]

And so the critical dispute swelled and burst and swelled again, soon growing far too voluminous to outline here. More important was the effect Masters had on other poets. That, too, was immediately apparent in the *Mirror*, where minor poets loved to attack the critics in verse, as did one minor bard, vainly seeking to catch Masters' rhythm:

> The critics are still squinting,
> And humming and hawing,
> "Is this poetry, or is it prose?"
>
> *And what of Truth?*
> Spoon River has flooded their pigeon holes
> And blurred their formulas.[42]

Even Sara Teasdale was impelled to depart from her tripping rhyme schemes and embark on free-verse dialogue. "Freedom calls all poets," remarked Reedy, as he reprinted her poem, "The Lighted Window," from the *Century*.[43] Reedy was soon being attacked in his own columns for the aid and comfort he gave to enemies of conventional prosody.

Carl Sandburg, on the other hand, acknowledged his indebtedness to Reedy in his dedication of *Chicago Poems* when it came out as a book in 1916, but even while the Masters epitaphs were running in the *Mirror* he had flung himself into the battle for freedom by sending Reedy his "Tribute to Webster Ford." There he alluded to the old schism between poetry and

THE MAN IN THE MIRROR

practical life, which Reedy—and now Masters—did so much to close.

A man wrote two books.

One held in its covers the outside man,
   whose name was on a Knox College diploma,
   who bought his clothes at Marshall Field's,
   had his name done by a sign painter in gilt
   on an office door in a loop skyscraper,
   and never did any damage to the code of morals
   set forth by the *Chicago Tribune.*
The other book held a naked man,
   the sheer brute under the clothes
   as he will be stripped at the Last Day,
   the inside man with red heartbeats
   that go on ticking off life
   against the ribs.[44]

Masters' most important function in *Spoon River Anthology* was to effect a fusion between poetry and the common life of the Middle West, something he could not have done without the example of Dreiser and Sandburg, the encouragement of Reedy. The part Reedy had played in shaping Masters was no accident. They had been formed by one another like neighbor boys in a city street. They had wrestled and bruised themselves on the same pavements. In fact, Reedy's reminiscences of Johnnie Cunningham and Jack Shea appeared just before the first of the "Anthology" poems, and the epitaph of Webster Ford with which the book drew to an end echoed the mood of Reedy's recollection of his boyhood friends.

Hitherto it had been Reedy's part to offer Masters needed resistance, force him to search out his inner resources, and to rid his verse of circumlocution and affectation. Now that the book was a success, he became Masters' apologist in the critical war. Dreiser seems to have feared that Reedy would spoil Masters and said as much in a letter, to which Reedy retorted:

"I don't think he quite appreciates how big a thing he's done." Reedy praised a humility no one else recognized in Masters. "Those Spoon Riverites are so real to him he feels as if he'd done nothing but report them. But he's done more. He has indicted Life of high crime and misdemeanor, more effectively than did Leopardi."[45] Reedy went on to admit Dreiser's charge that he was perhaps too tender in his treatment of his writers, but he refused to mend his ways.

In his dual role of editor and critic Reedy was generally not guilty of over-solicitude. It was usual for him to reject a poet for some time, as he had Masters, perhaps printing a contribution or two and then ignoring his work for a period of years. Then there would be a "Reflection," or a headnote over a set of poems, signifying tentative endorsement. Later might come interpretation, advocacy, and at last revaluation. Meanwhile, there would be poems accepted, and others inevitably rejected. In Masters' case Reedy made a regrettable exception. If he did not publish everything Masters sent him after "Spoon River," he certainly published far too much. He espoused him too loyally, pointing out that Masters' realism and modernism were balanced by profound knowledge of the classics, his minute observation of local detail by a cosmic wisdom.

At a time when both Pound and Dreiser could see Masters' need for restraint and discipline, Reedy in fact abdicated his critical function. Within a few years a disinterested critic like Conrad Aiken could see in Masters' voluminous output that he had lost selective skill and given up the compression forced on him by the epitaph form. He was developing neither in psychological insight nor in musical or formal sensibility.[46] When others made similar criticisms Reedy persisted in denying their validity.

Perhaps Reedy would have lost Masters as a friend had he continued to serve him as a critic. His decision not to take that risk was not only a grave misfortune for Masters; it kept Reedy from performing the most creative function criticism can ever attempt. It was Reedy's limitation that when the choice had to be made, he preferred the part of a friend to that of a critic. In the last analysis such friendship must necessarily defeat its own ends.

CHAPTER 18

THE WAR OF THE IMAGISTS AND THEIR ANTAGONISTS

Having championed Dreiser and Masters when their work was unknown, Reedy had identified himself with a new trend. Yet he tried to draw a distinction between the newness of Masters and the novelty Amy Lowell sought. Novelty-seeking was what he had complained of in Hamlin Garland twenty years before, and still despised.

Garland was no longer a novelty in 1915 but he was still in the limelight. His masterpiece, *A Son of the Middle Border,* had recently been published in *Collier's* and sealed his fame as a veteran literary campaigner. Garland had led off for Lindsay in 1911. He was to be a sponsor of *Spoon River Anthology* when it was introduced at a meeting of the Poetry Society of America the month before its publication as a book. The strategy he and Richard Burton planned was calculated to win the Society over to Masters with a minimum of debate. They wanted the poems read quietly, without emphasis or excitement, so that the applause of members who knew them from the *Mirror* might quell the doubts of those encountering them for the first time.[1]

Amy Lowell picked up her phone in Brookline to wedge her way into that same March 1915 meeting in New York. She was seeking a sensational debut, and so played into the hands of Masters' sponsors. The book she meant to introduce was an anthology, *Some Imagist Poets.* Besides her own verse, it contained examples of the work of Richard Aldington, Hilda Doolittle, D. H. Lawrence, John Gould Fletcher, and other London friends she had met through Ezra Pound. The book was also the battle flag of Miss Lowell's rebellion against Pound's leadership of what was still known as the *imagiste* movement. Those who heard her at the Poetry Society that night came away unperturbed by the radicalism of Masters. What all remembered was the hilarious image called up by one of Miss Lowell's own poems: the portly, cigar-smoking spinster of forty, lolling and laughing in her morning bath.[2]

Miss Lowell's name was still new to readers of the *Mirror*, though she had published some poems in *Poetry*, and the sister of the president of Harvard was never precisely an unknown. She had brought out one plodding book of rhymes, which Louis Untermeyer had been the only critic to attack or even notice. Her second book, *Sword Blades and Poppy Seed*, promised to be another disappointment. It had sold only seven hundred copies when Zoë Akins singled it out for attention in a series of articles on poetry she had suddenly decided to write for the *Mirror* that same spring of 1915. Miss Akins omitted any humorous reference to the bathtub incident, but instead, sincerely praised Miss Lowell's "devotion to sheer craftsmanship" and her "spiritual congeniality with change and progress and strength." [3]

Zoë Akins' series, "In the Shadows of Parnassus," had reflected the atmosphere of distraction in which she always worked. The Lowell poems discussed in the fifth of her essays were inadvertently printed in the fourth. Irrelevantly she coupled Miss Lowell with Lindsay, and went out of her way to express her resentment of Gertrude Stein and Ezra Pound, all in the same article. She accused Pound of charlatanism, presumption, and lack of taste. Where Pound had denied that Miss Lowell's poem "The Taxi" was an example of *imagisme*, Miss Akins showed that its congeries of sharp, hard images evoked by sinewy verbs

WAR OF THE IMAGISTS

and nouns does succeed in building a mood and stating a situation:

> When I go away from you
> The world beats dead
> Like a slackened drum.
> I call out for you against the jutted stars
> And shout into the ridges of the wind.
> Streets coming fast,
> One after the other,
> Wedge you away from me,
> And the lamps of the city prick my eyes
> So that I can no longer see your face.
> Why should I leave you,
> To wound myself upon the sharp edges of the night? * 4

Whether or not Pound was right in denying that this was *imagisme*, the poem showed the influence of a group of French poets almost unknown in America—even to those who had read *Mlle. New York*, the *Chap-Book*, and the *Mirror* in the nineties. Miss Lowell had been lecturing on de Régnier, Jammes, Paul Fort, Remy de Gourmont, and other French poets who called themselves *imagistes*. Her *Six French Poets* was scheduled for fall publication. It introduced a fresh influence from a source America had neglected for the better part of fifteen years. Sara Teasdale, who was nothing if not *au courante*, told a correspondent that her own knowledge of French poetry was "bounded on all sides by Verlaine." 5

Miss Akins did not score again so surely as she had with her timely tribute to Miss Lowell, though her series came to include sixty poets. She omitted some names as important as William Carlos Williams, Wallace Stevens, and T. S. Eliot. But she drew attention to some she included, especially when Braithwaite in his *Anthology* for 1915 contradicted her statement that America

* Quoted in full with permission of the publisher from *Sword Blades and Poppy Seeds*. Copyright 1921 by Houghton Mifflin.

THE MAN IN THE MIRROR

had yet to produce a great poet. He felt that *Spoon River Anthology* and Robert Frost's *North of Boston,* the two "great successes of the year," were both likely to live. Impressed nevertheless with Miss Akins' poetical essays, he took a new interest in the *Mirror,* which he had disregarded the year before. Braithwaite had his friend Miss Teasdale ask Reedy for a file of the magazine. Reedy complied, modestly regretting that he had published "practically no original verse except Mr. Masters' *Spoon River.*" On that he was "content however to rest." [6]

Miss Lowell rapidly made herself the field commander in an aggressive drive to force the public to accept the "New Poetry." Reedy was characteristically averse to seeing anything new in the movement she wanted to lead. In one of his essays which Braithwaite lists among the important discussions of poetry published that year Reedy tries to define imagism as a method that is "Japanesque, or early Greek." The imagist, he says, "gives you a word-picture of a person, a thing or a scene . . . He doesn't tell you the thoughts or emotions these evoke in him or should evoke in you. He tells you the thing, though, so that it makes you clothe it with appropriate vesture of thought and emotion. He makes you see the invisible colors in his picture, hear the inaudible music of his song . . . He gives you three lines and it is the means to your sensing the horror of war, the quality of a character, the beauty of a scene. He calls out the poet in the reader." [7]

Reedy went on to consider "the Pope of the imagist cult," Ezra Pound, whose *Cathay* had just come to him from London. It was the first in a series of translations from the Chinese, based on notes Pound had inherited from the American orientalist Ernest Fenollosa. Reedy called the poems too cryptic to be read without excessive explanation. Their symbolism was "a kind of sublimated slang" no one could read unaided. Pound's imagism was made brilliant by his notes, Reedy said, but he himself preferred the imagism of Sappho or Theocritus, for no one had to tell him what they meant or how he was supposed to respond to them.

Readers of the *Mirror* were seldom as tolerant of the new movement as its editor. Some objected strenuously to Miss Lowell on the same grounds as those which had led the *Mirror's* reviewer of the *Lyric Year* to question its invocation of the "Time Spirit." They felt that an appeal to modernity was a confession of weakness in a poet. The leading exponent of this negative view was a Chicagoan, John Lewis Hervey, who now became a frequent contributor of articles that invited and exulted in Miss Lowell's wrath. Hervey was an eccentric critic with an aggressive and passionate love for poetry. He and Miss Teasdale's friend, John Myers O'Hara, spent years translating *Les Trophées*, the exquisite neoclassic poems of the Cuban leader of the Parnassians, José Maria de Heredia. But by profession Hervey was an expert judge of fine harness horses, the editor of the *Horse Review;* and he wrote an official history of American racing published by the Jockey Club.[8]

Like Reedy, Hervey noted that imagism had an Oriental root, but he objected to Miss Lowell's imagism because it lacked the spontaneity of Oriental art and seemed overrational and contrived. Comparing her unfavorably with a Japanese poet long familiar to *Mirror* readers, he quoted Yone Noguchi as saying it was "the sadness of the age that we must have a reason even for poetry."

Miss Lowell, he exclaimed, "is so conspicuously, so insistently, a poet with a reason." He accused her of reading into her poetry the theories expressed in her *Six French Poets* and her preface to *Sword Blades*. He regarded her not as a bad poet but as a general threat to all poetry. "I demand of poetry above all else that it shall move me," he declared. "Alas, the reading of Miss

Lowell's verses proved the most miscalculated poetical adventure in which I have lately indulged. It was like taking ship for Cythere and disembarking in Brummagem." [9]

What Hervey resented was in part Miss Lowell's efforts to attract publicity to further her cause. The critical attentions of Braithwaite, John Gould Fletcher, and Louis Untermeyer provoked him, as did Miss Akins'. He took issue with her for admiring "Patterns," a poem he subjected to cruel analysis. It was true that Miss Lowell felt it an advantage to the new poetry to stir up as much dissent as possible; she had had her fill of being ignored. So she welcomed Hervey's assault and promptly mobilized her forces to repel him. This, she confided to her publisher, was her studied plan. "*Reedy's Mirror* has also published an attack on me, this time for my poem 'Patterns.' But Mr. Fletcher has answered it in the *Mirror,* if only they will publish it; and Mr. Untermeyer is to answer it in the *Chicago Evening Post.* You always said that you wanted me to be a storm-centre, and I hope you are satisfied." [10]

John Gould Fletcher was no fit opponent for Hervey and his howling cavalry charge. He was a foot soldier. His knees shook in battle and his voice turned squeaky when he grew excited. The *Mirror* did print his answer to Hervey, though, and it had a certain cogency. It was Hervey, not Miss Lowell, who was reading theories into her verse, Fletcher said. What Hervey objected to in her dramatic monologue "Patterns" could for the most part apply to Browning. As to innovation, she was a pioneer and explorer only because new forms were needed to fit her thought. Did Hervey expect her to write ballades and couplets? Did Mr. Hervey *dare* say that she had not attempted new forms? [11]

Perhaps Hervey dared, but he shifted his strategy when Miss Lowell carried the war into his own camp by coming to Chicago to lecture. She came, she saw, she overcame. She met Masters and Arthur Davison Ficke and made a lifelong friend of Carl

WAR OF THE IMAGISTS

Sandburg. She addressed a sold-out house at Maurice Brown's Little Theatre, with an overflow crowd listening out of sight in a nearby tearoom and a hundred or so turned away. In his account of his "Evening with the Imagists" Hervey gave only the faintest inkling of the success of the occasion. He tried to turn the imagists' weapons against them, saying he had gone to hear Miss Lowell merely out of curiosity: he wanted to see "how the wheels go round. And the New Poetry," he added, "is literally full of wheels—pin wheels, cart wheels, catherine wheels, fly wheels . . . They whizz, they grind, they crunch, they roar, they rumble, they clatter; raising, altogether, a very insistent rumpus and scattering clouds of dust and vapor." Then, calling on his sporting vocabulary to pile up metaphors, Hervey wished the little stage where Miss Lowell spoke had been a roped arena with a couple of bare-knuckle fighters to decide the issues she raised. Out there alone to do single battle, she had half disarmed him with her glowing countenance, her "ample" person, and ready smile, and he had found himself laughing despite himself and applauding with the rest. But he came away still skeptical. These new poets, "their mouths full of the shibboleths of freedom," were cumbered with rules. They claimed that they had restored humor to poetry. He had not known that it ever needed restoring.

"But I do agree," he ended, "that the Imagists have injected a whole lot of fresh humor into it—the most humorous thing of all being their own unconsciousness of how very, very funny they so often are."[12]

Reedy doubtless enjoyed these articles, for he went on printing Hervey's critical essays for several years, giving prominence to a series that was signed "Alliteraricus." But as the satire against the imagists became bitter, Reedy began to conceive a particular liking for the doughty Miss Lowell. He took pride in her allowing him to introduce another of her experiments, "An

Aquarium," which D. H. Lawrence found her finest poem. When her next book, *Men, Women and Ghosts,* appeared, in the fall of 1916, with "Patterns" in the van and "An Aquarium" bringing up the rear (all in good military order), Reedy was unequivocal in his praise.

Miss Lowell was reported to have said that God made her a businessman; she had made herself a poet. Reedy dissented. His reply was as graceful an appreciation as he knew how to write: "Amy Lowell is a poet by the grace of God, and to that grace is added a scrupulous art of form in seeming formlessness, whatever the unshakable adherents of the classical tradition may say to the contrary." He particularly liked her attitude toward the life around her, the tolerance she maintained even under stress of indignation or pity. It was this tolerance that endowed her work with genuine humor—"a spirit of conceding to life its liberty to be what it is." Her latest book was "poetry as authentic as any we know." It was "individual, innocent of echo and imitation, and in the main unique, with the uniqueness that comes of personal genius." [13]

To those who complained that the new poetry was lacking in melody, that it was obscure, hard, or doctrinaire in its conception, Reedy had other answers equally sweeping. He came as a peacemaker, like Fergus. "There is more poetry and good poetry being written to-day," he said in 1916, "than in the past twenty years." [14] His accounts of his reading were studded with similar remarks.

And now other voices were raised like swords in the *Mirror* to offset those of Hervey, and of his sympathizers in the letter columns. Odell Shepard wrote of the problems involved in using modern themes in place of ancient ones with their wealth of connotation and "all the immense accretion of suggestion" that attached to great events and ideas and names from the past. Vachel Lindsay begged the public to be satisfied with "good poets" and not to expect every talent to produce greatness. He advised his contemporaries to return not only to their home towns but also to the "old poets," whose discipline they needed to master if they were to succeed with the difficult new forms.[15]

Then Roger Sherman Loomis resumed the attack against "poetic truth" which he had begun when he supported Masters in the *Dial*. The realists, he said in the *Mirror*, were not out to shatter the fabric of morality. "They merely maintain that the whole truth is a better basis for a system of ethics than a partial or distorted truth." Poetry must deal with the problem of evil in all its shapes—political, religious, and psychological. Poetry must inspire the emotional reaction against evil in all its disguises.[16]

It was when she came to deal with these questions—especially those broached by the realists—that Amy Lowell broke with the *Mirror* a year later, in 1917. Her next book, *Tendencies in Modern American Poetry*, ignored a number of poets whose work had been given prominence in the *Mirror*. It omitted both Lindsay and Pound. Masters and Sandburg were chosen to represent the realist tendency, and Miss Lowell gave a harsh, unsympathetic comment on Masters. Here she parted company with Reedy, but by then both Reedy and Miss Lowell were being attacked on another front—or, to be precise, in the copious and vulnerable area, their rear. It was a guerilla attack executed with lethal skill by most wily enemies—the wiliest that imagism and "Amygism" had yet called forth.[17]

CHAPTER 19

ATTACK FROM THE REAR

For several years Reedy had fueled the poetic rage of Witter Bynner, who contributed his first little lyric to the *Mirror* in 1905 and in 1909 won an accolade: one of his poems reminded Reedy of Emily Dickinson. A strikingly handsome young man, popular with lecture audiences, Bynner endeared himself to fellow alumni with his "Ode to Harvard." But despite the wistful, nostalgic appeal of his ode and the neat craftsmanship of all his verse, Bynner sang small. As the poetic revival surged ahead and battle lines were drawn, his oaten treble was soon lost beneath the brassy tantaras and lilting band music. For six years the *Mirror* heard no more of his verse.[1]

"I ain't got no money to pay for poetry," Reedy told him just before acknowledging his recommendation of Lindsay in 1910. "And when I ain't got no money, you poets needn't come around."[2]

Bynner, like Masters, throve on rejection. Even in 1911, when two or three of his lyrics came out in the *Mirror*, Reedy was testing his mettle with sardonic comments on rejected poems and dyspeptic slurs on those that other editors had seen fit to buy. "It must be a new school of dryness you are trying to found. It doesn't get into me at all, but this may be because I'm getting old, rusty and resentful of innovation. Your last poem in the *Forum*, for instance; I couldn't make head nor tail of it. Maybe I'm poetically deaf to actinic melodies beyond the violet rays. Your 'Lincoln' . . . so wars with my conceptions of poetry that

ATTACK FROM THE REAR

I cannot bring myself to give it even such slight currency as the *Mirror* might provide . . ."[3]

Even more infuriating to Bynner must have been Reedy's insistence on comparing him with Louis How, a St. Louis poetaster whose slim volumes he did not have the heart to review himself, and wished Bynner would. "You and How are a new school of odd fish . . . and I can't make you out at all. Where's your juice? Poetry without juice is like faith without good works. . . ."[4] When Bynner later had the honor of composing the Phi Beta Kappa poem and reading it at Harvard, Reedy asked to see it, saying he always enjoyed reading Bynner's poems in hopes of finding a cryptogram in them.[5]

As an editor who had once served *McClure's*, Bynner seemed to take pride in standing up to such tirades; and as editorial consultant to the Boston book publishers, Small, Maynard & Company, he even asked permission to bring out a collection of Reedy's essays. Reedy refused to be disarmed. Many such requests had come to him, he said, and they were always turned down. "I don't care very much for my writing, anyhow, to tell the truth," he added; "and I'm strictly honest and sincere in this."[6]

But their common taste for radicalism in economics and for convention in poetry laid the basis for a friendship that tolerated, and even subsisted on, such relentless frankness. Bynner was addicted to good causes. Reedy said he would not espouse the cause of woman suffrage as Bynner suggested, because it was well known in his home town that he had no character. He no longer objected to socialism in general, yet would not stand for socialism in Bynner's poetry. And although he found the social content of Bynner's plays more acceptable, it was not until Bynner wrote one without topical reference that he could praise him unreservedly. In 1915 Bynner wrote an English version of Euripides' *Iphigenia in Tauris* for Isadora Duncan, who wanted her dance troupe to interpret the choral odes. When the poet went on the road to give public readings of the play he won Reedy's support. The enticing advance notices in the *Mirror* helped sell out the house for three St. Louis performances.

This visit, in the early part of January 1916, gave the two men a chance to meet on more affectionate terms than the critical acerbity of Reedy's letters might have promised. What preoccupied Bynner most at the time (it was while Hervey's attacks on Amy Lowell were appearing in the *Mirror*) was what he considered the pretentiousness and downright charlatanism of the new poetic schools, notably the Imagists. Being averse to schools in general, Reedy listened sympathetically to Bynner's angry talk. "You have left a very pleasant and fragrant memory behind you here," he wrote, when Bynner had gone on to Chicago. "Because you have passed this way all other peripatetic poets will have a warmer and better welcome." He nevertheless ended his letter by rejecting another poem.[7]

In Chicago Bynner, still heatedly talking down imagism and the schools, dined one night with an old Harvard friend, Laird Bell, a lawyer who owned an interest in that venerable Chicago review, the *Dial*. Afterwards they went with another friend to the Russian Ballet to see Diaghilev's production of *Spectre de la Rose*. Apparently Bynner was still fuming about Miss Lowell and her poetic school during the intermission, for Bell remonstrated quietly, saying that it was, after all, something to have founded a school. Bynner replied that that was something he could do himself. Glancing through his ballet program ("*Je suis le spectre de la rose / Que tu portait . . .*"), he added that he not only could but would. He would call his school "Spectrism."[8]

His next stop was Davenport, Iowa, where he planned to stay with another college friend, Arthur Davison Ficke, lawyer and poet. At Harvard they had been drawn together partly by a

ATTACK FROM THE REAR

common dislike of Wallace Stevens, who edited a college magazine to which they both contributed. Although by now a conservative Hartford insurance man, Stevens associated himself in poetry with the most fanciful and extreme of all the coteries, those who contributed to Alfred Kreymborg's little magazine, *Others*.

On their first evening together Bynner excitedly proposed that he and Ficke start a school to "burlesque the various Imagist and other cults." The Spectrist school was born in a bibulous mood. It consisted of two leaders, for the time being without followers. Bynner would write as "Emanuel Morgan," an unprosperous American painter just back from Paris; Ficke as "Anne Knish," a Hungarian bluestocking whose only book had been published in Russia. Both were to use the home of a Pittsburgh friend of Bynner as their address. Ficke soon afterwards wrote a memorandum recording the atmosphere of abandon in which the project was conceived. They had sat down almost at once to compose some little poems they called "spectra." After a day or two the game turned into work. "Our first efforts were rather crude and exaggerated, and because we feared we could not fool anyone with them alone, we went on and wrote some others in a little more serious way . . . Toward the end we wrote a few that really pleased us; and it was only Bynner's opportune departure, this third day of March, that prevented us from becoming seriously interested in further and genuine experiments, and thus perishing at the hands of the monster we had created." [9]

Meanwhile Reedy, who had received no answer to his friendly farewell letter, wrote Bynner again. It was the day after Bynner left Davenport, and Reedy (by coincidence) wondered whether his friend had been "eaten up by a blind tiger" in the desert. He enclosed a kindly paragraph he had written on *Iphigenia,* and a poem Bynner had sent in—which he rejected as usual. "The poem you send me to-day has me guessing. You are the most cryptic fellow that ever crypt into an editor's affection, and you are so doggoned fine and subtle that an editor always fears not to like your stuff, lest thereby he demonstrate himself a bonehead." [10] Bynner must have set his teeth, determined to do what he could to help Reedy demonstrate what he feared. The hoax now became his chief occupation.

That month Ficke went to Chicago, where he was invited to a luncheon to meet Miss Lowell, whose lecture at the Little Theatre was to take place the following week end. Soon afterward he sent her the manuscript of an article, "Modern Tendencies in Poetry"; and she replied superciliously, saying she feared that his wish to make a rhetorical point had run away with him. He spoke of schools of poetry—the obscure "Patagonians" and "Spectrists" among them. *Others* was a magazine, not a school, she retorted. "And I have already told you what I think of the Patagonians. I have never heard of the Spectric School." [11]

That exchange took place in April 1916, and Ficke's article did not come out until September. But meanwhile Bynner had begun to mention Spectrism, with an offhand air, in his lectures. He added a note to his copy of the memorandum Ficke had written about their first efforts, initialing it, "W.B., who two days ago began to perish of the monster by lecturing on it." [12]

In June the *Forum* contained an article which, although Ficke had written it, was signed by Emanuel Morgan and Anne Knish. It was illustrated by their poems, and mentioned casually that the authors had a book called *Spectra* coming out shortly. Kennerley was to be the publisher. Miss Lowell sent the article to her friend Fletcher, who told her he had never read worse rubbish. But Reedy reprinted the article.

Deftly, Bynner began to sow hints about the Spectrists where they would fall on fertile ground. He appealed to the snobbery of those who do not like to admit that they have not yet heard of a new name or a new thing. His skill at name-dropping won him an invitation to review the forthcoming book *Spectra* for the *New Republic,* founded in 1914 "to start little insurrections." Still incredulous that Kennerley would "print the fool thing" when he and Ficke completed it, Bynner accepted the assignment to review their own book with feigned reluctance.[13]

The Spectrist movement twined through all the intricate politics that had overtaken the poetic revival. As Ficke explained in Morgan and Knish's *Forum* article, which he turned into the preface for their book, the Spectrists had to go their own way because the other movements were destroying one another. Imagism had committed suicide when it consented to be "advertised by a concerted chorus of poet-reviewers." Vorticism, which Pound had created to take its place when Amy Lowell ran off with the leadership of the imagist movement, had meanwhile "died an ignominious death in London." Reedy at the time was irritating Pound by pretending to confuse him with Professor Roscoe Pound of Harvard, and adding to his annoyance by saying in a correction that Ezra Pound was now "head" of the Vorticist movement—to which Pound retorted that Vorticism *had* no head; he could not imagine his fellow-Vorticist Wyndham Lewis being "anyone's elbow or shinbone." [14]

When Miss Lowell's "An Aquarium" appeared she explained it as one of those poems calculated to give "the color, and light, and shade, of certain places and hours." [15] The *Forum* article and the preface covertly alluded to Miss Lowell's remark and her first book, *A Dome of Many Colored Glass,* with a skillful prose parody of the passage in "Adonais" from which she had taken its title. "The subject of every Spectrist poem has the function of a prism, upon which falls the white light of universal and immeasurable possible experience; and this flood of colorless and infinite light, passing through the particular limitations of the concrete episode before us, is broken up, refracted and diffused into a variety of many-colored rays." [16]

THE MAN IN THE MIRROR

Spectrism had another topical connotation. For more than a year St. Louis had been the focus of an international sensation arising out of the quasi-poetic utterances of a wraith named Patience Worth—ostensibly a seventeenth-century ghost. Patience produced long tales and poems through the Ouija board of a spiritualist medium, Mrs. John H. Curran. Sober editors and professors of literature and psychology were fascinated. Ouija boards became a national fad. And Reedy had been partly responsible, for he acknowledged that Patience Worth did produce poetry, of a sort. By 1916 the accumulation of ghost literature had become appalling and Reedy was bored with it, but that year one of Mrs. Curran's friends, an occasional contributor to the *Mirror*, received on *her* Ouija board what purported to be a novel by the late Mark Twain. Kennerley proposed to bring out the book and persuaded Reedy to write an introduction for it. Grumbling that he was "tired of this spook business" and that the medium who had heard from Mark Twain was one of his "pet afflictions and aversions," Reedy nevertheless allowed himself to be cajoled into writing the preface.[17] And the fad persisted. Amy Lowell and John Livingston Lowes made a point of calling on Mrs. Curran and conversing with her ghostly familiar.[18]

So the *Forum* article treated poetic connotations as specters that "haunt all objects both of the seen and the unseen world." These grotesque and shadowy projections or associations were what gives reality "its full ideal significance and its poetic worth." (Perhaps, too, its "Patience Worth.") "These spectres are the manifold spell and true essence of all objects,—like the magic that would inevitably encircle a mirror from the hand of Helen of Troy." [19] (Perhaps, too, a *Mirror* from the hand of William Marion Reedy?)

As they worked over their meticulous manuscript for the book, Bynner and Ficke became more than half serious. They traced their method to Poe's "Ulalume" and proposed to dedicate the volume to Poe, but later scratched out that dedication and inserted the name of Remy de Gourmont, Miss Lowell's "instructor in verbal shades." A passage in the Preface, likewise canceled, mentioned their old bête noire Wallace Stevens as Poe's literary descendant, and claimed him as the only living Spectrist besides themselves. "In his work," they had said of Stevens, "appears a subtle and doubtless unconscious application of our own method." [20]

So there was method in their madness. What it was came out later in an article Bynner wrote to explain the hoax. "The procedure was to let all reins go, to give the idea or phrase complete head, to take whatever road or field or fence it chose. In other words it was a sort of runaway poetry, the poet seated in the wagon but the reins flung aside." [21] One might say it was a technique in which the subconscious did the writing and the artistic censor was asked to sit back and pay no attention. Other poets to whom the Spectrists secretly tried to teach their method found it unlearnable. Some simply could not give rein to their fancy. Others turned out verse too bawdy to print. Only one was successfully indoctrinated—or rather coerced—into writing "spectra." Marjorie Allen Seiffert, a gifted and charming woman, was locked in her bedroom while her guests waited to be served dinner. With this inducement, passing out proof of her new-found skill under the bedroom door, she became a Spectrist. Later she explained that while Spectrism was basically a joke, "sub-basically it loosened up our styles, injected a lively sense of irony into our poetry, and did us all a lot of good." [22] Mrs. Seiffert took the Spectric pen name, Elijah Hay.

As the game went on the three conspirators succeeded in creating for themselves personalities so real that some swore they had met and talked with them. Alfred Kreymborg, the editor of *Others*, was bringing out a special number devoted

THE MAN IN THE MIRROR

to their poems. He spoke with "a gleam in his eye" of Anne Knish's great beauty. William Carlos Williams, who served as guest editor of the Spectrist Number of *Others*, wrote to Mr. Hay contrasting the virility of *his* lines with the female vagaries he noted in Miss Knish's. Former President Roosevelt, visiting his daughter, Mrs. Douglas Robinson, in New York, heard Bynner discuss the work of Morgan. A little later, in the same house, Reedy vainly tried to persuade Bynner that those spectra he talked about were better imagism than Miss Lowell's. And Masters, who was also there, followed up by writing a letter telling Morgan that Spectrism was at the core of things, Imagism at the surface.

A competent study of the hoax recently published by William Jay Smith contains the entire text of *Spectra* as Kennerley brought it out in 1916, together with later poems, both published and unpublished, by Morgan, Hay, and Miss Knish. There is no need to describe them here, therefore, save in a cursory way. In their grotesques Morgan and Miss Knish sought to build an emotional structure out of unguided verbal music, sharpen it with visual imagery, then shatter it with some outrageous sound or image whose wording might break the spell with comic dissonance. The musical factor is emphasized in their book, where the poems bear opus numbers rather than titles.

Morgan's Opus 15 opens with deep clarinet tones that bespeak longing, and continues,

> When the round and wounded breathing
> Of love upon the breast . . .

which a moment later is interrupted by the oboe's falsetto simile.

> Is not so glad a sheathing
> As an old vest . . .[23]

The sound that breaks the mood of his Opus 14 is more raucous.

ATTACK FROM THE REAR

> Beside the brink of dream
>   I had put out my willow-roots and leaves
> As by a stream
>   Too narrow for the invading greaves
> Of Rome in her trireme . . .
>   Then you came—like a scream
> Of beaves.[24]

The jabberwocky music of this seems to mean—one can't say what. Morgan has his moments of piety and tenderness, but madness predominates. Opus 6 is as catchy as Mark Twain's "Punch brothers, punch with care." He relies on rhyme schemes.

> If I were only dafter
>   I might be making hymns
> To the liquor of your laughter
>   And the lacquer of your limbs.[25]

Miss Knish, on the other hand, writes free verse. She is as female in her dark rages and harsh ironies as William Carlos Williams seems to have found her. She is more jagged than Morgan, though he has his disagreeable moods, too. In her Opus 181 she beckons beguilingly to a cat:

> Skeptical cat,
> Calm your eyes, and come to me.

Then suddenly her own feline nature asserts itself. "Come to me," she says,

> Or I will spring upon you
> And with steel-hook fingers
> Tear you limb from limb.[26]

When she writes parodies they are deadly. In Opus 187 she hits off Masters and the Freudians:

> I do not know very much
>   But I know this—
> That the storms of contempt that swept over us,

THE MAN IN THE MIRROR

> Ready to blast any edifice before them
> Rise from the fathomless maelstrom
> Of contempt for ourselves.[27]

She knows the "thousand sordid images" of T. S. Eliot, too, and mimics them in her Opus 195:

> Her soul was freckled
> Like the bald head
> Of a jaundiced Jewish banker.[28]

And her comment on the sanitary inadequacies of bohemian love affairs shows that, like Miss Lowell, she finds bath tubs poetic.

> If bathing were a virtue, not a lust,
> I would be dirtiest.[29]

Such lines were received by the newspaper columnists and the reviewers with derisive laughter or indignation. But then, that had been the reception accorded serious poets; as Bynner and Ficke had wanted to point out, mockery had served to make the names of Pound and Miss Lowell, of Kreymborg and the *Others* poets, familiar to the innocent public. They had invited it.

Reedy refused to be warned by the absurdities of the spectra or by any similarity he may have noted between the parodies and what they made fun of. "They are vitalized grotesques which at first seem like parodies of some recent poetry, but it is only seeming," he declared in an enthusiastic review of *Spectra*. He scented a trap, announced that it looked like a trap, then plunged rashly into it. Even without knowing who was their author, he found Bynner's poems cryptic, as usual. "Some of the poems read like riddles: they go along smoothly for a few lines and then leap a vast gap to some observation or reflection in startling contrast to what has gone before. In truth, these poems have the beauties and the oddities of

ATTACK FROM THE REAR

Chinese landscape painting . . ."[30] Frankly delighted by the Spectrists' "friskiness of thought and fancy," he warned that their enjoyment demanded a sense of humor. His own would soon be put to the test.

For his endorsement led others into the ambush. *Poetry* accepted some of the poems partly on the strength of his review. Three of the *Others* poems from the Spectrist Number found their way into *Current Opinion*. In July 1917 the *Little Review* printed one of Emanuel Morgan's spectra—with a parody of its own.[31] In a word, the Spectrists achieved as much recognition as several of the more zany schools they hoped to demolish.

John L. Hervey must have recognized the Spectrists as his allies, for he did not attack them. But he did attack the poetry of the subconscious, the kind they were writing. He singled out Conrad Aiken as his principal target, and in so doing again collided with Reedy, who was enthusiastic in his approval of Aiken's *Turns and Movies,* a work which had caused an editor to resign when *Poetry Journal* first brought it out. (It was Miss Lowell who induced Houghton Mifflin to accept *Turns and Movies* for their Poetry Series.)

Aiken, a more recent graduate of Harvard than Bynner, Ficke, and Stevens, was exploring the subconscious minds of vaudeville actors in his poetry. Like the Spectrists, he sought to use verbal music to convey feelings as inchoate as dreams. Unlike them, he was intentionally seeking to implement Freudian theory in his work. His poetry is full-fledged surrealism.

> My blood was tranced at night by the palest woman,
> But when I kissed her the blood in my veins went cold,
> Her mouth was as cold as the sea.
> Among the leaves she rose like fire;
> Her eyes were phosphor: her cold hands burned.
> But when the red sun clanged she fell from me.*[32]

* From *Collected Poems* by Conrad Aiken. Copyright 1953 by Conrad Aiken. Reprinted by permission of Oxford University Press, Inc.

THE MAN IN THE MIRROR

In these fantasies of a variety actor Hervey recognized elements directly inherited from the decadence. He called *The Jig of Forslin,* from which they are taken, a sample of the New Poetry's taboo on good taste. As he described the book, "We pass from the mauve wounds of the Saviour to a little, blue-eyed girl in Virgo loved by a syphilitic twice her age; from *fioriture* to fornication . . . It beats Gerard, promenading his live lobster through the boulevards at the end of a bright blue ribbon, to a pulp." [33]

Aiken replied in the *Mirror* to this scathing attack, revealing the serious purpose and thought animating his poetry. His answer is a terse, eloquent plea for a kind of poetic realism Masters had striven for, a realism that would conform not to a theory but to the newly recognized secret symbolism of man's buried life. "As the fairy-story, or the religious myth, or a melody, are wish-thoughts worked into beauty of outline . . . so the wish-thoughts presented in *The Jig of Forslin* are shaped as stories . . . presented with little or none of the self-consciousness which leads to analysis . . ." This reply to Hervey is one of the cogent and essential documents for a study of the influence of Freud and Jung on contemporary literature.[34]

Most of the discussion in the *Mirror* was on a lower plane. Reedy showed his sympathy for Freudian experiment not only by inviting Aiken to defend himself in the magazine, but by coming to Marjorie Allen Seiffert's defense when he published her "Portrait of a Lady in Bed," a poem which started a spate of ribald doggerel. There were *Mirror* readers ready to deny that even such psychoanalytic meditation as Mrs. Seiffert's contained anything genuinely new. One wrote:

> For my poor self I simply say:
> "Miss S. T. Coleridge! Please make way!
> 'The Ancient Mariner' of the 'hay!'" [35]

ATTACK FROM THE REAR

In a subtle way this implied that Mrs. Seiffert's lady in bed was afflicted with age-old concerns of the flesh, and that Coleridge had anticipated her poetic method by many years. The doggerel writer perhaps also wanted *her* to know that *he* knew Marjorie Allen Seiffert as Elijah Hay.

All this excellent fooling came to seem out of place as world conditions sickened. American troops were landing in France, and the world was about to be made safe for democracy. Ficke volunteered and went to France as captain in Ordnance. Later, he became Judge Advocate with the rank of major, finally earning decorations and a lieutenant colonelcy. In France, he had the exquisite pleasure of breakfasting with a brigadier general who knew all about the Spectrists. The school was a hoax, the general said, and admitted shyly that he himself was the real Anne Knish. By the following spring of bloody trench warfare, Bynner had grown weary of the business. It had been more than two years since his visit to St. Louis and his evening at the ballet with Laird Bell, the lawyer who owned an interest in the *Dial*. Conrad Aiken was now a *Dial* editor. Bynner must have asked one or the other of them to divulge the identity of the Spectrists. The exposé appeared in the *Dial*, but so unobtrusively as to escape the notice of the daily papers. So Bynner divulged again, this time while lecturing in Detroit. The *Detroit News* got the point. Within hours newspapers all over the country were regaling their readers with uproarious accounts of how learned critics and eminent poets had been duped, while their own editors and critics had seen through the hoax from the first. Reedy was, of course, one of the chief victims of their ridicule. Critics and editors of advance-guard reviews, squirming with embarrassment, turned on one another with recriminations.

Alice Corbin Henderson, who contributed to the *Mirror* as

THE MAN IN THE MIRROR

well as to *Poetry,* where she served as Miss Monroe's assistant, told in aggrieved tones of the perfidy of reckless poets, trifling with public confidence. While she said nothing of the spectra which *Poetry* had accepted (and not yet printed), she blamed Reedy for having "devoted an apparently serious review to *Spectra.*" Unaware that she was making matters worse, she accused all those who had misled her. "Mr. Alfred Kreymborg, the founder of *Others,* assured me solemnly that Emanuel Morgan and Anne Knish were . . . real persons, that he had had letters from them, and that he had actually met, I think he said, Elijah Hay . . ." [36]

The *New York Times* could take another tone; not having reviewed *Spectra,* it found the reviews Bynner showed its interviewer "delicious." The interviewer, Thomas Ybarra, was especially delighted with Reedy's remark about the poems being "vitalized grotesques" which seem like parodies—"but it is only seeming." Then he told how Reedy had taken his revenge. ("It was the only clever rejoinder of them all," Mrs. Ficke said later.) "When the story of the hoax came out . . . *Reedy's Mirror* got back at the graceless Bynner and Ficke by declaring that their work in *Spectra* was far more successful than anything else they had done before." [37] That was the line Reedy stuck to. He insisted that Bynner, in particular, had revealed his other self in the parodies, a poetic self far superior to the inhibited Harvard rhymster of the ode and the social causes.

Not unmindful of the wrath his efforts had inspired in their victims, Bynner seems to have thought that his best policy lay in the plea of split personality which Reedy had suggested. Or perhaps he was honestly persuaded that he was now two persons in fact. In any event he tried to make peace with those he had duped by blaming Emanuel Morgan for their deception. Impenitently he told Miss Monroe that Emanuel had been "enjoying himself in a manner not altogether foreseen by W.B.

ATTACK FROM THE REAR

In other words, he has got away from me and refuses to be called back."[38] He continued writing poems in Morgan's manner, and by July 1918 had accumulated nearly a hundred new ones, which he proposed to publish under his old pseudonym.

Reedy, who was staying in New York with Kennerley when he received Bynner's new manuscript, found the poems "peppered all over with tremendously good things." He persuaded Bynner to drop the name of Morgan. "You killed him, —let him stay dead." It was arranged that the *Mirror* should publish the poems anonymously as "Songs of the Unknown Lover." Later, Alfred Knopf, who had served out his apprenticeship under Kennerley and was now publishing on his own, would bring out the book as *The Beloved Stranger*. Reedy provided the preface.[39]

In it he tells something of his part in the *Spectra* story, admitting he was a victim of the hoax but claiming that the phenomenon of poetic *Doppelgängerei* has greater interest than the satiric deception and its effect. Morgan and Miss Knish reminded him of "Fiona McLeod," whose poems he and Mosher had printed from the turn of the century until William Sharp died in 1905 and was discovered to have been their author. What interested Reedy even more than those aspects of poetic schizophrenia, which he was happy to leave to the psychiatrists, was whether readers might discover in such poems *their* "unsuspected" other selves.

At least one reader flatly refused to try. "It is very 'sporting' of you to attempt the dual personality plea," Miss Lowell wrote Bynner after she had been exhaustively pilloried as the Spectrists' chief victim; "but how will it affect the dear public, so ignorant, and so fearful of being made a fool of?" She wondered in what terms a lady should acknowledge a gentleman's admission "that perhaps he had made a mistake in trying to cut her throat." Then she forgave him freely—and warned her friends privately to consider him her deadliest enemy, never to be trusted again. The correspondence between Miss Lowell and "Dear Emanuel" went on for months. It was not until after her death that Bynner learned how implacable her hatred had been.[40]

He sent one of her first letters to Reedy, who found it an "interesting exposition of Amy." Reedy was glad to find her friendly, as he supposed, for he had the strongest kind of liking for the dauntless lady and valued her sense of humor. What if her political and poetical views were not exactly his own? What if she still imagined that poetry could be bred in schools?

"I must confess," he said in this regard, "that I don't get her point of view at all. To me all these schools of literature are 'literature' when they're good and 'schools' when they aren't." [41]

PART FOUR

THE AFTER-IMAGE

CHAPTER 20

WAR AND REACTION

SHADOWS of war hang low over the land. Yet the greenness of the Ozarks after centuries of arson hints at a power of healing that might repair the scars of hellfire. Never were the amenities of country life more precious; Reedy's poise through the years of perilous neutrality partly reflects the loveliness of Clonmel and Mrs. Reedy's skill as its chatelaine.

"Clonmel is beautiful," writes a house guest, "even when its tall shade trees are naked; its orchard trees as lean and black as widows; its grass locked in ice." The land "lays high," as they say there; it is fair and cedar-pointed, edged with purple. Manchester Road, once a trail for Mexico-bound caravans, disappears into the Ozark uplift, hills heaved up from the primeval floor of an ocean. In spring the plowlands will be dotted after a rain with bits of flint tools older than the mounds themselves, and with fossils of seashells perhaps older than man. After spring the lonely whistle of quail and dove gives over, and summer nights are exuberant with katydid and whippoorwill and mockingbird. When the fierce heat of Sunday afternoon dies down the guests sit drinking in the shady grape arbor beside Mrs. Reedy's kitchen. The Madam (as Reedy says) sets a good table. Her pride is her produce: hams from the smokehouse, hens that foraged the barnlot, veal and sweet butter from her own dairy, iced melons and greens from her garden. On an autumn evening, walking up from the station, Reedy will be met by the scent of wood smoke and the yelp of delighted dogs—a hound named Beauty and Falstaff the Airedale, gift of a generous brewer. Though only a short walk from the devouring suburbs, Clonmel lies in a gracious countryside of neat German farms and whitened brick farmsteads with pollarded sycamores and duck ponds under willows.

Chatting across the fence with his farm neighbors, grandsons of Blair's and Brokmeyer's followers who still vote Republican in memory of Lincoln, Reedy cannot believe stories of German soldiers who cut off the hands of Belgian babies. "More democracy is the cure for the war-madness," he had written on his return from war-tossed England. "There is not enough of it now anywhere." [1] He had held high hopes for Wilson. From his observation point in the country, that hope dies hard. Even confronted with the newfangled horrors of mechanical warfare that invents refinements on famine and pestilence, poisoning the very air and sparing neither helpless age nor scared children, he sees a fleck of hope. "There is not a person on the planet who is not hurt by this war," he writes that first Christmas, wondering whether the dark ages have returned. But he remembers that man learns most from what most hurts him. "Maybe, I think, the world needed this shock of universal pain. The world has been growing too smug. It was undoubtedly too much concerned with progress and property. So much so that it wouldn't look behind them to see the suffering that was there, that is always there." [2] Somehow universality of anguish must restore the lost sense of brotherhood, and he wonders why there had been no peacetime fellowship in happy prosperity.

If the quiet pleasures of country life give one form of relief from the gloom of war, literary excitements afford another. The literary prestige of the magazine had been steadily rising, and Reedy's style achieved a corresponding dignity. Repose it never attained, but it won at times a quality verging almost on restraint. From the publication of *Spoon River Anthology* onward, Reedy's personal reputation continued to mount. He was constantly quoted or written up in the magazines and in newspaper columns. It was in this period that an editor in *Town and Country* captioned his portrait with the remark quoted earlier: "Not to know Reedy argues yourselves unknown." More and more young writers were attracted to him for stimulation, guidance, and a first hearing. Padraic Colum, William Rose Benét, Babette Deutsch, Carl Van Vechten, and Maxwell Bodenheim were among the newcomers.

Reedy had an important function to perform for young beginners striving for recognition in an increasingly clamorous arena. Most of those writers who had revitalized poetry and fiction in the prewar years had been nearing middle age when the revival began. Having published their first fugitive efforts around the turn of the century, they had been exposed to the confusions of the waning decadence. Yet most of them had had a decent respect for older traditions beaten into them by critics like Reedy, Pollard, and Huneker. However daring and rebellious they might become, their most radical efforts grew out of the conviction that older forms could not be made to fit the substance of what they had to say about America, an old industrial nation but a new world power. The younger hopefuls had to compete for the attention of an increasingly shock-proof public. Reedy's innate conservatism benefited them, discouraging innovation for its own sake and frowning on affectation. His hard-bought political radicalism won their confidence and led them to heed his fundamental respect for tradition in literary matters.

Hence his influence was especially salutary during a time of increasing political reaction that had begun with the election of William Howard Taft and had become intensified in the atmosphere of war. A counterrevolutionary reaction in poetry had begun during this time, too, and Reedy himself was

THE MAN IN THE MIRROR

affected by it. This he showed when he was chosen, with Bliss Perry of Harvard and Jessie B. Rittenhouse of the Poetry Society of America, to select a book of poetry to win the cash award to be dispensed by Columbia University along with the first Pulitzer prizes. (Joseph Pulitzer having omitted to offer a poetry prize—an omission eloquent of his time—the Poetry Society had found another patron to make up the deficiency for the first year or two, retaining the right to choose its own jury.) Reedy was the one member of the jury to whom Miss Monroe did not take exception.

"No one," she said, "could question Mr. Reedy's competence as a judge of modern poetry." [3]

Of the dozen competitors who could be considered, Pound, H.D., Lindsay, and Bynner all had suitable entries, books published in 1917. Reedy voted for Bynner's *Grenstone Poems,* which represented a return to convention after the dalliance with spectral surrealism. It was a choice Masters probably would have concurred in, since he soon afterwards wrote a preface for Knopf's new edition of *Grenstone*. But Professor Perry and Miss Rittenhouse insisted on giving the prize to Sara Teasdale for her *Love Songs*. It was a reactionary choice, but one Reedy could not quarrel with for long. He had been extravagant enough to class Miss Teasdale with Burns and Heine when he reviewed the poems, praising their poignancy. "The words fall into order with an entrancing inevitability and appropriateness," he had said. "Her songs are as nearly perfect as any songs may be. Their melody ever befits their thought." [4] So when the committee outvoted him he could only murmur that he would "get more credit in St. Louis" than he deserved.[5] And when the prize was announced there was little for him to add. The first poet he had introduced and could still acclaim had been rewarded for her devotion to craftsmanship. She had received the highest distinction her contemporaries could accord an American poet. Reedy could only say that the *Love Songs* were "as nearly flawless lyrics as ever were penned." [6]

Miss Teasdale had been somewhat affected by the revolutionary trends that set in around 1914, but she had recovered. No longer warbling of girlish frustrations, she had now come to know the reality of love and mourn its evanescence. Her voice gained a certain husky vehemence as she resented the finality of death:

> With envious dark rage I bear,
> Stars, your cold complacent stare;
> Heart-broken in my hate look up,
> Moon, at your clear immortal cup,
> Changing to gold from dusky red—
> Age after age when I am dead.* [7]

But her overriding loyalty was to song, and her prosody was what she had learned from Reedy's old friend William Vincent Byars. "All these new poets seem to think that because the Greeks didn't use rhyme, they wrote in free verse," she had told her husband while the *Spoon River* debate was raging. "Nothing could be further from the truth." She admitted that the new poets had put her under an "incalculable debt," but felt that melody was being neglected, and that it is indispensable. "It seems to me that these new poets are compressing and hardening their work until their poems are like pellets of condensed food.—They may contain a great deal, but they aren't palatable. If you take a poem like 'Under the greenwood tree' from *As You Like It*, you will find not a single image.—All is melody. There is not even a striking idea. Now the vitality of this poem is beyond question. It must appeal deeply to the human soul for some reason." [8] This was the point of view the first "Pulitzer" rewarded.

* Reprinted with permission of the publisher from *Collected Poems* by Sara Teasdale. Copyright 1937 by The Macmillan Company.

THE MAN IN THE MIRROR

And Masters, the most influential rebel against metric conventionality, seemed to have fallen into step. He had by now reverted happily to strict blank verse, as in "Autochthon," one of his many long poems first published in the *Mirror*. The broken rhythms, the jagged syncopations and true elegiac overtones of the *Spoon River* cadence had slipped away. Compare, for example, the last lines of his Anne Rutledge epitaph in the *Anthology*:

> Bloom forever, O Republic,
> From the dust of my bosom! [9]

with the last stanza of "Autochthon:"

> There is a windless flame where cries and tears,
> Where hunger, strife, and war and human blood
> No shadow cast . . . [10]

It is apparent at once that he has bought sonority at the expense of sharpness, accent, and exultation. The liberation he had won for poetry no longer belonged to his own poetry.

Among *Mirror* contributors only Miss Lowell held out in the face of the mounting tide of poetic reaction. When Reedy praised her *Can Grande's Castle* in 1918 it was because the other critics had "hammered" it—a fact of which the lady herself seems to have been blissfully unaware. This particular book won a surprising victory for Miss Lowell, for it was praised without qualification by her old enemy, John L. Hervey. The editor of the *Horse Review* even admired in it Miss Lowell's "Bronze Horses."

But it is worth noting that other readers of the *Mirror* more and more vehemently rejected Miss Lowell's experiments, which now explored territory opened up to her not only by Conrad Aiken's surrealism but by her mockers the Spectrists. Reedy reported to her that forty bewildered subscribers had written in for an explanation of her poem "Gargoyles." She obliged, saying the poem presented "the utter impossibility of amalgamation between the top and the bottom under the figure of an ordinary merrymaking." He printed the explanation, but being no friend to *explications de texte,* laughed it out of court. "There now," he exclaimed. "Is the poem a darn bit better after it is explained?" [11]

He himself complained to Miss Lowell that her "Chopin" (probably suggested to her by one of Anne Knish's cat spectra) was obscure. In this case her reply was of such significance that future editors would do well to append it to the poem at every reprinting.[12] But habitués of the *Mirror* remained hostile. The same reader who had greeted the first garlands of Masters' "Anthology" with a sympathetic prose-poem visualizing the Spoon River cemetery ("the shunned God's acre, baking under an August sun") responded to "Gargoyles" with vicious and tasteless doggerel. After having been exposed to the mimicry of the Spectrists, however, and after witnessing Hervey's surrender before *Can Grande's Castle,* no one seems to have been disturbed by such an image as Miss Lowell's "grinning jaw-bone in a bed of mignonette." The war had brought about a certain callousness to the macabre.

As it became apparent that America would enter the war, Reedy, one way and another, kept his poise. He tried hard to maintain an attitude of neutrality. Yet for a self-styled Irishman living both in an intellectual environment where German was spoken by the elite and in a countryside where the farmers' accent is thick with German, he was singularly open to arguments favoring the British.

"I've only read one pro-German article yet, in this country, that impressed me," he told his old friend Thekla Bernays in 1915; "that was Kuno Meyer's in a recent issue of the *Atlantic.*"[13] Miss Bernays had been writing articles on "The Soul of Germany" for the *Mirror,* and Reedy was trying conscientiously to coach her. He told her not to forget "the services of the Germans in digging up so many facts about early English literature, from *Beowulf* down" or what Kuno Meyer had done for her "Irish fellow-neutrals" and their poetry.[14]

By 1917 Reedy had acquiesced in the conclusion most Americans had reached, that we must go to war against Germany. But later, as the war dragged on, he was overcome by disenchantment with Wilson and the propaganda that had involved us in it. The reasons for having gone to war came to seem scarcely valid.

For one thing, Reedy was convinced that the causes of war were economic rather than political. All nations had shared the same economic fallacies. "Both sides," he wrote, "made the war inevitable. Both sides are wrong. And neither side can win save at such cost as may well give it pause." [15] Yet he could not concur in the *New Republic's* formula either, that the end object should be "peace without victory." Wilson had seized on that slogan, but like other Wilsonian aphorisms "peace without victory" resembled the propaganda of those who wanted a League to Enforce Peace. Such arguments seemed to Reedy merely a ruse intended to "perpetuate the supremacy of Great Britain as a world power." He kept going back to economic fundamentals, and his one hope was freer trade—"a world without tollgates." If this would not eliminate the national rivalries that had led to war, he said, "at least we would get rid of what all are agreed is the chief cause of war —the economic conflict that intensifies nationalism into madness." [16] A world of "free seas and free land," one where unused natural resources would be taken out of private hands by taxation, would remove restrictions on opportunity both for individuals and for nations. Such had been the contention of Henry George.

The war's greatest threat seemed to Reedy the willful sacrifice of that scale of values wherein the ultimate prize is personal freedom and human dignity. "We cannot abolish liberty to save liberty," he wrote soon after America joined the conflict. "We should not make war on German music, art, letters, philosophy, language. Our business is to smash German autocracy. And we should be as kind as possible to our own German-Americans while we are doing it. Now is the time to show them what American liberty means." [17]

Out in the country such home talk might sound reasonable, but it was by no means a popular line to take in town, where St. Louis Germans were being attacked in the streets, denounced by zealots if they went to the theater, and daily insulted in the press. Berlin Avenue was renamed Pershing Avenue, and South Side Germans were encouraged to stay on their side of the tracks that run through Mill Creek Valley. There was even talk of forbidding their crossing the bridges.

Reedy was as unafraid of being labeled pro-Communist as pro-German. From the signing of the Brest-Litovsk treaty between the Central Powers and the Russian revolutionists, at the start of 1918, he advocated cooperation with the Soviets as the only effective counter to German autocracy in the East. He maintained this stand while agents of Attorney General A. Mitchell Palmer were hauling alleged communists and anarchists out of their beds and loading them on ships headed for Russia, Reedy's friend Emma Goldman among the first boatload. From the time of their trial he also defended Thomas J. Mooney and Warren K. Billings of the International Workers of the World, who were convicted for their part in the Preparedness Day bombings in San Francisco and condemned to death. Reedy kept pointing out that it was well known they had been found guilty on the basis of perjured testimony and subornation of perjury. With similar indifference to consequences, he opposed the discharge of two pro-German professors from Columbia University, a patriotic gesture by President Nicholas Murray Butler which caused Professor Charles A. Beard to resign in protest.

Visiting New York in the autumn of 1919, Reedy learned of the secret hearings by which a zealous committee headed by New York State Senator Clayton R. Lusk sought to silence teachers and writers whose views its members did not share. Their method seemed an ironic commentary on Wilson's phrase-making. As Reedy said, "It can choke off eventually every plea for justice to little nations or mercy to political prisoners, every protest against the iniquity of coercion and the insolence of office. Such a thing as the Lusk Committee is doing was inconceivable before we went to war to make the world safe for democracy." [18]

He found himself constantly pleading the cause of literary friends against the efforts of government and patriotic volunteers to suppress their work. George Sylvester Viereck was evicted from the Poetry Society of America, and Reedy urged that he be reinstated. While lecturing at the University of California, Bynner was attacked for having petitioned Secretary of War Newton D. Baker on behalf of those who had been persecuted for their opinions. Reedy called the move to expel Bynner "Prussianism at Berkeley." [19]

But the friend whose German name and sympathies demanded Reedy's most frequent support was Theodore Dreiser, always the lone and sitting duck for censorship.

CHAPTER 21

DREISER AND HARRIS MERTON LYON

SINCE abandoning magazine work in 1910 Dreiser had established himself as a novelist, however controversial his standing. Yet despite his continuing need for supporters he had a way of sloughing off old friends. Arthur Henry, who first lured him into writing fiction, had slipped away, as had the young editorial assistant Harris Merton Lyon, who had been like a son. While still editing the *Delineator,* Dreiser had become more intimate with Henry Louis Mencken than he had ever been with either of them. But he still kept in touch with Reedy, in part because he valued the editorial support he could count on in the *Mirror,* but more because Reedy was his ally in an increasing number of battles for freedom of expression, starting with the critical debate over *Spoon River Anthology.*

Reedy had meanwhile taken over the sponsorship of Lyon, whom Dreiser had left behind on the *Broadway* to be spoiled (as Dreiser thought) by the magazine's publisher. Having already published a few stories and poems and having praised the irony of Lyon's *Sardonics,* which might have succeeded had not the publishers failed, Reedy was determined to keep the young man's work before the public. He reprinted several of the *Sardonics* stories in the *Mirror,* called Lyon to Kennerley's attention, accepted other stories Lyon could not sell to better-paying magazines, and in August 1913 invited him to contribute a regular column of letters, or familiar essays, to the *Mirror*. In January 1914 Reedy brought out a second collection of Lyon's stories under the title *Graphics,* one of Reedy's rare ventures into book publishing. Kennerley had probably turned the book down, like most publishers considering short-story collections by little-known authors a hopeless form of speculation.

Alexander Harvey of *Current Literature,* who was bringing out a story collection of his own that year, reviewed *Graphics* for the *Mirror*. He marveled at Lyon's power. "He is, indeed, I think, America's most powerful writer of short stories," Harvey wrote. "He arrests one like the ancient mariner who 'stoppeth one of three,' and for my part I am like the wedding guest—I cannot choose but hear. Harris Merton Lyon seizes his reader, bears his reader off like the heroic figure in melodrama who carries the heroine away in his arms." It was not always a pleasant experience reading Lyon, Harvey implied, but it was one nobody was likely to forget.[1] Harvey's calculation proved absurdly optimistic. Far from stopping one of three readers, *Graphics* sold less than fifty copies. It was a publishing venture more dismal than Percival Pollard's *The Imitator* had been, and far less successful than the publication of Ernest McGaffey's *Sonnets to a Wife,* whose second edition still enjoyed a trickle of sales after a dozen years. Reedy never published a book he thought anyone else would touch. No best-seller sailed under his ensign.

Not in the least daunted, he encouraged Lyon to go on with a second series of letters for the *Mirror*. The young writer had bought a farm at North Colebrook, near Norfolk, in the northern hills of Connecticut. His letters or essays, "From an Old Farmhouse," were anonymous. That was Reedy's method of piquing the curiosity of his readers. Mainly literary in theme, they covered a wide range of topics: Congreve, the spirit of satire, the low tastes and character of publishers, Mencken's opinion of H. G. Wells, the excellence of Fred L. Pattee's *History of American Literature since 1870*. A year after the series started Lyon got around to his old mentor Dreiser, whom he now considered superior to all other American novelists— "One man writing in this country to-day who is worth the lot of them." For Lyon the author of *The Titan* had both the inscrutability and the clarity that mark the prophet. Lyon did not assert the privilege of the prophet himself, but dealt with the novelist in unassuming, straightforward terms, relating Dreiser's success in fiction to his editorial training.

For years he prepared magazines for the simple people; and he seems in that work to have convinced himself that it will never do to take for granted that the mob is already apprised of a fact. Once, riding in the subway, he opened a copy of the *Evening World* and showed me the line: "Let us introduce you to the work of Rudyard Kipling." I scoffed, saying people already knew that work. Dreiser said, No, they don't; they have to be introduced to everything. To believe that, and yet to write novels, requires infinite patience. It also lays the ghost of "style"; for perhaps one-half of style is repression. The stylist is the man who withholds his pen.[2]

"Who the devil wrote this?" Mencken asked Dreiser in his next letter from Baltimore. "It is a fine piece of writing—the best thing about you ever printed."[3] Dreiser answered that he did not know. "From an Old Farmhouse" could have been the work of any one of three farm dwellers he knew, though Masters, whose epitaphs Mencken had not yet noticed in the *Mirror*, had told Dreiser the series was by Lyon.

"I wish you could find out," Dreiser told Mencken, Reedy being still away in England. "It would please me much if Lyon had done it."[4] He considered Mencken to be somewhat better situated to discover the authorship of the article than he was, because Mencken had for several months been the co-editor of *Smart Set* (formerly one of Colonel Mann's publications) and was therefore in a position to know what was going on in the magazine world. Despite the name he was making for himself with his novels, Dreiser still hankered after that world. He was perhaps a little envious of Mencken's editorship and even of Lyon's column in the *Mirror*, whose authorship he soon confirmed. He volunteered his impressions of the editorial policy of *Smart Set* in a detailed and withering letter to Mencken. "Take a tip from Reedy . . . and do the serious critical thing in an enlightening way." [5] Then, in the fall of 1915, he asked Reedy to let him write a regular New York letter for the *Mirror*. He wondered also whether he might be paid for such a series. "You were one of the few who praised *Sister Carrie* originally," he recalled with unwonted modesty, "and I have never lost your favor—not yet, anyhow." [6]

"Pay anything? Heavens!" Reedy answered, horrified, and went into elaborate protestations. One reason he could not pay Dreiser for such a column was that too many unemployed newspapermen depended on him for sustenance during these bitter times. "Good to hear from you though. Masters tells me your forthcoming novel is going to be a stunner. Glad of that. I've enjoyed all your work—its honesty, its care, its passionate intensity for truth, its lack of definite propaganda [or] programme." He went on to discuss Masters, ("a big fellow. This hit hasn't turned a hair on him.") and to take up a complaint Dreiser had made, that Reedy was too lenient in handling his writers.

Perhaps Dreiser had in mind Harris Merton Lyon: "As for Lyon, I give him a free hand because I believe that's best for a writer. I check him now and then, and bawl him out. But he's not a frequent mis-fire. I like the quality of his work, like that of good old sherry that you can chew the flavor of. He's got it on most of the contemporary writers in that he isn't treacly sweet nor a hysteric gloomster. Me for H.M.L. as a man due for a big strike. But—" [7]

It was a prophetic "but," for Lyon died the following year,

in June 1916, his work the delight of a number of professional writers though still unknown to the larger public. Doubtless Reedy had meant to disclose the authorship of the letters "From an Old Farmhouse" when the time should be right and public curiosity had reached a point where the disclosure might create a sensation. That had been done in the case of Masters' epitaphs and attempted in introducing Bynner's "Songs of the Unknown Lover." But Lyon had not yet arrived. After almost three years the letters still remained anonymous. It was only in an obituary written by Carl Sandburg and sent to the *Mirror* that one could begin to put together some of the roles Lyon had played in his obscurity. It told how O. Henry had admired Lyon's stories and asked Lyon to finish his own incomplete ones when he was dying. Whether Lyon did so he did not say, but Sandburg also told of letters he and others had written to Reedy urging him to persuade Lyon to write more. He told of Lyon's encouraging letters to Masters when Masters was working on the "Anthology."

"Harris Merton Lyon paid some of the costs of being a truth-telling artist," Sandburg concluded. "Yet, along with Stevie Crane, the big, free, glad way he roamed through most of his life makes a good life, a rich life to look back on." Unhappily it was also a short one; Lyon was just thirty-four.[8]

What Sandburg did not know (and few could) was the bitterness of Lyon's despair at having failed to attain his goal before he died. Reedy had seen him at Clonmel only a few months before the end. It was the third and last time they met, and he mentioned the occasion to Dreiser long afterwards, and with the greatest reluctance. "Poor Lyon—my God, how he burned for fame, for fame based on excellence; how he scorned the idea of writing for the market. I hurt in the heart every time I think of him—the more so since our last meeting was marred by a clash between women over something the nature of which I was never able to make out. Lyon and his wife decamped from my house, Lyon with his doom on him (as I knew from his doctors) . . . It sickened the soul of me, for I loved Lyon, and he was one man who really believed in me." [9]

Dreiser, who had once thought of Lyon as his wayward son and had afterward become convinced that the boy was a trifler, spoiled by his first taste of success, was overcome by a mixture of powerful feelings centering around Lyon. He may have envied the talent he thought Lyon had wasted. He had been too jealous to pay much attention to the letters "From an Old Farmhouse" after discovering who was writing them. Reedy had turned down his own offer of a New York letter, even when he proposed to write it gratis. Reedy rejected a one-act play of Dreiser's, saying simply that he did not like it. Unconsciously Dreiser may have felt guilty, having sometimes wished for Lyon's death (as he said) and feeling secretly relieved at his rival's removal. Now Lyon was dead Dreiser became avid for knowledge of all that concerned him. He asked Reedy for Mrs. Lyon's address and followed his suggestion of going to see her. When he came to write of his association with Lyon, he concluded the account: "On the last day, realizing no doubt how utterly indifferent his life had been . . . [Lyon] broke down and cried for hours. Then he died." * [10]

Whether Lyon had lived "a good life, a rich life," as Sandburg supposed, or a life embittered by frustration, as Dreiser assumed, no one will ever know. But for readers of the *Mirror* he became another Chatterton.

While Lyon's death served to renew the old ties between Dreiser and Reedy, the influence of Mencken tended to sunder them. Reedy had been interested in Mencken's study of Friedrich Nietzsche in 1908 and had been entertained by Mencken's collaboration with Willard Huntington Wright on a travel book,

* Quotations from *Twelve Men* by Theodore Dreiser are reprinted by permission of The World Publishing Company. Copyright 1919 by Boni & Liveright, Inc.; copyright 1949 by Helen Dreiser.

Europe after 8:15, just before war broke out. As his own feelings became more antagonistic toward German imperialism and reverence for supermen, Reedy grew impatient with the Nietzschean point of view and openly disapproving of Mencken's influence on Dreiser. "Mr. Mencken writes of things *à la* Nietzsche, smashingly, but he says that Nietzsche went soft before he died and there is danger that Theodore Dreiser will go soft too . . . and 'arrange himself with the tripe-sellers of orthodoxy,'" wrote Reedy. He recognized the bond of Germanic culture between Dreiser and Mencken, and regarded it as a threat. "In my opinion Dreiser has not found himself. And he won't find himself by becoming a Nietzschean or anything but Dreiser. The worst danger Dreiser is in is taking himself too seriously. He will suffer eclipse if he falls wholly into the school of Mencken and Willard Huntington Wright, riant amoralists and Teutomaniacs." [11]

The thought that Dreiser had not found himself was based on Reedy's evaluation of *The "Genius."* The summer Lyon died this novel had been attacked by the Society for the Suppression of Vice, which had forced booksellers to remove it from their shelves. Whatever his view of its literary shortcomings, Reedy was among the hundreds who joined in the battle against this form of censorship. He was collaborating with Dreiser on another project as well. Soon after Lyon's death Dreiser conceived the plan of bringing out a collection of the young man's short stories and enlisted Reedy's aid. Dreiser proposed to gather and edit them if Reedy would review the selection and write the preface.[12] While the battle against censorship of *The "Genius"* raged in the courts and in the press, Dreiser became absorbed in leafing through Lyon's manuscripts, tracking down missing stories, writing to Reedy, Mencken, and other editors for clues to published material. He worked at the project on and off for nearly four years, from the summer of 1916 until after the war ended. Meanwhile he published his own first collection, *Free and Other Stories,* with its reminis-

THE MAN IN THE MIRROR

cent yarn about Red Galvin. He asked Reedy's permission to include the "Old Rogaum" story the *Mirror* had printed in 1901, tactlessly offering to return the small sum Reedy had paid him for it in that dark hour.[13]

Although enthusiastic at first, Reedy presently became doubtful about the prospects for a collection of Lyon's stories, remembering how unsuccessful he had been in his effort to find Lyon a publisher when he was alive and promising. He nevertheless consented once more to help Dreiser carry out his plan. Again, in the spring of 1918, he promised to look through the manuscripts after Dreiser had made his selection. "I was exceedingly fond of that boy," Reedy explained, "and admired his work this side of idolatry." But he voiced a feeling he had had all along, that the best of Lyon was in his "Old Farmhouse" essays, not in the stories.[14]

It took another year for Dreiser to complete his selection and for Reedy to get around to examining them. Then, in the spring of 1919, three years after Lyon's death, Reedy came out with the regretful admission that they all seemed flat and dated now. "Not one of these stories *gets* me in the way a good story should. Lots of cleverness . . . but . . . I can hear the springs creak and the wheels click. So far as the unprinted things are concerned, I believe they justify the editors who rejected them." [15] By this time Reedy was having serious trouble with his eyes and lived in fear of blindness. He wished Dreiser would write the preface, though he would still do what Dreiser thought best. Dreiser felt Reedy's sponsorship was essential and kept pressing him for his copy. Reedy kept complaining of his eyes and of lethargy, putting off the task. Then Dreiser's *Twelve Men* came out, a collection of life studies including the pathetic yet shattering portrait of Lyon as "De Maupassant, Junior"— an ironic and ambiguous title. The story is successful in bringing to life the writer of the "farmhouse" letters. It is told by a magazine editor, who relates how the talented young writer came to him as an arrogant youth, became spoiled by the magazine's publisher, was lost or cast off when the editor took another job, reappeared from time to time as a would-be man of letters and gentleman farmer, and died leaving suitcases full of old manuscript, which his fatherly former editor sorted as best he could. "But they are still unpublished." Poignant as Dreiser's tale of the abortive literary career may be, it tells more about Dreiser than about its hero, "L———." Reedy's first reaction was "Wonderful!" [16]

But when Lyon's mother happened to call at his office he must have found her most unlike the "iron woman," the "rough man-woman," of Dreiser's tale. Mrs. Lyon had not heard of Dreiser's new book, but since she was bound to do so in time, Reedy gave her a copy. She returned a day or two later, in deep pain and towering indignation. She was distressed by the imputation of her son's illegitimacy, but far more so by what purported to be his savage impression of herself—"at times coarse and vulgar, but a mother to him 'all right.'" She suspected that Dreiser had got his impression not from her dead son, but from the jealous daughter-in-law she had lately been supporting.[17] Reedy was sympathetic and tried hard to convince the bereaved mother that Dreiser was writing fiction, not biography. He explained the principles of the novelist's art, but it was no use. The explanations didn't "appeal" to her, he told Dreiser.[18]

"I don't mean this in criticism of you," Reedy concluded his report to Dreiser. "Your literary methods and your conception of your art are your own and justifiable, and of course if you get hold of wrong facts or perverted facts you are not to blame." Yet clearly he feared Dreiser was to blame, and his session with Mrs. Lyon had been intensely disconcerting. Dreiser himself may have had misgivings, for in telling Mencken who the twelve men of his portrait series were, he wondered if Mrs. Lyon would "kick."[19] Then, with god-like indifference, he was off on his plans for a companion volume, *A Gallery of Women*.

It was about this time that Dreiser received a call from a

young woman who introduced herself as his distant cousin. After a brief interval she came to live with him and he shrugged off the wife he had brought from St. Louis years before. His cousin changed her name to his, became ambitious for a career in motion pictures, and soon persuaded him to move to Hollywood.[20]

Meanwhile there were events of greater moment for Reedy to deal with. The world was on fire, and a wave of repression seemed to have swept away all the liberties for which Americans had been told they must willingly fight and bleed. Reedy and Dreiser continued to collaborate on many causes aimed at reversing the prevailing mood of savagery and repression. Reedy published two Dreiser articles that summer, and in September 1919 went to New York on his annual holiday. Though Dreiser had not yet gone west, and though he acknowledged letters from Reedy's secretary in St. Louis, Reedy could not reach him, and Dreiser made no effort to welcome Reedy to his home in the Village.[21]

"Now I hope you don't think I'm going away without seeing you," Reedy wrote, after fruitless attempts to talk to him on the telephone; "for I'm not." When at last they met, toward the end of September, he insisted on keeping on the old, jovial footing. Dreiser had always been a hard one to jolly out of a churlish mood, but Reedy seems partly to have succeeded, for after their meeting he sent another note begging Dreiser to dine with him: "Had a bully time the night I was with you . . . And if you'll come I'll do the Lyon [preface] as soon as I get back home—honest to God." [22]

But some chord had snapped. The preface was never written nor Lyon's book published. And in January Dreiser thought it necessary to disclaim any part in a trifling joke about Mencken that had slipped out in the *Mirror*. He and Reedy were no longer friends, he told Mencken. So that was that.[23]

CHAPTER 22

POETS AND POLITICS
DA CAPO AL FINE

WHEN Woodrow Wilson returned from his catastrophic visit to the Paris peace conference of 1919, Reedy, writing in the *Mirror*, proffered sage advice. He recognized that there had been real obstacles to obtaining the vaguely benevolent sort of treaty the President had asked for. At the same time this proposed peace was "full of the promise of more war."[1]

Reedy found the reparation terms "as cruel as were the German bombardments of unfortified towns and the sinking of ships without warning." These and the continuing blockade that methodically starved whole populations incited in Germany and her allies a spirit of revenge almost sure to break out in renewed hostilities. Yet he insisted that neither Germany nor the United States could absolutely reject the terms without throwing Europe "back into endless wars between nations and the people into starvation, revolution, and a long night of semi-savage ignorance." Bad as the treaty had turned out to be, it was better than no peace at all. Now it was up to the President to take the people into his confidence, admit his failures, and gain the treaty's acceptance. Reedy agreed with Wilson that our joining the League of Nations offered the one hope for revising the treaty's harsh terms. "Americans are a common-sense folk. They know very well that the President could not get all the idealistic things he went after to Paris.

THE MAN IN THE MIRROR

They know it was give-and-take at the conference . . ." But Reedy could not suppress the sad thought that, having got nothing for ourselves, we had "got so little for so many other peoples struggling to be free." [2]

What was worse was the collaboration of our government in suppressing movements for freedom all over the world. A number of Hindu leaders had been arrested in the United States and held for deportation to India, where they were all but sure to be shot. "These men were arrested after the war," Reedy expostulated. "What for?"

> Why for exactly the thing of which Washington, Jefferson, Franklin, Adams and others held in immortal memory by all Americans, were guilty; they have been struggling to free their country from the rule of the stranger. They have been endeavoring to secure for their own people that self-determination about which Woodrow Wilson has been discoursing so eloquently for at least two years . . .
>
> The idea that our government should send these patriots to the firing squad is enough to make the blood of any true blue American boil in indignation.[3]

Reedy's indignation proved costly, for at fifty-seven his health could no longer tolerate these daily exasperations. But each incident of repression seemed a personal betrayal. Disgust with the results of the war, the throttling of civil liberties at home, and the constant spectacle of mindless zeal searching out new victims for its rage, was taking its toll. He went off to New York that September determined to shake off painful feelings that were now causing him acute physical distress. For Reedy suffered from hypertension. In New York he became aware of Dreiser's animosity. He picked up gossip of the vicious star-chamber proceedings of the Lusk committee. He tried to give himself over to cheerful conversation and meetings with all sorts of people. But clearly his heart was not in it.

Although Reedy's health had been precarious for years— and he seems to have given up drinking after an incident of nephritis in 1915—he continued to revel in the joys of conversation. But those who watched him closely were troubled. Even in 1916 Sara Teasdale had feared he had not long to live.[4] Now he crowded his calendar with engagements. He used Kennerley's Park Avenue office at the Anderson Galleries for his headquarters, as usual, and went out to Mamaroneck with his host on week ends. He made the rounds of Greenwich Village. He enjoyed the hospitality of his old St. Louis protégé, the restaurateur Barney Gallant. Kennerley's friend Richard Ederheimer, the art dealer, had just returned from Germany. Reedy was fascinated by his firsthand impressions and interested in his plan of becoming a portrait painter. He allowed Ederheimer to paint his portrait, while he listened to the artist's opinion that the world would not be safe from Germany until her people could halt unemployment. "We must help them to get busy," Reedy told his readers in the *Mirror*. The Ederheimer portrait turned out to be a striking "primitive." The *New York Times* published a reproduction ten days later in its Sunday magazine, together with a full-page interview with Reedy.[5]

The *Times* interviewer wanted his impressions of Greenwich Village and seemed disappointed that Reedy found the new bohemian fad no more than the inevitable pose of youth, which "naturally poses—imagines itself already the thing it wants to be." Reedy had more telling things to say about American freedom and free verse. Did he think the new forms expressed the American spirit? "'On the contrary,' he answered. 'I should say that some of the modern pieces are good in spite of the vehicle." Free verse had helped young poets find a new path, just as French symbolism had helped them out of old ruts. But all poetic forms were liable to ossify, and free verse was no exception. The real danger to American literature lay not in forms but in young fellows who thought all literature had begun with Oscar Wilde.

As to the two leading writers with whose careers he had had

most to do, he praised Masters once more for his intellect and knowledge of the classics, but now feared Dreiser was becoming too documentary, "too ready to get his material from the newspapers." "What we need in life and art," he concluded, "is a freedom involving responsibility." He looked to see a higher literature develop when Americans should achieve freer, more democratic conditions of life. The interviewer had the impression that Reedy spoke from the ripeness of wisdom and with "such authority as comes only from character, experience, thought." Struck by Reedy's eyes, he compared his gaze to the "concentrated search of a railroad engineer." [6]

Reedy continued to write his full quota of commentary during his visit to New York. He told of the powerful anti-labor feeling generated by an epidemic of strikes, of the indignation of a lieutenant colonel who had been one of his theater party at a play about a uniformed veteran turned revolutionary, and he remarked the beginnings of a movement to make Herbert Hoover a candidate for the presidency.[7]

After his return home Reedy became fascinated by the meeting in St. Louis of a strange national organization which called itself the "Committee of Forty-Eight" and sought to consolidate the political dissatisfactions of all the elements in the forty-eight states that were disillusioned with the two major parties. The numerous delegations which began to arrive early in December included radical as well as moderate dissenters, and the announcement of a congress of this stripe aroused reactionary opposition, especially that of the American Legion, one of whose Kansas City posts threatened to disband the gathering violently unless the Statler Hotel canceled its promise of a hall. After obtaining a court order to confirm its reservation, the committee began its meetings under close surveillance of Department of Justice agents. Its heads were not prominent. The best-known leader was Theodore Roosevelt's friend Amos

Pinchot, a lawyer and journalist who had held no public office since 1901.[8]

While Reedy was not listed as an active member of the Committee of Forty-Eight he covered the meetings himself and conferred with the many single-tax advocates there. The single-taxers succeeded in having their tenets included in a three-plank "postcard platform" worked out in a series of noisy discussions. On Christmas Day Reedy published both this capsule version and the lengthy program none of the great newspapers would print. If it were well received, the committee would form itself into a party and pick a presidential slate the following summer. The members had Senator Robert M. La Follette in mind as their candidate.

Their program called for public ownership of natural resources, utilities, and food-processing plants. It recommended taxation to "force idle land into use" and eliminate land speculation. It demanded a universal franchise, the restoration of free speech and other Constitutional rights suspended for the duration of the war, and the right of labor to bargain collectively and "share in the management of industry."[9]

Soon after the Forty-Eighters broke up, Reedy collapsed as a result of hypertension, which had induced a retinal hemorrhage in one eye. His friend Dr. Major Seelig had him taken to Jewish Hospital.

Reedy's various earlier sojourns there had become legendary. On one occasion, hearing him complain that his breakfast oatmeal was cold, Mrs. Reedy had bundled him out of the hospital, had been arrested driving him home, and braved the wrath of Dr. Seelig, nursing him at Clonmel, muttering the while, "God help me, I've done a grievous thing."[10]

Now the case was more serious. Reedy wrote his will. Leading specialists were called in consultation, and it was agreed that the eye must be removed. Reedy seems to have managed

THE MAN IN THE MIRROR

to get the operation at Jewish Hospital set for the day the *Mirror* went to press, so he could dictate his copy for the following week and not miss a number. On New Year's Day he entitled his leader "At Ease in Zion."

His sole complaint was still the meager diet. "In order to reduce the high blood pressure occasioned by my labors on the peace treaty, the railroad problem, the labor question and other matters which could not very well be settled without my sage advice, I am subsisting upon a ration that would not surfeit a canary." Could such a diet be enforced on the nation, as Prohibition had, it would solve the food shortage, he said. "If we can get along without free press and free speech there is no reason why we couldn't be made to subsist and flourish upon the bill of fare prescribed for me." [11] The Prohibition amendment to the Constitution enraged him more than his own privation.

But he went on to give reassuring details of his condition. Since only one eye was affected, he could still enjoy the vision of pretty nurses, on whom he hoped to exert renewed charm once his diet had done its work. His main objection to the operation was that it had interrupted his reading of Romain Roland's *Colas Breugnon,* a book he nevertheless proceeded to review.

A week later visitors waited in line to call, two at a time. Some had grievances to air, which reminded him of another stay in the hospital eleven years before, when Frederick Lehmann (now Solicitor General of the United States) had remarked: "He writes so well with a broken leg that I could almost hope for the sake of literature that he'd break his damn neck." Now the guests filed in, and if pairs overlapped a debate was sure to start before the hospital authorities could intervene. Reedy enjoyed that, only regretting the occasional caller "who has just dashed off a little thing in free verse."

"But considering all that I have done against poetry in the

encouragement of free verse," he added ruefully, "I guess this sort of thing is coming to me." [12]

One unexpected caller was the one-time perennial candidate for mayor whom he had opposed so often, around the turn of the century. "In comes no less a person than Lee Meriwether to invite me to a banquet in honor of Senator James A. Reed for his heroic fight against the peace treaty and the League of Nations." Reedy was still supporting the League but hoped to meet the Senate die-hard anyway. "I don't know whether I'll be out in time to attend the dinner to Senator Jim," he said; "but if I am, I will. I got to get a meal somewhere." [13]

After almost a month in the hospital Reedy was released. He quoted his physician's little speech telling him on what terms he might expect to resume his life. A bevy of pretty nurses standing there listening reminded Reedy of vestals attending a Roman sacrifice. Dr. Seelig began:

"You will have to go through life hereafter, Colonel, with one eye. But I take it you won't miss [the other,] because you have seen about everything. You will have to be very careful of yourself in the years to come, and in particular you must refrain from all excitement . . . Let me warn you most solemnly against falling in love." At these words there was an audible titter in the assemblage before me where I sat receiving sentence.

"But, doctor," said I, "the last is impossible. I am an old married man and falling in love is out of the question." Thereupon the medical man . . . reiterated his warning that this was one of the greatest dangers besetting the path of a man who was emerging into life with premonitory symptoms of arteriosclerosis. Of course as a dutiful patient I couldn't but accept the doctor's dictum. But —it is going to be a terrible world with me because all my life I have been falling in love with all sorts of things, theories, arts, sciences, ladies, etc . . . which have made of my career thus far a movie of innumerable startling scenes . . . [14]

Outside the hospital he stopped to gaze on a pretty ankle ascending a streetcar step, and on his way out to Clonmel he

THE MAN IN THE MIRROR

pondered the beauties of the new short skirts. He would be able to get along with one eye.[15]

Despite his doctor's admonition, Reedy managed to get to Senator Reed's dinner, admiring the sonorous oratory with whose burden he found himself in such outraged disagreement. He was disgusted, nevertheless, with the newspapers' pale renditions of Reed's heresy. No one who read them could have formed the "faintest idea of the texture of the argument, of the color and music of the words, of the play of many moods from irony to exaltation, which marked the stately process of the deliverance." [16]

A week later Reedy himself was proposed as the new party's candidate for senator from Missouri, a nomination he received with horror. It came from a member of the Committee of Forty-Eight, of course a single-taxer. To run for office on such a ticket was Reedy's idea of "zero in political endeavor—of zero with the circumference removed." "Suppose I should take the lure and make the race and be elected. More unlikely things than that are likely to happen in the scattered condition of political thought and feeling of this commonwealth and this country at this time. The people . . . are in a mood to elect anybody to anything." [17]

And yet, in March 1920, again ignoring his doctor's advice, he presided at a meeting of twelve hundred persons. It was the first in a series to be held around the country to consider the chances for a third party at the elections the following November, and when a speaker called attention to Reedy's career as a molder of liberal sentiment, the audience applauded loudly, increasing its cheers when someone in the rear of the hall shouted: "Nominate Reedy for United States senator." [18]

Meanwhile the magazine went on, bristling with controversies, and Reedy did what he could to stir up new issues. One gets an impression of his method from a correspondence he had had a year or so earlier with his old friend William Vincent Byars. Reedy wanted the learned reporter who had been his tutor on the *Republican* to discuss the prosody of the new poetic forms. He recalled Byars' theory of rhyme, which, had astonished readers of the *New York World* in the nineties. But Byars, overcome with the enthusiasm of a lone crusader, was still pedantic and opaque on this favorite topic.

"Make it simple, simple, simple, so the fellows can see it," Reedy urged. "I'm hoping I can get somebody to attack you and then you can demolish [him]." And when a small tiff resulted, Reedy himself plunged in as usual.[19]

He seems to have been convinced it was a time for more radical policies, by the very fact of the panic resistance to them. That summer of 1919, when William C. Edgar of Minneapolis had suspended publication of the *Bellman* after thirteen years, Reedy said there was only one conservative weekly of any importance left, the *Argonaut* of San Francisco. He spoke of the radicalism that had overtaken the *Nation* and the *Dial* and said that even the *Atlantic Monthly* now published articles by an I.W.W. organizer. "Radicalism is the order. Don't make any mistake about that . . . The worst thing I can say about this mood of the people is that its defiant discontent is desperate—hopeless . . . Conservatism is in a stupor from which it seems only to awake in fits and starts of senseless panic."[20]

This view was roundly denied by Maxwell Bodenheim, the young Mississippi poet, who felt that the radical journals, like the popular ones, were given over now to mere entertainment. In an angry letter to the *Mirror* he spoke of the difficulty poets like William Carlos Williams, Wallace Stevens, Conrad Aiken —and Maxwell Bodenheim—still experienced in getting their work printed.[21] His letter provoked a spate of protest. Howard Mumford Jones, who was now contributing to the *Mirror* a flood of earth-bound poesy, said Bodenheim's complaint was the expression of mere pique. If Bodenheim would write less disconnectedly he might be printed oftener. Another reader defended the *Atlantic* against Bodenheim's charge. And so the fracas grew.[22]

But for all these symptoms of life, Reedy had emerged from the hospital overcome with a weariness he could not shake off. The thought of death was much in his mind. "Immortality is a threat, not a promise," he told Masters. "The best we can expect is rest." [23]

Sometimes his choice of verse for the magazine betrayed this preoccupation. The poets sang continually of death. Discussing the propaganda of reaction he and Reedy were battling against, Carl Sandburg quoted from Edwin Arlington Robinson's new dramatic lyric, "John Brown":

> Bones in a grave,
> Cover them as you will with choking earth,
> May shout the truth to men who put them there,
> More than all orators.* [24]

Reedy filled out that column with a Bodenheim lyric on the death of a young bear:

> Nights and days grazed the horizon
> With their breath of birth and death.[25]

And Conrad Aiken contributed a new vaudeville poem depicting a dance macabre that harked back to his lyric, "This Dance of Life," one of the poets' backstage sketches that had delighted Reedy four years before.

Most poignant of all was the sudden reappearance of Edna St. Vincent Millay in the Easter number, in the spring of 1920. Miss Millay's "Renascence" had been reprinted from *Lyric Year* eight years earlier. Since her Vassar College graduation she had known poverty and struggle. What poetry she pub-

---

* Reprinted with permission of the publisher from *Collected Poems* by Edwin Arlington Robinson. Copyright 1937 by The Macmillan Company.

lished had added nothing to her prestige, and she seemed unlikely to regain the acclaim that had come to her as a perilous miracle, while a freshman. In 1918 she had published in *Poetry* the first of her very young, very jaded, little "Figs from Thistles"—

> My candle burns at both ends;
> It will not last the night . . .[26]

—which was to become the motto of a generation that chose to call itself lost.

Deeply involved in the postwar despair and still fancying herself in love with Arthur Davison Ficke, whom she had scarcely seen in the seven years since he and Bynner had expressed to her their admiration for "Renascence," Miss Millay eked out her precarious literary income by acting with the Provincetown Players in Greenwich Village and the Theatre Guild, a troupe still as impecunious as its more daring rival from Cape Cod.

Out of this atmosphere of war-sickness, frustration, and poetic bravado came two important works Reedy published that spring. In a way both were products of that poetic conservatism the war had encouraged. Miss Millay's biographer, Elizabeth Atkins, tells of the resistance the poet had met on all sides when she attempted to place her sonnets. Only Ficke and Reedy seemed to retain a tolerance for a genre which had come to seem a kind of "quack grass, cropping up in all the interstices between essays and stories in the magazines." The twenty sonnets Reedy now published were out of the ordinary, and if they were a pastiche they seemed a great deal more than that to Ficke, who wrote in the margin of one Miss Millay sent him in typescript: "I have sometimes hoped that I played some part in this, her greatest sonnet. But I cared too deeply to ever ask, lest I be disappointed." It was that remarkably Elizabethan love lyric, "And you as well must

THE MAN IN THE MIRROR

die, beloved dust." Reedy had waited three years for work of its quality from this poet. He had told Kennerley of his admiration for three of the sonnets scattered through *Renascence,* when Kennerley brought out that collection in 1917.[27]

But far more in keeping with the poetic spirit of the year before Eliot's *Waste Land* was the tragic playlet *Aria da Capo,* which Miss Millay had written for the Provincetown Players in December. Kennerley persuaded Reedy to buy it for his Easter issue that spring, and to pay fifty dollars for it, which was ironic; for Kennerley himself delayed publishing it as a book for three years, and churlishly withheld all royalties on Miss Millay's other three books, at a time when he himself was prospering.[28]

Aria da Capo is a remarkable achievement, if only from the structural point of view. It contains two plays, one within the other. One is a travesty on the war, the other a farce about the postwar disillusionment. And this all takes place within the bounds of a single act—no more than four hundred lines of freely metered blank verse. It is acted on a bare stage, intended to represent a café terrace in the first scene.

The badinage of sophisticated Pierrot chatting at the table inanely with his compliant, blasé Columbine is a telling satire on the "lost generation" that took Miss Millay to be its spokesman. The second scene—a miniature pastoral tragedy of Corydon and Thyrsis, the two shepherds who murder one another in a silly boundary dispute—is a finely honed indictment of the bickering statesmen who had held the stage at Paris the previous summer. The shepherds, playing at war on two sides of their paper wall while ostensibly rehearsing a play, act out a heartbreaking sketch of humanity torn between love and hate. The pathos of Corydon's last lines would be painful enough:

POETS AND POLITICS

> You've poisoned me in earnest. . . . I feel so cold. . . .
> So cold . . . this is a very silly game. . . .
> Why do we play it?—let's not play this game
> A minute more . . . let's make a little song
> About a lamb. . . . I'm coming over the wall,
> No matter what you say,—I want to be near you . . .
> Where is the wall?
>   There isn't any wall,
> I think.
> Thyrsis, where is your cloak? just give me
> A little bit of your cloak! [29]

But Miss Millay makes this yet more shattering by adding a brief scene: Pierrot and Columbine are ordered to cover the two bodies with a tablecloth and play out their farce. "The audience will forget," says tragic Cothurnus, their stage manager. And so they resume their empty chatter.

The poem is the more stirring for its lightness and delicacy. It is as mannered as the players' scene in *Hamlet,* and as relevant to the exterior tragedy—a play within a play, within a play. Its piping, childlike tones speak for all innocents straying to their slaughter in a world of toppling thrones. One thinks of the sheepcote Marie Antoinette left behind at Versailles, and remembers that it was in her crystal ballroom that the peacemakers of 1919 had concluded their fated labors. Miss Atkins is even justified in comparing the shepherds' tragedy to Chaucer's "Pardoner's Tale." Millay's doll-like creatures are more fragile in their ignorance, but they are as feckless, as helpless to arrest history, as were the "yonge folk that haunteden folye," and wanted to kill Death.

Miss Millay's standing has diminished since the day Amy Lowell wished *she* had written *Aria da Capo.* Her delicate satire is as much out of favor now as her sonnets were before Reedy printed them. But those fragile figures of hers achieved in their poignant way what Reedy had once feared no American poet would attempt—the fusion of political life and poetry into a meaningful whole.

Reedy himself did not comment on the play. Critics in the thirties were sometimes lavish in their praise. Perhaps the little work will be rediscovered by some future lost generation.

CHAPTER 23

LAST REFLECTIONS

THE most discussed book that spring of 1920 was John Maynard Keynes's *Economic Consequences of the Peace*. Reedy took evident satisfaction in summarizing it, for it confirmed by eyewitness testimony all he had guessed about the treaty, whose ratification was still being hotly debated as the time for the presidential campaign drew near.

"A pact utterly ruthless, wholly in violation of the principles upon which it was proposed that the war should be ended, and designed not only to the end of absolutely crushing Germany and the German people, but to bring about the utter disruption of European organization and invite a reign of anarchism"— so Reedy summed it up. He predicted that Keynes would profoundly modify American opinion and policy in the future. Thus began another battle in the *Mirror*, with Reedy getting useful support from Walter Lippmann when a contributor called Keynes a German propagandist.[1]

But the attenuated debate over the unsigned peace and the League now seemed a screen to gloss over general failure to come to grips with domestic problems. Again and again Reedy begged for mature discussion of real issues—meaning economic ones. His pleas provoked a few serious articles, notably those by the lawyer-poet Charles Erskine Scott Wood and by Clarence Darrow, but as it came time for the conventions to be held, it became clear that there was no viable leadership to implement any program. The heads of the

279

Committee of Forty-Eight were politically inept. They wanted Senator La Follette for their candidate but alienated him by their bickering. Splinter groups formed and sentiment swung to extremes. The single-taxers, among others, withdrew. And Reedy's interest waned.[2]

La Follette himself put forward a platform for the progressive wing of the Republican party, which Roosevelt's defection and death had left leaderless. Reedy printed it unenthusiastically. The Wisconsin senator opposed our joining the League of Nations. Yet the effort of others to make an issue of the League was, as Reedy remarked in the same issue, mere camouflage. "The politicians don't want to be called upon to tell what they propose . . . doing about the railroads, or taxation or labor or waterways or military training or trust regulation. They want to talk about the League of Nations in glittering generalities. They . . . are dodging the real issues of American life."[3] As for La Follette, he was sixty-five now, and bad health prevented his taking the leading role he had almost played in 1908 and always seemed on the point of taking thereafter. Reedy put forward only one positive proposal for the coming campaigns. He suggested that the Democrats nominate Brand Whitlock, a successful writer who had been Governor Altgeld's protégé in Chicago and "Golden Rule" Jones's successor as mayor of Toledo, before serving with distinction as Wilson's ambassador to Belgium. The *New York Times* took up Reedy's suggestion.

But as pre-convention skirmishing went on it became obvious that no one with views as positive as La Follette's *or* Brand Whitlock's would be considered. Nominations seemed up at auction in both camps, with Bernard Baruch reported to have offered to raise $5 million for the election of William Gibbs McAdoo, President Wilson's son-in-law and Secretary of the Treasury. Pre-campaign expenditures became the object of Congressional investigation, which Reedy called "a great success in discrediting pretty nearly everybody." He was more discouraged than ever, saying that all the politicians aped those at Paris who had "put the 'deal' in idealism." "Political democracy looks more and more like a failure," he continued. "The people can hope for nothing from political puttering with conditions. The way out is through popular organization for economic democracy, because in political democracy privilege is in power."[4] He asked if American democracy had not reached the "last limit" of degeneration Henry Adams had prophesied, and concluded: "After war's wild ecstacy of devotion and sacrifice for a better world—this descent to dungy earth. Give us an ounce of civet, apothecary, to sweeten our imagination, for the facts in the news of the day shake faith and poison hope." In his own semi-blindness he remembered Lear's remark on justice to the blinded earl.[5]

A week later Reedy went to the Republican convention in Chicago with his old friend George Tansey, who sported a big Harding button; and there he confirmed his direst fears. There was no trace of a progressive element. That had been killed off before Roosevelt's death. Reedy proclaimed the machine-like proceedings of the professionals "banausic," called the ripple of enthusiasm for Hoover the only spontaneous impulse, and said that the Republicans' candidate for president was so unpopular that one of his own managers had remarked a general movement "back to the Democratic party." Warren G. Harding struck him as another McKinley—"a stodgy person who can 'say an undisputed thing in such a solemn way,' who would rather be led than lead, who will never lose sight of the great business interests."[6]

During that spring Reedy had broken in an assistant who looked capable of taking over for him while he had a vacation. Charles J. Finger, a middle-aged Englishman who had followed a spell of adventuring in Africa and Alaska by a successful career in American railroads, hoped to become a writer. He apprenticed himself to Reedy, and as an assistant editor managed to keep things lively, featuring Edgar Lee Masters' fictitious contributor, "Elmer Chubb, LL.D., Ph.D.," a sanctimonious caricature of Dr. Percival Chubb of the St. Louis Ethical Society. The real Dr. Chubb, also an Englishman, an old Fabian and a disciple of the "greatest scholar in the world"—Tom Davidson—soon lost his temper. When he canceled his subscription to the *Mirror*, Finger preened himself on a victory. There was a harsh quality in his mockery, and his style was as heavy as unrisen dough. But Reedy decided to leave Finger in charge while he went to the Democratic convention.[7]

"Off for San Francisco," he announced late in June. "What will happen there one can only guess."

San Francisco was like a carnival, after the funereal gloom of Chicago. Bryan was there, determined to eliminate any candidate opposed to Prohibition. Wilson was represented by skilled generals—Burleson and Senator Carter Glass, among others. There was no danger of his being repudiated as Cleveland had been in 1896. Senator Reed of Missouri, his bitterest opponent within the party, was denied a seat.

Reedy covered the backstage maneuvering with joy and skill. He appeared to know the entire Missouri delegation and hundreds of others. His accounts, taken up with good-natured gossip and vivid personal sketches, suppressed the pessimism he had labored under all that spring. He omitted mention of his home state's jovial compliment to himself, when the delegates nominated him as their favorite son for president of the United States.

He was fascinated by Bryan's campaign for a dry plank and a dry candidate, which he detailed without any trace of rancor. Bryan was "bland and at his ease and wore that cat-fish smile which rivaled in radiance the reflection from his bald head," Reedy reported. "His voice was as clear as his eye, and he received everyone with what seemed the right and happy word." But after filling in this benign portrait Reedy could not suppress the thought that anyone life had tempered with tolerance must find something "terrible" about such a man. "He possesses immeasurable potentialities as a tyrant—a political 'sea-green incorruptible' Robespierre. He draws strength from defeat. He has no knowledge of economic fundamentals but he stands on the ten commandments . . . dealing out damnation to all who dissent from him, with the unqualified certitude of a god." [8]

While Reedy could take no satisfaction in the candidate at last selected—after a harrowing contest that dragged on through forty-four ballots—he was at least pleased that Bryan's power was broken and a slightly "damp" candidate picked in spite of him. That the nominee, Governor James M. Cox of Ohio, was a nonentity did not disturb him. It had been a good show. The weather was balmy and the atmosphere glowing with good fellowship. Reedy thoroughly enjoyed his first visit to San Francisco, taking no thought of his health. He told of tasting bootleg whiskey at his hotel, and climbed to the top of Russian Hill one evening for a champagne dinner with his friend, the veteran lawyer, soldier, and poet Charles Erskine Scott Wood. They sat up talking far into the night.[9]

Then he went to Hollywood for ten days. His host, a playwright and motion picture director, was the brother of Cecil B. de Mille the producer, and an occasional contributor to the *Mirror*. His hostess was the daughter of Henry George and "her father's best work." Mrs. William de Mille was a devout single-taxer, who wanted Reedy to pacify some of the bickering factions agitating for tax legislation in California.[10]

The visit was a joyous interlude, and Reedy was an enchanting house guest, as always, filling the spacious bungalow with laughter, charming the de Mille children with his stories, and winning the heart of the Irish cook by saying he wanted his

THE MAN IN THE MIRROR

breakfast eggs boiled for three Hail Marys. He worked on his copy for the magazine every day; there was no money to buy contributions, and Finger could not fill the columns unaided. But there was ample time to visit the movie studios with the vivacious Mrs. de Mille, to shop the secondhand book stores in Los Angeles, and to have a long chat with Upton Sinclair, who was running for Congress again on the Socialist ticket. He saw nothing of Dreiser, who was now living in Hollywood with his mistress.

On the week end Reedy accompanied his host on a big-game fishing trip to Catalina Island, afterward writing it up with astonishing verve and accuracy considering that he had never held a rod in his hand. But his chief delight was in his hostess— "a charming person and pretty, too," he boasted in a letter to Kennerley the day before he returned to San Francisco. He felt as much at home already as he had visiting the publisher's family at Mamaroneck, and loved them all as he loved the Kennerleys. Although he had begged not to be asked to make speeches, he gladly addressed fifty guests at the de Milles' house, and happily scribbled his copy throughout a series of earthquakes that caused consternation in Los Angeles the same day. Mrs. de Mille nursed and mothered him, greatly concerned about his health.[11]

"Never have I been happier than in your dear home," he told her the Tuesday he returned to San Francisco on a train bearing refugees from the earthquake. He was writing from the office of the *Star* with the pungency of printer's ink and the cheerful, familiar clutter of the city room around him. But he promised her he would remember to take his pills. She had not trusted him, and had sent along a letter of instructions for his care to James Barry, the editor of the *Star*, and to Mrs. Barry, who was to be his hostess for the next few days.

Meanwhile he went through the mountainous stack of mail that had accumulated, and inspected the *Mirror*, trying to de-

LAST REFLECTIONS

cide whether he could afford to extend his vacation, going home by way of Canada. He was worried about the shop, as he had told Kennerley the day before. "May have to go back straightaway. Isn't it hell to be unable to let go?" But he was determined to let Finger have his head. He wrote him that he had decided to give Cox "the benefit of . . . some votes among our kind of liberal," but only for lack of any other possible candidate. He hoped Finger would follow up the suggestion of an Ohio correspondent who called attention to some favorable aspects of Cox's record as governor—"unless you can't abide him at all, at all,' he added. "I don't want you to do anything against the grain." [12]

That evening Reedy dined out with the Barrys and talked at great length of his happy visit with their friends, the de Milles. His laughter was as hearty as ever, and when Mrs. Barry reminded him about his pill on their return home, he took it "like an obedient child." An hour or so after going to bed, he had what seemed an attack of angina pectoris, and called for help. While the family doctor tried to reassure him and he labored for breath and wrestled with the pain in his chest, he gasped that it wasn't dying he was afraid of. It was not being able to die.

It was around two o'clock when Reedy died. Next day, while James Barry struggled with his feelings of shock and loss, he recalled his efforts to dissuade Reedy from going to Canada alone.

"We had advised him not to do so," he told Mrs. de Mille. "He has gone by another route." [13]

The next day's issue of the *Mirror* carried a last-minute announcement of Reedy's death, his vivid account of William de Mille's two-hour battle with a giant tuna, and his prediction that Edgar Lee Masters' tale "Mitch Miller," then running serially in a magazine, would be a best-seller. There was also a letter from a correspondent who signed himself Lucius Atherton, M.D.—the "toothless, discarded, rural Don Juan" of Spoon River, perhaps?—saying that he was sick and tired of reformers like Elmer Chubb, LL.D., Ph.D., and William Jennings Bryan—"compelling everyone to like what they like, and do what they do." [14]

At Clonmel, where Mrs. Reedy had awaited his return, Reedy's body lay in state. His friend George Johns wrote an editorial for the *Post-Dispatch,* praising his astonishing gifts as a wit and a reader. Privately, he wrote his son Orrick of the wake, presided over by Mrs. Reedy in her negligée—the litter of empty glasses and stale cigars, the conglomeration of celebrities from the great world and the half world: "a bartender and a gangster praying, and . . . somewhat apart from them, a group of light ladies." Reedy's friend, the handsome young Irish archbishop—presently to become John Cardinal Glennon—authorized the funeral at St. Louis University and permitted his burial in the family plot at Calvary Cemetery. In Kerry Patch rumor had it that Reedy would be buried in sanctified ground only because he had accepted extreme unction.[15]

The obituaries all over the country were written, many of them, by old reporter friends. Others deluged the guest editor of the *Mirror* with tributes. George Johns spoke of Reedy's "divine gift and grace of understanding." The *New York Times* compared him favorably with Henry Watterson of Louisville, who had died that spring soon after sending his last contribution to the *Mirror.* Alexander Harvey called Reedy "a master of the intellectual life." Masters wrote a doleful elegy entirely lacking the epigrammatic bite of the *Spoon River* epitaphs. Vincent Starrett praised Reedy's ability to "see with other men's eyes"—oblivious of Reedy's jokes about his one-eyed state. Reedy's secretary told how he would borrow money to give it away to needy friends—ignoring the creditors she would now have to appease. William Rose Benét spoke for the younger writers Reedy had helped, predicting there would soon be an

LAST REFLECTIONS

anthology of his essays to astonish the world. Babette Deutsch contributed the one graceful compliment in verse, though she later regretted that even this sonnet was not satisfactory as a poem.[16] But (as is often the way with such eulogies) the general praise of Reedy's *mellowness* and *humanity* had the ring of cant, as so many mouthed the tired words. Kennerley was fulsome. He called Reedy "the greatest human being I have ever known, a man like Shakespeare," but added with telling simplicity: "He had a genius for understanding everybody." [17]

The flood of newspaper grief was suffocating. The only discerning obituary of them all, as the *Literary Digest* remarked when it printed a selection of them, was the one in the *New York Tribune*. "The most appalling thing about William Marion Reedy," it said, "was his lack of fame among his own countrymen. Here was a really great critical mind . . ." And the writer went on to talk of the brief recognition that had come with *Spoon River Anthology* and the rising influence Reedy had since exerted on writers. "Yet of general fame, of position in the larger sense, he had next to nothing." The writer maintained that this was by deliberate choice. Conventional success had been Reedy's for the taking. He had insisted on devoting his efforts to those whose gifts he valued more highly than his own. Thus his great influence on the nation's taste and opinion had gone largely unnoticed except among the little group on whom he had lavished his parental care and guidance.[18]

And now most of *them* were too busy to mourn for long or re-examine the mass of critical writing he had left behind—though all seemed convinced it was studded with gems. Full of her problems with a Long Island house swarming with guests and servants, Zoë Akins wrote to Thekla Bernays of the success that had come to her at long last. The word "work" reminded her of Reedy.

I've two new plays waiting to be finished and the managers and theatres crying out for them—but it's been next to impossible to work, so far. By the way, I was of course very upset about Billy's death. I wrote a little article for the *Nation*. They changed it because it was too long—and also from sheer presumption . . . It isn't a very good article, but it was the best I had time to do. I'm sure that life had become a great bore to him—and that he was glad to know that the end was just around the corner. I'm sorry he was so worried about money. It's such a thwarting sort of worry. Grace Johns has at last succeeded in getting started on a stage career . . .[19]

"I suppose you read of Reedy's death," remarked Dreiser in a letter to Mencken that week. "You didn't like him, but he was a great book man [—] a little vain, an ass in war, but still a fellow. I'm sorry he is gone." If he regretted not having spoken to Reedy when they spent the previous week end in the same town, Dreiser did not say so.[20]

The one protégé who had ample time to estimate Reedy's career (and Reedy's contribution to his own career) chose to write no articles on the subject. Albert Bloch had been back in St. Louis that April, had exhibited his paintings at the Artists' Guild, explained them in the *Mirror*, and writhed under the play of Reedy's irony. Now back in Europe with his wife and sons, Bloch read through the memorial issue of the *Mirror*, which had been sent him by Thekla Bernays. Repelled by the sentimental tributes, he unburdened himself to her.

Futile sincerity and mutual condolence: a typical bourgeois funeral! How Billy would laugh, of course! But I, thank God, have not attained his "mellowness" and all-embracing tolerance; and besides he means more to me than he ever meant to himself. Not a *manly* expression; not an outspoken word of anything. Nor any hint of forthright criticism of the writer and thinker! But perhaps . . . these people really do believe that this wonderful personality, which they have so singularly failed to grasp, actually *was* the great stylist, keen thinker, and intellectual giant they have saddled on his memory. It would not "have done," I suppose . . . to reveal the Billy Reedy that actually was— . . . pontifex of the gin-mill backroom, marvellous swearer of round oaths, utterer of unique blasphemy . . .[21]

LAST REFLECTIONS

This intimate and honest statement won Miss Bernays' gratitude, as it must our own. The starting point for an appraisal of Reedy must be the acceptance of his limitations as a man and a thinker. His personal charm robbed his admirers of their judgment. In his life of Vachel Lindsay, for instance, Masters treated Reedy's death as a disaster that left its permanent scar on literature and hastened Lindsay's suicide. For him Reedy had been the only mind in the West with scholarship, vision, and independence enough to "see the country as a whole and to know what a book meant, and where it had to be placed. Had Reedy lived," said Masters, "he would have prevented, very probably, the strangulation of Lindsay." [22]

Such adulation has conspired with the natural indifference of a hurrying younger generation to postpone any sound appraisal of Reedy's career. Though a rising curiosity is manifest in many quarters today, the first book to be published about him, celebrating the hundredth anniversary of his birth, concludes: "He was a genius, a word of awesome meaning." [23] Certainly Reedy had talent of a high order, yet he achieved only a modicum of what his gifts predicted. Delightful as his writing often is, he never perfected a style. One is continually embarrassed by his wilful insistence on writing himself down. When he was most careful his diction became ornate and pretentious; and when he was fresh and offhand, he wrote too much. Considering his profound respect for letters, this is baffling. Yet partial explanation may be found in a certain instability of his own nature, and certain shortcomings in the community he made so much a part of himself.

St. Louis is matter-of-fact. "We are a peculiarly self-centered people," said David R. Francis before he went off as ambassador to Russia. Be that as it may, St. Louis during Reedy's time was a city in cultural decline. Had Reedy shifted his center of activity to New York, as his successful contemporaries usually did, he would have achieved more—though at the cost of that "autochthonous" quality he prized above success. Part of his distinction grew out of his identity with his fellow townsmen. ("Reedy was a bigger man in the provinces than he would have been in the city," writes B. W. Huebsch in a recent letter from New York; "but was all the more important for that."[24]). St. Louis lacked the magnanimity to return the compliment. So he remained an unfulfilled genius, doomed to magnificent mediocrity, though ever on the hunt for excellence. Had he not confessed this critical failing in a hundred ways himself, he might have surmounted the limitations of his environment and overcome that inner sense of frustration and inadequacy which bedeviled him, as it drove Dr. Johnson himself to melancholy.

Yet, whatever his shortcomings, they cannot efface Reedy's influence on his own and succeeding generations. He had a lofty conception of literature and a superbly independent recognition of its bearing on political and private life. The gap that separates our leaders from a kind of national self-knowledge which breeds greatness of vision is precisely the gap between life and letters. It is not yet closed, though Reedy was not altogether unsuccessful in his effort to close it. One cannot think of him for a moment as the prophet of a lost cause. He was the spokesman for a kind of individual and civic dignity which may be in abeyance yet is by no means lost, so long as we can see in the utterances of such a man the lively root threads of an American tradition.

It is our view of the past that will determine the directions we take. Our historians, both literary and political, have tended to adopt an official line in their interpretations. Many of them have fallen under the spell of such self-intoxicating rhetoric as Frederick Jackson Turner's frontier essay, which has been responsible for inflating the reputation of writers like Hamlin Garland and even Theodore Dreiser. As one reads what Reedy had to say of the exaggerated respect sometimes accorded such

LAST REFLECTIONS

literary frontiersmen, and as one watches him dissect the mentality of a leader like Bryan (whom some historians have mistaken for a great intellect), one is brought back with a thump to comfortable, solid earth. Scholars who want a new insight into our culture in its political and economic, or its aesthetic and literary ramifications, can do worse than turn to the files of the *Mirror*.

There they may hear a belly laugh where the historians led one to expect debate over principle. They may hear the mocking voices of poets mimicking the high-flown rhetoric of materialism. They will also hear obscure voices—reporters and lawyers and housewives by the thousand—demanding an end to American hypocrisy and sham. And they will hear the voice of Reedy himself, voluble in its insistence on a policy of charity and decency in a world whose only faith is in force. It was a voice listened to by many worthies in its day.

Carl Sandburg felt he *had* to know what Reedy thought, from week to week; a prefatory note to his *Chicago Poems* thanked Reedy and the editors of *Poetry* for services that "heightened what values of human address herein hold good." [25] Dreiser leaned on Reedy in his years of despair and counted on his support when he was embattled. Masters needed Reedy to show him where his talent lay. Many others did their best work trying to answer Reedy's mocking objections. Soon after Reedy's death Witter Bynner managed to persuade poets from forty states to attend the annual meeting of the Poetry Society, of which he was now president. It was Sandburg's first appearance there, and Amy Lowell's last. One feels it was partly Reedy's influence that brought such unlike minds to join in plotting (insofar as it *can* be plotted) the future of American poetry.

Always the mediator, Reedy had less political than critical influence. Casting back over the years one sees him as one of a minute yet potent splinter group of critics who bridged the chasm between pre-Raphaelites and moderns, between Pater

THE MAN IN THE MIRROR

and Ezra Pound. His brilliant early intuitions about Hardy, Wilde, Pater, Emily Dickinson, Francis Thompson, Joyce, Verlaine, and J. M. Synge, among so many others, built tolerance of the most disparate tendencies. He shored up confidence in tradition—especially native tradition. Some of the names he made familiar have ceased to be mentioned, but others, like Dickinson and Hawthorne, owe some of their aura of veneration to his constant, respectful allusions.

As one considers the disparity between the various aims and methods of all these writers Reedy admired, one realizes, too, that part of his function was to effect compromises. He began by affronting the genteel and vaunting a decadence he learned to contemn. In the process he helped win a hearing for new frankness in literary expression and social criticism. By the time the repressive element staged its counterattack, the *Mirror* was unassailable. It could slash at the censorious without being censored. It could defend classic values without estranging itself from militant innovators. Thus it was at once a liberalizing and a steadying influence—the advocate of that middle way Reedy himself instinctively sought and often stuck to, *via media et speciosa*. Not being the property of a cult, his magazine spoke in various accents, but never suppressed the coarse native idiom that was a rebuke to preciosity and fine jargon.

"Make it simple, simple, simple, so the fellows can see it." That might have been Reedy's motto. Yet he was always in touch with trends as recondite as nuclear physics, depth psychology, Thomism; the nominalism of Ockham, the ecology of Kropotkin, the demand theories buried in Thorstein Veblen's gnarled prose. For the most important thing that needed doing in those years of schism and desperate departures was to establish a meeting ground. Reedy helped bring the most diverse minds together. He espoused reform while deriding its righteous excesses, encouraged cultivated men to assume the burdens of politics, and tempered the business mentality by helping re-establish the dignity of poetry in the minds of those who regarded it as effete and remote from their practical concerns. A certain ruggedness and a common touch were what was needed, and these Reedy supplied—though he never altogether succeeded in stemming esoteric tendencies or the cultism he despised.

Harriet Monroe, who sought to build her public around an exclusive principle, differed from Reedy in most essentials. But jealous as she was of rivals, she recognized the *Mirror* as an ally, and saw that its standards were as high as her own. Because of the utter dissimilarity of their aims and their natures, because they preserved for one another the politeness of rivals and could never have been friends, her final comment on Reedy has weight, in contrast to the vacuity of most obituary praise.

"He could have held his own," she said, "in the Mermaid Tavern, or across the table from Dr. Johnson, or under the dialectics of Socrates or at the Gargantuan feasts of Rabelais. Indeed, his spirit really belonged to more spacious times."[26]

SELECTED BIBLIOGRAPHY
NOTES · INDEX

ABBREVIATIONS USED IN BIBLIOGRAPHY AND NOTES

- AL   *American Literature*
- DAB   *Dictionary of American Biography*
- Harvard   The Houghton Library at Harvard University
- LHUS   *Literary History of the United States*, ed. Robert E. Spiller *et al.* (rev. ed., New York: Macmillan, 1953)
- MHR   *Missouri Historical Review*
- MHS   Archives of the Missouri Historical Society
- MHS Bull.   *Bulletin* of the Missouri Historical Society
- Newberry   Newberry Library
- NYP   Manuscript Division, the New York Public Library
- SLP   St. Louis Public Library
- UP   University of Pennsylvania Library
- WMR   William Marion Reedy
- Yale   Yale Collection of American Literature at Yale University

SELECTED BIBLIOGRAPHY

THE SOLE criterion used in choosing this short list is its possible utility for investigators of Reedy's career and associations. While checklists of *Mirror* authors would be more valuable than what the bibliography contains, the most selective ones I could devise would run to thousands of entries and require separate publication. My own unpublished checklists are available and will be deposited at Yale when my work on Reedy is terminated. Arranged by authors, they include separate entries for the two hundred fifty or so I considered most significant.

There are also incomplete indexes to the *Mirror* at St. Louis Public Library, the Mercantile Library of St. Louis, and the University of Pennsylvania (though the last is now superseded), and these may be of use to anyone wishing to locate items by subject or author.

The list that follows merely complements the footnotes, and I have generally tried to omit works referred to therein, except those cited by short title. I have also sought to include helpful though obscure books and contemporary commentaries of historic interest, rather than well-known books and critical contributions. This must not be interpreted as ingratitude for the many excellent studies that have been indispensable to my own work.

I. PRIMARY SOURCES

1. Writings of William Marion Reedy, Separately Published or Contained in Books

A Golden Book and the Literature of Childhood (Cedar Rapids, Ia., Torch Press, 1910). Two essays edited by Joseph Fort Newton.
"Burns, the World Poet," in *St. Louis Nights Wi' Burns,* ed. Walter B. Stevens (St. Louis: Burns Club, 1913).
Burns, Robert, *The Jolly Beggars, A Cantata* (Portland, Me.: Mosher, 1914). Introduction by WMR.
Bynner, Witter, *The Beloved Stranger* (New York: Knopf, 1919). Preface by WMR.

BIBLIOGRAPHY

"Christmas Lyric," in W. H. Pommer, *Eight Songs* (1914).

Frisco the Fallen, pamphlet (San Francisco: L. S. Robinson, 1916); also published as *The City that Has Fallen* (San Francisco: Book Club of California, 1933).

Friendship's Garland or the Escape Valve of an Enthusiast (East Aurora, N.Y.: Roycroft [1899?]).

Hazlitt, William, *Liber Amoris* (Portland, Me.: Mosher, 1908). Introduction by WMR.

Hot Springs of Arkansas, The ([St. Louis?]: Missouri Pacific Railways, n.d.).

[Hubbard, Elbert, subject.] *The Feather Duster: Is He Sincere?* (East Aurora, N.Y., Roycrofters, 1912). Essays by WMR *et al.*

Law of Love, The: Being Fantasies of Science and Sentiment . . . (East Aurora, N.Y.: Hubbard, 1905). Seven pirated essays, all but two reprinted from Mirror Pamphlets.

Leith, W. Compton, *Sirenica* (Portland, Me.; Mosher, 2nd ed., 1927). Introduction by WMR.

McGaffey, Ernest, *Sonnets to a Wife* (St. Louis: Mirror Co., 1901). Preface by WMR.

Mirror Pamphlet Series

Series I
No. 1. September 1899. *A Message to Hubbard*
2. October 1899. *The Deaths of Friends*
3. November 1899. *What's the Matter with St. Louis?*
4. December 1899. *The Pope and the Virgin*
[5?] January 1900? *Anglo-Saxondom's Immoral Immortals*
6. February 1900. *Joe Jefferson, My Joe*
7–8. [Missing]
9. *Be a Coward*
10. [Extra] June 1900. *The Story of the Strike*
11. [July?] 1900. *Literature of Childhood*
12. August 1900. *A Gipsy Genius* [Sir Richard Burton]

Series II
No. 1. September 1900. *A Golden Book*
2. October 1900. *Nell Gwyn*
3. November 1900. *Ginx's Baby*
4. December 1900. *Machiavelli*
5. January 1901. *Brichanteau, Actor*
6. February 1901. *The Law of Love: A Fantasie of Science*
7. March 1901. *A Nest of Singing Birds*
8. April 1901. *The Greatest Woman Poet . . . Sappho of Mitylene*

BIBLIOGRAPHY

  9. May 1901. *The Two Eaglets* [Maude Adams and Sarah Bernhardt]
 10. June 1901. *Equality: A Beautiful Dream* [Edward Bellamy]
 11. July 1901. *Two Roles of Richard's* [Richard Mansfield]
 12. August 1901. *A Neronian Novel:* Quo Vadis

Series III
 No. 1. September 1901. *William McKinley*
      2. October 1901. *The Dreamers of Jewry*
      3. November 1901. *The Eugene Field Myth*
      4. December 1901. *The Divorce Problem*
      5. January 1902. *The War on Trusts*
      6. February 1902. *President of the United States*

The Mirror Pamphlets were superseded by the *Valley Magazine, q.v.*

Myth of a Free Press, The: An Address Delivered Before the Missouri Press Association at Excelsior Springs, Mo., May 28, 1908 (St. Louis: The Mirror, 1908).

Pater, Walter, *Marius, the Epicurean* (Portland, Me.: Mosher, 1900). Foreword by WMR.

"St. Louis, 'The Future Great,'" in *Historic Towns of the Western States*, ed. Lyman P. Powell (New York: Putnam, 1901). Vol. 4 in Historic Towns ser.

Snoddy, J. S., ed., *A Little Book of Missouri Verse* (Kansas City, Mo.: Hudson-Kimberly, 1897). Contains three poems by WMR.

Tyranny or Freedom: Three Articles on the Proposed Amendment . . . (St. Louis, 1910).

2. Books and Periodicals Published by William Marion Reedy

As You Like It, a magazine. Founded in the early nineties and published for about five years by Charles E. Meade, John E. Mohan, and WMR. (See *Mirror,* 25:391 [June 9, 1916]).

Cox, James, *Old and New St. Louis: A Concise History . . . with a Biographical Appendix* (St. Louis: Central Biographical Co. and The Sunday Mirror, 1894).

Lyon, Harris Merton, *Graphics* (St. Louis, 1913).

Makers of St. Louis, The: A Brief Sketch of the Growth of a Great City, with Biographies . . . (St. Louis: The Mirror, 1906).

McGaffey, Ernest, *Sonnets to a Wife* (St. Louis, 1901; augmented ed., [1910?]).

Mirror, The. Published weekly under one of three variants of that title from February 1891 to September 1920. No copy earlier than vol. 4, no. 1 (February 25, 1894), has been found. That

BIBLIOGRAPHY

issue and succeeding ones are entitled *Sunday Mirror* and published by The Sunday Mirror Company of St. Louis. On February 28, 1895, when day of publication was changed, title became *The Mirror*. The company failed in October 1896, was bought by James Campbell, and was given to WMR, who became publisher in December 1896. The subtitle *Reedy's Paper* was added later, and from May 30, 1913, until his death, in July 1920, the title was *Reedy's Mirror*. Publication was continued from August 5 to September 2, 1920, under same title by Charles J. Finger, who called himself "Editor in Charge," and the magazine was revived under title of *The Mirror*, sporadically thereafter. The last issue of this trivial ghost that I have seen is marked vol. 14, no. 21, is dated December 1944, and was edited by Barry Lewis.

The system of numbering volumes and issues broke down several times, so that date of publication is the only safe reference. In 1910 the printers neglected to alter the volume and number series, so that there are two volumes numbered 19. From that time on (February 1910) all volume numbers are erroneous, and the confusion is compounded by efforts of librarians and their binders to re-order the files. Continuous pagination was introduced in September 1915. There were several "mug issues" of more than two hundred pages issued earlier, the most useful being vol. 21, no. 11 (May 9, 1912), containing biographical sketches of several of Reedy's friends, including James Campbell, which I attribute to WMR.

The only good files are at the Mercantile Library of St. Louis, which owns the office file, containing a partial index inserted, and at SLP, which owns the unique fourth volume and duplicates of the following: vol. 14–16 (1904–1907) and vol. 18–24 (1908–1915). All duplicates have been microfilmed by the University of Chicago Library, apparently for its own exclusive use and not for loan or distribution. Duke University has under consideration a complete microfilm of available files.

Contrary to information in Miss Gregory's *Union List of Serials,* there is no broken file of early issues at Salt Lake City; and Howard Mumford Jones is incorrect in stating in his *Guide to American Literature and its Backgrounds Since 1890* (Cambridge, Mass., 1953, p. 54) that the *Mirror* was a "wandering periodical, St. Louis being only one of its homes . . ." The magazine seems never to have missed an issue during Reedy's tenure, was always published from St. Louis, and always contained his share of copy even when he was in the hospital or abroad.

BIBLIOGRAPHY

Mirror Pamphlets. See listing under "1. *Writings of William Marion Reedy* . . .", above.

St. Louis Sunday Tidings. Only one report, Miss Fox's, attests the existence of this magazine, which is said to have come out in 1890 or thereabouts, and to have been superseded by the *Mirror.* No copy has been seen, and its having existed at all is doubtful.

Valley Magazine, The. Published monthly in St. Louis by WMR, from August 1902 until November 1903, when it was sold to the Mead-Biggers Company and superseded by their *Valley Weekly.* Volume 1, containing six issues, 322 pp. (6" x 9") and running from August 1902 through January 1903, may be seen at the Mercantile Library of St. Louis and the State Historical Society of Missouri, at Columbia. Volume 2, in a larger format (10" x 14"), containing nine issues, dated from February through November 1903, is at the State Historical Society, which also owns a third volume (December 1903 through July 1904), and a broken run of subsequent issues. Miss Gregory reports other broken runs at the Library of Congress, the Chicago Historical Society, and the University of Texas. Reedy edited the first two volumes, Claude H. Wetmore and Robertus Love the third. Reedy was also author of a column, "As the World Goes," which he signed "Touchstone." This ceased when he sold the magazine.

3. *Manuscript and Letter Collections*

Akins, Zoë, to Thekla Bernays, 1913–1920. MHS. More than 40 sheets of intimate correspondence, often supplementing Reedy's.

Barry, James H., to Mrs. William C. de Mille, July 1920. MHS. Two letters and a telegram concerning Reedy's final visit and his death.

Bloch, Albert, to Thekla Bernays, 1920–1921. MHS. More than 30 sheets in English and German, written after Reedy's death.

Braithwaite, W. S., to Thomas Bird Mosher. Harvard.

——— to Carl Sandburg, November 14, 1920. Harvard.

Byars, William Vincent, Correspondence, 1867–1942. MHS. Contains several hundred items, including letters from his parents and WMR, and a long exchange with Arthur Brisbane.

——— Notebooks, holographs, and annotated books, some with correspondence laid in. The library, containing some 4,000 volumes is at the home of Byars' daughters, Mrs. C. H. Dawson, Miss Mary, and Miss Katharine L. Byars, 425 North Taylor Ave., Kirkwood, 22, Mo.

Bynner, Witter. MS., "Iphigenia," [1915?]. Harvard.

BIBLIOGRAPHY

———— and Arthur Davison Ficke, typescript, "Spectra: A Book of Poetic Experiments." Yale. Original inscribed "To the Yale University Library . . . Emanuel Morgan."

———— Typescript, "Spectra . . ." A bound copy of same. Yale. Ficke's copy with numerous marginalia and a memorandum initialed by Bynner and Ficke, laid in, together with discarded poems.

———— to Arthur Davison Ficke, June 7, 1904–December 6, 1945. Yale. Some three hundred sheets with many enclosures and envelopes, but with letters of the Spectrist period apparently removed by Ficke.

———— to Amy Lowell, September 8, 1916–October 11, 1917. Harvard.

Chubb, Percival. The "Elmer Chubb" correspondence. St. Louis Ethical Society. Letters from several members of the Society attempting to put an end to the satiric letters and comments of Edgar Lee Masters and Charles J. Finger on "Elmer Chubb, LL.D, Ph. D."

Filley, Chauncey Ives. "Scrap Book," 1908. SLP. Annotated electrotype reproduction of a collection of clippings and letters.

Filsinger, Ernst, to Eunice Tietjens, 1914–. Newberry. Contains some 20 items of biographical interest.

Filsinger, Sara Teasdale. See "Teasdale," below.

Glaenzer, Richard B., to W. S. Braithwaite, November 14 and 19, 1918. Harvard.

Harris, Frank, to Thekla Bernays, August 5, 1916. MHS.

Kennerley, Mitchell, to W. S. Braithwaite, 1911–1914. Harvard. Concerns *Lyric Year* and Braithwaite's *Anthology*.

———— to [Charles van Ravenswaay], Director, MHS. Indicates that Kennerley gave his letters from WMR. to Fred W. Wolf prior to August 15, 1949.

———— to Thomas Bird Mosher (and his secretary Miss F. M. Lamb), 1897, 1924. Contains 48 items.

———— to Alfred Stieglitz, 1916–1923. Yale. Includes letter on death of Mosher, "my oldest friend in America," September 5, 1923.

Lowell, Amy, to Witter Bynner, 1917–1921. Harvard. Contains 16 items plus carbon copies, mainly about poetry, after the "Spectra" hoax.

———— to John Livingston Lowes, 1916–1924. Harvard. Contains 22 items, some written while he was in St. Louis.

Masters, Edgar Lee, to W. S. Braithwaite, 12 November 1918. Harvard.

———— to Theodore Dreiser, 1912–1914. UP. Some 36 sheets out of a much larger correspondence are pertinent to this study.

BIBLIOGRAPHY

———— to Arthur Davison Ficke. Yale. Belongs largely to a later period.

———— to Carter H. Harrison, Jr., 1913–1948. Newberry. Peripheral, but warrants further inspection.

Masters Collection. Huntington Library. A "sizable collection of Masters MSS., but only one letter and that is about one of his MSS.," according to a report from Guy Adams Cardwell, June 9, 1955.

Masters Collection. UP. On deposit; this large collection is more fully discussed below under the Reedy correspondence.

Newberry Library. Among headings too numerous for separate listing here are the following collections: Dell-Ficke, Dell-Deland, Ficke-Hambledon, Rice-Garland, and Mosher (Misc.). In the Carter Harrison Collection, the following: Altgeld, Bryan, Darrow, Garland, and Yerkes. Among collections analyzed for the MLA American Literature Group, are the following MS. holdings: Anderson (An), Cowley (Cow), Dell (De), Hambledon-Ficke (Ham), Little Room (Li), Agnes Freer (Fre), O'Hara (Oh), Teasdale (Oh), Tietjens (Ti); also, Aiken (Ti), Benét (Ri, Ti, Cow), Bloch (Ti), Bodenheim (Ti), Braithwaite (Ti), Bynner (Cow, De, Ri, Ti, An), Chatfield-Taylor (Li, Pa), Fuller (Fu, We); also the following: Darrow (Ri, Ha, Be), Deland (De), Deutsch (De), Dreiser (An), Ficke (De, Ti, Ham), Garland (Ri), Kennerley (Ti), Kreymborg (Ti, An, De), Lindsay (De, Ti, Misc.), Masters (Ha, Ti), Mencken (An), Monroe (Ti), Mosher (M), Roosevelt (Ha), Sandburg (Ti), Teasdale (Ti, Oh), Viereck (An), Wheelock (De).

Reedy, William Marion, to Zoë Akins. Huntington. Said to contain about 100 items. This collection is not available for inspection.

———— to Thekla Bernays, 1897, 1908–1917. MHS. About 35 items.

———— to Albert Bloch, 1909–1913. MHS. Most revealing collection of WMR letters that has yet come to light.

———— to W. S. Braithwaite, 1915–1917. Harvard. Three items of minor significance.

———— to William Vincent Byars, 1895–1918. MHS. Contains some 30 items, including some carbon copies of Byars' letters to WMR.

———— to Witter Bynner, 1909–1920. MHS. Collection of some 34 letters courageously presented to the Society with a revealing letter of transmittal.

———— to Anna George de Mille (Mrs. William C. de Mille), 1920. MHS. Letters covering the last three months of Reedy's life.

———— to Babette Deutsch, 1917–1919. Miss Deutsch. Collection

BIBLIOGRAPHY

of 26 letters containing suggestions for and reactions to her critical articles for the *Mirror*.

———— to Theodore Dreiser, 1901–1919. UP. Contains about 65 items, of great importance.

———— to Frank Harris, July 17, 1916. Gertz Collection, Chicago. A letter owned by Mr. Elmer Gertz, 120 South LaSalle Street, Chicago.

———— to W. B. Huebsch, 1917. Newberry. Six letters, chiefly interesting because of Reedy's enthusiastic remarks on James Joyce.

———— to Edgar Lee Masters. On deposit, UP. The collection contains 188 sheets, according to Mrs. Ellen Coyne Masters, who says it represents 1,400 correspondents. It will not be available for inspection until catalogued and sold. According to William S. Dix, Librarian of Princeton University, who had custody of it for several years following Masters' death, it represents "a considerable mass of miscellaneous papers . . . including manuscripts, correspondence, and books from his library . . . contained in some five or six locked trunks." (Letter of September 20, 1955.)

———— to Harriet Monroe, 1915–1919. University of Chicago. Consists of seven rather formal letters.

———— to Lincoln Steffens, June 6, 1910. Columbia University Library.

———— to Eunice Tietjens, 1917, 1919. Newberry. Two letters giving permission to reprint poems and mentioning Masters.

———— to Mrs. Minnie McIntyre Wallace, 1906, 1912. University of Chicago. Contains reference to John L. Hervey and Oliver White.

Reedy Collection, SLP. Acquired from Mrs. Reedy, May 24, 1924, contains annotated and presentation copies of books. A program of exercises in connection with the presentation of a bronze portrait medallion of WMR contains the only list of 78 presentation copies of books from his library of some 500 volumes. The collection was not kept together, but presentation copies are held by the Library's Reference Service and may be consulted after referring to the printed program.

Sandburg, Carl. Correspondence. University of Illinois, Urbana. John T. Flanagan reported on May 31, 1957 that the University had acquired "the Carl Sandburg library," but that Mr. Sandburg was retaining his papers for the time being, while writing his autobiography. Reedy's letters are presumably included, but no description is available.

Teasdale, Sara, to W. S. Braithwaite. A collection said to consist of

BIBLIOGRAPHY

60 autographs was offered to SLP in 1941 by R. F. Roberts, a New York dealer. It has not been found.

——— to Ernst Filsinger, 1915–1927. MHS. This large collection contains not only her letters to her husband but other family papers dating from 1911.

——— to Orrick Johns, 1912. Yale. Three letters enclosing poems.

——— to John Myers O'Hara, 1908–1914. Newberry. Contains some 300 items.

——— to Eunice Tietjens, 1913–1932. Newberry. Several hundred sheets, including familiar discussion of the writer's friendship with Vachel Lindsay, John Hall Wheelock, John Myers O'Hara, and others.

Tietjens, Eunice, MS., "Biographical Notes on Edgar Lee Masters, March 1923." Newberry.

II. SECONDARY SOURCES

1. Unpublished Dissertations, Theses, and Articles

[Brann, William Cowper.] See Randolph, John.

Byars, Mary Warner, "Reminiscences of William Vincent Byars," article at MHS. A mass of other Byars material (referred to under "Manuscript and Letter Collections," above) includes unpublished articles and marginalia.

[Dreiser, Theodore.] See Saalbach, Robert.

Elta, Thomas, "Missouri Poets of the Twentieth Century," M.A. thesis, William Jewell College, Liberty, Mo., 1928.

Ficke, Arthur Davison, "The Spectric School of Poetry," article, Yale.

Fox, Marjorie Eileen, "William Marion Reedy and the St. Louis *Mirror*," M.A. thesis, University of Illinois, Urbana, 1947.

Huntress, Keith G., "Thomas Bird Mosher: A Biographical and Critical Study," diss., University of Illinois, Urbana, 1942. (Diss. abstract also available, Urbana, 1942.)

Mosher, Frederick L., "*The Dial,*" diss., University of Illinois, Urbana, 1951.

Randolph, John, "Apostle of the Devil: W. C. Brann," diss. Vanderbilt University, Nashville, Tenn., 1939.

Reedy, Margaret Rhodes (Mrs. William Marion Reedy), "Chapter: I Kidnap My Editor," Typescript carbon copy of book chapter or serial installment, given to Miss Preston Settle of the Mercantile Library of St. Louis by Mrs. Reedy.

Saalbach, Robert P., "Collected Poems of Theodore Dreiser," diss., University of Washington, Seattle, 1951.

Schlich, Ross, "The *Mirror*: A Reflection of William Marion Reedy,"

BIBLIOGRAPHY

incomplete draft of M.A. thesis in the hands of the author, Dr. Ross Schlich, 1208 Spivey Building, East St. Louis. Ill.

Seelig, Clover H., "William Marion Reedy: A St. Louis Titan," article by the widow of Reedy's physician, Mrs. Major Seelig, of Atherton, Cal.

Wolf, Fred Wilhelm, "William Marion Reedy: A Critical Biography," diss., Vanderbilt University, Nashville, Tenn., 1951. (Issued as No. 7180 in Doctoral Dissertation Series, Ann Arbor, Mich., University Microfilms, 1954.)

2. *Published Books and Articles*

Åhnebrink, Lars, *The Beginnings of Naturalism in American Fiction* (Upsala: Lundquist; and Cambridge, Mass.: Harvard University Press, 1950).

André-Johnson, Anne, *Notable Women of St. Louis: 1914* (St. Louis, privately printed).

Archer, William, "The American Cheap Magazine," *Fortnightly Review,* 87:921 (1910).

Bernays, Thekla, *Augustus Charles Bernays: A Memoir* (St. Louis: Mosby, 1912).

——— "Currents of Modern Literature," *St. Louis Globe-Democrat,* April 15, 1894.

——— "Studies in Contemporary Literature: *Gaston de Latour,*" *Criterion* (St. Louis), 15:7 (August 7, 1897).

[Bloch, Albert.] See Derrickson, Howard; also Valentin, Curt, Gallery.

Bodenheim, Maxwell, *Minna and Myself* (New York: Pagan Press, [1919]).

Brashear, Minnie M., "Missouri Literature Since the First World War," *MHR,* 18:315 (April 1924).

Burke, Harry Rosecrans, *From the Day's Journey: A Book of By-Paths and Eddies about St. Louis* (St. Louis: Miner, 1924).

Byars, William Vincent, *Glory of the Garden, The . . . With a Note on the Relations of the Horatian Ode and the Tuscan Sonnet* (New York, privately printed, n.d. [c. 1896?]).

——— *Homeric Memory Rhyme*[s] (South Orange, N.J.: privately printed, 1895; rev. ed., St. Louis: privately printed, 1916).

——— *Origins of Modern Verse, The* ([St. Louis:] privately printed, n.d., [1924]).

——— *Poets and Poetry: A Lecture* (St. Louis, New York, Chicago: American University Society, n.d.).

——— *Practical Value of the Classics, The; A Lecture* (Lebanon, Ill.: McKendrie College, 1901).

BIBLIOGRAPHY

——— *Studies in Verse with Certain Melodies* ([St. Louis], privately printed, 1933).

Carpenter, Margaret Haley, *Sara Teasdale: A Biography* (New York: Schulte, 1960).

Carver, Charles, *Brann and the Iconoclast*, with intro. by Roy Bedichek (Austin: University of Texas Press, 1957).

Chandler, Josephine C., *The Spoon River Country*, offprint from *Journal of Illinois State Historical Society*, vol. 14, nos. 3–4 (n.d. [1923]).

Clark, Harry Hayden, ed., *Transitions in American Literary History* (Durham, N.C.: Duke University Press, for the Modern Language Association, 1953).

Cowley, Malcolm, "Magazine Business," *New Republic*, 115:521 (1946).

Damon, S. Foster, *Amy Lowell: A Chronicle* (Boston: Houghton Mifflin, 1935).

De Menil, Alexander N., "A History of Missouri Literature," *MHR*, 15:74 (October 1935).

Derrickson, Howard, "Art and Artists: Albert Bloch and 'The Blue Rider,'" *St. Louis Post-Dispatch*, December 12, 1954.

Dreiser, Theodore, *A Book About Myself* (New York: Boni & Liveright, 1922); originally appeared as "Out of My Newspaper Days," *Bookman*, 54:42, 208, 542; 55:12, 118 (November 1921 through April 1922) and was republished as *Newspaper Days* (New York: Liveright, 1931).

——— *Free, and Other Stories* (New York: Putnam, 1918).

——— *Letters of Theodore Dreiser: A Selection*, ed. Robert H. Elias, 4 vols. (Philadelphia: University of Pennsylvania Press, 1959).

——— *Twelve Men* (New York: Boni & Liveright, 1919; 6th printing, 1923).

Duffey, Bernard, *The Chicago Renaissance in American Letters: A Critical History* (East Lansing: Michigan State College Press, 1954).

Dunbar, Olivia Howard, *A House in Chicago* (Chicago: University of Chicago Press, 1947).

Eliot, T. S., *Ezra Pound: His Metric and Poetry* (New York: Knopf, 1917). A copy in WMR library at SLP.

Farrell, James T., "Some Observations on Naturalism, So Called," *Antioch Review*, 10:257 (1950).

Flanagan, John T., "Literary Protests in the Midwest," *Southwest Review*, 34:148 (1948).

——— "Reedy of the *Mirror*," *MHR*, 43:128 (1949).

BIBLIOGRAPHY

———— "Some Projects in Midwest Cultural History," *Indiana Magazine of History*, 47:239 (1951).
Garland, Hamlin, *Crumbling Idols*, ed. with intro., Robert E. Spiller (Gainesville, Fla.: Scholar's Facsimiles and Reprints, 1952).
Geiger, Louis G., *Joseph W. Folk of Missouri*, in University of Missouri Studies, vol. 25, no. 2 (Columbia: Curators of the University, 1953).
Gregory, Horace, and Marya Zaturenska, *A History of American Poetry: 1900–1940* (New York: Harcourt, Brace; 1946).
Hansen, Harry, *Midwest Portraits* (New York: Harcourt, Brace; 1923).
Harmon, Frances B., *Social Philosophy of the St. Louis Hegelians* (New York: Columbia University Press, 1943).
Heller, Otto, *Henrik Ibsen: Plays and Problems* (Boston: Houghton Mifflin, 1912).
Hoffman, Frederick J., Charles Allen, and Carolyn Ulrich, *The Little Magazines: A History and a Bibliography* (Princeton, N.J.: Princeton University Press, 1946).
Holliday, Robert Cortes, *Men and Books and Cities* (New York, 1920).
Hubach, Robert R., "St. Louis, Host of . . . Authors," *MHR*, 37:375 (1944).
———— "Walt Whitman Visits St. Louis," *ibid.*, 37:386 (1943); *AL*, 14:141 (1942).
Huneker, James, *Steeplejack*, 2 vols. (New York: Scribner, 1921).
———— *Letters*, ed. Josephine Huneker (New York: Scribner, 1922).
Hutcherson, Dudley R., "Poe's Reputation in England and America: 1850–1909," *AL*, 14:223 (1942).
Hyde, William, and Howard L. Conard, eds., *Encyclopedia of the History of St. Louis*, 4 vols. (New York, etc.: Southern History Company, 1899).
Johns, George Sibley, *Thekla Bernays: In Memoriam*, pamphlet (St. Louis: Artists' Guild, 1931).
Johns, Orrick, *Time of Our Lives: The Story of My Father and Myself* (New York: Stackpole, 1937).
[Johnson, Anne.] See André-Johnson, Anne.
Kelsoe, W. A., *St. Louis Reference Record* (St. Louis: von Hoffman, n.d. [1927?]).
King, Ethel, *Reflections of Reedy: A Biography of William Marion Reedy* (Brooklyn, N.Y.: Rickard, 1961).
Kramer, Sidney, *A History of Stone & Kimball and Herbert S. Stone & Co. . . . 1893–1905* (Chicago: Forgue, 1940).
Kreymborg, Alfred, *Troubadour: An Autobiography* (New York: Boni & Liveright, 1925).

BIBLIOGRAPHY

Lehmann-Haupt, Helmut, *The Book in America: A History* (New York: Bowker, 1951).

Lowell, Amy, *Tendencies in Modern American Poetry* (New York: Macmillan, 1917)

——— "Two Generations of American Poetry," in *Contemporary American Criticism*, ed. J. C. Bowman (New York, 1926).

[Lowell, Amy.] See Damon, S. Foster.

Masters, Edgar Lee, *Across Spoon River* (New York: Farrar & Rinehart, [1936]).

——— *Vachel Lindsay: A Poet in America* (New York: Scribner, 1935).

——— "Genesis of Spoon River," *American Mercury*, 28:48 (1933).

——— "Literary Boss of the Middle West," *American Mercury*, 34:450 (1934).

——— "William Marion Reedy," *American Speech*, 9:96 (1934).

——— "William Marion Reedy: Feaster," *Esquire* (October 1939), p. 67.

[Masters, Edgar Lee.] See Chandler, Josephine C.

[Menil, Alexander N., de.] See De Menil, Alexander N.

Millay, Edna St. Vincent, *Letters*, ed. Allan Ross Macdougall (New York: Harper, 1952).

Monroe, Harriet, *A Poet's Life* (New York: Macmillan, 1938).

Mott, Frank Luther, *American Journalism* (rev. ed., New York: Macmillan, 1947).

——— *Golden Multitudes: The Story of Best-Sellers in the United States* (New York: Macmillan, 1947).

——— *A History of American Magazines*, 4 vols. (Cambridge, Mass.: Harvard University Press, 1957).

Perry, Charles M., *The St. Louis Movement in Philosophy: Some Source Materials* (Norman: University of Oklahoma Press, 1930).

Pochmann, Henry A., *German Culture in the United States* (Madison: University of Wisconsin Press, 1957).

——— *New England Transcendentalism and St. Louis Hegelianism* (Philadelphia: Carl Schurz Foundation, 1948).

Pottle, Frederick A., "Aldi discipulus americanus," in [Thomas B. Mosher], *Amphora: A Second Collection of Prose and Verse* (Portland, Me.: Mosher, 1926).

Pound, Ezra, *The Letters of Ezra Pound: 1907–1941*, ed. D. D. Paige (New York: Harcourt, Brace; 1950). Microfilms of the original MSS. at the University of Chicago reveal many omissions and emendations.

——— Preface to *Poetical Works of Lionel Johnson* (London: Mathews, 1915).

BIBLIOGRAPHY

———— "Webster Ford," *Egoist*, 2:11 (January 1, 1915).

Rittenhouse, Jessie B., *My House of Life: An Autobiography* (Boston: Houghton Mifflin, 1934).

St. Louis University. *Memorial Volume of the Diamond Jubilee, 1829–1904*. (St. Louis, 1904).

Schwab, Arnold T., "James Huneker's Criticism of American Literature," *AL*, 29:64 (1957).

Seitz, Don C., *Joseph Pulitzer: His Life and Letters* (New York: Simon & Schuster, 1924).

Shoemaker, Floyd Calvin, "Missouri Literature: 1900–1940," in *Missouri and Missourians* (Chicago: Lewis, 1943).

———— "WMR," in *Missouri Day by Day* (Jefferson City: State Historical Society of Missouri, 1943).

Snider, Denton J., *The St. Louis Movement* (St. Louis: Sigma, 1920).

———— *A Writer of Books* (St. Louis: Sigma, 1910).

Stevens, Thomas Wood, and Percy Mackaye, *The Pageant and Masque of St. Louis* (St. Louis: Pageant Drama Association, 1914).

Tietjens, Eunice, *The World at My Shoulder* (New York: Macmillan, 1938).

Towne, Charles Hanson, "The One-Man Magazine," *American Mercury*, 63:104 (1946).

Untermeyer, Louis, *From Another World* (New York: Harcourt, Brace; 1930).

Vale, Charles, "The Lyric Year," *Forum*, 49:91 (1913).

Valentin, Curt [Gallery], *Der Blaue Reiter*, catalogue, with extracts from a letter by Wassily Kandinsky (New York: Valentin, December 1954).

Wells, Rolla, *Episodes of My Life* (St. Louis, privately printed, 1933).

Winkler, Jean, "William Marion Reedy," *St. Louis Review*, 2:5 (January 28, 1933).

———— "William Marion Reedy and the *Mirror*," *ibid.*, 2:7 (February 11, 1933).

Wood, James P., *Magazines in the United States: Their Social and Economic Influence* (New York: Ronald, 1949).

NOTES

CHAPTER 1: Persona non grata

1. Even mass media in that time enjoyed less currency than they came to have a decade or so later. *Harper's Weekly* boasted 80,000 subscribers, and there were only seventy or eighty magazines that exceeded 100,000. See Frank Luther Mott, *History of American Magazines* (Cambridge, Mass., 1938), III, 6–9; (Cambridge, 1957), IV, 17; and cf. N. W. Ayer, *American Newspaper Annual* (Philadelphia, 1897).

CHAPTER 2: A Boy in Kerry Patch

1. "St. Louis: The Future Great," in *Historic Towns of the Western States*, ed. Lyman P. Powell (New York and London, 1901), p. 331. For the previously unrecognized significance of the Camp Jackson episode see Jared C. Lobdell, "Nathaniel Lyon and the Battle of Wilson's Creek," *MHS Bull.*, 17:3 (October 1960), and James W. Covington, "The Camp Jackson Affair: 1861," *MHR*, 55:197 (April 1961); also Arthur Roy Kirkpatrick, "The Admission of Missouri to the Confederacy," *MHR*, 55:366 (July 1961), one of a series of revealing studies.

2. J. Elbert Jones, *A Review of Famous Crimes Solved by St. Louis Policemen* (St. Louis, n.d. [1924?]), p. 43.

3. Most of these details appear in Marjorie Eileen Fox, "William Marion Reedy and the St. Louis *Mirror*," M.A. thesis, University of Illinois, 1947; and Fred Wilhelm Wolf, "William Marion Reedy: A Critical Biography," diss., Vanderbilt University, 1951 (issued as No. 7180 in Doctoral Dissertation Series, Ann Arbor, Mich., University Microfilms, 1954). The last item is from Clover H. Seelig, "William Marion Reedy: A St. Louis Titan," unpublished article lent me by the author.

4. Reedy, "Jack Shea and I," *Mirror*, 23:4 (July 10, 1914).

5. However, cf. Ethel King, *Reflections of Reedy: A Biography* (Brooklyn, N.Y., 1961), p. 8.

6. Reedy, "Jack Shea and I."

NOTES TO CHAPTER 2

7. Reedy, *A Golden Book and the Literature of Childhood* (Cedar Rapids, Ia., 1910), p. 39.

8. Reedy to Albert Bloch, March 30, 1909. MHS.

9. Reedy, "A Funeral in the Family," *Mirror*, 14:3 (October 27, 1904). My copy of this issue is extensively annotated in blue pencil. My guess is that this was done by Tubman K. Hedrick, who edited it as Reedy's assistant. Over this article is scrawled: "The stuff seems born of keen sorrow—maybe fake, though it rings true."

10. *Ibid.*

CHAPTER 3: Literati in the City Room

1. See W. A. Kelsoe, *St. Louis Reference Record* (St. Louis, n.d. [1927?]), p. 249; W. B. Stevens, "Biographical Notes," *Mirror*, 29:606 (August 5, 1920); Reedy's article in the *St. Louis Republic* centennial issue, July 12, 1908.

2. Dreiser, *A Book About Myself* (New York, 1922), p. 206. See my article "Dreiser, Reedy, and 'De Maupassant, Junior,'" *AL*, 33:466 (January 1962).

3. Reedy in *St. Louis Republic* centennial issue, July 12, 1908. On Reedy's attitude toward Kelsoe see Reedy to Bernays, October 16, 1911. MHS.

4. Don C. Seitz, *Joseph Pulitzer: His Life and Letters* (New York, 1926), p. 112. Cf. the *Spectator* (St. Louis), 3:121 (October 21, 1882), 3: 261, 316 (December 1882), and 3:448 (January 27, 1883). For articles which played a part in the Slayback killing see *St. Louis Post-Dispatch*, October 13, 1882, p. 4, col. 4, and editorial in following issue, p. 4, col. 2. Cf. Ernest Kirschten, *Catfish and Crystal* (New York, 1960), p. 30.

5. "A Piece Patibulary," *Mirror*, 27:219 (April 12, 1918).

6. *St. Louis Republic* centennial issue, July 12, 1908.

7. The death of Jesse James is treated in front-page articles in *Missouri Republican*, April 4–6, and April 18, 1882. For the surrender of Frank James see *ibid.*, October 6, 1882, pp. 4–7; October 7, p. 2, col. 1; October 8, p. 9, col. 7; October 9, p. 1, col. 7; October 10, p. 6, col. 3; October 12, p. 3, col. 3; and October 14, p. 4, col. 5.

8. Wolf, "Critical Biography," p. 16, and *Mirror*, 7:4 (August 5, 1897).

9. *New York World*, March 17, 1895, p. 6, col. 1; *ibid.*, March 24, 1895, p. 14, col. 1; and see Reedy to Byars, April 8, 1895. MHS. Better statements of Byars' prosodic theories will be found in his essay "The Horatian Ode and the Tuscan Sonnet," *The Glory of the Garden* (privately printed, n.d.; probably in New York, June 1896). There are also two privately printed collections of essays, *The*

THE DECADENCE

Origins of Modern Verse (St. Louis, 1924) and *Studies in Verse with Certain Melodies* (St. Louis, 1933), which were generously presented to me by Byars' daughter Mrs. Clarence Dawson of Kirkwood, Mo. Richard Ohmann, who has examined some of Byars' works for me, is not impressed with their prosodic importance. "What animates him is a genuine love of language and poetry, without a corresponding analytic talent," he writes, in a letter dated February 13, 1961.

10. Clarence E. Miller, "William Marion Reedy: A Patchwork Portrait," *MHS Bull.*, 17:45 (October 1960). Mr. Miller has found more information about Reedy's obscure years in the city directory than had previously been found by biographical students.

CHAPTER 4: The Decadence—From Oscar Wilde to an "American Baudelaire"

1. My general authority, especially for the hypothesis that the idea of the decadence grows out of the myth of the noble savage, is A. E. Carter, *The Idea of Decadence in French Literature: 1830–1900* (Toronto, 1958). Other useful studies are Lois and F. E. Hyslop, *Baudelaire on Poe* (State College, Pa., 1952), William Eickhorst, *Decadence in German Fiction* (Denver, 1953), and R. W. B. Lewis, *The American Adam* (Chicago, 1955), notably chap. 1. I should have been much indebted to Oscar Cargill's analysis of the dichotomy of decadence and naturalism in *Intellectual America: Ideas on the March* (New York, 1941) but unfortunately did not know this valuable work when the chapter was written.

2. Reedy, "A Golden Book," in his *The Law of Love* ([East Aurora, N.Y.], 1905, p. 135. Originally appeared in *Brann's Iconoclast*, 7:70 (April 1897).

3. "He is a noble savage—in reverse." Carter, *Idea of Decadence*, p. 6.

4. See Octave Mirbeau, *Le Jardin des supplices* (Paris, 1899), tr. as *Torture Garden* (New York, 1948) by Alvah Bessie, with foreword by James Huneker. See also Joris Karl Huysmans, *Against the Grain [À rebours]*, with introduction by Havelock Ellis (New York, 1931), p. 325 et passim.

5. "Reflections," *Mirror*, 5:4 (January 23, 1896).

6. Harry T. Levin, "The Discovery of Bohemia," chap. 64 in *LHUS* (rev. ed., New York, 1953) appeared originally as "America Discovers Bohemia," *Atlantic Monthly*, 180:68 (September 1947). As a magazine article it was provocative and apt, but it is my contention that the same amusing matter sets up a false category in the

NOTES TO CHAPTER 4

context of a standard literary history. It should certainly not have been given the authority of such publication when Oscar Cargill's study (n. 1 above) had already been out for six years.

7. Or Frank O'Neil, who was city editor in 1881, but transferred to Scripps's *Chronicle* at about this time, taking Byars with him. See Kelsoe, *Reference Record*, p. 324.

8. A. Lloyd Lewis and Henry Justin Smith, *Oscar Wilde Discovers America* (New York, 1936), p. 205.

9. *St. Louis Post-Dispatch*, February 25, 1882, p. 1, col. 4; *ibid.*, February 27, p. 5, col. 1; and *St. Louis Globe-Democrat*, February 26, 1882.

10. *St. Louis Globe-Democrat*, February 26, 1882. Article cited in n. 9.

11. *Missouri Republican*, February 26, 1882, p. 13, col. 1; and *ibid.*, February 27, 1882, p. 4, col. 2.

12. *Missouri Republican*, February 27, 1882. Article cited in n. 11.

13. M. A. Fanning, "Chief O' the Clan," *Mirror*, 29:627 (August 12, 1920). Actually, Helena Petrovna Blavatsky had founded the Theosophical Society in New York and departed for India before Reedy and Fanning met, but Fanning apparently heard of her only later.

14. Carlin T. Kindilien, *American Poetry in the Nineties* (Providence, 1956), p. 188. See also Cupid Jones (pseud.), *Fact and Fancy* (New York, 1895), an anthology of Saltus's *Town Topics* poems.

15. See Edgar Saltus, *Parnassians Personally Recollected* (Cedar Rapids, Ia., 1923), p. 19; Marie Saltus, *Edgar Saltus: The Man* (Chicago, 1925), p. 28; and James Huneker, *Steeplejack* (New York, 1921), II, 11.

16. Marion Reed (pseud.), "The American Baudelaire," *Mirror*, 4:11 (May 6, 1894).

17. M. A. Fanning, "Chief O' the Clan," *Mirror*, 29:627 (August 12, 1920).

18. W. M. R., "Some Epigrams: Showing How Easy Oscar Does It," *Mirror*, 4:13 (April 29, 1894).

19. "Reflections," *Mirror*, 7:2 (April 8, 1897). Cf. "Reflections," 5:1 (April 11, 1895), in the course of which Reedy calls *Dorian Gray* "perhaps the most debasing production to which the human mind has set itself since the Marquis de Sade."

20. "A Weird Poem by a Weird Man," *Mirror*, 8:4 (July 21, 1898). Reedy's copy, given him by Ernest McGaffey, is in the Reedy collection at the St. Louis Public Library. See my note, "Masters's 'Maltravers,'" *AL*, 31:491 (January 1960).

21. "Reflections," *Mirror*, 13:3 (March 22, 1900).

FOUNDING OF THE *MIRROR*

CHAPTER 5: The Founding of the *Mirror*

1. "Announcement," *American Queen and Town Topics,* 13:3 (January 3, 1885). The title was shortened the following month, the prospectus repeated in slightly emended form. The publisher was then E. D. Mann, of whom nothing significant seems to be recorded. See also "More Press Comments," *American Queen and Town Topics,* 13:2 (January 17, 1885). Rare; copy at Yale.

2. *Collier's Magazine,* 36:25 (November 11, 1905); and cf. *World's Work,* 11:7369 (April 1906), and Mott, *History of American Magazines,* IV, 751.

3. Ludwig Lewisohn, *Expression in America* (New York and London: Harper, 1932), 314–316. Quoted by permission.

4. "Reflections," *Mirror,* 4:2 (July 8, 1894).

5. Dreiser's *A Book About Myself* (New York; Boni & Liveright, 1922). Another edition entitled *Newspaper Days* (New York: Liveright, 1931). Was originally published as "Out of My Newspaper Days," *Bookman,* 54: 42, 208, 542; 55: 12, 118 (November 1921 through April 1922).

6. Articles referring to the early history of the magazine will be found in *Mirror,* 7:6 (February 17, 1897) and 7:1 (December 16, 1897).

7. "Reflections," *Mirror,* 4:2 (July 8, 1894).

8. Kelsoe, *Reference Record,* pp. 165, 242.

9. A. N. De Menil, "A Century of Missouri Literature," *MHR,* 15:97 (October 1920), and "Magazine Literature" in *Encyclopedia of the History of St. Louis,* ed. William Hyde and H. L. Conard (St. Louis, 1899). Hyde was Reedy's former editor-in-chief.

10. "Miscellaneous Journals" in *Encyclopedia of St. Louis,* ed. Hyde and Conard.

11. De Menil, "Magazine Literature," in *Encyclopedia of St. Louis.*

12. Denton J. Snider, *A Writer of Books* (St. Louis, 1910), pp. 387–389. See also his *The St. Louis Movement* (St. Louis, 1920).

13. See Charles M. Perry, *The St. Louis Movement in Philosophy: Some Source Material* (Norman, Okla., 1930), Frances Harmon, *Social Philosophy of the St. Louis Hegelians* (New York, 1943), and Henry A. Pochmann, *New England Transcendentalism and St. Louis Hegelianism* (Philadelphia, 1948) and *German Culture in America* (Madison, Wis., 1957).

14. Reedy, "What I've Been Reading," *Mirror,* 19:4 (May 26, 1910). A corroborative account unlisted in the bibliographies of works cited above (n. 13) is Augustine Warner, "Kultur in St. Louis," *Mirror,* 26:650 (October 12, 1917).

NOTES TO CHAPTER 5

15. Reedy, "Kindly Caricatures: No. 191," *Mirror*, 18:8 (February 18, 1909); see also "A Writer of Books," *ibid.*, 19:4 (May 26, 1910). According to Pochmann, Brokmeyer "lived the life of a hermit, pondering questions regarding 'whence we come and whither we go.'" *Transcendentalism and Hegelianism*, p. 9.
16. "Reflections," *Mirror*, 4:3 (April 8, 1894).
17. H. L. Mencken, *Prejudices: First Series* (New York: Knopf, 1919), p. 129. Quoted by permission.

CHAPTER 6: Toward Naturalism

1. "Currents of Literature," *St. Louis Globe-Democrat*, April 15, 1894. The full title is restored by hand in the author's copy. MHS.
2. Reedy to Bernays, August 8, 1897. MHS. The article appeared in Miss Bernays' "Studies in Contemporary Literature," *Criterion*, 15:7 (August 7, 1897).
3. Ethel L. Voynich obit., *New York Times*, July 29, 1960.
4. *The Second Common Reader* (New York: Harcourt, Brace, 1932), p. 291.
5. "Reflections," *Mirror*, 6:3 (February 27, 1896).
6. "The Black Rider," *Mirror*, 5:3 (May 23, 1895), and cf. "Reflections," *Mirror*, 8:3 (May 5, 1898).
7. "New Books," *Mirror*, 6:13 (July 10, 1896).
8. "Reflections," *Mirror*, 5:1 (February 21, 1895).
9. *Illustrated American*, 19:366 (March 1896).
10. "Reflections," *Mirror*, 6:3 (February 27, 1896).
11. *Crumbling Idols* (facsimile ed.), ed. Robert E. Spiller (Gainesville, Fla., 1952), p. 190.
12. "Culture in the West," *Mirror*, 6:5 (April 30, 1896).
13. "Zola: The Man and His Work," *Mirror*, 8:5 (March 10, 1898).
14. "Thomas Hardy's Art," *Mirror* 6:13 (June 25, 1896).

CHAPTER 7: The *Mirror's* "War Boom"

1. Clarence E. Miller, "William Marion Reedy: A Patchwork Portrait," *MHS Bull.*, 17:45 (October 1960), supplies details of his occupation and residence.
2. *Mirror*, 4:iii (March 4, 1894) carries an advertisement for Dr. Keeley's "double chloride of gold remedies" for alcohol and opium addiction. Reedy was presumably treated at the Keeley center in nearby Kirkwood, Mo., rather than at Dwight, Ill., as Wolf suggests ("Critical Biography," p. 48.)

3. Wolf, "Critical Biography," p. 50. Dr. Wolf interviewed Sullivan.

4. Miss Fox, "Reedy and the *Mirror*," (thesis), p. 17, refers to these data as "confirmed by intimate friends still living in St. Louis."

5. Wolf, "Critical Biography," p. 47, says the priest was Father J. J. Harty, who later became archbishop of Manila. See "Reflections," *Mirror*, 7:2 (March 4, 1897).

6. *Ibid.*, 5:3 (January 2, 1896).

7. *Ibid.*, 6:3 (June 18, 1896).

8. Cf. G. W. Auxier, "Middle Western Newspapers and the Spanish-American War," *Mississippi Valley Historical Review*, 26:523 (1940), and M. W. Wilkerson, *Public Opinion and the Spanish-American War* (Baton Rouge, 1932), pp. 62–63.

9. "Reflections," *Mirror*, 5:1 (January 23, 1896).

10. "Reflections," *Mirror*, 8:4 (March 24, 1898); and see Harold and Margaret Sprout, *Toward a New Order of Sea Power* (Princeton, 1940), pp. 9ff, 21ff.

11. "Reflections," *Mirror*, 6:1 (June 18, 1896); and cf. Margaret Leach, *In the Days of McKinley* (New York, 1959), pp. 78–80.

12. "Degenerate Democracy," *Mirror*, 6:1 (July 16, 1896); see also James A. Barnes, "Myths of the Bryan Campaign" in *William Jennings Bryan and the Campaign of 1896*, Amherst College Problems in American Civilization series, ed. Theodore P. Greene (Boston, 1955). Jones had been Pulitzer's managing editor on the *New York World* after reorganizing the *Republican* (as the *St. Louis Republic*) and editing it for five years. He took over the *Post-Dispatch* under a partnership contract, defied the publisher, and was at last removed by litigation. During the dispute he discharged Byars for budgetary reasons, thereby giving him an opportunity to write his biography of Richard Parks Bland.

13. "Reflections," *Mirror*, 6:1 (November 19, 1896).

14. *Ibid.*, 7:6 (May 20, 1897), and for other details see *ibid.*, 7:7 (September 30, 1897) and 21:204 (May 9, 1912).

15. "James Campbell," in James Cox, *Old and New St. Louis* (St. Louis, 1894), p. 247, and cf. *Mirror*, 21:204 (May 9, 1912).

16. *Mirror*, 21:204 (May 9, 1912).

17. Reedy to Bernays, December 10, 1908; Reedy to Bloch, March 30, 1909. MHS.

18. "Reflections," *Mirror*, 6:6 (November 19, 1896); see also L. H. Jenks, *Our Cuban Colony* (New York, 1928), p. 40, and Walter Millis, *The Martial Spirit* (Cambridge, Mass., 1931), p. 68.

19. "National Quixotism," *Mirror*, 7:1 (June 27, 1897).

20. "Reflections," *Mirror*, 7:2 (September 30, 1897).

NOTES TO CHAPTER 7

21. *Ibid.*

22. I am indebted to Mrs. Dorothy Garesché Holland of St. Louis for information from her forthcoming study of the Garesché, Bauduy, and Keating families, and for referring me to the article on Dr. Bauduy in *Eminent American Physicians and Surgeons,* Indianapolis, 1894. Eulalie Bauduy was born in St. Louis in 1872, educated at convent schools there and in Ohio, and had made her debut some years before marrying Reedy, in February 1897.

23. "Archbishop Kain," *Mirror,* 7:7 (June 24, 1897); see also *Mirror,* 7:1 (June 17, 1897).

24. *Mirror,* 7:3 (February 18, 1897).

25. *Mirror,* 7:2 (March 4, 1897), and 7:1 (June 17, 1897).

26. "The President and the Peace," *Mirror,* 8:1 (March 31, 1898), and see leading articles in the issues of February 24, and March 3, 10, 17, and 24.

27. For references to circulation see "Seven Years Old," *Mirror,* 8:6 (February 17, 1898), "Our War Boom," *ibid.,* 8:1 (April 28, 1898), and figures published below masthead in issues of April 28 through May 26, 1898. Circulation seems to have risen from around 23,000 in February to 32,250 the week after the Battle of Manila Bay, afterward falling to 31,992.

28. "Reflections," *Mirror,* 8:6 (February 17, 1898).

29. "Some War Reflections," *Mirror,* 8:2 (April 21, 1898).

30. *Ibid.*

31. "Our Sudden Imperialism," *Mirror,* 8:1 (May 26, 1898); "The Revolution," *Mirror,* 8:2 (June 2, 1898).

32. *Ibid.*

33. "Our War Boom," *Mirror,* 8:1 (April 28, 1898).

34. "Problems of World Politics," *Mirror,* 8:1 (June 16, 1898).

35. "Bryan's Recrudescence," *Mirror,* 8:1 (December 22, 1898). See Andrew Carnegie's account of Bryan's explanation and Carnegie's conclusion: "One word from Mr. Bryan would have saved the country from the disaster. I could not be cordial to him for years afterwards." *Autobiography of Andrew Carnegie* (Boston: Houghton Mifflin, 1920), p. 364.

36. "Reflections," *Mirror,* 8:1 (June 5, 1899), and cf. Albert Weinberg, *Manifest Destiny* (Baltimore, 1935), pp. 304, 314.

CHAPTER 8: Streetcars and Corruption

1. "Once a Year," *The Criterion* (St. Louis), 2:67 (October 1, 1882), and "Big Thursday," *MHS Bull.,* 12:45 (October 1955).

2. "Reflections," *Mirror,* 6:1 (April 30, 1896), one of a series of essays on the same theme.

3. *Mirror,* 9:1 (November 2, 1899), reprinted as Mirror Pamphlet ser. 1, no. 3 (November 1899). See bibliography for list of titles in this series and dates of publication.

4. *Ibid.* See also "Reflections: The Matter with St. Louis," *Mirror,* 9:1 (November 16, 1899); 9:3 (November 23, 1899); and "The Sleeping Beauty," *ibid.,* 9:1 (December 7, 1899).

5. Louis G. Geiger, *Joseph W. Folk of Missouri* (Columbia, Mo., 1953), p. 40. Also see Harold Zink, *City Bosses in the United States* (Durham, N.C., 1930), pp. 302ff, and John D. Lawson, *American State Trials* (St. Louis, 1918), vol. 9. Campbell probably had a hand in Reedy's article "St. Louis Street Railway Securities," *Mirror,* 10:2 (March 2, 1901).

6. "Another Strike," *Mirror,* 10:2 (April 19, 1900).

7. "Strikeography," *Mirror,* 10:1 (June 21, 1900).

8. *The Story of the Strike* (pamphlet, 2nd printing, St. Louis, 1900). Also see *Mirror,* 10:1 (June 14, 1900).

9. *Ibid.*

10. For comment on Henry George, see *Mirror,* 6:5 (October 8, 1896); 7:3 (October 14, 1897); 7:3 (November 4, 1897); 8:4 (February 9, 1899); 10:7 (January 3, 1900); 13:6 (December 3, 1903). For comment on Johnson, see *Mirror,* 11:2 (February 14, 1901); 11:6 (August 8, 1901); 12:3 (August 21, 1902); and obituary, 20:1 (August 10, 1911). See also M. A. Fanning, "Municipal Reform," *Mirror,* 10:4 (May 24, 1900).

11. Announcement of union contract was made in *Mirror,* 12:6 (September 11, 1902). George's condensed explanation of his theory, "The Single Tax," *Mirror,* 11:4 (February 28, 1901), was reprinted from *Christian Advocate.* See also Reedy, "The 'Key of Wall Street' and a Key to the Rights of Man," *ibid.,* 15:1 (June 15, 1905).

12. "The Rising Tide of Reform," *Mirror,* 10:1 (August 30, 1900); "Reform in St. Louis," *Mirror,* 10:3 (September 13, 1900); "Reform and the World's Fair," *ibid.,* 10:1 (October 4, 1900); and "Now to Reform St. Louis," *ibid.,* 10:1 (November 8, 1900).

13. Reedy, "Prominent Citizens in Politics," *Mirror,* 10:1 (February 7, 1901); James L. Blair, "Novel Municipal Conditions," *Harper's Weekly,* 45:695 (July 13, 1901); and Lee Meriwether, *My Yesteryears* (Webster Groves, Mo., 1942), pp. 176–184.

14. William Allen White, "Folk: The Story of a Little Leaven in a Great Commonwealth," *McClure's Magazine,* 26:115 (December 1905); and cf. Ernest Kirschten, *Catfish and Crystal* (Garden City, N.Y., 1960), pp. 315–318.

15. Geiger, *Folk of Missouri,* chap. 2.

16. Quotation from Charles Nagel, "Municipal Situation in St.

NOTES TO CHAPTER 8

Louis," *Proceedings of the National Muncipal League*, 7:105 (May 1901). Also see Meriwether, *My Yesteryears*, p. 159; Meriwether, *My First 98 Years* (Columbia, Mo., 1960), chap. 24; *The Commoner*, 1:3 (March 15, 1901), 1:1 (March 22, 1901), 1:6 (April 5, 1901), 1:1 (April 12, 1901). On July 15, 1960 I asked Mr. Meriwether, then in his ninety-eighth year and about to fly to Istanbul for a holiday, whether he thought Reedy had opposed him because of Campbell's influence. He was positive that Reedy had considered him "a dangerous man" and had opposed him for no other reason.

17. *Mirror*, 11:3 (April 4, 1901).

18. Meriwether, *My Yesteryears*, pp. 176–184; Lawson, *American State Trials*, IX, 342, n. 7.

19. "The City Beautiful," *Current Literature*, 31:257 (September 1901).

20. G. J. Tansey, "Lalitte Bauduy-Reedy," [sic] *Mirror*, 11:10 (November 7, 1901). The cause of Mrs. Reedy's death is given by Dr. Amand Ravold, the physician who attended her, in a letter to Wolf ("Critical Biography," p. 55) as "hyperthyroidism, the result of an obscure bacterial infection" with myocardial involvement.

21. "Thanksgiving," *Mirror*, 11:1 (November 28, 1901), and miscellaneous short items in same issue.

CHAPTER 9: At the Fair

1. A[lma] Meyer, "W. M. R., the Heart Within," *Mirror*, 29:605 (August 5, 1920). Miss Meyer was Reedy's secretary and office manager for seven years

2. Oral sources and D. H. Harris, *A Brief Report of the Meeting Commemorative of the Early St. Louis Movement*. (St. Louis, 1921), p. 146.

3. Rolla Wells, *Episodes of My Life* (St. Louis, 1933), chap. 19 and pp. 147, 209.

4. Claude Wetmore, *The Battle Against Bribery* (St. Louis, 1904), p. 27.

5. Geiger, *Folk of Missouri*, p. 28; and see Lincoln Steffens, *Autobiography* (New York, 1931), p. 370; Steffens, *Shame of the Cities* (New York, 1904, rev. ed., 1957), p. 27; James L. Blair, "The St. Louis Disclosures," *Proceedings of the National Municipal League*, 9:87 (1903).

6. Geiger, *Folk of Missouri*, pp. 28–29; see Wetmore, "Folk and the Force behind His Boom for the Presidency," *The Reader*, 4:124 (July 1904).

7. Wetmore, "Joseph Wingate Folk: The Man and His Methods," *Valley Magazine*, 2:2 (August 1903).

8. "$140,000 Boodle Story," *Mirror*, 11:1 (January 30, 1902); "The Boodlers," *ibid.*, 11:3 (February 6, 1902); "The Bribery Conviction," *ibid.*, 12:1 (April 3, 1902). The Wainwright Building, designed by Louis Sullivan, has been called the prototype of all skyscrapers.

9. "Our Garbage and the Grand Jury," *Mirror*, 12:1 (April 10, 1902).

10. William Allen White, "Folk: The Story of a Little Leaven in a Great Commonwealth," *McClure's Magazine*, 26:115 (December 1905); and cf. Geiger, *Folk of Missouri*, p. 46, and the introduction to vol. 9 of Lawson's *American State Trials*.

11. "That Man Folk," *Mirror*, 13:1 (November 12, 1903).

12. See Wetmore article cited in n. 7 above.

13. Blair, "The Ideal in Public Life," *Valley Magazine*, 2:9 (August 1903). See also his articles, "What Is a Good Citizen?" *Mirror*, 12:5 (March 13, 1902), and "The St. Louis Disclosures," *Proceedings of the National Municipal League*, 9:87 (1903). James Blair's disgrace is not mentioned in William Ernest Smith, *The Francis Preston Blair Family in Politics* (New York, 1933), though his relations with his father are described at II, 459.

14. *New York Times*, October 25, 1903, p. 1; and further articles on October 27, 28, and 29. *St. Louis Globe-Democrat*, November 6, 1903, p. 1; November 8, 1903, p. 1; November 10, 1903, p. 10; and November 14, 1903, p. 9.

15. "A Homily on Mr. Blair," *Mirror*, 13:1 (October 29, 1903).

16. Walter B. Stevens, *St. Louis: The Fourth City* (St. Louis, 1909), I, 1131.

17. Wells, *Episodes*, p. 230.

18. "The Fair in the Fall," *Mirror*, 14:2 (October 27, 1904).

CHAPTER 10: Roosevelt and the Free Press

1. Lawson, *American State Trials*, IX, 463.

2. "Reflections," *Mirror*, 8:4 (July 14, 1898).

3. "Reflections: Teddy and the Trusts," *Mirror*, 10:3 (October 4, 1900).

4. "President Roosevelt," *Mirror*, 11:1 (September 19, 1901).

5. "The President and the Negro," *Mirror*, 11:1 (October 31, 1901).

6. "Three Notes," *Mirror*, 11:1 (December 26, 1901); see also "In Washington," *ibid.*, 11:1 (December 12, 1901).

NOTES TO CHAPTER 10

7. "Swinging Round the Circle," *Mirror*, 17:4 (September 12, 1907).

8. *The Myth of a Free Press* (St. Louis, 1908) has become a rarity. The only copy I have found is one Reedy gave to the Library of Congress about a year after he published it under the *Mirror's* imprint.

9. *The Myth of a Free Press*, p. 15.

CHAPTER 11: Theodore Dreiser

1. *Theodore Dreiser*, American Men of Letters Series (New York, 1951), p. 94.

2. See Dreiser, *A Book about Myself* (New York, 1922), *Free and Other Stories* (New York, 1918), and *Twelve Men* (New York, 1919). Useful information on Dreiser's St. Louis experience as witnessed by others will be found in Harry R. Burke, *From the Day's Journey* (St. Louis, 1924), p. 165.

3. See "Collected Poems—Theodore Dreiser," ed. R. P. Saalbach, diss., University of Washington, 1951.

4. Robert H. Elias, *Theodore Dreiser: Apostle of Nature* (Philadelphia, 1949), chap. 4.

5. "Reflections," *Ev'ry Month*, 2:6 (September 1896).

6. *Ibid.*, 4:21 (June 1897).

7. *Ibid.*, 2:5 (September 1896).

8. *Ibid.*, 4:2, 20 (June 1897).

9. "Notoriety: The Craze for It a New Disease," *Mirror*, 7:7 (April 22, 1897). The two Reedy essays appeared in *Ev'ry Month*, 3:13 (December 1896), and 3:23 (February 1897).

10. Dreiser to Mencken, May 12, 1916, in *Letters of Theodore Dreiser: A Selection*, ed. Robert H. Elias (Philadelphia, 1959), I, 210. Cf. Elias, *Apostle of Nature*, chap. 6. The impression Dreiser tried to give, that the stories enjoyed quick acceptance, is not borne out by evidence of publication.

11. In his introduction to the Grosset & Dunlap reprint of *Sister Carrie* (New York, n.d.) and the Modern Library edition (New York, 1932), Dreiser ascribes the suppression of his novel to the strong dislike expressed by Mrs. Frank Doubleday, who "read the novel and was horrified by its frankness." As this retrospective charge is not borne out by primary evidence it should perhaps be received skeptically.

12. *Letters*, ed. Elias, I, 51–63.

13. Reedy to Dreiser, January 4, 1901. UP.

14. "Sister Carrie: A Strangely Strong Novel in a Queer Milieu," *Mirror*, 10:6 (January 3, 1901).

REAL WOMEN AND LOVE LYRICS

15. Reedy to Dreiser, January 4, 1901. UP.
16. Review cited in n. 14 above.
17. Reedy to Dreiser, January 4, 1901. UP.
18. Reedy to Dreiser, January 25, 1901. UP.
19. Reedy to Dreiser, February 1, 1901. UP.
20. *Mirror,* 11:4 September 26, 1901.
21. Reedy to Dreiser, October 24, 1901. UP.
22. The article is by John Raftery, "By Bread Alone," *Mirror,* 11:5 (December 5, 1901). Dreiser's story, "Butcher Rogaum's Door," *Mirror,* 11:15 (December 12, 1901), was later collected, as "Old Rogaum and His Theresa," in *Free and Other Stories.*
23. See Orrick Johns, *Time of Our Lives* (New York, 1937), pp. 128, 163. The remark from Reedy to Dreiser, October 25, 1918 (UP), is quoted approximately in *Twelve Men* (at p. 223), where Dreiser attributes it to "a certain Western critic and editor."
24. *Twelve Men,* p. 216 et passim.
25. *Ibid.,* pp. 218, 220.
26. Dreiser to Reedy, March 19, 1907. *Letters,* ed. Elias, I, 80.
27. Reedy to Dreiser, March 23, 1907. UP. The letter is marked for Dodge's attention in Dreiser's hand.
28. See my article "Dreiser, Reedy, and 'De Maupassant, Junior,'" *AL,* 33:466 (January 1962), n. 36, and chap. 22 below.
29. "Jennie Gerhardt," *Mirror,* 21:4 (November 30, 1911); "The Financier," *ibid.,* 21:2 (January 2, 1913); and "Dreiser's Titan," *ibid.,* 23:3 (May 29, 1914). See also Lawrence Carroll, "Sister Carrie," *Mirror,* 21:6 (April 25, 1912), reporting that the success of *Jennie* revived interest in *Carrie.*
30. "Dreiser's Titan," Mirror, 23:3 (May 29, 1914).
31. Reedy to Dreiser, November 13, 1912. UP.
32. Reedy to Dreiser, January 15, 1913, and enclosure. UP.
33. "Reflections: Dreiser's Great Book," *Mirror,* 21:2 (January 2, 1913).

CHAPTER 12: Real Women and Love Lyrics

1. "Blue Jay's Chatter," *Mirror,* 15:11 (October 26, 1905).
2. Reedy to Mosher, November 19, 1905. Harvard. Cf. "Blue Jay's Chatter," *Mirror,* 15:14 (November 30, 1905). Quoted by permission.
3. "Blue Jay's Chatter," *Mirror,* 15:7 (February 23, 1905).
4. That Reedy himself wrote the column was confirmed for me by Mrs. Albert P. Greensfelder of St. Louis, who was contributing to the *Mirror* in 1905.
5. Apart from newspapers, see Anne André-Johnson, *Prominent*

NOTES TO CHAPTER 12

Women of St. Louis (St. Louis, 1914), p. 12, and Edwin Björkman's introduction to Miss Akins' *Papa* (New York, 1913).

6. "Blue Jay's Chatter," *Mirror*, 18:12 (May 21, 1908).

7. Quoted from two undated letters in Reedy's hand, presented to MHS by Miss Akins in 1951. My approximate dating is based on internal evidence, a reference to the forthcoming engagement of the Ben Greet Players in one (which contains conflicting references to Reedy's "Christmas number" and "the Easter grind"; and a reference to Julia Marlowe in the second. Most of the above is from the "Ben Greet letter."

8. Reedy to Akins, n.d., the "Marlowe letter." MHS.

9. "Reflections: Akins for Mexico," *Mirror*, 15:2 (August 10, 1905). On Miss Akins' ambition see, for example, Reedy to Bernays, December 19, 1908, March 26, 1909, and March 19, 1914. MHS. Also Akins to Bernays, July 25, 1913, and n.d. [1914]—"I wonder what waits for me in New York." MHS.

10. "Huneker's *Iconoclasts*," *Mirror*, 15:16 (July 20, 1905).

11. Huneker to Reedy, August 3, 1905, in *Letters of James Gibbons Huneker*, ed. Josephine Huneker (New York: Charles Scribner's Sons, 1922), p. 41. Mrs. Huneker identifies Reedy but not his "young friend."

12. W. G. Eliot, *Home Life and Influence* (St. Louis, 1880), p. 180.

13. "Blue Jay's Chatter," *Mirror*, 15:12 (June 1, 1905). There is a diary of Miss Teasdale's European trip at Yale.

14. See Margaret Haley Carpenter, *Sara Teasdale: A Biography* (New York, 1960); and Louis Untermeyer, *From Another World* (New York, 1939), p. 162.

15. Johns, *Time of Our Lives*, p. 179.

16. "The Heart's Hearth," *Mirror*, 17:42 (December 19, 1907), and in Sara Teasdale, *Collected Poems* (New York: Macmillan, 1937). Other items referred to are "The Little Love," *ibid.*, 16:7 (November 22, 1906), "The Crystal Cup," *Mirror*, 16:4 (May 17, 1906), and Reedy's comments on Miss Teasdale in "Swinging Round the Circle," *ibid.*, 17:4 (September 26, 1907).

17. *Mirror*, 17:43 (December 19, 1907). Quoted by permission of the Akins Estate.

18. See her *Collected Poems* (New York, 1937), pp. 9–20. See also *Helen of Troy* (New York, 1911).

19. *Mirror*, 19:7 (March 17, 1910). Reprinted from February *Forum*.

20. Reedy to Bernays, December 10, 1908, and Reedy to Bloch, March 30, 1909. MHS. Wolf confirmed the facts in interviews with

Mrs. Rhodes, whom Reedy generally refers to as Margery or Gretchen; her legal name was Margaret Helen Chambers. See Wolf, "Critical Biography," chap. 8.

21. Reedy to Bloch, April 29, 1909. MHS.
22. Reedy to Bloch, November 9, 1912. MHS. See also Lothar-Günther Bucheim, *Der Blaue Reiter* (Feldafing, 1961).
23. *Augustus Charles Bernays: A Memoir* (St. Louis, 1912).
24. Saunders Norvell to Bernays, February 16, 1910. MHS.
25. Reedy to Bernays, December 19, 1908. MHS.
26. Reedy to Bernays, March 26, 1909. MHS.
27. Reedy to Bernays, November 24, 1908. MHS.
28. Reedy to Bloch, May 28, 1909. MHS.
29. "Women and Love Songs," *Mirror*, 18:4 (March 4, 1909).
30. "Letters," *Mirror*, 19:13 (March 25, 1909). Charles August Sandburg changed his signature to "Carl Sandburg" some time after serving as secretary to the Mayor of Milwaukee in 1910–1911.
31. Reedy to Bernays, March 24, 1909. MHS.
32. Reedy to Bloch, March 30, 1909. See also Reedy to Bernays, March 26, April 14, 1909. MHS.
33. Reedy to Bloch, n.d. [1909]. Also Reedy to Bernays, July 24, 1909. MHS.
34. Reedy to Bloch, August 2, 1909. MHS.

CHAPTER 13: Three Critics in Search of an Art

1. The series ran intermittently from the *Mirror* of March 25, 1909, into 1917.
2. On Norton, see "Bad Logic and Bad Sentiment," *Mirror*, 16:2 (June 11, 1906); on Peck, see "Peck on Vulgarity," *ibid.* 9:3 (April 6, 1899).
3. See Pollard, "Censorship and Criticism," *Mirror*, 12:5 (May 1, 1901), and Reedy, "Reflections," *Mirror*, 5:4 (January 23, 1896).
4. Pollard, "A Heroine Swears," *Mirror*, 14:11 (January 26, 1905); "Yule-Tide Books," *ibid.*, 11:9 (December 19, 1901); "Our Alexander the Great," *ibid.*, 12:7 (April 10, 1902); and "Writing Revolutionaries," *ibid.*, 12:6 (April 24, 1902).
5. See Huneker, *Melomaniacs* (New York, 1902), and Reedy's review of it, *Mirror*, 12:2 (March 13, 1902).
6. H. L. Mencken, "James Huneker," *Mirror*, 25:292 (April 28, 1916), an article reprinted from the *Baltimore Sun*.
7. *Mirror*, 20:8 (September 7, 1911), and cf. *Their Day in Court* (Washington, 1909). Cf. Huneker to Mencken, April 11, 1916. *Letters of James Gibbons Huneker*, p. 209. "I hope you will

NOTES TO CHAPTER 13

not endorse the legend . . . Pollard . . . did me an injustice."

8. Reedy, "A Conflict of Critics," *Mirror*, 20:2 (September 21, 1911).

9. "Reflections," *Mirror*, 9:1 (August 3, 1909). The account of the poem's success is from William L. Stidger, *Edwin Markham* (New York, 1933), p. 143, the quotations being taken from *Edwin Markham: Living Praise and Final Appraisal*, pamphlet issued by the Markham Memorial Association (New York, 1941).

10. Huneker, "A Visit to Walt Whitman," *Ivory Apes and Peacocks* (New York, 1917), p. 22.

11. "The Salt of Old Walt," *Mirror*, 19:5 (April 22, 1909).

12. For a valuable discussion of the gradual increase of Whitman's influence, which mentions Traubel but touches only lightly on the period 1900–1910, see Clarence A. Brown, "Walt Whitman and the 'New Poetry,'" *AL*, 33:33 (March 1961). Reedy, "Reflections: With Walt in Camden," *Mirror*, 16:3 (March 8, 1906), "Swinging Round the Circle," *ibid.*, 17:1 (September 12, 1907), *ibid.*, 18:4 (December 24, 1908), and Orrick Johns, "*Optimos*," a review, *Mirror*, 20:18 (March 9, 1911). There are other Whitman and Traubel items in the *Mirror* for the period.

13. "The Hotel," *Mirror*, 19:5 (April 22, 1909); cf. Mr. Brown's article, n. 12 above.

14. *Mirror*, 21:7 (May 27, 1911), and *ibid.*, 21:16 (May 4, 1911).

15. "Losses to Letters," *Mirror*, 19:5 (April 22, 1909).

16. Reedy, "To a Charming Little Lady in the West End," *Mirror*, 16:2 (March 12, 1906).

17. Reedy to Bloch, n.d. [late 1909] and March 10, 1910. MHS. Later, in the *Mirror* of September 22, 1910, Reedy brags of having discovered Galsworthy for America. That would have been in 1906.

18. See, for example, the title essay of Reedy's *The Law of Love* (East Aurora, N.Y., 1905) and "Some English Poets," *Brann's Iconoclast*, 7:170 (August 1897) [very rare; copy in Library of Congress], with which cf. "A Dead Poet," Henley's obituary, *Mirror*, 13:2 (July 16, 1903). On Swinburne, see "Ave atque Vale," *ibid.*, 19:1 (April 15, 1909).

19. E.g., Reedy, *The Law of Love*, p. 146.

CHAPTER 14: Ezra Pound, Poet in Exile

1. On Eliot's recollection of the *Mirror* I am referring to a letter from Mr. Morley Kennerley of Faber & Faber, Ltd., dated June 22, 1959. On Miss Teasdale my informant is Professor Donald Gallup. The Prufrock advertisements were especially prominent in 1907–

POETS IN THE MARKET

1908. See also Sean O'Faoláin, "New Spirit of St. Louis," *Holiday,* 27:80 (May 1960), and Walter J. Ong, a note in *AL,* 33:522 (January 1962).

2. Eliot, *Ezra Pound: His Metric and Poetry* (New York, 1917), p. 9; and cf. Pound MS. dated February 1, 1909, "What I Feel about Walt Whitman." Yale. The last is discussed by Charles Willard, "Ezra Pound's Debt to Walt Whitman," *Studies in Philology,* 54:573 (1957).

3. Eliot, "Ezra Pound," *Poetry,* 68:326 (1939).

4. Reedy, "Browning's 'Rabbi Ben Ezra,'" *Mirror,* 8:3 (March 31, 1898); "Childe Roland," *ibid.,* 11:8 (July 25, 1901); also Reedy's preface to Witter Bynner, *Songs to the Beloved Stranger* (New York, 1919).

5. "Browning's Optimism," *Mirror,* 21:3 (May 16, 1912).

6. *Provença* (Boston, 1910) contained most of the poems in *Personae* and *Exultations* (London, 1910) and *Canzoni* (London, 1911). See also "Mesmerism," *Mirror,* 19:17 (March 10, 1910); "A Ballad for Gloom," *ibid.,* 19:7 (March 10, 1910); and "The Goodly Fere," *ibid.,* 22:12 (July 18, 1913).

7. Quoted from *Mirror,* 19:17 (March 10, 1910). Published also in *Personae: The Collected Poems of Ezra Pound* (New York: New Directions, copyright 1926, 1954, by Ezra Pound), p. 13.

8. Will Schuyler, "A Friend of Dante's," *Mirror,* 21:6 (May 16, 1912).

9. Reedy to Babette Deutsch, December 1, 1917. From a file of twenty-six letters graciously made available to me by Miss Deutsch. Quoted by permission.

10. Reedy to Miss Deutsch, November 22, 1917. Quoted by permission.

CHAPTER 15: Poets in the Market

1. See Fannie Hurst, "Joy of Living," *Mirror,* 19:4 (May 27, 1909), "Etchings," *ibid.,* 19:7 (July 8, 1909), and so on, and Reedy to Bloch, August 2, 1909. MHS. Reedy figures in Miss Hurst's *Hallelujah* (New York, 1944).

2. Akins to Bernays, n.d. (on letterhead of Missouri Athletic Association). MHS.

3. Henry Seidel Canby and Malcolm Cowley, "Creating an Audience," *LHUS,* I, 1119f, 1237, 1317. For statistics of book production see compilation from *Publishers' Weekly* in Howard Mumford Jones, *Guide to American Literature and Its Backgrounds Since 1890* (Cambridge, Mass., 1953), p. 46.

NOTES TO CHAPTER 15

4. Mott, *History of American Magazines*, vol. 4.

5. Mott, *History of American Magazines*, IV, 506–510. The title *Current Literature* was changed to *Current Opinion* in 1913.

6. See Kennerley correspondence, NYP, and Kennerley-to-Mosher correspondence, Harvard. See also "A Wandering Poem," *Mirror*, 15:22 (October 5, 1905).

7. Lehmann-Haupt, *The Book in America: A History* (New York, 1951), p. 333.

8. *Publisher's Weekly*, 157:1428 (March 18, 1950); see also *New York Times*, February 23, 1950, p. 28, and Sidney Kramer, *A History of Stone & Kimball* (Chicago, 1940), p. 88. Facts on Kennerley's early career are hard to come by; these have been checked by Mr. Laurence Gomme, while he was at work on a biography of Kennerley, not yet published.

9. Reedy to Mosher, January 2, 1917. Harvard. The generalization is based on numerous unpublished letters in the Ficke collections at Newberry Library and Yale, the Dreiser collection, UP, the Teasdale collections at MHS and Yale. See also Eleanor Ruggles, *The West-Going Heart: A Life of Vachel Lindsay* (New York, 1959), pp. 221, 223, 227.

10. *Publishers' Weekly* and *New York Times* articles cited in n. 8 above.

11. Reedy to Bernays, February 18, 1910. MHS. There appears to have been a Moffat, Yard & Co. edition of *Confessions* in addition to Kennerley's.

12. "Is Oscar Wilde Alive?" *Mirror*, 15:24 (May 19, 1905); Verdant Green (pseud.), "The Truth about G.S.V.," *ibid.*, 19:6 (May 19, 1910); see also Bloch, "Gotham Comment," *ibid.*, 17:33 (December 19, 1907); and Frances Porcher, *ibid.*, 19:5 (May 12, 1910).

13. Reprinted from the *Academy*, *Mirror*, 20:13 (October 20, 1910). See also Reedy to Bloch, June 16, 1909. MHS. Viereck was a protégé of Huneker and defended him from Pollard's attack. See *Mirror*, 20:14 (October 19, 1911).

14. "Reflections: Sylvester Viereck's Swan Song," *Mirror*, 21:2 (April 4, 1912).

15. "The Poetry Society of America," *Mirror*, 20:7 (November 3, 1910).

16. Johns, *Time of Our Lives*, pp. 129, 170, 175, 239.

17. "Affinity Sonnets," *Mirror*, 20:16 (February 16, 1911).

18. Johns, *Time of Our Lives*, pp. 202–204.

19. See, however, Braithwaite to Kennerley, October 15, 1912, NYP, Wheeler to Kennerley, October 24, 1912, NYP, and Earle to Kennerley, October 15, and October 25, 1912, NYP. See also

VACHEL LINDSAY

Nelson F. Adkins, "The Lyric Year: A Bibliographic Note," *American Book Collector* (March 1933), p. 148.

20. On Earle's misfortunes see *New York Times*, November 30, 1911, sec. 2, p. 1, col. 5; November 11, 1913, p. 10, col. 2; November 25, 1913, p. 6, col. 4; April 9, 1913, p. 8, col. 3; and the following issues in 1914—January 3, p. 1, col. 5; January 6, p. 4, col. 2; February 28, p. 1, col. 4; March 17, p. 4, col. 3; April 9, p. 8, col. 3.

21. "Reflections: The Poets' Tourney," *Mirror*, 21:2 (November 28, 1912).

22. Elizabeth Waddell, "Salon of American Poetry," *Mirror*, 21:4 (December 26, 1912).

CHAPTER 16: Vachel Lindsay, Poet on Native Ground

1. Reedy to Bynner, June 23, 1910. MHS.
2. "An Illinois Art Revival," (anon.) *Current Literature*, 50:320 (March 1911).
3. Hamlin Garland, *Companions on the Trail* (New York, 1931), pp. 462–475; and cf. Eleanor Ruggles, *West-Going Heart* (New York, 1959), p. 172.
4. Reedy to Bloch, June 29, 1910. MHS. See obituary in *Mirror*, 20:4 (June 20, 1910). O. Henry stories had begun appearing in the *Mirror* at an early date. See "The Ransom of Mack," *Mirror*, 14:8 (December 15, 1904).
5. "The Knight in Disguise," *Mirror*, 21:7 (June 13, 1912).
6. *The Letters of Ezra Pound*, ed. D. D. Paige (New York: Harcourt, Brace, 1950), p. 66. References to these published letters should be checked against originals at the University of Chicago.
7. *Letters of Ezra Pound*, p. 49.
8. "Autobiographical Foreword," *Collected Poems*, p. 8.
9. The Campbellites are moderates, avoiding the severity of Presbyterians and the enthusiasm of Baptists. In the Civil War they held together by opposing both slavery and abolition.
10. "Alexander Campbell," *Collected Poems*, p. 352. See also George Scoufas, *Vachel Lindsay: A Study in Retreat and Repudiation*, diss. abstract, University of Illinois, 1951; Bernard Duffey, *The Chicago Renaissance in American Letters* (East Lansing, Mich., 1954), p. 222, and articles "Campbell" and "Disciples of Christ," *Encyclopedia Britannica*, 11th ed.
11. Edgar Lee Masters, *Vachel Lindsay: A Poet in America* (New York, 1935), p. 67.
12. Harriet Monroe, *A Poet's Life* (New York, 1938), p. 279; Ruggles, *West-Going Heart*, chap. 33.

NOTES TO CHAPTER 16

13. "Rhymes for Bread," published in the *Mirror*, 22:5 (March 7, 1913). Lindsay's letter is dated from Springfield, January 6, 1913.

14. "The City That Will Not Repent," published in the *Mirror* 22:7 (June 27, 1913).

15. The letters, which are at Yale, were not open for citation when I read them. The first, dated August 3, 1913, does not appear to have initiated the correspondence, which contains 251 letters to Sara Teasdale, 1913-1931. See accession item, *Yale University Library Gazette*, 33:78 (October 1958).

16. "The Kallyope Yell," published in the *Mirror*, 22:7 (November 14, 1913).

17. "Calliope or Callyope?" *Mirror*, 22:9 (November 21, 1913). See also Reedy to Byars, February 24 and 25, 1913, and Byars to Reedy, March 22, 1913. MHS.

18. "I Heard Immanuel Singing," *Mirror*, 22:11 (December 19, 1913); the accompanying letter is dated Springfield, December 11, 1913. See Masters, *Poet in America*, p. 179; Lindsay, *Last Song of Lucifer* (New York, 1908), and *The Tramp's Excuse* (Springfield, Ill., 1909); and Lindsay, "The Gospel of Beauty," *Mirror*, 22:7 (January 9, 1914).

19. Lindsay-Teasdale correspondence. Yale. Teasdale to Orrick Johns, April 5, 1912, and n.d., 10:30 Wednesday. Yale. Teasdale to Eunice Tietjens, March 1, 1914. Newberry.

20. Louis Untermeyer, *From Another World*, p. 175.

21. George P. Baker, "The Pageant and Masque of Saint Louis," *World's Work*, 28:389 (August 1914); *Mirror*, 23:1 (May 29, 1914). Filsinger to Tietjens, June 5, 1914. Newberry. On Lindsay's recitations see Angus Lodowis (pseud. Louis Albert Lamb), "Orotundo Poetics," *Mirror*, 23:3 (July 31, 1914).

22. Filsinger to Tietjens, June 21, July 10, 1914. Newberry.

23. Lindsay to Teasdale. Yale.

24. Olivia Howard Dunbar, *A House in Chicago* (Chicago, 1947), p. 111.

25. "Spring Night," *North American Review*, 199:599 (April 1914); *Mirror* 23:7 (April 17, 1914). Note emendations in *Rivers to the Sea* (New York, 1915), p. 1. See also Teasdale to Tietjens, March 14, 1914. Newberry.

26. Nicholas Vachel Lindsay, "Twelve Poems on the Moon," *Mirror*, 23:3 (June 12, 1914); with extended headnote signed W.M.R.

27. See headnote cited in n. 26 above.

330

CROSSING SPOON RIVER

CHAPTER 17: Crossing Spoon River

1. See my note "Masters's 'Maltravers': Ernest McGaffey," *AL*, 31:491 (January 1960). Since writing it I have wondered whether the pseudonym Masters used for McGaffey was suggested by Lord Lytton's *Ernest Maltravers* (1837). For McGaffey's essay see *Mirror*, 9:4 (April 11, 1901).
2. Masters, *Across Spoon River* (New York, 1936), pp. 259, 336, 341. For variant accounts see also his articles "Genesis of Spoon River," *American Mercury*, 28:48 (January 1933); "Literary Boss of the Middle West," *ibid.*, 34:450 (April 1935); and "Introduction to Chicago," *ibid.*, 31:49 (January 1934).
3. Masters, "William Marion Reedy," *American Speech*, 9:96 (April 1934).
4. "William Marion Reedy," *Songs and Satires* (New York: Macmillan, 1916), p. 82.
5. "*Maximilian*, A Play," *Mirror*, 12:10 (August 28, 1902). Although Masters refers to the review as highly favorable, the reviewer complains that his style is overelaborate and anachronistic, citing Edmund Gosse's recent objection to such pastiche.
6. *Mirror*, 29:11 (June 23, 1910).
7. Johns, "Webster Ford's *Songs and Sonnets*," *Mirror*, 20:17 (March 23, 1911); Reedy, "Mr. Pound on Mr. Masters," *Mirror*, 24:3 (May 21, 1915). Reedy's expostulation is quoted by Harry Hansen, *Midwest Portraits* (New York, 1923), p. 246; Hansen heard it from T. K. Hedrick, an assistant editor of the *Mirror*.
8. *Across Spoon River*, pp. 323–325 et passim. Also see Eunice Tietjens MS., "Biographical Notes" on her conversations with Masters, March 1923; Masters to Carter Harrison, April 14, 1913; January 23, 26, and 28, 1914; and Woodrow Wilson to Harrison, January 27, 1914—all at Newberry. See also Masters to Dreiser, December 9, 1912. UP. "I am going to try my hand at something later this winter just to do it and without any particular hope. I am about past that."
9. Subsequently she had written competent studies in English, French, and American literature. Her *Journal of a Recluse* had enjoyed a success, and Thekla Bernays had introduced her to Reedy when she came to teach school in St. Louis. See Anne André-Johnson, *Notable Women of St. Louis*, pp. 66–69, and Durward Howes, ed., *American Women* (Los Angeles, 1939), vol. 3. See also Fisher to Bernays, n.d. MHS.
10. Masters, "M.F.'s *Kirstie, Mirror*, 21:6 (November 7, 1912).
11. Masters to Dreiser, November 27, December 3 and 9, 1912.

NOTES TO CHAPTER 17

UP. Quoted by permission of Mrs. Ellen Coyne Masters. See Duffey, *Chicago Renaissance*, p. 158. Masters read *The Titan* in galley proof; see Masters to Dreiser, January 22 and 28, 1914. UP.

12. "Chicago," *Poetry*, 3:191 (March 1914); *Mirror*, 23:8 (March 20, 1914). Quoted by permission of Carl Sandburg.

13. *Spoon River Anthology*, rev. ed. New York: (Macmillan, 1915, 1916), p. 41. See also Masters to Dreiser, April 20, 1914. UP. Masters urges Dreiser to get the *Greek Anthology*—"good book for spring days—for the mood when one watches a craw-fish. Moreover you will there see the original of which the enclosed is my imitation."

14. Kimball Flaccus, *The Vermont Background of Edgar Lee Masters;* also bound as *Edgar Lee Masters: A Biographical and Critical Study* (diss. abstract, New York University), reprinted in *Vermont History*, January–October 1954, January 1955.

15. *Across Spoon River*, p. 341.

16. Reedy, "Vacation Notes," *Mirror*, 24:1 (August 20, 1915).

17. *Mirror*, 23:6 (May 29, 1914). See also *Spoon River Anthology*, rev. ed., p. 1.

18. Masters to Dreiser, May 31, 1914. UP.

19. Harry B. Kennon, "Spoon River Cemetery," *Mirror*, 23:6 (July 3, 1914).

20. Louis Albert Lamb, "Reflections: The Spoon River Plutarch," *Mirror*, 23:1 (July 31, 1914). From the Dreiser correspondence one knows that Mosher and Kennerley were among the "cognoscenti everywhere" who already foresaw the success of the anthology when it should appear as a book. Its success was, in fact, fairly clear within a month.

21. *Spoon River Anthology*, rev. ed., p. 16. Here it is one of a group "Benjamin Pantier," "Mrs. Benjamin Pantier," "Reuben Pantier," "Emily Sparks," and "Trainor, the Druggist." Its significance will be better appreciated if all these are taken in context with the preceding epitaph, "Kinsey Keene," and the following one, "Daisy Fraser."

22. *Ibid.*, p. 15.

23. "Oaks Tutt," *Spoon River Anthology*, rev. ed., p. 168.

24. *Ibid.*, p. 220.

25. *Ibid.*, p. 224.

26. *Ibid.*, p. 230.

27. Reedy, "Saving the Country," *Mirror*, 21:1 (November 7, 1912). The election in question was that of Woodrow Wilson, but the single tax was a concurrent state issue. See Norman L. Crockett, "The 1912 Single Tax Campaign in Missouri," *MHR*, 56:40 (October 1961). Clonmel, at Manchester and Berry roads, lay in a farm area between the suburbs of Rock Hill and Webster Groves.

28. "John Cabanis," *Spoon River Anthology*, rev. ed., p. 125.
29. "George Trimble," *ibid.*, p. 49. Quoted by permission.
30. "Reflections," *Mirror*, 23:1 (September 18, 1914).
31. "The Writer of Spoon River," *ibid.*, 23:1 (November 20, 1914).
32. Pound to Monroe, October 12, 1914. *Letters of Ezra Pound*, ed. D. D. Paige (New York, [1950]), p. 43. "Please observe above instructions as soon as possible," he adds. Quoted by permission of Harcourt, Brace & World, Inc.
33. "Webster Ford," *The Egoist*, 2:11 (January 1, 1915).
34. Pound to Monroe, March 5, 1916. *Letters*, ed. Paige, p. 71. Quoted by permission of Harcourt, Brace & World, Inc.
35. "Affirmations: Edgar Lee Masters," *Mirror*, 24:10 (May 21, 1915).
36. Masters to Dreiser, April 8, 1915. UP. Quoted by permission of Mrs. Ellen Coyne Masters.
37. *Publisher's Weekly*, 87: 226, 245 (1915), and 89:239 (1916). Also see Amy Lowell, *Tendencies in Modern American Poetry* (Boston, 1917), pp. 139, 160, 196; Alice P. Hackett, *Fifty Years of Best-Sellers* (New York, 1945); and Frank Luther Mott, *Golden Multitudes* (New York, 1947), p. 373.
38. "Mr. Masters' *Spoon River Anthology*," *Forum*, 55:109 (January 1916).
39. *Dial*, 60:325 (March 30, 1916); 60:415 (April 27, 1916); 60:498 (May 25, 1916); and 61:14 (June 22, 1916); and cf. *Mirror*, 25:3 (January 7, 1916), and 26:601 (September 21, 1917).
40. "Powys," *Mirror*, 24:3 (April 2, 1915). Powys was later proud to claim that he had been one of Reedy's literary discoveries.
41. Letter, "Mr. Pound's Disgust," *Mirror*, 24:26 (June 25, 1915).
42. Richard Butler Glaenzer, "To Edgar Lee Masters," *Mirror*, 24:8 (June 19, 1915); reprinted in Braithwaite's *Anthology of Magazine Verse* (New York, 1915), p. 96.
43. *Mirror*, 24:5 (June 18, 1915); and cf. Teasdale, *Rivers to the Sea* (New York, 1915), p. 7.
44. Sandburg, "To Webster Ford," *Mirror*, 23:7 (November 27, 1914). Quoted by permission of Carl Sandburg.
45. Reedy to Dreiser [dated, apparently by Dreiser], September 16, 1915. UP.
46. Aiken, "The Two Magics: Edgar Lee Masters," *Scepticisms* (New York, 1919), conclusion. Aiken speculates on the nature and function of realist poetry.

NOTES TO CHAPTER 18

CHAPTER 18: The War of the Imagists and Their Antagonists

1. S. Foster Damon, *Amy Lowell: A Chronicle* (Boston, 1935), p. 292; and Jessie B. Rittenhouse, *My House of Life* (Boston, 1934), p. 256. Cf. Masters to Dreiser, April 2 and 8, 1915. UP.

2. Louis Untermeyer, *From Another World* (New York, 1930), pp. 99ff.

3. "In the Shadow of Parnassus," *Mirror*, 24:7 (March 19, 1915).

4. *Ibid.*, 24:7 (March 12, 1915). Also published in *Sword Blades and Poppy Seed* (Boston: Houghton, Mifflin, 1921), p. 96.

5. Lowell, *Six French Poets* (New York, 1915), Preface; and Teasdale to Tietjens, n.d. (summer of 1913?). Newberry. Quoted by permission of Miss Margaret Conklin, literary executor of Sara Teasdale.

6. Reedy to Braithwaite, July 30, 1915. Harvard.

7. "A St. Louis Imagist," *Mirror*, 24:3 (April 23, 1915). The subject of the article is David O'Neil.

8. See *The Trophies and Other Sonnets* (New York, 1929) and Charles J. Finger, *Seven Horizons* (Garden City, N.Y., 1930), p. 415. There is a mass of autograph and manuscript material relating to Hervey and O'Hara at the Newberry. It is of some interest that Miss Lowell admits her "immense debt" to the Parnassians, notably Heredia and Leconte de Lisle, in the preface to *Sword Blades*, p. viii.

9. Hervey, " 'The New Poetry'," *Mirror*, 23:7 (April 10, 1914); "Apropos Poetical Patterns," *ibid.*, 25:39 (January 21, 1916).

10. Damon, *Amy Lowell*, p. 337.

11. Fletcher, "Patterns in Criticism," *Mirror*, 25:74 (February 4, 1916). This appears to be Fletcher's only contribution to the *Mirror*. Reedy knew his work but took no interest in it; see Reedy to Bynner, October 31, 1918. MHS. The numerous iterations of the statement that Reedy first published Fletcher and Julia Peterkin probably originate with Charles J. Finger's article on Reedy in *DAB* and have no basis.

12. Hervey, "An Evening with the Imagists," *Mirror*, 25:216 (March 31, 1916).

13. "What I've Been Reading," No. 10, *Men, Women and Ghosts*, *Mirror*, 25:503 (August 4, 1916), and see *ibid.*, 25:708 (November 10, 1916), as well as pp. 466, 479, 662 et passim in same volume. With regard to "An Aquarium," *Mirror*, 25:453 (1916), correspondents cite Heredia's "Le Recif de corail," a challenge to Miss Lowell's "extended staccatos."

14. "What I've Been Reading," *Mirror*, 25:662 (October 20, 1916).

ATTACK FROM THE REAR

15. Odell Shepard, "The Stuff of Poetry," *Mirror*, 25:664 (October 20, 1916); and Vachel Lindsay, "Home Rule in Poetry," *Mirror* 25:740 (November 24, 1916).

16. Loomis, "Poetic Truth," *Mirror*, 25:601 (September 22, 1916).

17. See Reedy, "Amy Lowell on Our Poets," *Mirror*, 26:692 (November 2, 1917). He called it "a bright and pungent book . . . immensely enjoyable," but took issue with every critical judgment it contained. (The pun on "imagism" was Pound's.)

CHAPTER 19: Attack from the Rear

1. William Jay Smith's *The Spectra Hoax* (Middletown, Conn., 1961) was received too late to be considered in formulating this chapter, though it was consulted in revising it. It includes the text of *Spectra* (New York, 1916) plus some additional poems by the Spectrists.

2. Reedy to Bynner, June 8, 1910. MHS. This correspondence was presented by the poet in 1949 with a letter indicating that he had been unable to recover "a batch of letters [lent] to someone who purported to be writing a life of Reedy." It is nevertheless the most valuable evidence that has come to light illustrating Reedy's method of helping to form a poet.

3. *Ibid.*, February 1, 1911.

4. *Ibid.*, April 15, (?), 1911. The letter begins, "Dammit, Mr. Bynner, I've no doubt that these are poems to you, but I can't see 'em."

5. *Ibid.*, June 9, 1911.

6. *Ibid.*

7. *Ibid.*, January 19, 1916.

8. "Soulful Spectrism," an interview with Bynner ascribed by Mr. Smith to Thomas Ybarra, *New York Times Magazine*, June 2, 1918, p. 11.

9. Memorandum initialed by Ficke, March 3, 1916, and afterwards by Bynner; found with typescript "Spectra." Yale. For remarks regarding Wallace Stevens see same typescript and Kreymborg, *Troubadour* (New York, 1925), pp. 218–223. Ficke's tragic war sonnet, "These are the thunders," is dated March 5, 1916, right after Bynner's departure. Manuscripts cited in this chapter are quoted by permission of Mr. Bynner, Mrs. A. D. Ficke, and the Yale Library.

10. Reedy to Bynner, March 4, 1916. MHS.

11. Lowell to Ficke, April 20, 1916. Harvard. See also Damon, *Amy Lowell*, p. 353; and cf. pp. 261, 346, 408, 453f, and 457.

335

NOTES TO CHAPTER 19

Quoted by permission of the Houghton Library at Harvard University.

12. Ficke's article was published in *North American Review*, 204:445 (September 1916). For Bynner's note, see "Spectra" memorandum cited in n. 9 above.

13. Bynner, "The Story of the Spectric School of Poetry," *Palms*, 5:207 (1928).

14. Reedy, "What I've Been Reading," *Mirror*, 25:462 (July 14, 1916), and letter, "Mr. Pound Files Exceptions," *Mirror*, 25:535 (September 8, 1916).

15. "An Aquarium," *Mirror*, 25:662 (October 20, 1916).

16. *Forum*, 55:675 (June 1916); *Mirror*, 25:416 (June 23, 1916). I am indebted to Professor Gordon S. Haight for his insistence that in this passage the Spectrists were paraphrasing lines 460–464 of Shelley's "Adonais." Those who attended the English Institute meetings of 1956 may recall an unrecorded discussion led by Professors William K. Wimsatt, Jr., and Cleanth Brooks which took a line strikingly parallel to the Spectrists'.

17. Reedy to Kennerley, June 26, July 7, July 17, 1916. Manuscript of the preface to *Jap Herron* is enclosed under cover of August 16, 1916. NYP.

18. Wolf, "Critical Biography," chap. 10; and see "Miss Lowell's Visit," *Mirror*, 26:118 (February 23, 1917).

19. "Spectra," typescript, Yale.

20. *Palms* article cited in n. 13, above; and see MS. of an article by Ficke written in reply to it but apparently unpublished. Yale.

21. *Palms* article cited in n. 13 above.

22. Quoted by Vincent Starrett, "Grey Cells at Play," *Coronet*, 2:37 (February 1939); and see Elijah Hay (pseud.), "Spectra," *Mirror*, 26:179 (March 16, 1917).

23. *Spectra* (New York: Kennerley, 1916), p. 6; William Jay Smith, *The Spectra Hoax*, p. 84. First four lines are omitted.

24. *Spectra* (1916), p. 51; Smith, *Spectra Hoax*, p. 116. Quoted in full.

25. *Spectra* (1916), p. 56; Smith, *Spectra Hoax*, p. 121. First of three quatrains.

26. *Spectra* (1916), p. 62; Smith, *Spectra Hoax*, p. 127. Fragment; nine lines omitted.

27. *Spectra* (1916), p. 58; Smith, *Spectra Hoax*, p. 123. Opening lines of 15-line poem.

28. *Spectra* (1916), p. 55; Smith, *Spectra Hoax*, p. 120. Opening lines of 8-line poem.

29. *Spectra* (1916), p. 7; Smith, *Spectra Hoax*, p. 85. Opening couplet of 8-line poem.

WAR AND REACTION

30. "Spectral Poetry," *Mirror,* 25:768 (December 1, 1916).
31. Smith, *Spectra Hoax,* pp. 11, 24; Damon, *Amy Lowell,* p. 454.
32. Aiken, *The Jig of Forslin* (Boston, 1916), p. 8. See also *Collected Poems* (New York: Oxford, 1953), p. 79.
33. J.L.H., "Mr. Aiken's Symphony," *Mirror,* 26:211 (March 30, 1917).
34. "Poet Aiken's Reply,' *Mirror,* 26:260 (April 13, 1917); and cf. Frederick J. Hoffman, *Freudianism and the Literary Mind* (New York, 1959), p. 274.
35. "Matters Grow Worse," *Mirror,* 26:416 (June 22, 1917).
36. "Our Contemporaries," *Poetry,* 12:169 (June 1918).
37. "Soulful Spectrism," *New York Times Magazine,* June 2, 1918, p. 11.
38. Monroe, *A Poet's Life,* p. 408.
39. Reedy to Bynner, August 1, 6, 14, 27, and 30, 1918. MHS. The book was published by Knopf (New York) in 1919.
40. Damon, *Amy Lowell,* p. 455; and see her letter to D. H. Lawrence, *ibid.,* p. 621; cf. Smith, *Spectra Hoax,* pp. 39–42.
41. Reedy to Bynner, September 18, 1918. MHS.

CHAPTER 20: War and Reaction

1. "Reflections," *Mirror,* 23:5 (October 20, 1914).
2. "A Hell of a Christmas," *Mirror,* 23:1 (December 18, 1914).
3. H.M., "Sara Teasdale's Prize," *Poetry,* 12:264 (August 1918).
4. "What I've Been Reading," *Mirror,* 26:736 (November 23, 1917).
5. Teasdale to Filsinger, May 12, 1918. MHS. Miss Teasdale was staying at a New Jersey inn, where she received from Miss Rittenhouse a first-hand account of the deliberations of the jury.
6. "Reflections," *Mirror,* 27:335 (June 7, 1918).
7. Quoted from the second stanza of "The Wind in the Hemlock," *Collected Poems* (New York: Macmillan, 1937), p. 159; and cf. holograph dated March 19, 1918, submitted to Filsinger with an urgent request for his judgment. MHS.
8. Teasdale to Filsinger, July 14, 1916. MHS.
9. *Spoon River Anthology,* rev. ed., 1916, p. 220.
10. "Autochthon," *Mirror,* 25:461 (July 14, 1916), and *The Great Valley* (New York, 1916), p. 42.
11. "Reflections: Explaining a Poem," *Mirror,* 28:255 (April 25, 1919).
12. See Damon, *Amy Lowell,* p. 508.
13. Reedy to Bernays, January 23, 1915. MHS.
14. *Ibid.,* February 3, 1915.

NOTES TO CHAPTER 20

15. "Still Hope for Peace," *Mirror*, 26:1 (January 5, 1917).
16. "The League to Enforce Peace," *ibid.*, 26:47 (January 26, 1917).
17. "Reflections: Don't Work up Hate," *ibid.*, 26:289 (May 4, 1917).
18. "Third Degree for the Liberal Press," *ibid.*, 28:644 (September 25, 1919).
19. *Mirror*, 28:159 (March 14, 1919). Reedy braced his support with a check for $200 in payment for "Songs of the Unknown Lover."

CHAPTER 21: Dreiser and Harris Merton Lyon

1. Harvey, "Harris Merton Lyon," *Mirror*, 23:4 (March 13, 1914); and see Reedy, "A Book I've Published," *Mirror*, 22:2 (January 9, 1914).
2. "From an Old Farmhouse: The Author of *The Titan*," 2nd ser., no. 11, *Mirror*, 23:7 (August 21, 1914).
3. Mencken to Dreiser, quoted in *Letters*, ed. Elias, I, 177, n. 27.
4. Dreiser to Mencken, September 11, 1914, *Letters*, ed. Elias, I, 176.
5. *Ibid.*, April 20, 1915. *Letters*, ed. Elias, I, 187. Masters had called Lyon's *Graphics* to Dreiser's attention a month before. See Masters to Dreiser, March 19, 1915. UP.
6. Letter partially printed in *Mirror*, 24:265 (October 15, 1915).
7. Reedy to Dreiser [dated, apparently by Dreiser], September 16, 1915. UP.
8. Sandburg, "No Regrets," *Mirror*, 25:508 (August 4, 1916). See also "Reflections," *Mirror*, 25:383 (June 9, 1916).
9. Reedy to Dreiser, January 31, 1919. UP.
10. Dreiser, *Twelve Men* (New York, 1919), p. 235.
11. "Reflections," *Mirror*, 26:495 (August 3, 1917).
12. Reedy to Dreiser, September 5 and 19, 1916. UP. See also Reedy to Dreiser, March 21, 1917, February 25, 1918. UP.
13. Reedy to Dreiser, February 25, 1918. UP. "Nix on that refund for that story," Reedy begins. "I had more than value received." He makes Dreiser welcome to use it in any way he sees fit, with or without credit to the *Mirror*.
14. Reedy to Dreiser, March 8, 1918. UP.
15. *Ibid.*, February 22, 1919.
16. *Ibid.*, May 12, 1919.
17. *Twelve Men*, p. 237.
18. Reedy to Dreiser, June 28, 1919. UP.
19. Dreiser to Mencken, April 8, 1919. *Letters*, ed. Elias, I, 263.

POETS AND POLITICS

20. Helen Dreiser, *My Life with Dreiser* (Cleveland, 1951).
21. Reedy to Dreiser, note dated "Sunday, P.M.," and A[lma] Meyer to Dreiser, September 4 and 10, 1919; Reedy to Dreiser, September 24, 1919.
22. Reedy to Dreiser, September 24, 1919. UP.
23. Dreiser to Mencken, August 4, 1920. *Letters*, ed. Elias, I, 265.

CHAPTER 22: Poets and Politics: *da capo al fine*

1. "How the President Can Save His Peace," *Mirror*, 28:431 (July 3, 1919).
2. *Ibid.*
3. "Doing Britain's Dirty Work," *Mirror*, 28:547 (August 14, 1919).
4. Teasdale to Filsinger, July 23, 1916. MHS.
5. Reedy's temperance during his last years is discussed by Clover Seelig (wife of his physician) in an unpublished article, "William Marion Reedy: A St. Louis Titan," which the author kindly lent me. See also Reedy to Dreiser, September 24, 1919, and note to Dreiser dated "Sunday P.M." UP. The interview with Ederheimer will be found in "Reflections," *Mirror*, 28:630 (September 18, 1919). The portrait was also reproduced on the cover of Kennerley's catalogue for Ederheimer's first one-man show held at the Anderson Galleries in December 1920. A letter to Kennerley from the painter reproduced therein contains the following: "After my return from Europe in September, 1919, I met our friend the late William Marion Reedy and found a fitting subject in him for a portrait in which I tried to come nearer my ideal—the style of the primitive Dutch and German masters." The original was recently donated to Yale by Mrs. Ederheimer, to whom I am obliged for the relevant references.
6. "Human New York and Young Greenwich Village," (anon.), *New York Times*, September 28, 1919, sec. 7, p. 11.
7. "Reflections," *Mirror*, 28:649 (September 25, 1919).
8. See *Nation*, 108:460 (March 29, 1919) and 109:821 (December 27, 1919); *New York Times*, December 14, 1919, sec. 3, p. 1; September 21, 1919, sec. 3, p. 2; and September 22, 1919, p. 7; *St. Louis Post-Dispatch*, December 7–13, 1919, pp. 1, 2, in all issues; editorials in issues of December 10 and 13, and article, December 16, 1919, p. 1.
9. "Platform and Argument of the Committee of Forty-Eight," *Mirror*, 28:954 (December 25, 1919).
10. Typescript and MS., "Chapter: I Kidnap My Editor," lent to me by Miss Preston Settle of the Mercantile Library, to whom it was

NOTES TO CHAPTER 22

given by Mrs. Reedy. Clearly the work of a newspaper reporter, this appears to be one of a series of reminiscences, probably the one referred to by Miss Fox in her bibliography as follows "Margaret Rhodes Reedy, "Reedy Lives On," *Slant*, II (Winter 1945–1946), No. 3." No other reference to this periodical has been found.

11. "At Ease in Zion," *Mirror*, 29:3 (January 1, 1920).
12. "Digressions, on a Diet," *ibid.*, 29:19 (January 8, 1920).
13. *Ibid.*, p. 20.
14. "The Escaped Editor," *ibid.*, 29:35 (January 15, 1920).
15. *Ibid.*, p. 36.
16. "At Senator Reed's Big Speech," *ibid.*, 29:36 (January 15, 1920).
17. "Declining a Nomination," *ibid.*, 29:51 (January 22, 1920).
18. *St. Louis Post-Dispatch* (March 20, 1920), p. 3.
19. Reedy to Byars, December 7, 1918. MHS.
20. "The Growth of Radicalism," *Mirror*, 28:434 (July 3, 1919).
21. Bodenheim, "American Magazines," *Mirror*, 28:952 (December 25, 1919).
22. See letter column, *Mirror*, 29:27 (January 8, 1920), 29:42 (January 15, 1920); and 29:58 (January 22, 1920).
23. As reported by Masters to Harriet Monroe; see *Poetry*, 16:328 (September 1920).
24. Sandburg, "Propaganda," *Mirror*, 29:74 (January 29, 1920).
25. Bodenheim, "Rattlesnake Mountain Fable," *Mirror*, 29:74 (January 29, 1920).
26. First published in *Poetry* for June 1918, then as a pamphlet, *A Few Figs From Thistles* (New York, 1920). The publisher was Frank Shay. Quoted by permission of Norma Millay Ellis.
27. *Mirror*, 29:348 (April 29, 1920), and following issues. See also *Letters of Edna St. Vincent Millay*, ed. Allan Ross Macdougall (New York, 1952), p. 88; Elizabeth Atkins, *Millay and her Times*, chap. 3, "The *Reedy's Mirror* Sonnets;" typescript in Ficke Notebook, Yale; and Reedy to Kennerley, n.d. (December 10–12, 1917). NYP.
28. Wolf, "Critical Biography," pp. 149, 223, cites a letter he received from Kennerley dated July 8, 1938.
29. *Mirror*, 29:199 (March 18, 1920); and see *Aria da Capo* (New York and London, 1920), p. 28. I have omitted stage directions. Quoted by permission of Norma Millay Ellis.

CHAPTER 23: Last Reflections

1. "An Englishman's Plea for Germany," *Mirror*, 29:90 (February 5, 1920). See Histor (pseud.), "Is Keynes' Book German Propa-

ganda?" *Mirror,* 29:331 (April 22, 1920), and Reedy, "To What Did Germany Yield?" *Mirror,* 29:387 (May 13, 1920), containing Lippmann's reply to Histor; and see Histor's rejoinder, "The Baby on the Doorstep," *Mirror,* 29:428 (May 27, 1920).

2. On failure of the Committee of Forty-Eight, see *New York Times Index* of articles too numerous to list here, which appeared in July and August 1920. See also Arthur Warner, "Christenson's Convention," *Nation,* 111:92 (July 24, 1920), Allen McCurdy, "The Forty-Eighters' Position," *Nation,* 111:126 (July 31, 1920), and Swinburne Hale, "What Has Happened to the Forty-Eighters," *Nation,* 111:243 (August 28, 1920). Reedy followed the events recorded therein at a distance, but see his "Convention in Chicago," *Mirror,* 29:557, and "Third Party Talk," *ibid.,* 29:556.

3. Reedy, "The Putridity of Politics," *Mirror,* 29:443 (June 3, 1920).

4. *Ibid.,* p. 444.

5. *King Lear,* IV:6, 132.

6. "The Plutes Put Harding Over," *Mirror,* 29:491 (June 17, 1920).

7. "A Card from Elmer Chubb, Ph.D., LL.D.," *Mirror,* 29:547 (July 8, 1920). The Chubb items in the *Mirror* for 1920 are too numerous to list. Investigators will find baffling many others in Masters' correspondence at the Newberry, UP, and so on. There are handbills announcing Chubb's lectures at the Scopes trial in Dayton, Tenn., some preserved at Yale. A file of correspondence intended to put an end to the running lampoon was made available to me by James F. Hornback, Leader of the St. Louis Ethical Society.

8. Reedy, "All Bosses Rolled Flat," *Mirror,* 29:539 (July 8, 1920).

9. Sara Bard Field, "Reedy's Last Party," *All's Well,* 1:114 (May 1921). Finger edited this journal from Fayetteville, Ark., after giving up his effort to keep the *Mirror* alive. In the *Mirror* of August 12, 1920 Finger had made a fevered plea for $15,000 of new capital to keep the *Mirror* going. He was still filling the magazine with obituaries for Reedy, which clearly failed to hold the interest of readers, and the magazine suspended publication five weeks after Reedy's death.

10. See Agnes de Mille, "A Note about the Author," in Anna George de Mille, *Henry George: Citizen of the World,* ed. Don C. Shoemaker (Chapel Hill, 1950), pp. vii–xii. See also Reedy to Anna George de Mille, May 10, 1920. MHS.

11. Reedy to Kennerley, July 26, 1920. NYP. Reedy to Anna George de Mille, July 27, 1920. MHS. And see Reedy, "Editing in Earthquakes," *Mirror,* 29:571 (July 22, 1920), and "Our Tuna," *ibid.,* 29:587 (July 29, 1920).

NOTES TO CHAPTER 23

12. Charles J. Finger, "Reflections: Reedy's Choice for President," *Mirror*, 29:624 (August 12, 1920).
13. James H. Barry to Anna George de Mille, July 30, 1920. MHS.
14. *Mirror*, 29:587ff (July 29, 1920).
15. Orrick Johns, *Time of Our Lives*, p. 173, and oral sources.
16. Deutsch, "To William Marion Reedy," *Mirror*, 29:608 (August 5, 1920). Her regret is expressed in a letter dated September 6, 1962.
17. Kennerley, "The Free Lance," *Mirror*, 29:607 (August 5, 1920).
18. Editorial, "Reedy and His Mirror," *New York Tribune*, July 30, 1920, and *Literary Digest*, 66:32 (August 21, 1920), and "Reedy's Last Story," *ibid.*, 66:53 (August 28, 1920).
19. Akins to Bernays, n.d. (letter from Locust Valley, L.I.). MHS.
20. Dreiser to Mencken, August 4, 1920. *Letters*, ed. Elias, I, 269.
21. Bloch to Bernays, [September 15, 1920], and October 21, 1920. MHS.
22. Masters, *Vachel Lindsay: A Poet in America*, p. 366.
23. Ethel M. King, *Reflections of Reedy* (Brooklyn, N.Y., 1961), p. 142.
24. Letter from B. W. Huebsch, dated January 26, 1962.
25. "Mr. Reedy's paper gave me a postgraduate education," Sandburg recently told Harry Golden, who communicated the remark to the *Saturday Review* (February 9, 1963, p. 48) to correct an earlier article he had written on personal journalism.
26. "The Death of Mr. Reedy," *Poetry*, 16:328 (September 1920).

INDEX

Abercrombie, Lascelles, 151
Academy (London), 53, 173
Adams, Henry, 113, 281
Aguinaldo, Emilio, 90
Aiken, Conrad, 215, 237–238, 239, 250, 273, 274; *The Jig of Forslin*, 238
Akins, Thomas J., 136
Akins, Zoë, 136–139, 140, 141, 142–143, 145, 168, 172, 173, 176, 185, 218–219, 222, 287; reviewer for *Mirror*, 137; romance with Reedy, 138–139; *Interpretations: A Book of First Poems*, 142; "In the Shadows of Parnassus," 218–219
Alcott, Bronson, 53, 55, 58
Aldington, Richard, 217
Altgeld, Governor John Peter, 54, 100, 182–183, 189, 193, 280
American Magazine, 169, 177, 181, 182
Anderson Galleries, 171, 267
Anthology of Magazine Verse, 175
Aria Da Capo. See Millay, Edna St. Vincent
Arena, 170
Argonaut, 273
As You Like It, 51
Atherton, Gertrude, 66, 152
Atkins, Elizabeth, 275, 277
Atlantic Monthly, 4, 87, 124, 157, 169, 256, 273, 274

Baker, Newton D., 254
Baldwin, Agnes. See Reedy, Agnes Baldwin
Balzac, de, Honoré, 65, 121
Barbey d'Aurevilly, Jules Amédée, 43

Barry, James, 284, 285
Baruch, Bernard, 280
Baudelaire, Charles, 35, 43
Bauduy, Eulalie. See Reedy, Eulalie Bauduy
Bauduy, Dr. Jerome Keating, 85–86
Beard, Charles A., 254
Beerbohm, Max, 152
Bell, Laird, 228, 239
Bellamy, Edward, 54
Bellman, 169, 273
Benét, William Rose, 247, 286
Benton, Thomas Hart, 14
Bernays, Dr. Augustus Charles, 62, 135
Bernays, Thekla, 62, 73, 144–146, 147, 148, 168, 251, 287, 289; "Currents of Modern Literature," 63
Bernoudy, Ellen, 31
Bibelot, 169, 170
Bierce, Ambrose, 61, 64, 155; *Tales of Soldiers and Civilians*, 61
Billings, Warren K., 253
Bixby, W. K., 171
Björkman, Edwin, 171
Blair, Francis Preston, Jr., 11, 13, 140
Blair, James L., 98, 99, 102, 109–111, 130
Blake, William, 61, 179
Blavatsky, Mme. Helena Petrovna, 42, 46
Bloch, Albert, 135, 143–144, 148, 172, 178, 288; "Kindly Caricatures," 135
Blossom, Henry, 135
"Blue Jay's Chatter." See *Mirror*

INDEX

Bodenheim, Maxwell, 247, 273, 274
Bookman, 150, 169
Boston Transcript, 175
Bourget, Paul, 63
Braithwaite, William Stanley, 175, 212, 219–220, 222
Brann, William Cowper, 25
Broadway, 128, 129, 255
Brokmeyer, Henry Conrad [Brockmeyer], 14, 55, 56, 57, 140
Brookings, Robert, 62
Brooks, Van Wyck, 155
Browning, Robert, 61, 163, 164–166, 176, 203
Bryan, William Jennings, 32, 82, 90–91, 100, 122, 182, 195, 282, 286, 291; Reedy's impression of, 282–283
Burgess, Gelett, 169
Burroughs, John, 193
Burton, Richard, 217
Butler, Edward ("Ed"), 94, 99, 102, 107, 108, 120–121
Butler, Nicholas Murray, 254
Byars, William Vincent, 31–32, 33, 42, 82, 186–187, 249, 273
Bynner, Witter, 177, 178, 189, 226–228, 240–242, 248, 259, 275, 291; translation of *Iphegenia in Tauris*, 227–228; as "Emanuel Morgan," 229, 233, 234, 237. *See also* Spectrism

Cabell, James Branch, 152
Caine, Hall, 123
Campbell, Alexander, 180
Campbell, James, 14, 82–84, 94, 98, 107, 110, 114, 120, 130, 143, 200; "reform by bribery," 99–101
Camp Jackson, capture of (1861), 11
Cardoner, A. B., 51
Carman, Bliss, 5, 66, 103, 146, 170, 212
Carpenter, George Rice, 156
Cavalcante, Guido, 166

Century, The, 169, 213
Chambers, Mrs. Margaret Helen. *See* Reedy, Margaret Rhodes
Channing, William Ellery, 53
Chap-Book, 66, 67–68, 169, 170, 219
Chapman, John Jay, 151
Chopin, Kate, 61
Chouteau, Pierre, 13
"Chubb, Elmer, LL.D., PhD.," 282, 286
Chubb, Percival, 282
Clemens, Samuel. *See* Twain, Mark
Cleveland, President Grover, 24, 54, 183
Clonmel, 205–206, 245–246, 260
Cockerill, John A., 28
Colum, Padraic, 247
Committee of Forty-Eight, The, 268–269, 272, 280
Commoner, 100
Couperus, Louis, 63
Cowley-Brown, John S., 169
Cox, Governor James M., 283, 285
Crane, Stephen, 67, 123, 259; *Red Badge of Courage, The*, 67
Criterion, 59–60, 62
Critic, 172
Cross, Victoria, 171
Cunningham, Johnnie, 15, 17, 65, 215
Curran, Mrs. John H., 232
Current Literature, 102, 169, 172, 175, 177, 256
Current Opinion, 237

Darrow, Clarence, 182, 193, 195, 279
Darwin, Charles, 36, 39, 53, 63
Davidson, Thomas, 58, 282
Decadence, the, 35–36; influence on Reedy, 46
Delineator, 129, 255
De Menil, Alexander, 52–53
de Mille, Anna George, 283, 284
de Mille, Cecil B., 283
de Mille, William C., 283, 285

344

INDEX

Detroit News, 239
Deutsch, Babette, 167, 247, 287
Dewey, Admiral George, 89
Dewey, John, 14, 53, 55, 160
Dial, 4, 169, 225, 239, 273
Dickinson, Emily, 7, 61, 157, 226
Dickinson, G. Lowes, 146
Dodge, B. W., 129
Donne, John, 61
Doolittle, Hilda, 217, 248
Dostoevski, Fyodor, 63
Doubleday, Frank, 123
Dreiser, Paul, 121
Dreiser, Theodore, 6, 23–24, 26, 49, 64, 73, 120–131, 158, 189, 195, 196, 197, 198, 211, 214, 215, 254, 257–258, 260–264, 266, 268, 284, 288, 290, 291; "Butcher Rogaum's Door" ("Old Rogaum"), 127, 262; *The Financier,* 130, 131, 196; *The "Genius,"* 261; *Jennie Gerhardt,* 130; *Sister Carrie,* 7, 123–127, 129, 130, 258; *The Titan,* 130, 196; *Twelve Men,* 262–263
Dresser, Paul. *See* Dreiser, Paul
Dreyfus, Captain Alfred, 71
Dumay, Henri, 60
Duncan, Isadora, 227
Dyer, R. A., 51

Earle, Ferdinand Pinney, 174–175
Ederheimer, Richard, 267, 339
Edgar, William C., 273
Edwin, William C., 169
Eliot, George, 15, 63
Eliot, T. S., 162–163, 168, 219, 236
Eliot, Dr. William Greenleaf, 13, 140
Ellis, Havelock, 54, 71
Emerson, Ralph Waldo, 53, 55
Ev'ry Month, 121–123

Fanning, Michael A., 33, 42, 44, 77, 97, 99; co-edits *Sunday Mirror,* 47, 49, 59

Ficke, Arthur Davison, 177, 222, 228–230, 232, 239, 275; as "Anne Knish," 229, 234–236. *See also* Spectrism
Field, Eugene, 25, 120, 154; *Sharps and Flats,* 154
Filsinger, Ernst, 189
Finger, Charles J., 281–282, 284
Fisher, Mary, 195, 331
Fitch, Clyde, 168
Flagg, James Montgomery, 5
Fletcher, John Gould, 218, 222, 230
Folk, Governor Joseph Wingate, 100, 106, 107, 108–109, 111, 114, 117, 119, 130
"Ford, Webster," *See* Masters, Edgar Lee
Forum, 170, 172, 175, 177, 185, 212, 226, 230
Foy, James, 51
Francis, David R., 42, 97, 112, 289
Frémont, General John C., 83
French, Alice ("Octave Thanet"), 61
Frohman, Charles, 139
Frost, Robert, 220
Fuller, Henry B., 65, 158, 177

Gallant, Barney, 267
Galsworthy, John, 158, 159
Galvin, James ("Red"), 49, 51, 106, 121, 262; co-edits *Mirror,* 50; and Suburban Railway Scandal, 106
Garland, Hamlin, 64, 67, 68–70, 129, 177, 217, 290
Gautier, Théophile, 153
George, Henry, 9, 54, 97, 98, 252, 283; *Progress and Poverty,* 42, 97, 98
Glass, Senator Carter, 282
Glennon, John Cardinal, 286
Godkin, E. L., 88, 89, 90
Goldman, Emma, 10, 253
Gomme, Laurence, 175
Gompers, Samuel, 95
Goose-Quill, 169

345

INDEX

Gourmont, de, Remy, 219, 233
Granville-Barker, Harley, 171
Greek Anthology, 197, 198

Hanna, Mark, 81
Harding, President Warren Gamaliel, 281
Hardy, Thomas, 7, 9, 64, 158, 212; Reedy's opinion of, 72–73; *Jude the Obscure*, 72
Harper's Monthly, 169
Harper's Weekly, 102
Harris, Frank, 171
Harris, William Torrey, 53, 58; Reedy's impression of, 58–59
Harrison, Mayor Carter, 194, 195
Harvey, Alexander, 170, 256, 286
Hauptmann, Gerhart, 63
Hawes, Senator Harry B., 96, 98, 99, 111, 200, 201
Hawthorne, Nathaniel, 7, 65–66, 68–69, 146, 147; *The Scarlet Letter*, 65–66
"Hay, Elijah." *See* Seiffert, Marjorie Allen
"H.D." *See* Doolittle, Hilda
Heany, Mrs. Martin P. *See* Reedy, Margaret Rhodes
Hearst, William Randolph, Jr., 80, 118
Hegel, Georg Wilhelm Friedrich, 53, 55, 57
Heller, Dean Otto, 151
Henderson, Alice Corbin, 239–240
Heney, Francis J., 119
Henley, William Ernest, 158, 160
Henry, Arthur, 121, 123, 255
Henry, O. *See* Porter, William Sydney
Heredia, de, José Maria, 221
Hert, B. Russell, 169
Hervey, John Lewis, 221–223, 237, 238, 250
Hesperian, 52, 53
Hiram College, 180
Homer, 32–33, 40
Hoover, President Herbert, 268
Housman, Alfred Edward, 171
How, Louis, 227

Howells, William Dean, 66–67, 70, 90, 153, 155, 158
Hubbard, Elbert, 105, 169
Huebsch, Benjamin W., 170, 290
Hugo, Victor, 69
Huneker, James Gibbons, 43, 48, 139, 144, 152–154, 155–156, 158, 247; writes for *Mirror*, 60
Hurst, Fannie, 168
Huysmans, Joris Karl, 36, 37, 42, 63
Hyde, William, 23, 24, 34

Ibsen, Henrik, 63, 64, 69, 151
Illustrated American, 68, 70
Imagism, 219–221, 223
Impressionism, 160
Irwin, Orvis B., 212

Jackson, Governor Claiborne, 11
James, Frank, 30–31
James, Henry, Sr., 53
James, Henry, 63, 64, 68, 136, 158
James, Jesse, 30
James, William, 53, 155, 160, 203
Jewett, Sarah Orne, 69
Johns, George Sibley, 174, 286
Johns, Orrick, 141, 156, 172, 173–175, 185, 195, 286; "Second Avenue," 175–176
Johnson, Mayor Tom L., 97, 98, 119
Jones, Charles H., 82, 280
Jones, Howard Mumford, 151, 273
Journal of Speculative Philosophy, 53, 59, 62, 167
"Journalism," Address on, 117–119
Joyce, James, 64, 73

Kain, Archbishop John Joseph, 79, 86
Kandinsky, Wassily, 143
Keeley, Dr. Leslie, 78, 316
Kelsoe, W. A., 25, 31
Kennerley, Mitchell, 241, 255, 256, 267, 284, 285, 287; career as publisher, 170–172; publishes Vachel Lindsay, 177, 185, 187; publishes Edna St. Vincent Mil-

INDEX

lay, 276; publishes *Spectra*, 230–232, 234; director of the Anderson Galleries, 171, 267
Kenrick, Archbishop Peter, 79
Keynes, John Maynard, 279
"Kindly Caricatures." *See* Bloch, Albert
Kipling, Rudyard, 61, 69, 150–151, 152, 158
Klee, Paul, 144
"Knish, Anne." *See* Ficke, Arthur Davison
Knopf, Alfred, 241
Kreymborg, Alfred, 229, 233–234, 236, 240

LaClède, Pierre, 13
La Follette, Senator Robert, Sr., 119, 269, 280
Lane, John, 170
Lang, Andrew, 151, 166
Lark, 169
League of Nations, 265, 280
LeBerton, A. [LeBerthon], 51
Lehmann, Solicitor General Frederick W., 98, 101, 105, 114, 135, 148, 270
Lehmann-Haupt, Helmut, 170
Le Gallienne, Richard, 5, 170
Lenalie, Aimee, 170
Leslie's Monthly. See American Magazine
Levin, Harry (T.), 38–39, 313
Lewis, Wyndham, 231
Lewisohn, Ludwig, 48
Lippmann, Walter, 159, 279
Lindsay (Nicholas), Vachel, 176, 177–192, 193, 217, 218, 224, 225; Reedy's opinion of, 190–191; "The City That Will Not Repent," 183–184; "The Eagle That Is Forgotten," 183; "Gloriana: Poet of St. Louis," 190; "I Heard Immanuel Singing," 181, 187; "The Kallyope Yell," 185–186; "The Knight in Disguise," 177–178, 179, 181; *Rhymes To Be Traded for Bread*, 181, 182

Literary Digest, The, 104, 287
Literary History of the United States, 174
Little Book of Missouri Verse, 70
Little Review, 237
Lombroso, Cesare, 54
Loomis, Roger Sherman, 212, 225
Lôme, de, Minister Dupuy, 87, 88
Lorimer, George Horace, 169
Lowell, Amy, 8, 217–224, 230, 231, 232, 236, 241–242, 250–251, 277, 291; Reedy's opinion of, 224; "An Aquarium," 224, 231; *Can Grande's Castle*, 250, 251; "Chopin," 251; "Gargoyles," 250–251; "The Taxi," 218–219
Lowes, John Livingston, 232
Louisiana Purchase Exposition. *See* World's Fair
Lounsbury, Thomas R., 151
Lusk, Senator Clayton R., 254, 266
Lyon, Harris Merton, 130, 141, 255–260, 262; relationship with Dreiser, 128–129, 260; "From an Old Farmhouse," 256–257; *Graphics*, 256; *Sardonics*, 255
Lyon, Mrs. Harris Merton, 260, 263
Lyric Year (contest), 175, 176
Lyric Year, The, 175, 176, 177, 221, 274

Mackaye, Percy, 168, 188, 189
Macke, August, 144
Maeterlinck, Maurice, 63
Mahan, Admiral Alfred Thayer, 54, 81, 85
Mann, Colonel William D'Alton, 48–49, 257
Marc, Franz, 143
Markham, Edwin, 155, 174, 189; "Man With the Hoe," 155
Marlowe, Julia, 138, 139
Masefield, John, 171
Masters, Edgar Lee, 5, 182, 193–216, 222, 225, 234, 235, 250, 258, 259, 268, 274, 282, 285, 286, 289, 291; "The Hill," 197, 198–199. *Spoon River Anthology*, 7, 198–199, 201–205, 211,

347

INDEX

Masters, Edgar Lee (*continued*) 217, 220, 246, 255, 287; Reedy's analysis of, 207–208; Pound's remarks on, 209–210
Mathews, Elkin, 162, 170
Matthews, Brander, 48, 151
Matthiessen, F. O., 120
McAdoo, William Gibbs, 280
McClure's Magazine, 107, 169, 177, 227
McCullagh, Joseph B., 26–27, 34, 120, 123
McGaffey, Ernest, 193, 194, 256
McKinley, President William, 81–82, 122, 281
"McLeod, Fiona," 141, 241
Mencken, Henry Louis, 59, 153, 155, 255, 256, 257, 258, 264, 288; influence on Dreiser, 260–261
Mercantile Library, 3, 40, 62
Meriwether, Lee, 100–101, 182, 271, 320
Meyer, Kuno, 151, 251, 252
Millay, Edna St. Vincent, 175, 176, 274–278; "And you as well must die," 275; *Aria Da Capo,* 276–278; "Figs from Thistles," 275; "Renascence," 175, 176, 274, 275
Miller, Joaquin, 40, 152, 155
Mirror, 4, 102; name adopted, 61; failure, 82; given to Reedy, 83; circulation, 87, 90, 91; publication stopped, 341, n. 9; "Reflections," 48, 60, 69, 122; "Kindly Caricatures," *see* Bloch, Albert; "Blue Jay's Chatter," 135–137, 140; "What I've Been Reading," 150. See also *Sunday Mirror*
Mirror Pamphlets, 94, 105, 298–299
Missouri Republican, 23–25, 39, 40–41, 42, 62, 120, 121, 273; Reedy as reporter for, 30–31, 33
Mlle. New York, 46, 219
Mobile Register, 48
Molnar, Ferenc, 171
Monahan, Michael, 169, 170
Monroe, Harriet, 156, 157, 178, 179, 181, 196, 208, 209, 240, 248, 293
Moods, 169
Moody, William Vaughn, 168
Mooney, Thomas J., 253
Moore, George, 152
"Morgan, Emanuel." *See* Bynner, Witter
Mosher, Thomas Bird, 7, 9, 46, 61, 130–131, 156, 170, 172

Nagel, Charles, 58, 135
Nation, 4, 87, 88, 89, 273
Naturalism, 63–64, 70–71
Neihardt, John G., 171
New Age, 210
New Republic, 231, 252
New York Journal, 80, 87
New York Sun, 152
New York Times, 116, 118, 240, 280, 286; interview with Reedy, 267–268
New York Tribune, 287
New York World, 32, 80, 121, 273
Nietzsche, Friedrich Wilhelm, 260–261
Noguchi, Yone, 171, 221
Noonday Club, 98, 99, 111, 200
Norris, Frank, 123, 124, 146
North American Review, 170
Norton, Charles Eliot, 150

O'Faolain, Sean, 163
O'Hara, John Myers, 221
O Sheel, Sheamus, 212
Others, 229, 230, 233, 236, 237, 240

Page, Walter Hines, 123, 124
Palmer, Attorney General A. Mitchell, 253
Papyrus, 169
Pater, Walter, 7, 36–37, 46, 61, 63–64, 144
Pattee, Fred L., 257
Patti, Adelina, 43
Peck, Harry Thurston, 150, 169
Peirce, Charles S., 53
Perry, Bliss, 248

348

INDEX

Phelps, William Lyon, 150–151, 155
Philistine, 169
Philippines, U.S. annexation of, 89, 90–91
Phillips, David Graham, 146
Pinchot, Amos, 269
Pindar, 186
Pochmann, Henry A., 56
Poe, Edgar Allan, 35, 38, 43, 46, 146, 155–156, 161, 177, 178, 233
Poetry: A Magazine of Verse, 178, 179, 181, 182, 189, 208, 218, 237, 240, 275, 291
Poetry Society of America, 6, 177, 187, 217, 218, 248, 254, 291
Pollard, Percival, 46, 48, 144, 150, 151–152, 172, 173, 247; writes for *Mirror*, 60; attack on Huneker, 153–154; *The Imitator*, 152, 256
Populism, 54
Porcher, Frances, 51, 138–139, 140
Porter, William Sydney, 178, 259
Pound, Ezra, 162–167, 168, 177, 178–179, 191, 192, 195, 215, 218, 225, 236, 248; "Mesmerism," 164–165; *Provença*, 164; *Sonnets and Ballate of Guido Cavalcante*, 166–167; comments on Masters, 208–210, 212–213, 215; Reedy discusses his imagism, 220–221; vorticism, 231
Pound, Roscoe, 231
Powys, John Cowper, 212
Pragmatism, 159–160
Priest, Judge H. Sam, 114
Prohibition, 270
Publisher's Weekly, 211
Puck, 59
Pulitzer, Joseph, 3, 26, 27–29, 34, 80, 118, 248
Pulitzer Prize, 248

Quiller-Couch, Sir Arthur, 151

Raleigh, Walter, 151
Ralston, Carol, 103

Realism, 159–160, 211–212, 225
Reavis, L. U., 26
Record-Herald (Chicago), 127
Reed, Senator James A., 271, 272, 282
Reedy, Agnes ("Addie") Baldwin (first wife), 77–78, 103
Reedy, Ann Marion (mother), 14, 15, 17
Reedy, Daniel (brother), 18, 20
Reedy, Eulalie ("Lalite") Bauduy (second wife), 85–86, 102–103, 115, 318, 320
Reedy, Frank (brother), 18, 19–20, 113
Reedy, Patrick (father), 12–13, 19–20
Reedy, Margaret Rhodes (third wife), 136, 143, 147–149, 171, 205, 206, 245, 269, 286
Reedy's Mirror. See *Mirror*
Reedy, William Marion: early life, 14–16, 17–21; education, 16–17; religion, 14, 21–22, 79–80, 86–87; as reporter, 23, 25, 29–30, 33–34; first marriage, 77–79; divorce, 79, 86–87; second marriage, 85–87; death of second wife, 102–103; third marriage, 147–149; ill health, 266–267, 269–270; proposed as senatorial candidate, 272; closing days and death, 282–286; and critical method, 65; and critical standards, 158–161, 98, 206, 209
"Reflections." See *Mirror*
Rhodes, Margaret. See Reedy, Margaret Rhodes
Richards, Grant, 142
Riley, James Whitcomb, 155
Rittenhouse, Jessie B., 177, 187, 248
Robinson, Edwin Arlington, 157, 274
Rolland, Romain, 270
Romanticism, 65
Roosevelt, President Theodore, 85, 111, 115–117, 139, 148, 193, 234

INDEX

Rossetti, Dante Gabriel, 34, 166, 173
Rousseau, Henri, 144
Rousseau, Jean-Jacques, 38, 145
Ruskin, John, 40

Sade, de, Marquis, 43
St. Louis: social structure, 13–14; Census of 1880, 25–26; "October Fair," 92–93; "Veiled Prophet," 29, 34, 92, 113, 120; street-car strike (1900), 94–97, 100; "reform by bribery," 98–102; Suburban Railway Scandal, 106–107
St. Louis Chronicle, 27
St. Louis Globe-Democrat, 23, 24, 25, 26–27, 33, 39, 40, 63, 80, 93, 120, 186; Reedy as reporter for, 33–34
St. Louis Mercantile Library Association. See Mercantile Library
St. Louis Movement, 55, 166, 167
St. Louis Philosophical Society, 14, 55–56
St. Louis Post-Dispatch, 24, 27–29, 82, 108, 174, 286
St. Louis Republic, 101, 121
St. Louis Star, 51, 77, 106; Reedy as editor of, 4, 33–34
St. Louis Sunday Tidings, 49, 51
St. Louis University, 3, 14, 16, 79
Saltus, Edgar, 43
Saltus, Francis Saltus, 42–43; Reedy's opinion of, 43–44
Sandburg, Carl (Charles), 6, 145–146, 156, 195, 196–197, 198, 213, 223, 225, 259, 260, 274, 291; "Tribute to Webster Ford," 213–214
San Francisco Examiner, 155
San Francisco Star, 284
Saturday Evening Post, 169
Saturday Review (London), 126, 127
Savoy (London), 71
Schoenberg, Arnold, 144
Schurz, Carl, 3, 14, 27, 56, 90
Schuyler, William, 135, 166–167

Scribner's, 157, 169
Scripps, Edward Wyllis, 27
Seelig, Dr. Major, 269, 271
Seiffert, Marjorie Allen, 233, 238–239. See also Spectrism
Sewanee Review, 169
Shakespeare, William, 69, 72
Sharp, William, 241. See also "McLeod, Fiona"
Shaw, George Bernard, 7, 152, 158
Shea, Jack, 17–18, 215
Shepard, Odell, 224
Sidney, Sir Philip, 178
Sigel, Franz, 12
Sinclair, Upton, 159, 284; *The Jungle*, 158
Single tax, 98, 206, 269
Sinnett, A. P., 42, 46
Slayback, Colonel Alonzo, 28–29, 30, 94
Slupsky, "Colonel" Abe, 135
Smart Set, 257, 258
Smith, William Jay, 234
Snider, Denton Jacques, 56, 135; Reedy's opinion of, 57–58
Soldan, Louis, 31, 58
Sothern, E. H., 138
Spanish-American War, 77, 80–81, 84, 85, 87–88
Spectra, 230; Reedy's review of, 236–237
Spectrism, 228–240, 251
Spoon River Anthology. See Masters, Edgar Lee
Stanley, Sir Hubert, 102
Star-Sayings. See *St. Louis Star*
Starrett, Vincent, 286
Stedman, Edward Clarence, 193
Steffins, Lincoln, 51, 107, 108, 109, 114, 130
Stein, Gertrude, 218
Stendhal, Henri, 145
Stevens, Wallace, 219, 229, 233, 273
Stone, Herbert S., 68, 69, 70
Sudermann, Hermann, 63
Sullivan, John J. ("Jack"), 51, 78, 143
Sunday Mirror, 4; founded, 49–50; format, 50–51, 53–55, 61

INDEX

Swinburne, Algernon Charles, 34, 41, 42, 158, 173
Symmonds, John Addington, 166
Symons, Arthur, 158

Taft, President William Howard, 247
Tansey, George J., 78, 98, 103, 281
Teasdale, Sara, 139–142, 157, 163, 168, 172, 175, 176, 184, 185, 188–189, 191, 197, 213, 219, 220; *Love Songs*, 248; *Sonnets to Duse*, 142; "Spring Night," 189–190; wins first "Pulitzer," 248–249
"Thanet, Octave." *See* French, Alice
Thomas, Augustus, 25
Thomas, William, 51
Thompson, Francis, 9, 158
Thompson, Vance, 46
Tietjens, Eunice, 189
Toledo Blade, 121
Tolstoy, Leo, 63, 64, 73
Town and Country, 247
Town Topics, 42, 47–49, 50, 153
Traubel, Horace, 156
Treaty of Versailles, 265–266, 279
Turner, Frederick Jackson, 54, 70, 290
Twain, Mark, 25, 52, 66, 90, 120, 158, 178, 232, 234

Untermeyer, Louis, 175, 188, 189, 218, 222
Upward, Allen, 171

Valley Magazine, 105, 109
Vechten, Carl Van, 247
Verlaine, Paul, 9, 38, 46
Viereck, George Sylvester, 170, 172–173, 174, 254; *The Candle and the Flame*, 173; *Confessions of a Barbarian*, 172, 174
Village Magazine, 177
Villon, François, 45, 46, 166
Vorticism, 231
Voynich, Ethel Lilian, 65

Waddell, Elizabeth, 176, 182
Wainwright, Ellis, 107

Watterson, Henry, 109, 118, 286
Wayland, Francis, 56
Wells, Rolla, 93, 99, 100, 101, 104, 105, 111, 112–113
Wetmore, Claude, 108–109
Weyler, General Valeriano, 80, 84
Wharton, Edith, 136, 137
"What I've Been Reading." *See Mirror*
"What's the Matter with St. Louis?", 93–94
Wheeler, Edward J., 170, 175, 177
Wheelock, John Hall, 187, 189
Whistler, James McNeill, 173
White, Sara, 121, 123
White, William Allen, 93, 143
Whitlock, Brand, 129, 280
Whitman, Walt, 40–41, 46, 152, 154, 155–156, 161, 163, 176, 178, 185, 209
Wilde, Oscar, 35, 39, 42, 43, 46, 152, 153, 173, 267; interviewed by *Missouri Republican*, 39–41; *Ballad of Reading Gaol*, 45; *Picture of Dorian Gray*, 42, 314
Williams, Walter, 117
Williams, William Carlos, 219, 234, 235, 273
Wilson, President Woodrow, 195, 246, 252, 265
Wolf, Fred Wilhelm, 86
Wood, Charles Erskine Scott, 279, 283
Woolf, Virginia, 65
World War I, 246, 251–254
World's Fair (1903), 93–94, 111–113
Worth, Patience, 232
Wright, Willard Huntington, 212, 260, 261

Yeats, William Butler, 7, 8, 46, 158, 163, 179, 210
Yerkes, Charles T., 130, 196

Zangwill, Israel, 64
Zola, Émile, 36, 64, 73, 212; Reedy's opinion of, 71; *J'accuse*, 71